ABORTION RITES

ABORTION RITES

A Social History
Of Abortion
In America

Marvin Olasky

Regnery Publishing, Inc.
Washington, D.C.

First Regnery edition published 1995.

Library of Congress Cataloging-in-Publication Data

Olasky, Marvin N.
    Abortion rites : a social history of abortion in America / Marvin Olasky
        p.   cm.
    Originally published: Wheaton, Ill. : Crossways Books, c1992.
    Includes bibliographical references and index.
    ISBN 0-89526-723-3
        1. Abortion--United States--History. 2. Pro-life movement--United States--History.
    3. Pro-choice movement--United States--History.
    I. Title.
    HQ767.5.U5043   1995
    363.4'6'0973--dc20   95-24312
                                                                    CIP

Published in the United States by
Regnery Publishing, Inc.
An Eagle Publishing Company
422 First Street, SE, Suite 300
Washington, DC 20003

Distributed to the trade by
National Book Network
4720-A Boston Way
Lanham, MD 20706

Printed on acid-free paper.
Manufactured in the United States of America

10 9 8 7 6 5 4 3 2 1

Books are available in quantity for promotional or premium use. Write to Director of Special Sales, Regnery Publishing, Inc., 422 First Street, SE, Suite 300, Washington, DC 20003, for information on discounts and terms or call (202) 546-5005.

For Susan, Peter, David,
Daniel and Benjamin

CONTENTS

ACKNOWLEDGMENTS

For those who glumly mail income tax returns on April 15, I have one suggestion: pretend that all your tax payments are going to the Library of Congress. This book owes much to the deeds of long-dead librarians who placed curious books on shelves now dusty, perhaps in the faith that someone decades later would care. The Library of Congress stacks were particularly energizing because employees took along their boom boxes as they reshelved books, and I could listen in. Astronomers travel from stars to shopping malls only after they go off duty; it made strange sense to read accounts of seventeenth-century abortion with rap music in the background.

For those who cynically suspect that all grant-makers require scholars to toe their line, I have another suggestion: meet Guy Condon and other leaders of Americans United for Life. A foundation grant provided through AUL allowed me to walk the stacks of the Library of Congress, with forays to the Chicago Historical Society, the New York Public Library, and the History of Medicine Library of the National Institutes of Health. AUL's acceptance of my requirements for academic freedom was exemplary; I was never requested to cover up findings that undercut pro-life myths.

For those who think all book publishers have become cold and calculating, I suggest a meeting with Lane and Jan Dennis of Crossway Books. Authors often become irritated with publishers, but Lane and Jan have now brought into the world six of my books, and I continue to be impressed with their combination of reason and passion. Many members of their staff, particularly managing editor Ted Griffin, also deserve my thanks.

And for those on both sides of the abortion debate who view women as second-class citizens . . . I can argue theoretically, but I think of my wife Susan. Her Biblical thinking and fine writing go along with her steadfast love in marriage and steady compassion in child-raising. This book is dedicated to her and to our four children. Peter, David, Daniel, and Benjamin continue to make me proud as they daily undercut my arrogance.

Many other individuals have given me helping hands or needed shoves: Hadley Arkes, Joe McIlhaney, Frederica Mathewes-Green, Cathy Showalter, Mary Krane Derr, Joseph Dellapenna, Howard and Roberta Ahmanson, David Coffin, Mary King, and Bill Smith come to mind. They are in no way responsible for my writing transgressions, of course, but my dissertation committee chairman sixteen years ago — Stephen Tonsor of the University of Michigan History Department — is partly responsible for what I have written, because without his kind and courageous support I would not have been able to begin a scholarly career.

PREFACE

by William J. Bennett

In thinking about Marvin Olasky's contribution to the current abortion debate, I am reminded of a passage from C. S. Lewis' *The Screwtape Letters*. The devil Screwtape is tutoring his young nephew and disciple, Wormwood, in the art of corruption. The trick, he explains, is to keep men from acquiring wisdom, a trick accomplished by keeping them ignorant of the past and by cultivating a devotion to present-mindedness. "Since we cannot deceive the whole human race all the time," Screwtape says, "it is important to cut every generation off from all others; for where learning makes a free commerce between the ages there is always a danger that the characteristic errors of one may be corrected by the charateristic truths of another."

Abortion Rites: A Social History of Abortion in America is a contribution to learning between the ages. While much has been written about abortion since the Supreme Court's *Roe v. Wade* decision, very little thoughtful work has been done on the history of abortion in America pre-1973. The old axiom that those who cannot remember the past are condemned to repeat it is true enough. But the converse is also true; those who cannot remember the past are unable to draw constructively from it. Professor Olasky takes the debate beyond political slogans and invective; he provides us with an intellectually serious examination of this nation's complex history regarding abortion. His findings may surprise you. There are lessons from the past that should appeal to virtually everyone.

Nevertheless, I suspect that some advocates on both sides of the abortion debate will not be completely happy with Professor Olasky's analysis. He will probably incur the wrath of some radical feminists and abortion-on-demand advocates who ascribe the same moral seriousness to abortion as they do to, say, the removal of an unsightly blemish. On the other hand, some pro-life activists may not consider Olasky sufficiently "pure" in his views, rhetoric, and recommendations. I hope that this is not the case; America's pro-life movement has a great deal to learn from the pro-life movement of the late nineteenth century, and from Professor Olasky.

For those of us who believe that 1.6 million abortions a year is a tragic feature of modern American life, the most pertinent question now (as it was a century ago) is not how to pass laws against all abortions, but rather *how best to reduce the number of abortions.* Professor Olasky makes a compelling argument for employing the strategy of containment as a first step toward rollback. He challenges pro-life leaders to tailor their approach to real-world realities, to content themselves with small victories, to provide women with positive, pro-life alternatives to abortion, and to continue to fight for laws restricting abortion while not making laws their primary focus. As Olasky writes, "Protective laws and enforcement help, but the most effective pro-life efforts have always concentrated on one life at a time."

The massive number of abortions in America is something about which no one — pro-life or pro-choice — can be pleased. We must begin the long, hard task of reestablishing a moral consensus if we hope to see any significant reduction in the number of abortions.

Marvin Olasky has injected civility, compassion, and cool reason into the most difficult, divisive issue in American political life. We are better off because of it.

INTRODUCTION

At a Moscow meeting in March 1991, Russian military historian Dmitri Volkogonov found out firsthand the dangers of delving too deeply into archives. Leading Soviet generals took turns lambasting Volkogonov for the history he had written of events leading up to World War II. A transcript of the session, as published in *Nezavisimaya Gazeta*, showed hatred for a book that portrayed "all that is negative." Volkogonov, however, fought back, saying the military officials desired "to control history, as usual, and for them, World War II can only be the victory of socialism and nothing else. I don't want to write a fake history."[1]

Volkogonov and others had tough going for a time, but that insistence on telling the truth contributed to the demise of the Soviet Union. A new look at American abortion history could also be helpful, because both sides have simplified the past and made assumptions favorable to their current campaigns. Opponents of abortion often look at the good old, pre-1960 days as a golden age in which abortion was rare. Advocates of legalized abortion criticize those bad old days of "back-alley abortionists" but argue that all along most Americans accepted the practice.

It's not that the history of abortion has been ignored completely; the events of the past three decades have been the subject of hundreds of articles and dozens of books. Reasons for the emphasis on recent history are obvious: not only is that history vital to understand, but information concerning the past several decades is readily available. Ease of research

---

[1]Washington *Post*, June 21, 1991, p. A-21.

is important. When we have lost a dollar at night and are deciding whether to invest a minute in looking for it, we have a much greater pos-sibility of success if the dollar was lost in an area illuminated by a street-light. The problem, however, is that only a few historians have invested time in the earlier, non-illuminated stretches of abortion history. And only one, James Mohr, to his credit, took the time to write a full-length history of nineteenth-century American abortion.[2]

Mohr in the 1970s walked bravely into the darkness of old and hard-to-find records. Like all historians, he had a sheaf of assumptions in one hand and a flashlight in the other. Mohr's book shows his assumptions: that abortion before "quickening" – the time in the fourth or fifth month when a woman can feel fetal movement – was acceptable in America at least until the mid-nineteenth century; that abortion was widely diffused throughout the population in the nineteenth century; that anti-abortion laws passed during that century were an aberration in American history; and that the legalization of abortion over the past two decades thus rep-resents a return to the true American consensus, rather than a sudden deviation from past practice. Mohr's key research question thus became: How did the nineteenth-century anti-abortion aberration occur?

Seeking to answer that question, Mohr used his flashlight in a very efficient way. He explained mid-nineteenth-century changes concerning abortion by arguing that a well-placed pressure group, the American Medical Association, had thwarted the public will. Mohr and his research assistants dutifully read articles in old medical journals and books. In following Mohr's trail, and often reading the same volumes that Mohr read, I have found his survey of the medical literature to be thorough. I respect his work, but in the pages to come I will have to take sharp exception to parts of it – because, as I have found, Mohr walked only one straight path and presented only one simple thesis. History is rarely so straightforward – and in the case of abortion, it is complex and convoluted.

This book examines curved paths, the mysteries of abortion history. The story is not a simple one – individual cases described in the histor-ical record often hinged on nuances of evidence rather than grand prin-ciples – but it is one that must be told if we are to go beyond bumper stickers. This is not a happy book. Since it cuts against the established views and convenient villains of both sides in the abortion wars, I won-

---

[2]James Mohr, *Abortion in America* (New York: Oxford University Press, 1978).

der whether many partisans will have the desire to read it. This is not the book I wanted to write. But after tramping the library stacks and finding information that could just as well remain buried – since it is in no one's real interest to disinter it – I have no choice but to tell what I have found.

The telling is as straightforward as I could make it. The first three chapters of Part One describe the three groups of women who were having abortions through the mid-nineteenth century; Chapter Four then examines the controversial and complicated question of what early anti-abortion laws accomplished and what they did not. Part Two examines the limited successes of pro-lifers as they tried to develop a culture in which abortion was shunned in deed as well as word. Chapters within that section assess the roles of doctors, ministers, journalists, and early social workers. Part Three carries the story into the twentieth century by examining the transition among physicians and the impact of changing values and economic pressures.

A final introductory note: This book was written during 1991 and the first two months of 1992, well before the Supreme Court's *Casey* decision. That decision makes it even more important to tell the real story of mixed victories and defeats over the centuries, rather than spectacular, immediate turn-arounds. I am adding these sentences to the page proofs on the evening of June 29, 1992, as leaders react to the *Casey* decision announced earlier in the day. Many of the statements from both sides are apocalyptic in tone, predicting imminent revolution of one kind or another. As the nations rage it is all the more essential to examine the evidence with calm resolution, and then to act in ways that provide long-term protection for children and mothers.

PART ONE

Abortion Emerges

1

Seduced, Abandoned, and Pregnant

In January 1973, as the Supreme Court was announcing its *Roe v. Wade* decision, construction began in Philadelphia on a shopping mall and restaurant complex known as the New Market. An entire city block along Pine Street had to be excavated. During the excavation, a brick-lined privy pit was uncovered at the rear of the property that is now 110 Pine Street. Archaeologists who dug into the pit found fragments of over one thousand ceramic, glass, and metal artifacts, along with a variety of pins, beads, buttons, dresshooks, lead counters, and wax seals from the 1750-1785 period. The pit also contained over eleven thousand pieces of bone, most of which were animal bones left over from long-ago dinners. However, archaeologists were surprised to discover fifty-two human bones which, after study, were seen to represent the remains of two infants who had been victims of late-term abortions or infanticide.[1]

Were those killings rare occurrences, or were they part of an early American quilt of death? Solid statistics concerning early abortion and

---

[1]Sharon Ann Burnston, "Babies in the Well," *The Pennsylvania Magazine of History and Biography*, Vol. 106 (1982), p. 152. Burnston explains that the bones would not have been those of a newborn dying of natural causes because they were so unceremoniously discarded.

even unwed pregnancy are unavailable,[2] but I have looked at enough pre-1800 records of infanticide and abortion to see a pattern emerging; let's look at some typical cases.

VIRGINIA, 1629: SUSPICION BUT INSUFFICIENT EVIDENCE

Many of us read about Captain John Smith in elementary school, but we probably did not hear about the time he was called in to hear depositions concerning Dorcas Howard. Miss Howard, an unmarried servant, was arrested after she gave birth in secret to a son who was soon found dead; he may have been America's first recorded victim of abortion, or he may have died during birth or through infanticide immediately after birth. Miss Howard was found out after Elizabeth Moorecode and other neighbors saw the dead baby and testified that "the mould of the head was bruised. . . ."[3] In this case John Smith and others found there was insufficient evidence to determine whether the child had died of natural causes or foul play. Similarly ambiguous incidences were scattered through the seventeenth century.[4] However, colony records of October 27, 1665, do show an "indictment against a man and woman for killing a bastard child."

MASSACHUSETTS, 1648: EXECUTION FOR INFANTICIDE

Another giant of American history, John Winthrop, observed the plight of a twenty-one-year-old servant, Mary Martin, seduced by a married man who was "taken with her, and soliciting her chastity. . . ."[5] The man "obtained his desire . . . divers times," Winthrop wrote; Miss Martin soon was "with child, and not able to bear the shame of it, she concealed it."[6] Although a midwife who observed the pregnant woman was suspicious, tight binding kept the concealment intact until December 13, 1648.

---

[2]As one scholar notes with understatement, "The numerical base for the history of American prenuptial pregnancy and illegitimacy has serious gaps and limitations [beyond] the normal problems of data reliability." Daniel Scott Smith, "The Long Cycle in American Illegitimacy and Prenuptial Pregnancy," in Peter Laslett *et al.*, eds, *Bastardy and Its Comparative History* (Cambridge: Harvard University Press, 1980), p. 364.

[3]*Minutes of the Council and General Court*, April 8, 1629, in the Library of Congress; see also the *Virginia Historical Magazine*, Vol. 31 (1923), pp. 210-211.

[4]See *Virginia Magazine of History and Biography*, Vol. 8 (1900-1901), p. 237.

[5]John Winthrop, *Journal [History of New England]; Original Narratives of Early American History*, James K. Hosmer, ed. (New York: Scribner's, 1908), pp. 317-318.

[6]Original spellings have been retained except when to leave them as is would render text unreadable to those unacquainted with colonial spelling and typography.

Then, "in the night, and the child born alive, she kneeled upon the head of it till she thought it had been dead. . . ." But horror was not yet done: "the child, being strong, recovered, and cried again. Then she took it again, and used violence to it till it was quite dead."

Mary Martin did not get away with her crime. The suspicious midwife confronted her and called the authorities. Miss Martin could have burned the tiny corpse, but "search being made, it was found in her chest," that place where unmarried women stored their most precious belongings in an attempt to keep hope alive. When a surgeon found a fracture in the skull, and Miss Martin "confessed the whole truth," she was executed.[7]

MARYLAND, 1652: FIRST CONVICTION FOR INTENTION TO ABORT

Captain William Mitchell was a member of the Maryland governor's council because Cecil Calvert, proprietor of Maryland, pronounced him a man of "honour, worth, and good abilities."[8] However, as Mitchell in 1650 voyaged from England to Maryland accompanied by his twenty-one-year-old bondservant, Susan Warren, Calvert's judgment proved poor. Mitchell tried to convince her to abandon Christianity; he did succeed in convincing her, or forcing her, to sleep with him.[9] When she became pregnant, Captain Mitchell forced her to drink an abortifacient – a potion designed to produce abortion – which caused her to "break into boils and blains, her whole body being scurfy, and the hair of her head almost fallen off."[10]

---

[7]*Ibid.*

[8]Raphael Semmes, *Crime and Punishment in Early Maryland* (Baltimore: Johns Hopkins Press, 1938), pp. 174-177.

[9]*Proprietary v. Mitchell* in *Archives of Maryland*, Vol. 10 (Baltimore: Maryland Historical Society, 1936), p. 176. Martha Webb, a servant, reported that Mitchell tried to persuade Susan Warren that there is no God and that Jesus and the Holy Spirit were but "a man and a pigeon." Susan Warren testified "That when she hath been sick calling on God to help her, Captain Mitchell hath replied, What was that which I called God, Did I know him, had I ever any conference with him, I said not on this person, but by his works, I was confident that I should have help. So He hath left me a while and then come again, How now hath your God help you, Ah thou may'st well be called a woman that will believe anything that is told you, such a thing as God, believe it not thou art merely lead away with what thou parents have told you, that if you do amiss, O, it is a sin, O thou art a fool . . ." (p. 173). Many thanks to Joseph Dellapenna, who told me about this case.

[10]*Ibid.* Susan Warren testified in her deposition "that when Capt. Mitchell perceived she bore a child by him, he prepared a potion of physick overnight." He put the potion into

Susan Warren survived, but the baby was stillborn, and a grand jury indicted Mitchell for having "Murtherously endeavoured to destroy or Murther the Child by him begotten in the Womb of the Said Susan Warren."[11] It could not be proven that Mitchell had murdered the child, but he was convicted of "adultery, fornication, and murtherous intention," fined five thousand pounds of tobacco, and required to give a bond for his future good behavior.[12] Lord Baltimore forced him to resign as a member of the governor's council, and he was forbidden to hold any public office in Maryland. Susan Warren received a whipping for fornication but was freed and discharged from any further service to Mitchell. Court records show Mitchell in repeated trouble thereafter.[13]

MARYLAND, 1656: FROM ABUSE TO ABORTION

Francis Brooke (or Brooks – spellings in the legal records vary) impregnated his servant and was angry about it. Witnesses testified to brutal treatment:

> He did beat her with a cane and he break it all to pieces because she would not give the dog a pail to lick before she fetched water in it. Another time, he had a loin of veal roasted and she was going to take a rib of the said veal and he took an oaken board and broke it to pieces on her. He followed her with pair of tongues [sic] and did beat her with the great end, and your deponent followed him and asked him if he longed to be hanged and he said he did not care if she did miscarry. . . .[14]

Finally, Brooke went all the way: "he gave her wormwood to drink and she fell in labor one night . . . the midwife came and when the child came it was all bruises and the blood black in it."[15] Midwife Rose Smith

---

a poached egg and came to her as she was in bed and "bid take, and she requesting to know for what, he said if she would not take it he would thrust it down her throat, so she being in bed could not withstand it. . . ."(p. 176).

[11]*Ibid.*, pp. 182-185.

[12]Mitchell's actions were seen as a natural result of his beliefs: he made "a Common practice by blasphemous expressions and otherwise to mock and deride God's Ordinances and all Religion, thereby to open a way to all wicked lustfull licentious and prophane Courses."

[13]*Archives*, Vol. 10, p. 529.

[14]Testimony of Elizabeth Claxton in *Proprietary v. Brooks*, in *Archives of Maryland*, Vol. 10, p. 464.

[15]*Ibid.*

testified that when she delivered the tiny unborn child, "he was a man-child about three months old. . . ." Even though the child had died before "quickening," court records state that "Brooke was brought before this court on suspicion of murder."[16] Brooke managed to escape punishment by marrying his servant and thus disqualifying the principal witness against him. The provincial records do not tell us whether Mr. and Mrs. Brooke lived happily ever after, but his arrest for murder does indicate the seriousness of abortion in the colonial mind.[17]

MARYLAND, 1663: RAPE AND ABORTION

Seven Maryland residents signed depositions charging a Maryland surgeon, Jacob [aka John] Lumbrozo, with committing an abortion on his twenty-two-year-old maidservant, Elizabeth Wieles. The incident allegedly began with rape; it was said that Lumbrozo had thrown Miss Wieles on a bed, covered her mouth with a handkerchief, and had "the use of her body." Later he gave her a strong abortifacient, and she soon passed "a clod of blood as big as a fist."[18]

Details were vivid: Joseph Dorroseol testified that Miss Wieles said "the Physick that the doctor did give her did kill the child in the womb . . . the doctor did hold her back for she was in such pain and misery that she thought that she would die."[19] Richard Trew testified that Miss Wieles had told him of the rape and the use of an abortifacient that made her feel as if "her back broke asunder." George Harris said that Miss Wieles told him "that the Doctor took her to bed and had lain with her whether she would or no, whereof before she could consent to lie with him, he took a book in his hand and swore many bitter oaths" that he would marry her.[20]

After hearing such testimony, a jury of twelve men charged

---

16 *Ibid.*

17 *Ibid.*, pp. 464-465, 486-488.

18 *Proprietary v. Lumbrozo*, in *Archives of Maryland*, Vol. 53 (Baltimore: Maryland Historical Society, 1936), pp. 387-391, 496-497.

19 *Ibid.*

20 *Ibid.* Elizabeth Wieles complicated matters by saying on June 29, 1663, "What I have said concerning John Lumbrozo it is false for he left me no such thing as I have reported and for the physick I thought it was Sak, whereupon I drank it." The next day, however, Margaret Oles put that testimony in perspective by saying that Miss Wieles had asked her advice on how to testify: "whether it was best for her to clear him or no. This deponent made answer to her again, by God He knows. . . . I do not know such things and further sayth not."

Lumbrozo with a felony because "she was with child when John Lumbrozo, he did give her physick to destroy it. . . ."[21] Lumbrozo evidently married Elizabeth Wieles, as he had promised earlier, and in that way disqualified her from testifying; all the depositions had to be treated as hearsay, and Lumbrozo escaped punishment.[22]

MASSACHUSETTS AND MARYLAND, 1680s: ABORTIFACIENT USE

Potions designed to bring about abortion sometimes were forced on bondservants, and some desperate women ingested them on their own. Elizabeth Robins took oil of savin – the product of bitter-tasting juniper berries (*Juniperus sabina*) – in colonial Maryland when she became pregnant after committing incest with her brother and adultery with another man.[23] Similarly, when a fourteen-year-old in Charlestown, Massachusetts, was pregnant in 1681, some of her family members allegedly "gave her boyld Saffin."[24]

NEW YORK, 1719: MURDER OF A NEWBORN

Anna Maria Cockin said a man had gotten her "half Drunk," promised her a pair of shoes, and impregnated her. She argued, however, that she was no murderer. While in agitated labor, she said, she had gotten out of the bed and the baby "fell from her upon the ground." She said she did not know whether the baby was stillborn or had come out alive. There was no proof of infanticide. A jury acquitted her of murder but sentenced her to thirty-one lashes and banishment from the county.[25]

---

[21] *Ibid.*, p. 391.

[22] A bill of sale by John Lumbrozo and his wife Elizabeth is dated from November 16, 1663. Also in the records (p. 496) is a bill of sale from September 4, 1660, by John Lumbrozo and his wife Elizabeth, but that appears to be a slip of the pen. Lumbrozo was involved in many other colonial activities under the name of Jacob or John. See *Archives*, Vol. 49, pp. 30, 52, 53, 76, 84, 85, 104, 111, 112, 142, 145, 147, 156, 161, 354, 455.

[23] Semmes, *Crimes and Punishment in Early Maryland*, pp. 203-204.

[24] Roger Thompson, *Sex in Middlesex: Popular Mores in a Massachusetts County, 1649-1699* (Amherst, MA: The University of Massachusetts Press, 1986), p. 183.

[25] Douglas Greenberg, *Crime and Law Enforcement in the Colony of New York, 1691-1776* (Ithaca, NY: Cornell University Press, 1976), pp. 117-118.

MAINE, 1712: TREATMENT OF
AN UNWED PREGNANCY

On April 1, 1712, a grand jury that included Mathew Austine charged Mathew's son Ichabod with being "the reputed father of a bastard child begotten on the body of Sarah More." The jury acted after Miss More testified that Ichabod was the father; he was sent to jail until he posted bond, and was told that he had better be "of the good behavior towards her Majesty and her Liege people & Especially toward the sd Sarah More."[26] On July 1 the case was continued, for Sarah More was not yet "Delivered of sd child," and it may have been hoped that marriage would ensue.[27] By October 7, however, she had given birth, and Ichabod had not come through; he was ordered to pay child support (two shillings six pence per week). Although he had not acknowledged paternity, Sarah More was "constent in sd accusation in court face to face, also Mary Black who did the office of Midwife & did examin sd Sarah More in the time of her Travell she did accuse sd Austine & no other man."[28]

By 1718 Sarah More was married, to one Jonathan Ireland.[29] Ichabod Austine stayed in trouble, with convictions for public drunkenness in 1713 and 1714 and fornication in 1718, at which time he was sentenced to either a whipping (ten stripes on his naked back) or a fine of thirty shillings; his choice is not recorded.[30] During those seven years the court also required paternity payments from Samuel Hill, Jr., "he denying the fact but the sd Abigail Chapman continuing constant in her accusation," and from Paul Williams and Joseph Woodson, under similar circumstances.[31] In each case payment was to continue "during this court's pleasure," which could be until marriage of the woman or majority of the child.[32]

---

[26] *Province and Court Records of Maine: The Court Records of York County, Maine, Province of Massachusetts Bay, April 1711 – October 1718* (Portland, ME: Maine Historical Society, 1928), p. 128.

[27] *Ibid.*, p. 130.

[28] *Ibid.*, p. 132.

[29] *Ibid.*, p. 209.

[30] *Ibid.*, pp. 138, 140, 153, 167, 207, 208.

[31] *Ibid.*, pp. 139, 163, 196-197.

[32] *Ibid.*, p. 197.

MASSACHUSETTS, 1670-1807:
FIFTY-ONE INFANTICIDE CONVICTIONS

Massachusetts colonial records show that children who were illegitimate at birth made up a high-risk population.[33] Only about 2 percent of all Massachusetts children during the colonial period were illegitimate; 90 percent of the neonates legally found to have been murdered were. A typical tragedy: unwed Elizabeth Emmison of Haverhill, Massachusetts, was executed in 1693 after she slept with Samuel Lad, became pregnant, gave birth to twins in her father's house, and murdered them.[34]

There is much more in the colonial records, but even this group of episodes shows why colonial officials expressed concern about the number of unmarried woman servants who had "been gotten with child" and then compounded the crime with killing. Maidservants repeatedly were urged to maintain chastity or at least to demand, prior to intercourse, a written promise of marriage.[35] (If the evidence satisfied the court, an unmarried freeman had to marry her or "recompense her abuse.") Courts in Virginia showed sympathy to female servants: When Margaret Connor charged her master with attempting to "prostitute her body to him," the court accepted the charge and forced her master to provide a cash bond to secure good behavior.[36] But infant killings continued. The case of one unmarried woman, Anne Barbery, who was called up "upon suspicion of felony" when her baby died shortly after birth, had hundreds of echoes. (Miss Barbery had hid her newborn in a tobacco house and said she had planned to take the baby to Joseph Edlow, the father of the child. There was no mark on the baby, and since the child may have died from lack of proper care, the accused received thirty lashes but was not convicted of murder.)[37]

The records suggest that, overall, infanticide was probably the most frequent way of killing unwanted, illegitimate children. Ballads do not

---

[33]See Peter C. Hoffer and N. E. H. Hull, *Murdering Mothers: Infanticide in England and New England, 1558-1803* (New York: New York University Press, 1981), pp. 38-39. There were fifteen more convictions in Connecticut.

[34]*Ibid.*, pp. 55, 59-60 and statistics on p. 109. Also see Joseph Dellapenna, "Brief Amicus Curiae of the American Academy of Medical Ethics in Support of Appellants in *Turnock* and Cross-petitioners in *Hodgson*," Supreme Court of the United States, October Term, 1989, pp. 17-18, for citation of Delaware and Virginia cases in which the outcome was unknown.

[35]Semmes, *Crimes and Punishment in Early Maryland*, p. 188.

[36]John d'Emilio and Estelle B. Freedman, *Intimate Matters* (New York: Harper & Row, 1988), p. 12.

[37]Semmes, *Crimes and Punishment in Early Maryland*, p. 195,

always reflect actual practice, but the existence in both America and England of many ballads about infanticide – such as "The Cruel Mother"– is suggestive:

> There was a lady come from York / All alone, alone and aloney, / She fell in love with her father's clerk/ Down by the greenwood siding.
>
> When nine months was gone and past / Then she had two pretty babes born. . . . She took her penknife keen and sharp / And pierced those babies' tender hearts.
>
> She buried them under a marble stone / And then she said she would go home. / As she was in her father's hall / She spied those babes a-playing at ball.
>
> "O babes, oh babes if you were mine / I would dress you up in silks so fine." / "Oh mother dear when we were thine / You did not dress us up in silks so fine."

The ballad concluded, "You took your penknife keen and sharp/ And pierced us babies' tender hearts."[38]

Physical and social reasons made abortion the less preferred mode of infant murder. Surgical abortion was virtually a guaranteed double-killer, due to poor knowledge of anatomy and the great risk of infection. Abortifacients were known and used in early America, however. Along with oil of savin, Tansy Oil (*Tanacetum vulgare*) was "a tradition among American women for its certainty as an abortifacient," one doctor recalled in later years.[39] Although pharmacologists today know of tansy as a deadly poison capable of killing not only unborn children but their mothers as well, southern doctors reported that it was "commonly cultivated in our gardens" and used by some desperate slave women.[40] Ergot, the popular name for the fungus *Claviceps purpurea*, a hard protru-

---

[38]"The Cruel Mother," in B. H. Bronson, *The Traditional Tunes of the Child Ballads*, Vol. 1 (Princeton, NJ: Princeton University Press, 1959), p. 292.

[39]See Ely van de Warker, "The Criminal Use of Proprietary or Advertised Nostrums," *New York Medical Journal*, Vol. 17 (January 1873), pp. 23-35.

[40]See John H. Morgan, "An Essay on the Causes of the Production of Abortion among the Negro Population," *Nashville Journal of Medicine and Surgery*, Vol. 19 (1860), pp. 117-118. Morgan noted that tansy was sometimes used among slaves; how often, neither he nor recent statistical analyses say. The legal documents and church records that are the major sources for studying illegitimacy in early America often leave us stranded at third base concerning the whole population; the records concerning blacks do not even get us to first base. For further discussion see Dr. John Metcalf, "Statistics in Midwifery," *American Journal of the Medical Sciences*, Vol. 6 (October 1843), p. 339.

sion from stalks of rye and other infected grain, was sometimes administered in small doses during labor to strengthen contractions or to aid in expulsion of the plaçenta, but it had an abortion-related reputation as well and in Germany was sometimes called *Kindesmord,* or "infant's death."[41] Other substances also had their supporters. Rue *(Ruta graveolens)* was called by some "more effectual than tansy to procure abortion."[42]

Historians have differed on how often abortifacients were used in colonial days and how "effectual" they were; the anecdotal evidence, which is all we have in this and many other abortion-related issues, is mixed. Oil of savin, for example, often was ingested in Europe, with some users reporting that it had not killed their unborn children, and others not reporting at all because it had killed them.[43] Since abortifacients worked by causing a horrible shock to the entire body of the maternal user, dosage was key, and effects could range all the way from a slightly upset stomach to death of child or death of mother and child. The few researchers who have looked into savin use have differed about its impact, perhaps because its impact could vary so immensely. When Elizabeth Wells of Massachusetts in 1668 took savin boiled in beer, her pregnancy continued.[44] Ten years later, however, another Massachusetts resident, Hannah Blood of Groton, was said to have used savin and lost "her great belly" that made her "as big as a woman ready to ly in."[45]

Results upon ingestion were difficult to predict precisely for at least four reasons. First, the orally transmitted recipes varied considerably, "some midwives urging the mother to drink two or three glasses of the concoction in an afternoon, others counseling that it be consumed over

---

[41]Morgan in 1860 *(ibid.,* p.120) wrote that three white women had taken ergot during their third or fourth months of pregnancy, and two of them had aborted.

[42]*Ibid.,* p. 118, quoting an elderly black woman.

[43]Daniel Defoe described use of savin, or another abortifacient, in *Conjugal Lewdness* (1727): "I have heard of a certain Quack in this Town, and knew him too, who gave the Directions to his Patients, as follows:

No. 1. If the Party or Woman be young with Child, not above three Months gone, and would miscarry without Noise, and without Danger, take the Bolus herewith sent in the Evening an Hour before she goes to Bed, and thirty drops of the Tincture in the Bottle, just when she goes to Bed, repeating the Drops in Rhenish Wine, right Moselle.

No. 2. If she is quick with Child, and desires to miscarry, take two papers of the Powder here enclosed, Night and Morning, infused in the Draught contained in the Bottle; taking it twice, shall bring away the Conception."

[44]Thompson, *Sex in Middlesex,* p. 25.

[45]*Ibid.*

a period of days."[46] Second, the amount of volatile oil in the plants varied widely, depending on soil conditions, the month of harvesting, the amount of rain, the particular plant parts used, and the technique of extracting the oil.[47] Third, the presence of active ingredients depended on how long a plant was stored and how long it was cooked; boiling the leaves for hours probably cooked away much of the oil.[48] Fourth, abortifacients that were harvested by someone other than the user might be adulterated, as illegal drugs now often are.

Overall, to label abortifacient use as *either* ineffective or suicidal is oversimplifying; since dosage was crucial, those who were desperate might try to get the amount and potency that would kill unborn children but not themselves. The emphasis was on desperation and on powerless women being forced or tricked into ingesting these substances by the men who had seduced or raped them. Since ingesting savin or other abortifacients was like playing Russian roulette with three bullets in the chambers, it is unlikely that colonial women would use the substances voluntarily unless they felt they had no other choice. How often they would feel such hopelessness brings us to consideration of the social climate concerning premarital sexual relations and consequent out-of-wedlock conceptions.

Those of us who imbibed myths of the good old days might be shocked to learn how frequent those activities and outcomes were, particularly during the late eighteenth century. Before 1680, the best estimates are that only 3 percent of colonial brides had children within six months of marriage, and 8 percent within nine months. But by the 1760-1800 period the percentages had risen to 17 and 33 respectively.[49] Although there were variations from colony to colony, the trend in each was similar. Some of those premarital pregnancies were intentional, a way of forcing the issue if parents objected to a marriage, but most evidently were unwanted. There was a major societal difference between then and now, however: most of these children were legitimized at birth, largely due to moral pressure (internal and external) on fathers to do the right thing.

The pressure was largely religious, familial, and churchly, but addi-

---

[46]Edward Shorter, *A History of Women's Bodies* (New York: Basic, 1982), p. 188.

[47]Active ingredients normally reach their maximum presence about budding time.

[48]Shorter, *A History of Women's Bodies*, pp. 186-187.

[49]See Robert V. Wells, *Revolutions in Americans' Lives* (Westport, CT: Greenwood, 1982), p. 353.

tional convincers were forthcoming if more were needed. Beginning in 1668 Massachusetts law stipulated that unwed mothers during delivery were to be asked to name the father. The belief was that a statement in labor was akin to a dying declaration and that a woman facing a great test would not lie. Men accused could not be convicted of adultery, since confession or two witnesses were needed for that, but would be called the "reputed father" and required to pay support.[50] Other colonies developed similar procedures that lasted into the days of early statehood. In Princess Anne County, Virginia, Thomas Galt, Charles Smyth, Samuel Smith, and Thomas Walke posted bond after accusations by Sarah King, Mary Davies, Lovey Chappel, and Mary Nimmo respectively during the period from 1783 to 1790.[51]

These moral and legal pressures meant that few pregnant women were abandoned. Paternity suits often led to belated marriage. Maine midwife Martha Ballard delivered twenty out-of-wedlock babies and recorded in her diary the names of thirteen of the fathers, after having "taken testimony" as the law instructed.[52] The court action that frequently followed was often successful. Nineteen paternity suits in Lincoln County, Maine, between 1761 and 1799 resulted in only three acquittals. Most actions were settled out of court, often – when the imputed fathers were members of local families – by marriage. For example, Mary Crawford of Bath, Maine, certified "that Samuel Todd of said Bath hath agreed to make me satisfaction for getting me with child by promising to marry me, therefore, I wish that the prosecution I commenced against him for so doing may be squashed."[53] Similarly, Martha Ballard's son Jonathon, when identified as the father by the unmarried Sally Pierce, married her in 1792, four months after the child was born and a month before his scheduled trial.[54]

Unmarried women undergoing crisis pregnancies, in short, had high expectations of marriage by birth. In one Massachusetts county dur-

---

[50]Minnesota had a similar law in 1920.

[51]*Virginia Antiquary: Princess Anne County Volume I, Loose Papers, 1700-1789*, pp. 83, 116, 119, 149, 154, 171-173.

[52]Laurel T. Ulrich, *A Midwife's Tale* (New York: Knopf, 1990), p. 151. More of the diary is available in print as a major section of Charles E. Nash, *The History of Augusta* (Augusta, ME: Charles E. Nash & Son, 1904).

[53]Ulrich, *ibid.*, p. 155.

[54]*Ibid.*, pp. 151-155. Martha Ballard delivered Sally Pierce's baby and obtained the testimony implicating her son, as the law required. Martha Ballard then made the new bride welcome and wrote in her diary (March 2, 1792), "Helped Sally nurse her Babe." Jonathon and Sally remained married for 46 years, until Jonathon died in 1838.

ing the 1760s over 80 percent of non-maritally conceived births were legitimated by the marriage of their parents, and counties in other colonies had similar records.[55] To be married under such shotgun circumstances might seem hard on some women, except that the procedure was common and did not carry disgrace; besides, most marriages were by (at least informal) parental arrangement anyway. Furthermore, through such means the overall illegitimacy rate was less than 1 to 3 percent of all births through 1750. Where fathers resolutely refused marriage, courts in Virginia and other colonies ordered payment. Thus economic desperation was unlikely to drive most unmarried, pregnant women to infanticide or abortion.

A remarkable Maine case from 1724 shows the extent of economic protection. Let's read along in the colonial records (with original spellings maintained):

March 16th: 1724. Daniel Paul Jun'r of Kittery in the sd County Shipwright being brought before Joseph Hammond Esq'r One of his Maj'tys Justices of the peace for sd county and being Accused by Bathsheba Lydston of sd Kittery Singlewoman for begeting her with Child of which She was delivered the 24th of Dec'r Last, He denying the fact."[56]

[3] Mistress Mary King Testifyeth that about the 24th day of Dec'r Last She was with Bathsheba Lydston in her Travail & asked her who was the father of her Child She then Travailed with. She Said it was Daniel Pauls.[57]

Sarah Allen Testifyeth that about the 24th of Dec'r Last She was with Bathsheba Lydston in her Travail & heard Mistress King who was the Midwife ask sd Bathsheba who was the father of her Child. She said it was Daniel Paul The Same Question being Asked her Several times She Continued Constant in the Same. . . .[58]

But then some questions were raised:

Abigail Lydston the wife of John Lydston Testifieth, I heard Bathsheba Lydston Say the Last Sumer past At my father Pauls House, And there She was a telling what a great Liberty a Young woman has to what a

---

[55]Daniel Scott Smith on Middlesex County, in Laslett, *Bastardy and Its Comparative History*, p. 373.
[56]Court of General Sessions, 7 April 1724, in *Province and Court Records of Maine*, p. 150.
[57]*Ibid.*
[58]*Ibid.*

young man hath for, Said She, I will Let any Young man get me with child and then, Said She, I can lay it to who I please because a woman has that Liberty granted to them.[59]

Samuel Remich Testifyeth that Sometimes the Last Summer he Saw Joseph Hill go in to Mr Lydstons house And Soon after he the Deponant went after him and saw him Sitting on the bed with Bathsheba Lydston & he saw no other person in the house.[60]

Sarah Paul the wife of Daniel Paul Testifyeth I heard Bathsheba Lydston Say the Last Summer past that Thomas Ham & Abigail Hill and She used to lye together in Naked bed for above a year & a halfe off & on upon times and I heard Bathsheba Lydston Say that Sometimes they used to do it once a night Sometimes twice a night And sometimes Three times a night & Bathsheba Lydston Said that Sometimes Abigail Hill used to get up and leave Thomas Ham & She together in the bed.

Was Sarah Paul trying to get her son off, or was Daniel Paul, Jr., guilty?

Susannah Lydstone of full Age testifieth and saith that Sundri times she saw Daniel Paull Juner and Bathshabe Lydstone [sic] In company one with Another and further the said Susannah Lydstone saith that the Last Spring Past She saw Paull and Bathshabe Lydstone [and] several others with them and the all went Away Except the said Paull and Bathshabe Lydstone.[61]

John Ledstone of full age Sayeth that he has seen Daniel Paull and Bathsheba Ledston often together Loveing and familor at Said Paulls fathers house and saw them walk away together after it was night at Severall times, this was last Spring. He further Saith that he has Seen Josep Hill Sitting on the bed with Bathsheba Also Thomas Ham and Lemuel Bickford.

Lydia Phillaps of full age Sayeth Shee was att Abegille Ledstones talking concerning Bathsheba Ledston and Daniel Paull Sum time in desember last and Abegille Ledston told this Deponant that Daniel Paull told her father Ledston that Said Bathsheba Ledstons Child was none of his for he had not lyed with her Since January.[62]

Nevertheless, once it was shown that Daniel Paul, Jr., had slept at some point with Bathsheba Lydston, he was liable. The official order came:

---

[59] *Ibid.*, p. 151.
[60] *Ibid.*
[61] *Ibid.*, pp. 151-152.
[62] *Ibid.*, p. 152.

"an order of his Maj'tys Justices of the Court of Gen'l Sessions . . . for the sd Daniel Paul Jun'r his paying Two Shillings & Sixpense per week unto Bathsheba Lydston of Kittery aforesd Singlewoman Toward the maintainance of her child from the birth therof Dureing the Courts pleasure."[63] That pleasure would generally last until the apprenticeship age of thirteen or so – and until then the child would be provided for out of the deepest liable pocket the mother could find.

A disgraced woman cannot live by bread alone, of course, so questions of social pressure are important even when material support is available. Significantly, in colonial times the pressure largely was on a father who would not do the right thing, not on the mother.[64] Abandoned unwed mothers were not shunned, and court records show them marrying other men of the community."[65] In any event, the woman could know that her child's life would not be one of obloquy; as Daniel Smith has noted, "by and large, the colonists were unwilling to punish children for the sins of the parents."[66] Illegitimate children could inherit property and become indentured to learn a trade; some, such as William Franklin (the last royal governor of New Jersey) and Alexander Hamilton, were able to become political leaders.

Behind the physical and social checks on abortion loomed the theological and the scientific. In an age of frequent Scripture reading it was difficult to avoid noticing that the Bible over forty times states that human life begins with conception.[67] At a time when sermons were the major means of communication and public affairs analysis, New England was filled with Presbyterian and Congregationalist churches founded on the doctrines of John Calvin, who wrote that an unborn child, "though enclosed in the womb of its mother, is already a human being" and should not be "rob[bed] of the life which it has not yet begun to enjoy."[68]

---

[63] *Ibid.*, p. 153.

[64] Nathaniel Hawthorne's character Hester Prynne wore her scarlet letter when she would not reveal the name of the father.

[65] The marriage of Sarah More to Jonathan Ireland in 1718, previously noted, is one example.

[66] Laslett, *Bastardy and Its Comparative History*, p. 36.

[67] Many books and articles have examined Biblical views of abortion; three of the most useful are John J. Davis, *Abortion and the Christian* (Philadelphia: Presbyterian and Reformed, 1984); Harold O. J. Brown, "What the Supreme Court Didn't Know," *Human Life Review*, Spring 1975, pp. 5-21; and John Warwick Montgomery, "The Fetus and Personhood," *Human Life Review*, Spring 1975, pp. 41-49.

[68] *Calvin's Commentaries*, Vol. 3 (Grand Rapids, MI: Baker Book House, 1981), p. 42; translated from the original Latin by Rev. Charles W. Bingham. Calvin added, "If it

A host of other Calvinists criticized "those who, by the same forbidden lust or violent abortions of offspring, destroy it before it was born. . . ."[69] The Anglican Church dominant in other parts of the country, and Lutheran churches as well, strongly opposed abortion, in the spirit of Conrad Dannhauer's attack on the "Molech-sacrifice to the god of the whorish spirit. . . ."[70]

English books available in the American colonies also included strong injunctions against abortion. One popular book written by a person who called himself "Aristotle" instructed midwives to refuse "to give directions for such Medicines as will cause abortion, to pleasure those that have unlawfully conceived, which to do is a high degree of wickedness, and may be ranked with Murther."[71] Nicholas Culpeper, writing about drugs that could be used in cases of menstrual obstruction, told midwives, "give not any of those to any that is with Child, lest you turn Murtherers, wilful Murther seldom goes unpunished in this World, never in that to come."[72] Benjamin Wadsworth, later to be president of Harvard College, declared in 1712 that "If any purposely endeavor [sic] to destroy the Fruit of their Womb (whether they actually do it or not) they're guilty of Murder in God's account."[73] Dr. John Burns gave a medical lesson with a moral emphasis:

Acrid substances such as savine . . . may produce abortions. Such medicines, likewise, exert a violent action on the stomach or bowels, where upon the principals formerly mentioned certainly excite abortion; and very often are taken designedly for that purpose in such quantity to produce fatal effects; here I must remark that many people at least pretend to view attempts to excite abortion as different than murder, upon the principle that the embryo does not possess of life [for] it

---

seems more horrible to kill a man in his own house than in a field, because a man's house is his place of most secure refuge, it ought surely to be deemed more atrocious to destroy an unborn child [Latin: *foetus*] in the womb before it has come to light."

[69]Andre Rivet (1573-1651), in Charles D. Provan, *The Bible and Birth Control* (Monongahela, PA: Zimmer, 1989), p. 87.

[70]Lindsay Dewar, *An Outline of Anglican Moral Theology* (London: A. W. Mowbrey, 1968), p. 85; George Hunston Williams, "Religious Residues and Presuppositions in the American Debate on Abortion," *Theological Studies*, Vol. 31 (1970), pp. 43-46; Dannhauer (1603-1666) quoted in Provan, p. 69.

[71]*Aristotle's Masterpiece, Or The Secrets of Generation Displayed in All the Parts Thereof* (London: n.p., 1684), p. 101.

[72]Nicholas Culpeper, *A Directory for Midwives* (London: n.p., 1671), p. 69.

[73]Benjamin Wadsworth, *The Well-Ordered Family* (Boston: Green, 1712), p. 45.

undoubtedly can neither think or act, but upon the same reasoning we should conclude it to be innocent to kill the child in birth. Whoever prevents life from continuing, until it arrives at perfection, is certainly as culpable as if he had taken it away after that had been accomplished.[74]

Scientific understanding of when human life began (as far as that understanding pushed into the popular consciousness, a transition difficult to measure) also may have undermined any inclinations to abort. During the seventeenth and eighteenth centuries many scientists essentially believed human life to begin not *after* quickening but *before* conception. Anton von Leeuwenhoek's discovery of microscopic "animalcules" in 1674 gave a boost to old theories that humans were actually "preformed" and existed as little people within the sperm. Those who were "animalculists," such as Leeuwenhoek, believed that men provided not only sperm but, essentially, entire babies: Children were "implanted" rather than "conceived."[75] Some philosophers, bothered by the loss of so many little people in unused sperm, became "ovists" and asserted that the baby already existed within the mother and was activated by contact with the sperm.[76] Overall, as historian Francis Kole notes, "From about 1674 the Preformation Doctrine was generally accepted and it was only a question of whether the miniature was in the egg or in the sperm."[77]

Preformationists, and particularly animalculists, remained dominant until almost 1800; even in the nineteenth century scientists such as Cuvier were preformationists. Karl Ernst von Baer's discovery of ova in dogs in 1827 finally illuminated the process of conception, but even after that the old theories stuck around for a while.[78] How much these preformationist theories influenced general popular attitudes is hard to say,

---

[74]John Burns, *Observations on Abortion* (New York: Collins and Perkins, 1809), p. 34.

[75]For an early American discussion of theories of conception and implantation, see Dr. Thomas Denman, *Introduction to the Practice of Midwifery* (New York: James Oram, 1802), pp. 94-97.

[76]However, Erasmus Darwin in 1794 typified the Enlightenment emphasis on natural process by saying that if millions of young fish perished while a few lived, the seminal animalcules could do likewise.

[77]Francis J. Kole, *Early Theories of Sexual Generation* (Oxford: Clarendon Press, 1930), pp. 53, 61, 63, 121.

[78]See Arthur W. Meyer, *The Rise of Embryology* (London: Oxford University Press, 1939), pp. 54-194; Shirley A. Roe, *Matter, Life, and Generation: Eighteenth-century Embryology and the Haller-Wolff Debate* (Cambridge: Cambridge University Press, 1981), pp. 1-123, and Joseph Needham, *A History of Embryology* (Cambridge, MA: The University Press, 1934), pp. 115-240.

but they did find their way into popular works of the eighteenth and nineteenth centuries that described how the "animalcule enters the ovum, where, being surrounded with albuminous fluid with which it is nourished, it gradually becomes developed. . . ."[79] As late as 1860 a popular American medical text was stating that semen contains "a vast number of animalcules, and that one or more of these was conveyed through the fallopian tubes to the uterus and there became the fetus, and that the female performed no other function than that of nourishing the germ till it reached a sufficient degree of development to be expelled."[80] It does seem that those who accepted "preformation" ideas would be unlikely to smile at abortion just because it was before quickening.[81]

In any event, with physical, social, theological and "scientific" reasons all making abortion unacceptable, only those in extreme duress or with contempt for existing standards would resort to it. Since there were no pregnancy tests and early signs of possible pregnancy could be misleading, few women were likely to attempt early abortions, even if they wished to play abortifacient roulette. (Until the late nineteenth century, determination of pregnancy before quickening was extremely uncertain.) Since pregnancy frequently led to marriage, with its provision of social and economic protection, few women would attempt mid-term abortions that would preclude that generally welcome possibility. Since late abortions were very dangerous to the mother, the tendency at that point, even if desperation was setting in, would be to wait until birth.[82]

How frequent was abortion? We know of the occasional incidents, but we have no reliable statistics. It is worth noting that colonial court records are filled with reports of flogging, fornication, and fraud; colonies and municipalities adopted statutes directed at the everyday crimes, but

---

[79]Charles Knowlton, *The Fruits of Philosophy* (Chicago: G. E. Wilson, 1870), pp. 11, 14. This was obvious, Knowlton argued, because "the offspring generally partakes more or less of the character of its male parent."

[80]Dr. B. L. Hill, *Midwifery Illustrated* (Cincinnati: J. W. Sewell, 1860), p. 44. Hill may have been behind the times, but as late as 1849 one of America's leading obstetricians, Dr. Charles Meigs, was writing that no one really knew how conception occurred. See Meigs, *Obstetrics* (Philadelphia: Lea and Blanchard, 1849), p. 149.

[81]See also John Noonan, *Contraception: A History of Its Treatment by the Catholic Theologians and Canonists* (Cambridge: Harvard University Press, 1986), pp. 232-237. Preformationist ideas also went well with the medieval theological tradition that treated contraception as homicide.

[82]Hoffer and Hull, *Murdering Mothers*, note that "Neonaticide was for some of these vulnerable unwed mothers a deliberate form of delayed abortion. The similarity and relationship between the two crimes is impressive" (p. 154).

they evidently had far less need to act on abortion. However, along with common law traditions, many colonies had statutory proscriptions on the concealment of birth, a practice closely related to abortion and infanticide, as Chapter Four will show.[83] Furthermore, New York City on July 27, 1716 enacted an ordinance that forbade midwives to aid in or recommend abortion, and thus severely limited access to abortion services.[84] All midwives were required to swear that they would "not Give any Counsel or Administer any Herb Medicine or Potion, or any other thing to any Woman being with Child whereby She Should Destroy or Miscarry of that she goeth withall before her time."[85]

The abortion and infanticide questions that historians *can* answer for the colonial period and the early years of the Republic do not so much involve *how many*, but *why?* Repeatedly the women involved in the crimes were not only unwed but among the minority of the pregnant unmarried who fell outside the informal and legal society safety nets. In South Carolina the four unmarried women during the period from 1794 to 1836 who were charged with infanticide had, for a variety of reasons, neither family nor friends to fall back on.[86] In Pennsylvania, Barbara Young was sentenced to three years of hard labor for "Concealing the death of her Bastard child."[87] Phoebe Cromwell was sentenced to five years of hard labor, half to be spent in solitary confinement, for "Concealing the birth and death of her Bastard child," and Elizabeth Bumberger, Sarah Taylor, Catharin Schneider, and Tenea Draper also went to prison on those charges.[88] On June 10, 1809, twenty thousand people in Reading, Pennsylvania, watched as Susanna Cox was hanged for infanticide. Eight years later a thesis by John Brodhead Beck com-

---

[83]See, for example *Calendar of Virginia State Papers*, Vol. 1 (1710), p. 143, and *Hening's Statutes of Virginia*, Vol. 3, pp. 516, 517. See also Samuel Evans Massengill, *A Sketch of Medicine and Pharmacy* (Bristol, TN: Massengill Co., 1942), p. 294. (The assumption was that an unwed mother who gave birth *secretly* to a child who died immediately had nothing good in mind.)

[84]*Minutes of the Common Council of New York City*, Vol. 3, p. 122; quoted in Dennis J. Horan and Thomas J. Marzen, "Abortion and Midwifery: A Footnote in Legal History," in Thomas W. Hilgers, Dennis J. Horan and David Mall, *New Perspectives on Human Abortion* (Frederick, MD: University Publications of America, 1981), p. 199.

[85]*Ibid.*

[86]Jack Kenny Williams, *Vogues in Villainy: Crime and Retribution in Ante-bellum South Carolina* (Columbia: University of South Carolina Press, 1959), p. 54

[87]See Sharon Ann Burnston, "Babies in the Well," *The Pennsylvania Magazine of History and Biography*, Vol. 106 (1982), p. 176.

[88]*Ibid.*, p. 177.

mented on the relation of seduction and abortion and suggested the degree of desperation involved:

> A young female of character and reputable connexions, and possessed of tender sensibility, may have been betrayed by the arts of a base seducer, and when reduced to a state of pregnancy, to avoid the disgrace which must otherwise be her lot, may stifle the birth in the womb, or after it is born, in a state of phrenzy, imbrue her hands in her infant's blood.[89]

Sadly, more isolated women come into the historical record in the early nineteenth century. Urbanization (small-scale by our standards, but still a movement out of small villages) touched off a change in the nature of households. As historian Peter Holloran has noted, "The early American household was not an isolated self-centered institution, but rather a semi-public institution with community-ordained and protected roles far beyond modern family functions."[90] Within those families, homeless and wayward children could learn family discipline and honest work. After 1800, however, the apprenticeship system began its decline, and masters came to regard servants more as hired hands than family members. Servants were less likely to be the children of friends and neighbors and more often migrants to Boston from rural New England, or Irish, Canadian or British immigrants. Furthermore, seduction and abandonment became easier as towns began to grow; a woman's family was not present to press for marriage when extramarital activity resulted in pregnancy.

Soon stories of servants seduced and abandoned were on the increase. One young woman came from rural New Jersey to Philadelphia and "lived some months in a family, conducting herself with perfect propriety, when in an unfortunate hour, she formed an acquaintance with one who, under a marriage engagement, planned and effected her ruin and then absconded."[91] Another woman, seventeen-year-old Isabelle Boltwood, worked as a housemaid and nurse in Rochester and was "'ruined' by a young man who worked in a

---

[89] J. B. Beck, "An Inaugural Dissertation on Infanticide," *Medical Dissertations and Theses* (New York: J. Seymour, 1817), p. 84.
[90] Peter C. Holloran, *Boston's Wayward Children: Social Services for Homeless Children, 1830-1930* (Rutherford, NJ: Fairleigh Dickenson University Press, 1989), p. 18.
[91] Quoted in Faye Duden, *Serving Women* (Middletown, CT: Wesleyan University Press, 1983), p. 215.

hotel."[92] Dr. Elizabeth Blackwell worked in the women's syphilitic ward in the Philadelphia almshouse in 1848 and recorded that "Most of the women are unmarried, a large proportion having lived at service and been seduced by their masters. . . ."[93] Magazines ran stories of women pressured into sexual activity, and ballads published in almanacs also lamented "ruination."[94] The probability of premarital intercourse leading to marriage declined as mobility increased and community enforcement of moral codes decreased.

Men sometimes got away with their seduction but were at other times held up to public scorn and legal repercussions. In the Northeast, city-dwellers sat on couches of cherry and mahogany veneer with mohair upholstery and watched the flickering of oil lamps with cotton wicks. There they talked of Elisa Butler, a "poor, pretty and simple girl" who lived among the descendants of John Hancock and was coerced into intercourse and impregnated by Hancock, who settled with her out of court.[95] William Avery Rockefeller, father of John D. Rockefeller, had to flee the family home in Moravia, New York, in 1849 after he was indicted for the rape of Anne Vanderbeak, a "hired girl."[96] Other employees pressed their cases in church proceedings or in civil cases; one who claimed in a breach of promise suit that she was seduced by her employer under promise of marriage, was awarded three thousand dollars.[97]

Sometimes trials led to convictions for abortion following seduction. In 1839 Philadelphia physician Henry Chauncey was charged with causing the death of Eliza Sowers by producing an abortion at the instigation of William Nixon. The typical and sad details were: Miss Sowers, twenty-one, worked in a paper mill at which Nixon was superintendent. A boardinghouse owner swore that Chauncey

> Brought a young girl to my house in the beginning of October. . . . At breakfast, next morning, Dr. Chauncey came in. He made me make

---

[92] *Ibid.*

[93] *Ibid.*

[94] d'Emilio and Freedman, *Intimate Matters*, p. 44.

[95] Page Smith, *The Nation Comes of Age* (New York: McGraw-Hill, 1981), p. 755.

[96] Duden, *Serving Women*, p. 216.

[97] As Faye Duden relates, even very wealthy families could not dismiss the possibility of marriage with a "domestic," and many must have reflected with a shudder when they read the headlines, "Douglas Weds his Domestic: Aged Capitalist Fools His Relatives." Benjamin Douglas, a wealthy California social leader, was seventy-nine; Louise Dretzler, his bride and former servant, was thirty. The Douglas family was reportedly "crushed," especially when the bridegroom made a new will.

some tea of a powder that looked like black pepper. . . . At 2 o'clock the next morning, [Miss Sowers] called me, She said she was very bad. She said, 'I won't take any more of that doctor's medicine; it will kill me.'

Then Chauncey came back:

He did to her what doctors do to women when they are confined. He then washed his hands. He picked up something off the washstand, which shined and looked like a knitting needle, and wiped it. . . . Said she was the most difficult person he had ever operated on. Said the medicine he gave her was too powerful, and had acted too quick.[98]

It is at this time of evidently increasing abandonment that abortion also began to receive broader mention. Residents of Poughkeepsie, New York, told of a sixteen-year-old orphan and serving girl seduced by her master: "in a short time, he accomplished her ruin" and then sent her to the abortionist.[99] Towns relied on the city: from "every large town on the Hudson [women who] get in trouble run down here for a visit, just as a ship puts in for repairs. . . ."[100] In the North, every year before the Civil War brought new reports of tragedy. In 1858 Olive Ash was impregnated by the Vermont farmer for whom she was working; he paid one hundred dollars to a Dr. Howard, who operated three times on Miss Ash before she died.[101] In 1859 Marty Kirkpatrick, a sixteen-year-old mill worker in New Jersey at first accepted clothing from her employer and then intercourse; next came pregnancy, use of the abortifacients he procured, and death.[102] Abortion, in short, was the last resort of a particular segment of the unmarried: seduced, abandoned, and helpless women, generally between the ages of sixteen and twenty-five.[103] In an article published in 1835 John Beck observed that "the practice of caus-

---

[98]*Medical Examiner* (Philadelphia), Vol. 2, February 2, 1839, p. 73.
[99]John H. Warren, Jr., *Thirty Years Battle with Crime, or The Crying Shame of New York as Seen under the Broad Glare of an Old Detective's Lantern* (Poughkeepsie, NY: A. J. White, 1874), p. 161.
[100]*Ibid.*, p. 163.
[101]d'Emilio and Freedman, *Intimate Matters*, p. 64.
[102]The rate of induced abortion among seduced servants in the North may have been higher than that among slaves in the South. Morgan in 1860 wrote about abortions among slaves occurring spontaneously, sometimes through undernourishment or overwork, and minimized those occurring by surgery or drug.
[103]See Horatio Robinson Storer and Franklin Fiske Heard, *Criminal Abortion: Its Nature, Its Evidence, and Its Law* (Boston: Little, Brown, and Co., 1868), p. 65.

ing abortion was resorted to by unmarried females, who, through impru-
dence or misfortune, have become pregnant. . . ."[104]

The key pro-life question from the seventeenth through the early
nineteenth centuries, therefore, was: How could desperate unmarried
women be helped? Pre-marriage social pressure pushed most young men
to do the right thing, and legal action was a backup. At no time was abortion considered legitimate and legal, but the practice did occur when
some women fell through the cracks, taking their unborn children with
them.

---

[104]Beck, "Infanticide," in T. R. Beck, ed., *Elements of Medical Jurisprudence* (Albany, NY:
5th edition, 1835), p. 207.

2

Abortion and Prostitution

Shortly after the Civil War, as doctors examining the incidence of abortion tried to denote the social groups in which the practice raged, Dr. John Cowan cited "the licentiousness of the man and bondage of the woman," which together led to the "monstrous crime . . . the murder of the unborn."[1] Cowan emphasized "the old story" of women "seduced through misrepresentation by men of licentious natures."[2] Dr. John Trader of Missouri contended that men were pushing women into abortion: "We do not affirm, neither would we have you think for a moment, that the onus of this guilt lies at the feet of women. Far from it. In the majority of cases, they are more sinned against than sinning. . . ."[3] A "Special Committee on Criminal Abortions" made up of New York doctors reported in 1871 that abortion was "prevalent to an alarming extent, particularly in this city, to which, as to a place of refuge, flee, from all sections of the country, those who seek to hide or get rid of their shame."[4] Feminist Elizabeth Evans reported in 1875 that

---

[1] Dr. John Cowan, *The Science of a New Life* (New York: Cowan and Company, 1871), p. 275.
[2] *Ibid.*, p. 279.
[3] John W. Trader, M.D., "Criminal Abortion," paper read before the Central Missouri Medical Association, Sedalia, MO, October 6, 1874, Toner Collection, Library of Congress.
[4] Morris J. Franklin, H. Raphael, W. A. James, for the East River Medical Association, *Report*, December 5, 1871 (New York: S. W. Green, 1871).

"among all races and classes, it is probable that the cases wherein the least hesitation at committing this crime would be felt, are those where an illegitimate birth is in question."[5]

Dr. J. J. Mulheron, however, tried to be more precise. He observed in 1874 that not just one but three groups of women were having abortions, and that each group's crimes provoked a different reaction. The third group he designated "married women," who surprised him when they deviated from "the path of moral and professional rectitude. . . ."[6] (We will examine in Chapter Three the reasons for deviation.) The second group he named included "young girls who have been seduced under specious promises, and have afterward been deserted by their betrayers."[7] (We discussed that predicament in Chapter One and only note here Mulheron's plea that doctors "commiserate the condition of both mother and child.") The members of Mulheron's first group are the subjects of this chapter: "prostitutes, who in the pursuit of their unnatural calling, became pregnant . . . the prospects of the unborn challenge the sympathy of the physician. . . ."[8]

The mass prostitution to which Mulheron referred was a new phenomenon in America. In colonial days brothels had been rare. In 1672 Bostonians found Alice Thomas guilty of "giving frequent secret and unseasonable Entertainment in her house to lewd lascivious and notorious persons of both sexes, giving them opportunity to commit carnal wickedness. . . ."[9] Alice Thomas was whipped and sentenced to an indeterminate amount of jail time, with the court receiving the right to keep her away from society as long as necessary to assure her reformation. No similar cases arose for many years. When Virginian William Byrd tried to find a prostitute in Williamsburg in 1720, his search failed.

There was little for early opponents of prostitution to do. When Cotton Mather alarmed his congregation members in 1702 with a sermon on prostitution, he and forty compatriots formed a Society for the Suppression of Disorders, chief of which might be the presence of a

---

[5]Elizabeth Edson Gibson Evans, *The Abuse of Maternity* (Philadelphia: Lippincott, 1875), p. 13.
[6]J. J. Mulheron, "Foeticide," *Peninsular Journal of Medicine*, Vol. 10 (September 1874), p. 387.
[7]*Ibid.*
[8]*Ibid.* Mulheron was also a student of abortifacients and noted that they achieve success "by causing violent catharsis, spending their force on the lower bowel contiguous to the uterus, thereby stimulating that organ to contraction" (p. 389).
[9]*Records of the Suffolk County Court, 1671-1680*, in Vol. 29 of *Collections of the Colonial Society of Massachusetts* (Boston, 1933), pp. 82-83.

brothel. By 1714 the society essentially was defunct because it had no significant business to conduct. By the middle of the eighteenth century, however, vice was ripening, and prostitutes were working cities such as Newport, Rhode Island. Bostonians in 1753 discussed the case of Hannah Billey, who invited men "not of good Behavior or Fame" to come to her home where they "carnally layed with whores, which the said Hannah then and there procured for them."[10] Benjamin Franklin described women walking the streets and "expos[ing] themselves to sale at the highest bidder."[11] John Adams complained about taverns used "for extinguishing virtuous Love and changing it into filthiness and bruted Debauch."[12] Juries in Charleston, South Carolina, protested the "number of houses of ill fame or brothels throughout the city, which are an annoyance generally to the good citizens." Columbia, South Carolina, home of the state college, was called a "perfect haven" for the "sisters of riotous sensuality."[13]

As brothels became common, some citizens of the poorer areas of town tried to keep them out of their neighborhoods. In 1793 townspeople attacked brothels in Boston and New York and demanded their closure; Bostonians rioted again in 1799, 1823, and 1825. In 1825, two thousand rioters stormed brothels in Lenox, Pennsylvania. One person was killed and scores were injured during Portland, Maine, riots that same year, but the rioters were unsuccessful in their attempt to close down "prostitution dens."[14] These types of activities continued into midcentury. In 1857 Chicago citizens, led by the mayor, burned down a row of brothels.

And yet prostitution was Hydra-headed, and individual closures had little permanent effect. Soon every city had its sporting houses catering to all classes: holes in the wall for the poor, gilt for the gilded gentry, and for those in between, frame houses with low feather beds, unbeveled glass mirrors, tallow candles, and a pitcher, bowl, and cake of soap.

---

[10]See Alexander Hamilton, *Gentlemen's Progress* (Chapel Hill, NC: University of North Carolina Press, 1948; orig. in 1744), p. 151, and Vern and Bonnie Bullough, *Women and Prostitution* (Buffalo: Prometheus, 1987), p. 50.

[11]John d'Emilio and Estelle B. Freedman, *Intimate Matters* (New York: Harper & Row, 1988), p. 50.

[12]*Ibid.*

[13]Jack Kenny Williams, *Vogues in Villainy* (Columbia, SC: University of South Carolina Press, 1959), p. 58.

[14]For accounts of further opposition to prostitution, see Ruth Rosen, *The Lost Sisterhood: Prostitution in America, 1900-1918* (Baltimore: Johns Hopkins University Press, 1982), Chapter One.

There were many reasons for the increase in demand, including the theological changes to be discussed in the next chapter, but one was that business travel further from home made anonymity more likely. Journalist James McCabe commented that "the fashionable houses are largely patronized by strangers visiting New York: these, thinking themselves unknown in the great city, care little for privacy and boldly show themselves in the general parlors. The proportion of married and middle-aged men among them is very great. . . . Men who at home are models of propriety seem to lose all sense of restraint when they come to New York."[15]

Supply readily met demand as the same air of "freedom" was breathed in by young women with big eyes for fashionable clothes or jewelry but not much cash. Prostitution offered shorter hours and far higher wages than domestic service or mill work. Some young women clearly fell into prostitution after seduction and social ostracism, and others, to gain sympathy, said they did. (McCabe found out after ample mid-century interviewing that "No reliance whatever can be placed on the stories they tell of themselves.")[16] Other young women hated the way they were treated. Public health doctor William Sanger complained of northern employers who treated servants "in a manner which would bring a blush to the cheek of a southern slave driver. . . . Is it any wonder that girls are driven to intoxication and disgrace by this conduct?"[17] But for probably the largest group of recruits into prostitution, the attraction was like that of a teenager today who shovels hamburgers and sees a drug runner in fancy sneakers.

Dr. Hiram Root, in his *Lover's Marriage Lighthouse*, probably portrayed with accuracy the young woman "poor in worldly goods, struggling day by day with the world for an honest living, and faring scantily despite all her toil, dress[ed] in the cheapest calico. . . ."[18] He showed how she might meet a woman "who, but a few weeks gone by, was poor in garments as herself, but is now clothed in all the gorgeousness of high fashion, flaunting in feathers and glittering with jewels." At that point most young women, even if attracted by quick cash, would revile at the prospect and

---

[15]James McCabe, *New York by Sunlight and by Gaslight* (Philadelphia: Douglas Brothers, 1882), p. 479.

[16]*Ibid.*, p. 477.

[17]Quoted in Faye Duden, *Serving Women* (Middletown, CT: Wesleyan University Press, 1983), p. 218.

[18]Hiram Root, *Lover's Marriage Lighthouse* (New York: Root, 1859), p. 389.

say "no" to those ugly urgings, but others would want all that glitters: "The poor girl's mind becomes poisoned. She dwells more and more upon the subject as days go by, and finally yields to the monomania of prostitution."[19]

In any event, the number of prostitutes soared in the nineteenth century. Many observers made estimates; probably the best was that of William Sanger, who surveyed prostitution at mid-century in New York City, Buffalo, Louisville, Newark, New Haven, Norfolk, Philadelphia, Pittsburgh, and Savannah, and concluded that there were about sixty thousand prostitutes nationwide.[20] Sanger also touched on the process by which beautiful women descended from "first-class" to "fourth-class" brothels in old basements as their charms faded, and journalist McCabe described the downward ride in more detail: "The proprietress will have no other than attractive women in her house: and as soon as the inmates begin to show sign of the wretched life they lead, as soon as sickness falls upon them, or they lose their beauty and freshness, she sends them away and fills their places with more attractive women."[21] We soon will look at one type of sickness nineteenth-century prostitutes were likely to have, but let's first follow the descent: "After a woman is kicked out of a first class house, the wretched women has no recourse but to enter a second class house and thus go down one grade lower in vice," McCabe wrote. "Her health breaks fast and what is left of her beauty soon fades and in two or three years she [drops] still lower to homelessness and death."[22]

The urban scene was far from pastoral in other ways as well. In New York during the 1840s, poor families crowded into five-story tenements with names like Gates of Hell and Brickbat Mansion, and youth gangs roamed: the Slaughter House gang terrorized Chrystie and surrounding streets, and the Buckaroos and Swamp Angels fought passersby and each other in the East River area. The Plug Uglies of the Five Points area became so famous that they lent their names to the slang dictionary.[23] At the old

---

[19] William W. Sanger, *The History of Prostitution* (New York: Harper and Brothers, 1858), pp. 482, 586. This Sanger should not be confused with William T. Sanger, husband (a half-century later) of Planned Parenthood founder Margaret Sanger.
[20] *Ibid.*, p. 614.
[21] McCabe, *New York by Sunlight and by Gaslight*, p. 479.
[22] *Ibid.*, p. 480.
[23] Plug Ugly creativity anticipated football helmets; gang members wore plug hats filled with wool and leather and pulled them over their ears.

brewery on Murderer's Alley, labeled the Den of Forty Thieves, a murder per night was the standard attraction. George Templeton Strong wrote in his diary in 1853 that among the young men of New York there had never been "so much gross dissipation." When Strong walked down Eighth Street, he found that "whores and blackguards make up about two-thirds of the throng." Some young women, he sighed, were "brutalized already almost beyond redemption by premature vice."[24] At the end of the decade Strong was concluding, "We are a very sick people just now."[25] That sickness meant a boom time for prostitution.[26]

The typical brothel career – nasty, brutish, and short – was sad enough in its Hobbesian dimensions, but other observers chronicled an additional aspect of what Root called "the horrors that accompany [a prostitute's] course of life to an early and premature grave. . . ."[27] During the 1830s reformer John McDowall interviewed prostitutes who acknowledged that they had "done the criminal deed. One of them said that she had destroyed five of her own offspring; another said she had destroyed three." He recorded reports by ex-prostitutes "that in some houses of prostitution it is a common practice every three months to use means preventive of progeny."[28] He cited the "criminal deed" by name: "Abortion."[29] During the 1850s Dr. Sanger surveyed two thousand prostitutes who received medical help at Blackwell's Island, New York's main public hospital, and found they had many pregnancies but very few chil-

---

[24]*Diary of George Templeton Strong: The Turbulent 50s*, Allan Nevins and Milton Thomas, eds. (New York: Macmillan, 1952), p. 117. Strong complained that reformers were paying attention not to the "whorearchy" around the corner but to the fugitive slave law. He also noted the increase in New York street crime during the 1850s and wrote that "garotting and highway robbery" were frequent enough that "most of my friends are investing in revolvers and carrying them about at night. . . ."

[25]*Ibid.*

[26]It is hard to judge the significance in the history of prostitution and abortion of some fads of the 1830s and the Victorian Era. For example, Sylvester Graham, a popular lecturer in the 1830s and 1840s and the inventor of graham crackers, told married men that they should have intercourse with their wives only once per month; in Graham's words, "the mere fact that a man is married to one woman, and is perfectly faithful to her, will by no means prevent the evils which flow from venereal excess." It is doubtful that many Americans followed the advice of Graham and others to the letter, but the crucial question is *how* they disregarded the advice: did some take on the posture of upright citizen within the household, and then take their love to town? (See Graham, *Lectures to Young Men, On Chastity.* (Boston: C. H. Pierce, 1848), pp. 23-24.

[27]Root, *Lover's Marriage Lighthouse*, p. 389.

[28]*McDowall's Journal*, May 1833, p. 37.

[29]*First Annual Report of the New York Magdalen Society* (New York: John T. West, 1831), p. 23.

dren. He could not calculate precisely the number of prostitution-related abortions, but he estimated a "startling . . . sacrifice of infant life" and called that loss "one of the most deplorable results of prostitution."[30]

Many other observers also linked prostitution and abortion. William Acton wrote in a book on prostitution that abortion and infanticide in an amount "fearful to contemplate" occurred among brothel residents.[31] New York detective John Warren linked prostitution and "the business of the abortionist" as he complained that abortionists "flourish and grow rich from prostitution as a source of income. . . ."[32] The link was evident to Maryland's top appeals court in 1874, when it stated in *Hays v. The State* (a case concerning an abortion committed in a brothel) that "a house of ill-fame" was a place "most fitted for the perpetration of a crime like this."[33] In 1881 C. E. Rogers estimated that prostitutes only survived in the trade for four years on the average, as disease, beatings, alcoholism, drugs, and abortion took their toll. Abortion and prostitution were two leading "secret sins," Rogers wrote, with abortion "the most common crime among Americans. It is a national sin."[34]

Along with all the direct observation, proof of the prostitution-abortion connection also emerges as we study the working conditions of prostitutes and their ways of protecting themselves from one of the hazards of the trade: pregnancy. Contraceptives of various kinds had been

---

[30]Sanger, *The History of Prostitution*, pp. 482, 586. Sanger did not go as deeply into the prostitution-abortion connection as he might have, since he was more interested in tracking the incidence of venereal disease. He found that 2,090 cases of venereal disease were treated in Penitentiary Hospital in 1857 and that almost ten thousand venereal disease cases were treated in 1857 at the seventeen public hospitals in New York City. Since New York public hospitals were not supposed to care for venereal disease patients, Sanger concluded that probably half as many again were treated for venereal disease but were recorded as having received treatment for some respectable malady. Furthermore, Sanger believed that at least an equivalent number of patients received treatment from doctors in private practice.

[31]William Acton, *Prostitution* (London: J. Churchill, 1857), p. 206. See also Dr. Charles Robert Drysdale, *Prostitution Medically Considered, with Some of Its Social Aspects* (London: Robert Hardwicke, 1866), for its critique of "social conditions that much favor prostitution, and (in England, at present) infanticide." Judith R. Walkowitz, *Prostitution and Victorian Society* (Cambridge: Cambridge University Press, 1980), notes that few children conceived by prostitutes survived, due to disease, abortion, and infanticide.

[32]John H. Warren, Jr., *Thirty Years Battle with Crime, or The Crying Shame of New York as Seen Under the Broad Glare of an Old Detective's Lantern* (Poughkeepsie, NY: A. J. White, 1874), pp. 37-38.

[33]*Maryland Reports*, Vol. 40 (1874), p. 645.

[34]C. E. Rogers, *Secret Sins of Society* (Minneapolis: Union Publishing Co., 1881), pp. 76, 144.

around for centuries. European prostitutes had long put cloth or linen rags in their vaginas, or used beeswax as a suppository or as a specially molded cervical cap.[35] By 1800 they also were using vaginally inserted sponges that could be pulled out with strings.

European men had used condoms for centuries. In 1564 Fallopius described the use of a linen sheath, and by 1717 British physician Daniel Turner could write that "the Condum" was the "Preservative our Libertines have found. . . ."[36] French physician Johannes Astruc noted in 1738 that London "debauchees" were using "skins made from soft and seamless hides in the shape of a sheath, and called condoms in English."[37] By 1800 condoms made from skins and bladders were openly advertised in England and were available in America.

The problem in brothels, however, was that condoms were expensive and often ineffective.[38] They were especially unlikely to be used in brothels because men considered them unpleasant. Turner noted comments about "blunting the Sensation," and German researcher Christopher Girtanner complained in 1788 that "fish membranes which serve to protect the man's member during copulation . . . diminish pleasure."[39] Charles Knowlton's sexology book of 1832, *Fruits of Philosophy*,

---

[35]Contraceptives of varying effectiveness were used early on in other parts of the world as well. The Bridhadyogatarangini, an eighth-century Hindu work, stated that "The prostitute who has intercourse with a man, after having inserted into the vagina a piece of rock salt dipped into oil, never conceives." Some Japanese women used as tampons disks of oiled tissue paper made of bamboo. Norman E. Himes, *Medical History of Contraception* (New York: Schocken Books, 1970; first published in 1936), p. 119.

[36]*Ibid.*, p. 196. It is not clear where the name came from, but usually reliable sources say there was a Dr. Condom in the court of Charles II in the 1660s.

[37]*Ibid.* Astruc added, "They claim, I suppose, that thus mailed and with spears sheathed in this way, they can undergo with impunity the chances of promiscuous intercourse. But (in truth) they are greatly mistaken."

[38]They did not gain widespread use there or in America until the vulcanization of rubber in the mid-nineteenth century made production easier and lowered costs.

[39]Himes, *Medical History of Contraception*, p. 196. (Girtanner also wrote that "during coitus the membrane may tear by a strong strain.") In America such devices, including the vaginally inserted sponges that could be pulled out with strings, gained an association with prostitution. Contraceptives did not find a general market in an agricultural economy with wide open spaces, frequent infant mortality, and a general desire among married couples for as many children (to love and to work) as they could have. Even more fundamentally, the Leeuwenhoek-supported belief in the existence of little people in the semen made contraception seem to be the destruction of human life. Women who had taken up prostitution, however, usually saw themselves living outside God's Law and man's and were unlikely to let animalcule theories keep them from conduct essential for professional survival.

noted that use of condoms "required a great sacrifice of enjoyment" and produced in men a "demoralizing tendency."[40]

Since male purchasers of pleasure were unlikely to use condoms in those days, what methods might prostitutes themselves use to avoid pregnancy? Knowlton recommended that women seeking to prevent pregnancy use the vaginal sponge with pullout string, and this seemed to become the contraceptive of choice in brothels. Handbills distributed in London early in the nineteenth century by Francis Place also recommended use of "a piece of sponge, about an inch square, being placed in the vagina previous to coition, and afterwards withdrawn by means of a double twisted thread, or bobbin, attached to it." Knowlton pointed out, however, that "even a trifle of semen" can impregnate: the sponge "has not proved a sure preventive. As there are many little ridges or folds in the vagina, we cannot suppose the withdrawal of the sponge would dislodge all the semen in every instance."[41]

Although no one at the time precisely calculated the effectiveness of the sponge-on-a-string, testimony like that of Knowlton's suggests that it was far from surefire. (A century later, when the Birth Control Clinical Research Bureau in New York City interviewed 377 women who were sponge-users, 188 reported success in contraception and 189 failure.)[42] Fish-membrane condoms, even if used — and there is no evidence that they were commonly used in brothels, and much to suggest that they were not — also had only partial effectiveness. (Even today reliance on barrier methods leads to a pregnancy rate of 20 percent.)[43]

Some prostitutes also tried to prevent conception by using vaginal injections of carbolic acid, but they were warned against this by both madams and doctors.[44] Other pregnancy-avoiding douches used at various times in the nineteenth century included injections of solutions containing bicarbonate of soda, borax, vinegar, lysol, potassium bitartrate, and bichloride of mercury (which could cause mercury poisoning).

---

[40]Charles Knowlton, *Fruits of Philosophy: A Treatise on the Population Question* (Chicago: G. E. Wilson, 1870), pp. 5, 18. First published in New York during 1832, Knowlton's book went through over thirty editions and many reprintings. See second edition (London, 1833), p. 33: "As to the baudruche, which consists in a covering used by males, made of very delicate skin, it is by no means calculated to come into general use."
[41]*Ibid.*, pp. 18, 19 (Chicago edition); London edition, p. 34.
[42]Marie E. Kopp, *Birth Control in Practice* (New York: McBride, 1934), p. 133.
[43]Joe McIlhaney, *1250 Health-Care Questions Women Ask* (Grand Rapids: Baker, 1985), p. 560.
[44]Webb J. Kelly, "One of the Abuses of Carbolic Acid," *Columbus Medical Journal*, Vol. 1 (1883), pp. 433-436.

Some house physicians prepared vaginal suppositories of boric acid, tannic acid, cocoa butter, olive oil, or glycerine.[45] And yet there is no evidence that any of these substances, even when destructive to semen generally, proved an effective barrier to that "trifle of semen" that could impregnate. (As English contraception proponent Marie Besant warned her readers, "there is much uncertainty attending the use of all these injections [and] also many failures. . . .")[46]

Purveyors of the various substances at least did consumers a favor by denouncing the claims of their competitors. For example, Dr. Frederick Hollick attacked one potion "sold extensively by a person calling himself a French Professor, but who is really the husband of a noted Abortionist in New York."[47] Hollick noted that "The remedy is only a powder of colored alum, or sulphate of zinc, which is dissolved in water, and used with a syringe as an injection after connection. It fails as often as it succeeds, and often injures."[48]

In other words, there was no way for most prostitutes to avoid getting pregnant – sometimes later but usually sooner. There were some exceptions. Probably one out of ten women is naturally infertile.[49] Women who had undergone episodes of gonorrhea had reduced fertility.[50] Most prostitutes who had the more common venereal disease of the period, syphilis, were fertile, however.[51] Syphilis has dire consequences but does not prevent conception: When unborn children are infected with syphilis, 30 percent die before the mother goes into labor, and only one-fourth of those who make it to birth are healthy.[52] The prevalence

---

[45]For additional discussion see *The Physician and Sexuality in Victorian America* (Urbana, IL: University of Illinois Press, 1974), p. 118.

[46]Marie Besant, *The Law of Population* (London: Freethought Publishing Co., 1879), p. 34.

[47]Hollick was referring to Charles Lohman, aka "Dr. Mauriceau," husband of "Madame Restell." (We will hear more about her in Chapter Seven.)

[48]Frederick Hollick, *The Marriage Guide* (New York: T. W. Strong, 1850), p. 400.

[49]Interview with infertility expert Dr. Joe McIlhaney, February 25, 1992.

[50]Dr. McIlhaney: each episode of gonorrhea reduces fertility by about one eighth.

[51]Robert S. Morton, *Venereal Diseases* (London: Harmondsworth, 1966), p. 55. Gonorrhea blocks the tubes and makes women infertile; syphilis kills the unborn child late in pregnancy or causes disease which can kill soon after birth. William Sanger found two-fifths of New York's prostitutes admitting to syphilis and believed the actual incidences of disease to be even higher. Without blood tests, primary syphilis was often difficult to detect in women. Secondary syphilis, which occurred six weeks to six months after the initial outbreak, involves fatigue, fever, rash, and various diseases. One-fourth of untreated patients developed tertiary syphilis in four years, with resultant insanity, heart disease, and often death.

[52]McIlhaney, *1250 Health-Care Questions Women Ask*, pp. 314, 622.

of syphilis among prostitutes meant that a great many unhealthy and potentially deformed children (in today's parlance, "hard cases") would be conceived by women who did not want to bear them. Furthermore, many of these mothers would die. The accepted nineteenth-century cure for syphilis was treatment with mercury, as it had been for the past three centuries, but mercury was very dangerous to patients and had no guarantee of effectiveness.[53]

Another source of exceptions, in theory, might be some special infertility factor at work among prostitutes. Was there such an infertility factor? Rumor sometimes had it that there was, since so few prostitutes gave birth to children. No one appears to have studied the question scientifically in the United States, perhaps because prostitution almost always was illegal and thorough research into it very difficult. However, in Paris where regulated prostitution was legal, the leading public health researcher of the 1820s and 1830s, Dr. Alexandre-Jean-Baptiste Parent-Duchatelet, spent years looking into the question and arrived at startling results that, to my knowledge, have not been translated into English until now. (Parent was a highly respected physician and founding editor of the *Annales d'hygiene Publique et de Medecine Legale*, the most prestigious French journal of public health. Before he began his research into prostitution, he wrote about clogged sewers, polluted rivers, and dead horses.)

Parent faced the question head-on. "The examination of menstruation among prostitutes leads me naturally to a study of their fertility, an important question and one over which great darkness still reigns," Parent began.[54] He presented the myths: "It is generally believed that prostitutes don't have children, or if they do, they have so few that they can be considered to be sterile."[55] Then he presented evidence of prostitutes having children at the Maternity Hospital of Paris and quoted a midwife:

These girls don't make themselves known for what they are, but after several days of observation, we can easily tell them apart from the other women by their dress, their language, and especially by the remarks they

---

[53]In 1838, physician Phillippe Ricord demonstrated the difference between syphilis and gonorrhea, and gonorrhea began to be treated as a "local infection" by cauterization or by acid treatment of the sores. The breakthrough for both diseases did not come until the advent of penicillin in 1929.

[54]Parent, *De la prostitution dans la ville de Paris* (Paris: Balliere, 1837), two volumes, p. 232. These passages translated by Cathy Showalter.

[55]*Ibid.*

make in the rooms and the halls. The most curious thing that we have observed about them is that it is rare they have happy births; the slowness of labor necessitates the use of forceps. Their babies rarely live; often they are born dead, and the most serious complications constantly follow these births.[56]

Venereal disease had its effect.

Far more frequent than births, however, was abortion. Parent wrote, "According to the information given me in the prison and the hospitals, abortions are frequent during the first seven to eight months of pregnancy, and even more frequent during the less advanced stages."[57] He quoted one leading physician: "the youngest ones often have late periods, which end with the expulsion of what they call a 'bung'. For two years I paid no attention to this expression but [then] examined with care these productions, and found it easy to recognize all the characteristics of a human. . . ."[58] Parent noted these details of early miscarriage or abortion and commented, "even though these public girls bring a very small number of children into the world, they still have a[n] aptitude for conception. . . ."[59]

Parent then dealt with the question of whether induced abortions or miscarriages were occurring and asked the officials charged with registering and examining legal prostitutes:

I learned from the inspectors charged with finding them when they didn't show up for their appointments, that time after time they would find them lying in bed, recovering from an abortion . . . it is proven that they often induced them: my colleague, Mr. Velpeau, who has perhaps the largest collection of embryos in existence, gathered five belonging to prostitutes, and of these five, three bore traces of perforating instruments which caused their deaths. They were all three or four months from conception.[60]

Parent observed, "one sees from what I have said – and if one has respect for information which comes from all parts, one acquires the proof – that the occupation they practice is not an obstacle to fertility."[61]

---

[56] *Ibid.*
[57] *Ibid.*, p. 235.
[58] *Ibid.*, p. 236.
[59] *Ibid.*
[60] *Ibid.*, p. 237.
[61] *Ibid.*, p. 238.

He asked, "to what can we attribute these frequent, I would say, almost constant, abortions? Without speaking about direct maneuvers employed by some of them, is not their occupation itself sufficient reason to explain it all?"[62]

Parent concluded his discussion of abortion with a summary of findings: "if these public girls rarely bring their pregnancies to term, it is because they almost always abort them, whether these abortions take place through criminal acts or whether they can be attributed to the exercise of their occupation."[63] No one in the United States studied prostitution as did Parent, but the three sets of evidence – reports of contemporary observers, the lack of effective contraception, and the research of Parent which certainly seems applicable to America's prostitution – make the case for considerable abortion among U.S. prostitutes a strong one. How many prostitute-related abortions were there in America? Here some rough estimates are necessary, with the logic laid out in ten parts as follows:

(1) Since diaphragms used today have an average failure rate in actual use of 20 percent (lower among married couples in their thirties, higher among teenagers), barrier contraceptives then could not have been more effective and were actually far less effective.[64] On the other hand, since experienced prostitutes would be sure to use to maximum effectiveness whatever technology they had available, we might assume that 20 percent figure as a rough yardstick for the calculations that follow.[65]

(2) According to nineteenth-century testimony, the average full-time prostitute would have intercourse at least thirty times per week, which would make for at least 1,500 sexual acts per year. (Two weeks of vacation, of course.) For example, John McDowall calculated that the average prostitute had intercourse with thirty to forty men each week, including "three men or boys daily" during the week, and the bulk from

---

[62] *Ibid.*

[63] *Ibid.*, p. 242.

[64] Ernest Page *et. al.*, *Human Reproduction* (Philadelphia: W. B. Saunders, 1976), p. 89, gives a 15 to 20 percent actual use failure rate; Boston Women's Health Collective, *Our Bodies, Ourselves* (New York: Simon & Schuster, 1976), second edition, p. 185, gives a 20 to 25 percent rate. Effectiveness rates reviewed with Dr. Joe McIlhaney.

[65] See also Harry Rudel *et. al.*, *Birth Control and Abortion* (New York: Macmillan, 1973); Marianne Jackson *et. al.*, *Vaginal Contraception* (Boston: G. K. Hall, 1981); Daniel Mishell and Val Davajan, *Infertility, Contraception & Reproductive Endocrinology* (Oradell, NJ: Medical Economics, 1986).

"Saturday night to Monday morning [when] they will receive fifteen to twenty-five men and obtain as their reward from thirty to fifty dollars."[66]

(3) Some fertility experts estimate that one out of thirty-three contraceptive-less acts of vaginal intercourse, on the average, leads to clinical pregnancy.[67] One technical report in the 1968-69 volume of *Population Studies* showed that when couples had twenty non-contracepted coital acts during a particular month, the likelihood of pregnancy was 43 percent; the equivalent number of monthly coital acts for a prostitute using 80 percent effective contraception would be one hundred.[68]

(4) Not all acts of prostitution involved vaginal intercourse, and not all were completed. Furthermore, various factors, such as gonorrhea and a general state of poor health after a year or two of prostitution, may have reduced the number of conceptions; to be conservative, let's estimate a 50 percent decrease.

(5) Those calculations leave us with (using the lower part of the estimate) perhaps 1,200 acts of ejaculatory vaginal intercourse per prostitute year. Multiply by one thirty-third (conception rate), divide by five (80 percent contraception rate), and reduce the figure by half (the health factor), and we are at about 3.6 abortions per year.

(6) We can reduce that number further. Pregnancies occasionally were continued. The effect of repeat abortion made future conception less likely (fertility is cut by 10 to 20 percent after three abortions). Some time off would be necessary after an abortion. And so forth.[69] Estimating conservatively by reducing the rate by a further 50 percent for those reasons, we still have 1.8 abortions per prostitute per year.

(7) Arrived at by such abstract numbers-crunching, such a figure may seem merely theoretical, especially since prostitution and abortion were two topics generally swept under the rug and out of the pages of parlors and magazines in polite society. And yet such a figure is consis-

---

[66] *Magdalen Society Annual Report*, 1831, p. 23.

[67] Dr. McIlhaney tells patients that when couples have non-contracepted intercourse twice per week, within three months (about twenty-six acts of intercourse) 50 percent of the women will be clinically pregnant. (Perhaps half of pregnancies are ended by very early miscarriage before the woman even knows she is pregnant; "clinical pregnancies" are verified pregnancies.) Most of the remaining women will be pregnant before the year is out; 15 percent of couples will be unable to conceive within that time. Also see Nathan Keyfitz, *Population Change and Social Policy* (Cambridge, MA: Abt, 1982), pp. 216-232, for an interesting discussion of "How Birth Control Affects Population."

[68] J. C. Barrett and J. Marshall, "The Risk of Conception on Different Days of the Menstrual Cycle," *Population Studies*, Vol. 23 (1968-69), pp. 455-461.

[69] Prostitutes, however, were put back to work quickly.

tent with the observations of McDowall, William Sanger, Acton, Warren, Rogers and others.

(8) If anything, a 1.8 estimate may be low. McDowall wrote about prostitutes seeing abortionists once every three months, on the average. A British model of conception at a coital rate equal to that of 1860 prostitutes showed an "approximate duration of conception wait" of three and a half months; women who had six non-contracepted coital acts in a six-day period around the time of ovulation (the equivalent of thirty coital acts by an 1860 prostitute) became pregnant two-thirds of the time.[70]

(9) The abortion rate among prostitutes also helps to explain the low life expectancy – four years – of prostitutes who did not leave the trade within the first year or two. Only one historian, to my knowledge, has even mentioned abortion and prostitution in the same sentence. But when she did, Ruth Rosen acknowledged that "the many deaths associated with prostitution might have resulted from some of the medicines and procedures used for abortion."[71] That makes sense because venereal disease, suicide, and the occasional murderous customer by themselves do not seem sufficient to explain the frequency of prostitute death; having abortion operations, however, does.

(10) If the average prostitute had 1.8 abortions per year, Sanger's estimate of six thousand full-time prostitutes in 1858 in New York City and sixty thousand prostitutes nationwide suggests that there may have been at least one hundred thousand prostitution-related abortions annually in the United States on the eve of the Civil War.[72]

All such figures are estimates, of course. Governments and private observers did not compile many statistics of legal activities at that time, let alone the illegal. Given the illegality of abortion businesses, it is not surprising that financial records or other clues concerning customer load are not available. (Even today, with a massive tax enforcement structure and much more required paperwork, much of the income of certain escort services and massage parlors remains hidden.)

Descriptive material from the period, however, such as this para-

---

[70]Barrett and Marshall, "The Risk of Conception on Different Days of the Menstrual Cycle," p. 460; see also John Bongaarts and Robert G. Potter, *Fertility, Biology, and Behavior* (New York: Academic Press, 1983), pp. 32-36.

[71]Ruth Rosen, *The Lost Sisterhood: Prostitution in America. 1900-1918* (Baltimore: Johns Hopkins University Press, 1982), p. 99.

[72]Sanger, *The History of Prostitution*, pp. 579-680.

graph from *The Boston Medical and Surgical Journal*, helps us grasp the frequency of horror:

> There seems to be no diminution of the evil, notwithstanding the terrors which the law holds up to the view of the criminal. The murder of unborn children is fearfully common everywhere, if the great number of half-grown infants found floating in boxes upon the water, dropped in vaults, or otherwise brought to light, is any evidence of the fact. Both women and men abound, in all our large cities, who have a decided and acknowledged reputation for performing the murderous operation.[73]

This careless disposal was conventional among prostitutes from the 1850s through the 1870s. New York detective John Warren complained that "Social crimes like infanticide, that were once placed on the same level as murder, are now not only looked upon with complacency but overlooked altogether, but are defended on principle by certain theorists. . . ."[74] The prostitution-abortion link continued throughout the nineteenth century, which ended with journalists estimating that there were over one hundred thousand prostitutes in the United States with an average life expectancy within the trade of five years (death or rescue would take them out).[75]

Yet, improved contraception, particularly through the use of diaphragms and rubber cervical caps which began to be available in mass reliability following the vulcanization of rubber, led to a decreased incidence of pregnancy per prostitute.[76] Technological innovation helped in the containment of abortion among prostitutes – but early in the twentieth century abortionists still were giving pregnant prostitutes, in the words of one madam, a "black pill which, if taken for three days and with hot baths, usually brought a girl around."[77] Problem-related abortions were reduced but not eliminated. Journalist Clifford Roe could still write in 1911 that "In the center of Chicago's principal vice district is a resort that for years had a sign Le Moulin Rouge, which is French for The Red

---

[73] *The Boston Medical and Surgical Journal*, Vol. 51 (October 4, 1854), p. 224.

[74] John H. Warren, Jr., *Thirty Years Battle with Crime, or The Crying Shame of New York as Seen Under the Broad Glare of an Old Detective's Lantern* (Poughkeepsie, NY: A. J. White, 1874), pp. 37-38.

[75] Clifford Griffith Roe, *The Great War on White Slavery* (Chicago: Roe and Steadwell, 1911), p. 15.

[76] Some cervical caps were available beginning in the 1860s; Mensinga publicized the diaphragm in 1882.

[77] Nell Kimball, *Her Life as an American Madam* (New York: Macmillan, 1970), p. 17.

Mill. Paris has or had a resort of that name. All such resorts in Paris, Chicago and elsewhere are Red Mills – red with the heart's blood of mothers, red with the blood of murdered babies. If people only knew what grist such Red Mills grind they would not tolerate the murderous dens."[78]

The prostitution-abortion link is important to keep in mind because abortion historian James Mohr repeatedly has generalized about the "many American women" who sought abortions during the first two-thirds of the nineteenth century, for "this practice was neither morally nor legally wrong in the eyes of the vast majority of Americans, provided it was accomplished before quickening."[79] He repeatedly has suggested that everyone was doing it: "Abortion entered the mainstream of American life during the middle decades of the nineteenth century" and was "relatively common."[80] According to Mohr, at mid-century "the chief problems associated with abortion were medical rather than moral."[81] But the evidence suggests that most abortions during that period were related to prostitution, which was a muddy stream rather than a mainstream of American life, and was definitely not viewed as an issue unrelated to morality.

---

[78]Roe., *The Great War on White Slavery* p. 307.
[79]James Mohr, *Abortion in America* (New York: Oxford University Press, 1978), p. 16.
[80]*Ibid.*, pp. 102, 172.
[81]*Ibid.*, p. 75.

3

Abortion and Spiritism

T he growth of slums in the North and the continuation of slavery in the South were not the only problems gripping the states as mid-century approached. Although solid statistics again are lacking, many observers commented about abortion among *married* women during the 1840s and 1850s. The *Boston Medical and Surgical Journal* reminds readers in 1854 that times were changing: abortion was "not exclusively performed upon unmarried women" anymore.[1]

Some physicians' estimates of abortion incidence were heavily influenced by their own clientele. Michigan physician George Smith pointed out that some physicians had associated abortion with married individuals of the "better classes" because those were the people with whom they came in contact.[2] But the pattern is clear. The *Boston Surgical and Medical Journal* noted that "happy wives, strong in the affectionate regard of considerate husbands, rarely attempt this violence"[3] and implied that there were many unhappy wives. Were there? Was abortion becoming

---

[1] *Boston Medical and Surgical Journal*, Vol. 51 (October 4, 1854), p. 224.
[2] George Smith, "Foeticide," *Detroit Review of Medicine and Pharmacy*, Vol. 10 (1875), p. 211.
[3] *Boston Surgical and Medical Journal*, Vol. 75 (November 1, 1866), p. 275. The *Journal* observed, "There is but one stronger element known to society than that of a true woman's love for a worthy husband; one who is careful for her comfort and her preferences. . . . [When husbands are loving], let her but be convinced that her husband

acceptable among the troubled married as well as among those who had been unduly tempted by men or money?

The Mohr thesis is that abortion was general in the mid-nineteenth century; many observers at the time, however, linked abortion to seduction, prostitution, and some *specific* groups among the married, not the populace generally. "Feticide is not a vice of ignorance," Dr. Henry Gibbons, a president of the California Medical Society, declared. "It rather grows out of a certain kind of knowledge which has become popular in late years . . . the obscene literature of 'free love,' the delirium of spiritism, the impulse of passion, the concealment of shame. . . ."[4] Dr. E. M. Buckingham of Springfield, Ohio, connected abortion with the values of the "fashionable and intellectual communities."[5] The General Assembly of the Presbyterian Church in the USA (Northern) connected "the destruction by parents of their own offspring before birth" with the development of "unscriptural views of the marriage relation. . . ."[6]

Those critics were all *outside* the group allegedly having or promoting abortions among the married. But two doctors, Thomas L. Nichols and B. F. Hatch, gave *insiders'* views during the 1850s. Hatch in 1859 described how "women who have abandoned their husbands . . . and who are living in adultery with their paramours, produce abortion, and arise from their guilty couches and stand before large audiences as the medium for angels."[7] Hatch quoted a spiritist channeler: "Our spirit friends say all purely natural passions must have ample scope to work themselves out in their true order. The hoops which have bound the past must be . . . trampled under foot, and a high and holy freedom must take their places."[8] He described how 1850s New Agers

> boastingly speak of their freedom from what they call, social conventionalism and the superstitions of Christianity. They plant themselves

---

would be happier with little voices singing in his home, and let him sustain her, and pity her, and she will bear it all, even to the end, cheerfully."

[4] Henry Gibbons, "On Feticide," *Transactions of the California State Medical Society*, Vol. 8 (1877-1878), pp. 27, 212. I have adopted Gibbons' use of the term "spiritism" to describe the religious movement examined in this chapter, rather than the conventional "spiritualism" usage, because the religion focused on spirits, not spirituality.

[5] E. M. Buckingham, "Criminal Abortion," *Cincinnati Lancet and Observer*, Vol. 10 (1867), p. 139.

[6] Resolution of the General Assembly, in Hugh Hodge, *Foeticide or Criminal Abortion* (Philadelphia: Lindsay and Blackiston), p. 6.

[7] Benjamin F. Hatch, *Spiritualists' Iniquities Unmasked* (New York: Hatch, 1859), p. 51.

[8] *Ibid.*, p. 50.

upon the instincts of their nature. . . . They earnestly contend that no external authority, and no code of human laws can justly bind their affections, or interfere with their liberty to follow the impulse of their personal affinities.[9]

In Hatch's summary, "Adultery to effect a greater degree of spiritual and physical development – the breaking up of marriage to aid in a more perfect unfoldment – becomes to them mandates from heaven, which must be obeyed."[10]

Hatch also observed that spiritists claimed "a God-given right to rectify any mistakes they may have made, and do so as often as such mistakes occur."[11] Mistakes could include misplaced love or unintended pregnancies; unborn children did not have the right to get in the way of spiritual fulfillment, so trips to the abortionist were part of the spiritist tendency, in Hatch's words, to "open every flood-gate of iniquity. All who have yielded themselves to its influence and teaching have run the same sad course, slightly varied according to circumstances."[12]

Spiritism was intensely self-centered, and its "paramount doctrine," according to Hatch, was for believers to "seek such conjugal relation as, at the time, may best please them." Such self-gratification was seen as a spiritual duty, for the object of life was to cultivate all "faculties, sexual as well as the moral," Hatch wrote. The spiritist code, he noted was "if another can develop in me more love than my husband or wife, in virtue of that very love I am newly married, and the old should be absolved, for we should be true to nature and no law has any right to interfere in my affections."[13]

Hatch understood the spiritist movement because he and his wife had been prominent in it until he began witnessing its destructive effects. Thomas Nichols had similar experience and observations. Nichols' *Esoteric Anthropology* sold two hundred and fifty thousand copies during the two decades following its 1853 publication and included the argument that there was "no reason why any one should be compelled to bear children who wishes to avoid it." Nichols reported uncritically the

---

[9] *Ibid.*, p. 24.
[10] *Ibid.*, pp. 18-19.
[11] *Ibid.*, p. 24.
[12] *Ibid.*, p. 18.
[13] *Ibid.*, pp. 16-17.

experience of a wealthy woman who "six times had abortion procured, and by her family physician, too."[14] Prior to his abandonment of spiritism, Nichols and wife Mary Gove Nichols, a gynecologist and abortion counselor during her "free love" days, produced screeds that suggested abortion as a better alternative for some children than birth: "The hereditary evils to children born in a sensual and unloving marriage are everywhere visible . . . sickness, suffering, weakness, imbecility, or outrageous crime."[15]

Nichols later wrote of "the marked effect of spiritism upon American fact, feeling and character. Nothing within my memory has had so great an influence. It has broken up hundreds of churches and changed the religious belief of hundreds of thousands; it has influenced more or less the most important reaction and relations of multitudes."[16] The change was part of what was tormenting the United States during the decades known as "the Mad Forties" and (I would suggest) "the Enraged Fifties."[17] Although mid-nineteenth-century American spiritism has received little attention from recent historians, it was much remarked upon at the time. In New York in 1854, diarist George Templeton Strong thought spiritism was nonsense but its popularity remarkable:

> What would I have said six years ago to anybody who predicted that before the enlightened nineteenth century was ended hundreds of thousands of people in this country would believe themselves able to communicate daily with the ghost of their grandfathers? That ex-judges of the Supreme Court, Senators, clergymen, professors of physical sciences, should be lecturing and writing books on [spiritism]. . . . It is surely one of the most startling events that has occurred for centuries and one of the most significant. A new Revelation, hostile to that of the Church and the Bible, [is shaping] intellectual character and morals. . . .[18]

---

[14]Thomas Nichols, *Esoteric Anthropology* (New York: Nichols, 1853), p. 172.
[15]Thomas and Mary Gove Nichols, *Marriage: Its History, Character and Results* . . . (New York: Nichols, 1854), p. 223. Mary married in 1848 after she abandoned a marriage that produced one child and several "miscarriages."
[16]Thomas L. Nichols, *Forty Years of American Life*, Vol. 2 (London: John Maxwell, 1864, two volumes), pp. 40, 49.
[17]See Grace Adams and Edward Hutter, *The Mad Forties* (New York: Harper and Brothers, 1942).
[18]*Diary of George Templeton Strong: The Turbulent 50s* (Allan Nevins and Milton Thomas, eds. (New York: Macmillan, 1952), November 26, 1855, p. 245.

Strong was amazed at the number of "educated, intelligent people" who had embraced spiritism.[19]

During the 1850s newspaper after newspaper expressed amazement at spiritism's rapid spread. The New York *Times* said of spiritism, "Judging from its rapid extension and widespread effects, it seems to be the new Mahomet, or the social Antichrist, overrunning the world."[20] The *Cleveland Plain Dealer* reported that spiritism was "gaining ground on every side. One month ago, there were not fifty believers in the city; now there are hundreds including some of its best minds."[21] The *Cincinnati Daily Times* noted in 1854 an "astonishing" expansion of spiritism, whose adherents were now found "on every street and corner of the city."[22]

Spiritist inroads were small only in the South, where a "singular hostil[ity] to the introduction of spiritualism" was evident to movement leader Emma Britten.[23] As Dr. Thomas Nichols noted, "spiritualism is most common in New England and the northern states. The southern people have given themselves very little trouble about spiritualism and the many isms that have agitated their northern neighbors."[24]

The movement was powerful because it had both popular, sensational manifestations – "spirit-rapping" – and an ample intellectual base. Although Ralph Waldo Emerson criticized seances and other bizarre manifestations of spiritism, his transcendentalism fed the spiritist move-

---

[19]*Ibid.*, October 16, 1854, p. 133; see also November 15 diary entry. For other comments on those attracted to spiritism, see Burton Gates Brown, Jr., *Spiritualism in Nineteenth-century America*, unpublished dissertation (Boston University, 1972), pp. 71-73, 84, 273; also Hatch, *Spiritualists' Iniquities Unmasked*, pp. 13-15.

[20]New York *Times*, September 8, 1855, p. 2.

[21]*Cleveland Plain Dealer*, quoted in S. B. Britten, ed., *The Telegraph Papers*, Vol. 9 (New York: Chas. Partridge, 1857), p. 297.

[22]Emma Hardinge Britten, *Modern American Spiritualism* (New York: Britten, 1870), p. 351. Echoes of spiritism were heard even in small towns. Samuel Clemens, when writing *The Adventures of Huckleberry Finn* in 1885, used spiritistic references to give a realistic sense of a Missouri town in the 1850s: when slave Jim escapes from a farm in that border state, a neighbor says, "spirits couldn't have done better, and been no smarter."

[23]*Ibid.*, p. 406. Spiritists struck back by channeling George Washington in May 1861 in order to say that southerners, in comparison with northerners, "are not as intelligent, they have not the same free and independent feelings; they have not yet developed up to the idea that freedom of person, and freedom of thought, is the inalienable right of every human being. . . ."

[24]*Ibid.*, p. 66. Conservative southern ministers observed the growth of Unitarianism, Transcendentalism, spiritism, and other "isms" in the North and sometimes felt that North and South were engaged in not just a political battle but a religious one as well. The Confederate version of the Civil War song "Rally Round the Flag" includes the line, "Down with the eagle / Up with the cross."

ment; notable lines from his essays — "I become a transparent eyeball, I am nothing, I see all" — were passed around.[25] Harriet Beecher Stowe (married to Calvin Stowe, a medium) made sympathetic bows to spiritism, and writers such as John Greenleaf Whittier and Henry Wadsworth Longfellow regularly attended seances.[26] Spiritism gained respectability throughout the 1850s as Horace Greeley, Henry Ward Beecher, Emerson, William Lloyd Garrison, and Charles Sumner all attended seances of Judge John Edmonds.[27] Radical-turned-conservative Orestes Brownson observed,

> There are some three hundred circles or clubs in the city of Philadelphia alone. . . . The infection seizes all classes, ministers of religion, lawyers, physicians, judges, comedians, rich and poor, learned and unlearned. The movement has its quarterly, monthly, and weekly journals, some of them conducted with great ability.

Brownson complained that spiritism was "making sad havoc with religion, breaking up churches, taking its victims from all denominations. . . ."[28]

Spiritist theology reached its nineteenth-century peak on the eve of the Civil War. "About the opening of the year 1861, Spiritism had obtained a numerical strength and popularity," Britten wrote. "Regular Sabbath meetings and conferences were held in not less than 3,000 different places."[29] Soon northern spiritists were using the tune of "The Battle Hymn of the Republic" to sing of their self-granted immunity to concerns about Heaven and Hell:

> We have come unto the mountain, and the city of our God, / to the ways of truth and beauty by the souls perfected trod, / and the resurrection trumpet shall not wake us from the sod /as we go marching on. / Glory, Glory, Hallelujah . . . / and we need not ask St. Peter to be ready with his keys, / as we go marching on.[30]

---

[25]See Russell and Clair Goldfarb, *Spiritualism and 19th Century Letters* (Rutherford, NJ: Fairleigh Dickinson University Press, 1978), pp. 45, 60.
[26]See Slater Brown, *The Heyday of Spiritualism* (New York: Hawthorn Books, 1970), p. 151.
[27]Adams and Hutter, *The Mad Forties*, p. 220.
[28]Orestes Brownson, *The Spirit-Rapper* (Boston: Little, Brown, 1854), p. 138.
[29]Britten, *Modern American Spiritualism*, p. 493.
[30]*Ibid.*, p. 535.

Estimates of total spiritist support are difficult to make because, as Brownson wrote, "the age is indifferent, syncretic, and disposed to accept all religions and superstitions as true under certain aspects, and as false under others, and to pronounce one about as good and about as bad as another."[31] Perhaps two million persons (of a U.S. population of thirty million) espoused some spiritist beliefs or engaged in spiritist activities.[32] (Certainly the publishing record of spiritists was impressive; the Library of Congress stacks contain row after row of spiritist works from the 1850s and 1860s.) Spiritists themselves used a figure of five to seven million adherents in 1860, and one writer in 1867 quoted an even more exaggerated figure of eleven million (used at a Catholic convention).[33]

During the 1850s and 1860s spiritists and other theological radicals frequently met and passed resolutions that embodied their new faith. A typical product, unveiled at a "Free Convention" in Vermont, proposed

1. That the authority of each individual soul is absolute and final, in deciding questions as to what is true or false in principle, and right or wrong in practice.

2. That slavery is a wrong. . . .

3. That an intelligent intercourse between embodied and disembodied human spirits is both possible and actual. . . .

6. That the most sacred and important right of woman, is her right to decide for herself how often and under what circumstances she shall assume the responsibilities and be subject to the cares and sufferings of Maternity. . . .[34]

To understand more about the application of this last resolution, let's examine two popular books published in 1858 – the year of that Vermont convention – and then see how the faith worked out in practice.

---

[31]Brownson, *The Spirit-Rapper*, p. 236.

[32]See estimates in Brown, *Spiritualism in Nineteenth-century America*, pp. 70-72, 111, 112, 126, and in U. Clark, ed., *Fifth Annual Spiritualist Register* (Boston: Bela Marsh, 1861), pp. 5, 34, 36.

[33]Geoffrey K. Nelson, *Spiritualism and Society* (London: Routledge,1969), p. 24; Clark, *Fifth Annual Spiritualist Register*, pp. 34-35; Britten, *Modern American Spiritualism*, p. 258.

[34]*Proceedings of the Free Convention, Rutland, Vermont, July 25-27, 1858* (Boston: J. B. Yerrinton, 1858), p. 9.

WRIGHT AND ROOT

In 1858, when Henry Wright spoke at the Vermont convention and published *The Unwelcome Child*, both he and the spiritism he embraced were on a roll. At the convention Wright praised men who slept with women "not by any enactment, ceremony or license of Church or State . . . nor by any formal contract or bargain," but only as long as they desired.[35] Wright argued that an "unwelcome child" arising unplanned by father and mother would grow up doomed "to drunkenness, to lying, to revenge" and would become "a miser, a warrior, a slaveholder, a robber, a murderer, a pirate, or an assassin. . . ."[36] It was no wonder that a surprisedly pregnant woman would have "Grief, anguish . . . consternation [at the] necessity, for weary months, of drinking the bitterest cup of life."[37] Wright quoted reports of desire for abortion: "I have heard many women say they would gladly strangle their children, born of undesired maternity, at birth, could they do so with safety to themselves."[38] Wright himself did not explicitly advocate in writing such strangling before or after birth, but he was sympathetic to women who made that choice:

> No words can express the helplessness, the sense of personal desecration, the despair, which sinks into the heart of woman when forced to submit to maternity under adverse circumstances, and when her own soul rejects it. It is no matter of wonder that abortions are purposely procured; it is to me a matter of wonder that a single child, undeignedly begotten and reluctantly conceived, is ever suffered to mature in the organism of the mother. Her whole nature repels it. How can she regard its ante-natal development but with sorrow and shrinking?[39]

Wright argued that the mother of an unplanned child "is intent on its destruction, and her thoughts devise plans to kill it."[40]

Was such killing wrong? Wright in one passage presented conventional language to that effect, but his book overall was a justification of abortion as good for both the aborting mother *and* the aborted child.

---

[35]*Ibid.*, p. 10.
[36]Henry C. Wright, *The Unwelcome Child or The Crime of an Undesigned and Undesired Maternity* (Boston: Bela Marsh, 1858), p. 21.
[37]*Ibid.*, pp. 24, 25.
[38]*Ibid.*, p. 35.
[39]*Ibid.*, p. 35.
[40]*Ibid.*, p. 45.

First, a woman's task in life was to develop her own spiritual essence; when she saw the unborn child "as a sacrilegious intruder into the domain of her life; an invader of the holy of holies of her being," the woman had "a right to protect herself from further evil. . . ."[41] Wright even contended that whatever "god" he believed in was against the unborn child: "God, speaking through the body and soul of that mother, frowns on its conception, its development, and its birth."[42]

Second, one of Wright's spiritist doctrines was that a child conceived during "mere sensual indulgence" of husband and wife – as opposed to a spiritual union among true "affinity-mates" – would have problems throughout life:

> The mother imparts no vitality to the child in its conception. It is conceived in weakness, is developed in joyless, lifeless imbecility, or intense anguish. It is born an idiot; or without sufficient vital force to develop it into life with the ordinary energies and faculties of a man or woman.[43]

The father, for his part, had given an "exhausted, soulless life" to the child: "Can you commit against it a greater crime?" True love meant abortion when "A living death is its doom."[44] Repeatedly Wright suggested that only planned children should be born: a child's "first claim is, to a *designed* existence, if it is to exist at all. Only in such an existence can it hope for a true and noble nature."[45]

With such thinking common in the fashionable spiritist groups of the mid-nineteenth century, abortion also became common. Wright reported that two women

> made an estimate of the number of our near neighbors who, to our knowledge, had killed one or more of their children before they were born. Six, out of nine, had done the deed, or had procured the services of a 'family physician' to do it for them. . . . They all insisted it was less criminal to kill children before they were born, than to curse them with an unwelcome existence.[46]

---

[41] *Ibid.*, p. 108.
[42] *Ibid.*, pp. 46-47.
[43] *Ibid.*, p. 40.
[44] *Ibid.*, pp. 41, 42.
[45] *Ibid.*, p. 42.
[46] *Ibid.*, p. 111.

Continuing an unplanned pregnancy was not good for either party, because "War is declared between that mother and her child before it is born; a war that must be lasting as life, — a deadly conflict, to which the happiness, and, it may be, the life of the child must be victimized." Fathers also would suffer: "this internal, organic discord, this war, must extend to you, the father, as well as to the mother."[47] The child would be a terror: "Disobedience, ingratitude and defiance are constitutional, — bred in its bones, organized into every fibre of its being." A mother's alternative, under such circumstances, was logical: to procure abortion.[48]

Wright used the words "killing" and "unborn babe," but he defined abortion as a mother "killing her unborn babe to save it from a worse doom" and herself from "enforced, repulsive maternity. . . ."[49] He quoted one spiritist who had abortions "several times in four years" because, as she wrote, "I cannot consent to have the woman, *the real soul-and-spirit-woman* in me, obliterated."[50] "Feelings" were everything in the nineteenth century new age, and it was a sin to ask "the soul" to accept any obligations that restricted absolute freedom.

One woman killed three unborn children, including one who "was seven months old when she killed it." Had she not killed those children, however, she would have "give[n] existence to those whom her soul repels, and thus entail[ed] on them a mother's curse." Overall it was "no greater sin against the child, against herself, against society, and against humanity, for a mother to kill her child before it is born, than to give birth to it when her own heart loathes its existence."[51]

Wright told of how mothers and daughters came to agreement about the new gospel. In one family when a "pregnant daughter spoke to her mother about the child within her," the daughter spoke of her "loathsome and horrible feelings about it" and declared that "it would be a greater sin to give birth to a child, with the feelings I now have towards it, than to kill it before it is born." The mother debated the question with her daughter for several days, but realized that "if the child was developed and born, under such a state of mind in the mother, it must inevitably be a desperado, or a fugitive and vagabond on the earth." The mother

---

[47] *Ibid.*, p. 48.
[48] *Ibid.*, p. 59.
[49] *Ibid.*, p. 71.
[50] *Ibid.*, p. 80.
[51] *Ibid.*, p. 114

took her daughter "to a doctor, noted for his ante-natal murders, and he advised that the child should be killed, — and he killed it."[52]

Wright also showed how another pregnant woman was brought to her senses:

> My own soul, and the God whose voice was heard within, repudiated its existence. I could not help the feeling. . . . I consulted a woman, a friend in whom I trusted. I found that she had perpetrated that outrage on herself and on others. She told me it was not murder to kill a child any time before its birth. Of this she labored to convince me, and called in the aid of her 'family physician,' to give force to her arguments. He argued that it was right and just for wives thus to protect themselves against the results of their husband's sensualism, — told me that God and human laws would approve of killing children before they were born, rather than curse them with an undesired existence.[53]

The argument, much-used then as now, was, "It would be a greater sin against children to entail on them the curse of an abhorred existence, than to kill them before they are born!"[54]

Wright's book was solemn, but the mid-nineteenth century was also the era of patent medicines and P. T. Barnum; "spirit-rapping" sensationalism shared that flavor, as did some pro-abortion books. One of the significant spiritist Barnums was Harmon Knox Root, author of two books — *The People's Medical Lighthouse* and *The Lover's Marriage Lighthouse* — that sold hundreds of thousands of copies. Root was not above offering a prize of one hundred dollars for "the best poetical criticism of his celebrated medical work" and awarding the prize to one Owen Duffy for his ode, "Lines Suggested by Reading Dr. H. K. Root's Celebrated Work, *The People's Medical Lighthouse.*"[55] (Duffy's poem began "Hail, glorious beacon, great temple of light, / Whose effulgence of knowledge discloses the right, / And changes to daytime the darkness of night.")[56] But Root had a serious point to make: he argued that his theology, which he called "Deistical free spiritualism," would bring about a "good time" for all mankind.[57]

---

[52]*Ibid.*, p. 117.

[53]*Ibid.*, p. 102.

[54]*Ibid.*, p. 118.

[55]Harmon Knox Root, *The Lover's Marriage Lighthouse* (New York: Root, 1858), p. 222.

[56]The first three stanzas discuss men's longtime ignorance. The fourth stanza brings the good news, "All hail! On this sea of woe has appeared a light/ To guard us safe through this dark, dark night! . . . immortal ROOT . . . Hail, glorious beacon. . . ."

[57]Root, *The Lover's Marriage Lighthouse*, p. 7.

Root began by complaining that the Biblical worldview dominant in America to that point was constraining: "Man has not been allowed to lean upon and trust his own nature and wisdom as they gush from the divine foundation forever living, but is forced to drink from matrimonial and religious pools of filthy waters repugnant to his natural tastes."[58] Root argued that 1850s spiritists had taken human understanding a great leap forward:

> Why not, then, wisely construct the garments of the present generation to fit the child of to-day? . . . we want the liberty that allows each one alone to judge conscientiously for himself, in regard to matters pertaining to his affectional nature.[59]

The marriage bond was "of earth," Root concluded, but "the female or male who trusts to the strength and divinity of love and congeniality, requiring no other bondage, is of heaven." Root's sacrament was "the love of the sexes – that love which is stronger than death, which springs so freshly in youth. . . . Let mankind trust in this power."[60]

Root developed his position in several steps. First, despite all the evidence of seduction's sad consequences, he advised young women to go with the flow:

> The female that makes profession of love and of confidence and will not copulate without first binding her lover in an indissoluble marriage, lays her love open to the suspicion of hypocrisy, and shows that she considers her person as superior to her affection. But the woman who asks no pledge from her lover as security for her embrace, gives the strongest of all possible evidence of the truth of her heart, and the sincerity of her professions of love.[61]

Root praised

the affectionate mind of a young and passionate woman. There is within her very soul a love for the opposite sex as such, and in her physical organization an amative passion that counsels her to indulge in sexual

---

[58] *Ibid.*, p. 8.
[59] *Ibid.*, p. 9.
[60] *Ibid.*, pp. 9, 179.
[61] *Ibid.*, p. 178.

intercourse . . . she yields to the natural impulse of her organization, and allows her love its full fruitation in sexuality. . . .[62]

He even praised the second abortion-likely group, prostitutes, as "far above the so-called virtuous women who stick to an indissoluble marriage as the road to their sexuality. . . ."[63]

Root next turned to the plight of a spiritistically inclined married woman who was "like a fruitful vine, covered with the green leaves of affection, with the flowers of love and the fruits of sexual desire. . . ."[64] This "beautiful and loving being," sadly, was married to "a regular hedgehog in all his affections and passions – stuck full, mentally and physically, of bristles – making him as unapproachable as a fretful porcupine, with all his quills standing erect."[65] Some women in such a situation "choose to abuse themselves," Root stated: "the practice has of late years become so common, that some ingenious Frenchman, wishing to supply an increasing demand, has actually invented and manufactured a substitute . . . called in English, a 'dildo.'"[66] But Root's alternative choice for such a married woman was adultery, and that was much superior: "In the eye of the female who has sexual intercourse out of marriage, as distinguished from the self-polluter, there is a look of mildness and confidence. [Adultery] brightens up her womanly nature."[67]

Root acknowledged a drawback to his proposal: the possibility of pregnancy, which could lead to the trapping of a woman's spirit in new bondage. Root, however, had the solution. He told women to

make use of the French Instrumental Uterine Regulator. This beautiful and exceedingly useful little instrument should comprise a part of every lady's toilet articles, as being really indispensable. If used as directed, it will produce no irritation or trouble from its introduction into the neck of the womb. . . . The system and the mind are at once relieved; fear is banished, and nature resumes its healthful operation. The French

---

[62] *Ibid.*

[63] *Ibid.*, p. 179. Root also argued that government stay out of marriage but manage the economy: "Let the state erect large and convenient workshops . . . there should be not only mechanical shops, but studios for young American artists . . . in these institutions every person should be sure of employment . . . there should be no failure about it possible." (p. 315)

[64] *Ibid.*, p. 397.

[65] *Ibid.*

[66] *Ibid.*, p. 348.

[67] *Ibid.*

Instrumental Uterine Regulator can be had of the author, or it will be securely mailed, with the explicit direction for use, to any part of the world, on reception of the money. The cost of the instrument is $10.

Root concluded with a guarantee: His Uterine Regulator "will bring on contractions, and produce evacuation of the contents of the womb, commonly known as miscarriage, no matter at what period of gestation."[68]

FROM THEORY TO PRACTICE

Many spiritist leaders lived the lives Wright and Root recommended. Andrew Jackson Davis, probably the most influential American spiritist in the nineteenth century, called marriages "legalized adultery and bigotry" unless they were true spiritual marriages with "affinity-mates."[69] Children conceived in such a marriage were spiritually illegitimate and might be better off dead. "The female has the right to control all the manifestations of love," Davis asserted euphemistically.[70] He acknowledged that other children might be conceived as spiritists experimented with numerous individuals outside marriage until the real "affinity-mate" was found, and he noted that some of those children might live, but he wanted all spiritists to recognize that initial judgments concerning affinities could be mistaken. This meant that after several months of gestation, a woman might find her child to be wrongly conceived, doomed to misery, and needing abortion for his or her own good.

Dr. Thomas Nichols during his spiritist days also declared that since a woman "has the right to decide who'll be the father of her children, she has the equal right to decide the time to have children." He then added the logical conclusion: "Since the Woman alone has the right to decide whether her ovum shall be impregnated, she must also have the privilege of determining the circumstances which justify the procurement of abortion."[71] That logic caught on, and Nichols later related (in a book published in London and aimed at British readers), "it is scarcely known,

---

[68] *Ibid.*, p. 194.
[69] Andrew Jackson Davis, *The Great Harmonia*, Vol. 4 (Boston: Sanborn, Carter, and Bazin, 1856), pp. 426-445.
[70] *Ibid.*
[71] Adams and Hutter, *The Mad Forties*, p. 289. Nichols argued for surgery rather than abortifacient use: "A surgical operation is the simplest and the one accompanied by the minimal danger."

I believe, in England, to what extent the anti-life and marriage theory has been maintained in the Northern states of America."[72]

As Nichols noted, anti-marriage and anti-life doctrines went together. Minnesota spiritist-explorer Charles Carpenter reported that only "two or three families of spiritists in St. Paul were not spiritually mismated," and 90 percent of spiritist leaders "were in this unsettled state with an affinity."[73] The *Spiritual Telegraph*, one of the new religion's central organs, noted that all "advanced spiritists" substituted "the doctrine of affinities" for marriage.[74]

One observer noted that "Husbands have abandoned wives, and wives have abandoned husbands, to find more congenial partners, or those for whom they have stronger religious affinities."[75] Journalist William Dixon wrote that spiritists did "not mind people consorting when there is an attraction; else how is the affinity to be found?" The opening for sarcasm was obvious, and Dixon joked about the spiritists who "traveled from place to place finding a great many affinities everywhere."[76]

Dixon also detailed the relations of spiritism and other mid-century radical movements. "Free-love" doctrine, for example, shared with spiritism some "poets, orators, and preachers," but also had its own "lecture halls, excursions, picnics and colonies," he noted.[77] Diarist George Strong in New York City had fun commenting on the growth "of the 'free love' league . . . 'passionate attraction' its watchword, fornicating and adultery its apparent object."[78] Strong wrote that when abortion did not result, confusion did: "Mrs. A. was going to have a baby, was B. or C. its father?"[79] But developments quickly became more tragic than farci-

---

[72]Thomas. L. Nichols, *Forty Years of American Life*, Vol. 2 (London: John Maxwell, 1864, two volumes), pp. 40, 49.

[73]William Dixon, *Spiritual Loves* (Philadelphia: Lippincott, 1868), p. 339.

[74]Britten, *Modern American Spiritualism*, p. 119.

[75]See Alice Tyler, *Freedom's Ferment* (Minneapolis: University of Minnesota Press, 1944). Tyler describes a variety of cults and utopias, including those of Transcendentalism, Millerism, spiritism, religious communism, Shakerism, and utopian socialism.

[76]Dixon, *Spiritual Loves*, p. 399.

[77]*Ibid.*, p. 381. The commune movement was particularly colorful. Residents at the commune of Modern Times on Long Island, forty miles east of New York, "abolished the wedding ring . . . substitut[ing] instead the piece of string. . . . Should a lady show up at the eating place with a piece of string neatly tied in a loveknot above her little finger, this would mean that she had changed love partners in the night. Everyone would then look for the man with the finger tied likewise." Adams and Hutter, *The Mad Forties*, p. 288.

[78]Strong, *Diary of George Templeton Strong*, October 17, 1855, p. 235.

[79]*Ibid.*, p. 117.

cal, for abortion often was the outcome: "Unintended" children were called "children of chance, children of lust" and "abortions [with] no right to existence."[80] Their mothers sometimes followed literally what Henry Wright may have meant rhetorically when he told a cheering audience at the 1858 Vermont convention, "Die rather than give existence to children thou dost not want."[81]

How many spiritist-related abortions took place? We have no accurate statistics, but convention records show spiritists acknowledging a large number of abortions "in our midst."[82] Although few spiritists risked imprisonment by publicly confessing to illegal acts, they were willing to accuse others who had held to the faith but then backslid. For example, a Mrs. Stearns of Corry, Pennsylvania, told one spiritist convention that her estranged husband, who had investigated spiritism with her, had tried to abort their unborn baby, but the child was born anyway.[83] Public acknowledgment of abortion could have legal complications, but the *desire* for one could be freely described, so we can read statements such as that of Laura C. Owens of Indianapolis to the convention: "I went to a physician and offered him $500 to cause an abortion. . . ."[84]

Woodhull & Claflin's Weekly, which mixed spiritism and feminism – editor Victoria Woodhull was president of the American Association of Spiritualists – recorded story after story of abortion among those who had practiced spiritism and/or free-love.[85] "It is one of those things against which almost everybody willfully shuts his eyes and professes to think that it does not exist; and everybody pretends to everybody else that he knows nothing about it," the editors wrote. "Some wives procure a half dozen abortions per year."[86]

---

[80]Speech by Julia Branch, in *Proceedings of the Free Convention, Rutland, Vermont, July 25-27, 1858* (Boston: J. B. Yerrinton, 1858), p. 54.

[81]*Ibid.*, p. 72.

[82]*Proceedings of the Tenth Annual Convention of the American Association of Spiritualists* (1873), p. 91, in Houdini Collection, Rare Book Room, Library of Congress.

[83]*Ibid.*, p. 136.

[84]*Ibid.*, p. 137. She added, "the physician did nothing, and the child was born: but it died, and God knows that I am the occasion of its being in spirit land, for with tears of bitterness I prayed that she might be born dead."

[85]Victoria Woodhull also was known for consorting with Commodore Vanderbilt, exposing Henry Ward Beecher, and allegorically reinterpreting the book of Genesis so that the Garden of Eden was the human body and the four rivers referred to were the blood, the bowels, the urinary system, and reproductive organs.

[86]"The Slaughter of the Innocent," *Woodhull & Claflin's Weekly*, June 20, 1874, p. 8.

"Half a dozen" is an exaggeration, but contemporary testimony concerning the extent of spiritism and the propensity to abort among its adherents, makes it clear that many believers were having one, and perhaps half a dozen over a series of years. If pushed to make a reasonable estimate of the total, I suggest roughly forty-five thousand among the non-slave population, based on the following considerations:

(1) According to accounts in the 1850s, about 10 percent of the population had moved away from theological orthodoxy and its opposition to abortion. The most popular alternative religion was spiritism.

(2) There were six million non-slave women between the ages of fifteen and forty-four in 1860.[87] Relatively small portions of that number f-" into the abandonment or prostitution categories. Close to one out of a hundred probably was a prostitute committed to abortion by her lifestyle. Others who had been seduced and abandoned were desperate enough to fall into abortion in opposition to their theological beliefs.

(3) Here we are considering those fifteen- to forty-four-year-old women who would entertain notions of abortion usually because of their spiritist beliefs. If accounts in the 1850s are accurate, there may have been close to six hundred thousand such women. Census records in 1860 show that this number of women aged fifteen to forty-four was likely to bear about ninety thousand children annually.[88]

(4) We do not know exactly how many children these particular women, most of whom were married, did bear. But if half the time they "followed their bliss" (to use today's New Age expression) and chose abortion, forty-five thousand unborn children would have died.

(5) Again I stress that such a number is speculative – but it does explain why doctors at mid-century suddenly saw an influx of married women seeking abortions, even though American society as a whole considered abortion wrong. Such an estimate provides a numerical beat for the sirenic melody sung by publications such as *Woodhull & Claflin's Weekly*, which did not applaud abortion but did apologize for it.

(6) Keeping of vital statistics was so erratic in the nineteenth century that little in the way of scientific analysis can be done. And yet, some numbers developed by Dr. Elisha Harris, a public health reformer who became Registrar of Vital Statistics for New York City, are suggestive.

---

[87]Bureau of the Census, *The Statistical History of the United States* (New York: Basic Books, 1976), p. 16. Lack of information makes any estimate of abortion among slaves pure guesswork.
[88]*Ibid.*, p. 62.

New York first began to keep records of deaths of unborn children by miscarriage or abortion in 1805, when forty-seven were recorded from among a population of 76,770. By 1849 the number of fetal deaths had jumped almost thirty-fold to 1,320; the ratio of fetal deaths to population went from 1:1,633 in 1805 to 1:516 in 1840 and 1:341 in 1849.[89] Stated another way, the number of New York City fetal deaths (compared to total mortality) increased from 1 in 376 to 1 in 13.[90] That change showed the historical flow; what it meant in New York City of the 1860s, according to Harris, is that one of every five unborn children whose deaths were legally reported was suffering abortion or miscarriage.

Such numbers are only indicative, since the most abortion-prone members of the population – prostitutes – lived generally outside of the law and official records, and since mortality reporting varied from decade to decade. But they do suggest some rise of abortion among urban populations.

Woodhull and Claflin's Weekly did not approve of that practice, but the publication apologized for abortion by emphasizing "what compels woman to the terrible extremity of [choosing] the least of two evils." According to one woman who attended spiritist lectures,

> The laws of legal marriage have robbed woman of her sexual rights and placed them in the keeping of the man. Restore to woman her God-given right to control maternity and consider it a far more damnable wrong to keep a wife ever liable to pregnancy than it is for her to prevent as soon as possible the consequences of so flagrant an outrage upon her nature.

That writer asserted, as had Henry Wright before the war, "better to remain childless than to bear an unwelcome child. The right to parentage is evolved only from mutual love and mutual desire."[91]

Abortion was also the lesser of evils from the child's perspective, according to another argument left over from before the war. Children deserved pure spirits, but if begotten in the absence of true spiritual love, they would have "at the very dawn of their existence a curse that an eternity may not remove."[92] Another article proclaimed

---

[89]Horatio Storer and Franklin Fiske Heard, *Criminal Abortion: Its Nature, Its Evidence and Its Law* (Boston: Little, Brown, 1868), p. 24.
[90]*Ibid.* See also J. C. Stone, "Report on the Subject of Criminal Abortion," *Transactions of the Iowa State Medical Society*, Vol. 1 (1874), p. 28.
[91]"The Only Preventive," *Woodhull & Claflin's Weekly*, November 28, 1874, p. 12.
[92]*Ibid.*

that the mother makes the child just what it is; that, if during the gesta-
tive period, she loathe the father, quarrel with him, suffer from him, she
must expect her child to possess the same characteristics; that, if she conceives in lust and not from and in love, her child will be a child of lust
and subject to all its deep damnations; that, if she desire to rid herself of
her unwelcome burden, she makes her child a murderer at heart.[93]

A third article argued, "No mother can have a desire spring up in her
mind to be rid of the child she carries in her womb without imprinting
the thought, the possibility of murder, upon its facile mind."[94] The logic
was clear: think abortion, do abortion.

We might also understand better the consequences of ideas by examining the practice of Emily Dickinson's sister-in-law, Susan Dickinson,
who "thought it disgusting to have children." Susan Dickinson's husband, Austin, confided to his neighbor and mistress, Mabel Todd, that
his wife "had four killed before birth" by "Dr. Breck of Springfield."[95]
Ned, the first child of Austin and Susan, was born five years after the
wedding and only after Susan (according to another journal entry) had
"caused three or four to be artificially removed" and had failed in
repeated abortion attempts.[96] Ned became an epileptic – the result,
thought Mabel Todd, of Susan's efforts to "get rid of him" – and had
frequent "fits in his sleep. . . . His mother was afraid of him so his father
had to take care of Ned until he awoke with a sore mouth from having
bitten his tongue."[97] Susan Dickinson, while not a regular participant in
spiritist practices, had absorbed the self-centeredness and disgust for children that was rampant in spiritist circles.

It may be that by the post-war era the tide of spiritism was receding
for a time; fewer spiritist books were being published by the 1880s and
the 1890s. By then, however, many Americans had imbibed for several
decades the spiritist stress on "the individual or personal sovereignty of
man and of woman" and its condemnation of "all laws, ecclesiastical or

---

[93]"Motherhood," *Woodhull & Claflin's Weekly*, May 13, 1876, p. 4. The writer told mothers
"that it is you who are responsible for the groans and griefs and tears that make this
world a hell; that it is you who create the candidates that adorn the gallows; to fill the
prisons and other loathsome institutions. We would sound this in your ears until you
wake to your senses, now deadened, by the curse on Eve, to all the misery you make."
[94]*Ibid.*, p. 9.
[95]Todd journal (October 18, 1891) and scrap, quoted in Richard B. Sewell, *The Life of
Emily Dickinson*, Vol. 1 (New York: Farrar, Straus and Giroux, 1974), pp. 188-189.
[96]*Ibid.*
[97]*Ibid.*, p. 189.

civil, which conflict with the exercise of this right by adult human beings."[98] In practice this meant a stress on "love-unions between men and women; monogamic, if the parties forming them be naturally monogamic, or otherwise, if they be naturally otherwise."[99] And in practice that meant more unwanted pregnancies: unwanted if they occurred within a marriage that was not a true "love-union," and generally unwanted if they came outside of marriage, with the result that "society will [make the child] illegitimate and curse [the parents] as disrespectable. . . ."[100]

Overall, it is clear that the tendency of spiritists to blame social conventions for abortion led them to apologize for the abortion practice they sometimes criticized. "Where one [young woman] dies a physical death, the abortionist unquestionably saves scores if not hundreds from being morally murdered by society's damnation," the *Weekly* declared. "The trade of the abortionist ought to be looked upon as a blessing rather than a curse to the community."[101] Although we have no record of how many spiritist "blessings" took place, physicians such as P. S. Haskell were shocked at the number of young wives who requested abortions so as not to be deprived of "society and literary association."[102] In Vermont, far from the cities where prostitution was rampant, Dr. William McCollom reported that abortion "is frequent – and applications are continually made to apothecaries as well as physicians for drugs for this purpose."[103] Dr. E. M. Buckingham of the small town of Springfield, Ohio, suggested, "Perhaps there is no crime more frequently contemplated, and committed under a misguided judgement, than that of criminal abortion."[104] Dr. S. K. Crawford of Monmouth, Illinois, wrote that "Every practicing physician in the state of Illinois can see on his daily

---

[98] *Woodhull & Claflin's Weekly*, August 29, 1874, p. 9.

[99] *Ibid.* The *Weekly* also argued, in traditional spiritist fashion, that "man-made law or legal ceremony is not the tribunal for the free born, the spiritually unfolded, the free-love soul. Love and nature alone can give to two conjugally mated souls the precious right to the sacred blending of their beautiful sexual unfoldment."

[100] "Spiritualism and Abortion," *Woodhull & Claflin's Weekly*, May 31, 1873.

[101] "Down with the Babies," *Woodhull & Claflin's Weekly*, November 29, 1873, p. 10.

[102] Haskell, "Criminal Abortion," *Transactions of the Maine Medical Association*, Vol. 4 (1871-1873), p. 460.

[103] William McCollom, "Criminal Abortion," *Transactions of the Vermont Medical Society for 1865*, p. 40.

[104] E. M. Buckingham, "Criminal Abortion," *Cincinnati Lancet and Observer*, Vol. 10 (1867), p. 143.

rounds the land-marks [of] this criminal work, this ignoble business, this murderous practice."[105] Dr. O. C. Turner of Massachusetts reported that

> There is an ever-deepening shadow creeping over the face of the land, like a destroying plague. . . . Where the Asiatic cholera or any other dreaded pestilence takes one, this takes ten; and for every hundred that consumption, that scourge of our race, demands, this Moloch receives a sacrifice of thousands.

Turner called actions of those who had embraced a new idolatry "the slaughter which out-herods Herod, Criminal Abortion."[106]

From the vantage point of 1877, Dr. Henry Gibbons, former head of the California Medical Society, did a good job of summarizing what he called "the continuous stream of obscene feticide literature" that had been common in American life since the 1840s.[107] Gibbons traced the development of the idea that "spirit-affinity" was more important than marriage and concluded that

> Whatever tends to discourage marriage, and to remove it from the domain of the affections, and to make it the subject of calculation, tends in a greater or less degree to promote licentiousness, prostitution, and feticide. Our age and our country, alive with free and busy thought, have given birth to a number of anomalies, if not monstrosities, religious, intellectual, and moral.

Gibbons, in a speech, displayed a spiritist booklet that

> denounces marriage, 'as now instituted,' because it 'binds the parties in the slavery of ownership; refuses the soul the right of expressing itself beyond its imprisonment' . . . 'Will you,' the writer asks, 'will you, oh! man, be guilty of soul-murder by refusing woman the right of being the object of your love? Will you iron-case the crystal spring lest another thirsty soul may drink and be refreshed on the water of life?'[108]

---

[105]S. K. Crawford, "Criminal Abortion," *Transactions of the Twenty-Second Anniversary Meeting of the Illinois Medical Association*, (1872), pp. 74-81.
[106]O. C. Turner, "Criminal Abortion," *Boston Medical and Surgical Journal*, Vol. 5 (1870), pp. 299-300.
[107]Gibbons, "On Feticide," pp. 27, 212.
[108]*Ibid.*, pp. 217-218.

Gibbons suggested that such beliefs led to more adultery and more abortion.

Gibbons then turned directly to "the influence on private morals exercised by the host of clairvoyants, mesmerists, astrologers, fortune tellers, trance mediums, healing mediums, materializers, and spiritists of all kinds." Spiritism, he noted, "has now been on trial," and the result was clear: "It has crazed no small proportion of its devotees, and bewildered and intoxicated a still larger number . . . it builds a nest that receives the egg that hatches the serpent that tempts the woman to put to death her unborn offspring."[109]

Our examination of the three populations that were abortion-likely in America up to the Civil War era leads to one clear conclusion: individuals who were part of those three groups were at risk, but most American women were very *unlikely* to have an abortion. Concerning the incidence of AIDS in recent times, it was important in developing public policy to note that the disease was not diffused throughout the population but (with rare exceptions) was specific to several groups. Similarly, it is incorrect to conclude, as historian James Mohr and his followers have done, that abortion was widespread throughout early American society. Yes, by the time of the Civil War every city supported its abortionists, but (with rare exceptions) they were catering to the three specific clienteles.

The goal of most anti-infanticide and anti-abortion leaders was not abolition of the practice but containment – i.e., restriction of abortion to those three groups, and reduction of it within those groups. The hope was that pressure on members of those three populations would at the least lessen the likelihood of their committing infanticide or abortion, and might even bring them back into communion with a Biblical worldview.

---

[109]*Ibid.*, pp. 221-222. The connection of belief and action may have been particularly clear in the career of Dr. Sara B. Chase. Dr. Chase in 1874 wrote for the *Herald of Health* an article, "The Great Crime," in which she claimed concerning abortion, "The one great underlying cause which fosters this evil more than all other causes combined is the want of the recognition of one important truth . . . that she who is the continued originator of the race, she whose power and influence for weal or woe must be handed down through her posterity during all coming time, shall be granted the inalienable, indisputable right to determine for herself when she can lovingly take upon herself the responsibilities of maternity." A few years later, Sara Chase was arrested as an abortionist.

4

Abortion and
Legal Minimalism

During the eighteenth and early nineteenth centuries, legislative action was not the first recourse when social problems arose. Much of the pressure on individuals was to come from family, church, or associations. Parents, employers, heads of benevolent organizations, teachers, and church leaders were all representatives of different types of governing authorities that individuals were to respect. Newspapers typically argued that family, church, and charity, not civil government, should take leadership in dealing with social problems. Alexis de Tocqueville noted in *Democracy in America* in 1835 that

> Americans of all ages, all conditions, and all dispositions constantly form associations. . . . If it is proposed to inculcate some truth or to foster some feeling by the encouragement of a great example, they form a society . . . what political power could ever [do what Americans voluntarily] perform every day with the assistance of the principle of association?[1]

---

[1] Alexis De Tocqueville, *Democracy in America*, Vol. 2, book 2, chap. 5 (p. 116 in Vintage edition, New York, 1945).

A popular newspaper of the period, *The Boston Recorder*, had much more coverage of voluntary associations than it did of developments on Capitol Hill or Beacon Hill.[2]

Emphasis on initiative even undergirded one early nineteenth-century pro-life campaign, the battle against dueling. The *Boston Recorder* gave specific details on one duel and its bloody results and then noted that "The above mentioned murder shows the folly of resorting to a *duel* to settle differences . . . what madness it is to continue the practice, attended by such dreadful consequences." The *Recorder*, though, never proposed federal or state governmental action to deal with the problem. Instead, the *Recorder* frequently showed sons bowing to parental wishes and abandoning plans for duels.

The *Recorder* also showed how soft answers could turn away wrath, even when duels already were scheduled. An article in 1823 began with one man challenging another to a duel and the challenged man accepting on the condition that they should breakfast together at his house before going out to fight. After breakfast, the challenger asked if the host was ready.

"No sir," replied he, "not till we are more upon a par; that amiable woman, & those six innocent children, who just now breakfasted with us, depend solely upon my life for subsistence – and till you can stake something equal in my estimation to the welfare of seven persons, dearer to me than the apple of my eye, I cannot think we are equally matched." "We are not indeed!" replied the other, giving him his hand.[3]

Furthermore, the *Recorder* encouraged voluntary associations, schools, and churches to criticize duelists at every opportunity. Newspapers, for their part, were encouraged to print names of all those involved in duels. In opposition to those who saw dueling as heroic activity, the *Recorder* suggested that societal leaders should poke fun at duelists at every opportunity. One of its own stories told of a man awaiting his opponent's arrival until "he observed some bushes near him shaking, and supposing it was his adversary skulking," fired.[4] The man found out he had shot a cow. In addition, journalistic accounts of duels engaged in

---

[2]Marvin Olasky, "Finding and Losing a Macro-Story," *Christian Scholar's Review*, Vol. 20 (September 1990), p. 23.
[3]*Boston Recorder*, April 22, 1823, p. 57.
[4]*Ibid.*, March 21, 1826, p. 52.

by famous leaders often were structured so as to end *with* blood but *without* honor. In 1820 when Admiral Stephen Decatur fought and died, the *Recorder* was pointed in its criticism:

> The brave Decatur, who was ever ready to launch his country's thunder against his country's enemy, and who was calm and fearless in the very tempest of battle, – the brave DECATUR, grew pale at the thought, that a man who sought his blood, might post his name as a coward! [He forgot] . . . that there is no honor, which is valuable and durable, save that which comes from God.[5]

Other accounts of dueling also emphasized man's responsibility before God, not civil government. It is in this context that we should look upon the early development of legislation to protect unborn children. Today's mood in many areas is pro-legislation; given the mood of an earlier America, it is no surprise that abortion legislation emerged only when the number of abortions grew and non-governmental means of containment seemed inadequate.

Two abortion/infanticide scenarios were in the background of early legislation not explicitly connected to abortion. The first occurred when the prostitute or despairing victim of seduction took into her confidence a mother, friend, or madame and plotted the death of the child. Legislators, seeing this threat, passed laws to dissuade the confidant from counseling infanticide. Delaware in 1719 instructed its residents, ". . . And if any person or persons shall counsel, advise or direct such woman to kill the child she goes with, and after she is delivered, of such child, she kills it, every such person so advising or directing, shall be deemed accessary [sic] to such murder, and shall have the same punishment as the principal shall have."[6]

Other colonial (and then state) legislatures took similar action over the next century. The *Georgia Penal Code* in 1811 included the sentence, "And be it further enacted, That if any person or persons advise or counsel another to kill a child before its birth, and the child be killed after its birth, in pursuance of such advice, such adviser of advisers is or are declared accessory to the murder."[7] These laws did not guard against the rare abortion; they applied themselves to the task at hand, safer-for-

---

[5] *Ibid.*, April 22, 1820, p. 57.
[6] *Delaware Laws*, chapter 22, section 6, p. 67 (1797).
[7] *Georgia Penal Code*, section 17 (1811).

mother infanticide. They did presuppose a fundamental continuity of unborn and born child; a person charged with advising killing of the child was not to get away with saying, "I merely advised the killing of a fetus."

Desperate women who did not confide might conceal – and it was this second prospect, that of a woman concealing her pregnancy and killing the child immediately after birth, that other laws were designed to counteract. The task of concealment in an era of loose dresses and an ideal feminine build heftier than that now fashionable was not as difficult as it would be today. Colonies and states both north and south moved against concealment whenever it threatened to become a problem, with the first such law emerging in the most populous colony, Virginia, in 1710. Since the statute is very instructive and also very difficult to find in libraries at present, it is worth quoting at length:

An Act to prevent the destroying and murdering of Bastard Children

I. WHEREAS several leud women, that have been delivered of bastard children, to avoid their shame, and to escape punishment, do secretly bury or conceal the death of their children; and after, if the child be found dead, the said women do allege, that the said child was born dead; whereas it falleth out sometimes, (although hardly it is to be proved) that the said child or children were murdered by the said women, their leud mothers. . . .

II. Be it enacted by the Lieutenant-Governor, council and Burgesses, of this present General Assembly, and it is hereby enacted by the authority of the same, That if any white or other woman, not being a slave, after one month next ensuing the end of this present Session of Assembly, be delivered of any issue of her body, male or female, which being born alive, should by law be a bastard, & that she endeavour privately, either by drowning, or secret burying thereof, or any other way, either by herself, or the procuring of others, so to conceal the death thereof, as that it may not come to light, whether it were born alive, or not, but be concealed; in every such case, the mother so offending, shall suffer death, as in case of murder, except such mother can make proof, by one witness at the least, that the child (whose death was by her so intended to be concealed) was born dead.

III. And to the end, this Act may be made public, Be it further enacted, by the authority aforesaid, That the same shall be read yearly, on some Sunday in May, in all Parish Churches and Chapels within this colony, by the Minister or Reader of each Parish, immediately after

Divine Service, under the penalty of five hundred pounds of Tobacco
for every omission and neglect therein. . . .[8]

The act was passed after debate and amendments that — much to our
loss — were not recorded in the legislative journals.[9] The details of that
Virginia legislation are instructive in many ways. Significantly, lawmakers perceived the problem not as one of infanticide or abortion generally,
but one specifically deriving from the conduct of "leud women."
Furthermore, the legislature was acting not on a theoretical basis but
because of real incidents — "it falleth out sometimes" — that required a
response if further "great mischief" was to be avoided. The act only covered women who were not property; slaves were considered part of the
owner's body, which was not to be touched by the state. The mother of
the child, once found to have practiced concealment, was treated as if
guilty of murder unless she could prove her innocence. Finally, church
services were key communication vehicles, and churches that neglected
reading the Act were fined.

Each of those aspects was fraught with difficulties. The provision
that very quickly caused legislative second thoughts was that which
potentially provided capital punishment for concealers. The executive

---

[8]William Waller Hening, ed., *The Statutes at Large*, Vol. 3 (Philadelphia: Desilver, 1823),
pp. 516-517.

[9]A general frustration for colonial historians is embodied in the scanty records of the
General Assembly of Virginia called in October 1710. On October 31, the Council of
Colonial Virginia (essentially, the upper chamber of the legislature) agreed "That a Bill
be prepared and brought in to prevent the destroying and Murdering of a bastard
child. . . ." (See *Legislative Journals of the Council of Colonial Virginia*, Vol. 1 [Richmond:
Virginia State Library, 1918], p. 493.) On November 2 "*an act to prevent the destroying and
murdering of bastard Children* [was] read the first time"; on November 6 the bill was "read
the second time and amended"; on November 8 the bill was read the third time —
"Resolved that the Bill do pass" — and sent to the House of Burgesses (pp. 494-495).
But nowhere in all this is any record of what was changed in the amendments.

The record of the House of Burgesses (lower chamber) is equally taciturn. The bill
was discussed on November 8 (*Journals of the House of Burgesses of Virginia, 1702-1712*
[Richmond: Virginia State Library, 1912], pp. 259, 261, 262, 265, 268, 298), read the
first time on November 9, and the second time on November 10. "Thereupon some
amendments being agreed to" (p. 262), the bill was read the third time on November
11, with the House deciding, "Resolved that the bill with the amendments, do pass." The
House of Burgesses that day asked the Council to concur in the amendments. The
Council did, but came back on November 15 with its own amendments, to which the
Burgesses agreed. The Governor passed the Act to prevent *The Destroying and Murthering
of Bastard Children* on December 9. All this, and still we do not know what transpired
during the legislative discussions.

journals of the Council of Virginia in 1713, only three years after passage of the Act, include a request for leniency for Jane Ham, who was

> indicted [by] this General court upon the Law of this Colony, for concealing the death of her Bastard Child, and found guilty: And the Judges of the General court this day representing to the governor that there did not appear on the tryal any proof of the said jane Ham's having done any violence to the said Child, to occasion its death, but only endeavored to conceal her being delivered thereof; and further that the said jane appeared to be a very ignorant person, and not like to be apprised of the Law which makes such Concealment penal, And therefore recommending her as a fitt object of mercy.[10]

The governor, after some jockeying, signed a reprieve; the records suggest that Jane Ham was pardoned shortly before Christmas 1714.[11]

Perhaps because of such difficulty, the law evidently fell into disuse, was omitted from Virginia legal codes from 1769 on, and was then repealed in 1819, "doubts existing whether it was in force or not."[12] In the meantime, other colonies – and then states – were passing similar laws, in four waves. First, colonies such as New Hampshire passed acts similar to those of Virginia and found out during the course of the eighteenth century that they had set the penalty too high for juror comfort. New Hampshire's "Provincial Act of 1714" was virtually word for word that of Virginia's four years before, but the Granite State's revision in 1791 provided a nerve-racking warning of the death penalty rather than the real thing:

> And be it further enacted That if any Woman shall endeavour privately to conceal the Death of any Issue of her body which if born alive would by Law be a Bastard so that it may not come to light whether it were born alive or not, or whether it was murdered or not, in every such Case the Mother so offending on being thereof convicted shall be set on the

---

[10]Meeting of May 2, 1713, in *Executive Journals of the Council of Colonial Virginia* (Richmond: Virginia State Library, 1925), p. 344.
[11]*Ibid.*, pp. 346, 391. The reprieve was signed on June 10, 1713, but complications were involved: "The Governor declaring that the Crime of which the said Jane Ham is found guilty, making her liable to the same punishment as in case of willful Murder he was restrained by this Commission from pardoning the same: Whereupon the Council do request the Governor to represent the said Case to her Majesty and in the mean time to reprieve the said Criminal, untill her Majesty's pleasure be known therein."
[12]*Revised Code of the Laws of Virginia*, Vol. 1 (Richmond: State of Virginia, 1819), p. 594.

Gallows for the space of one Hour, and may be imprisoned not exceeding two years. . . .[13]

The New York City statute for midwives, noted in Chapter One, followed its attack on abortion with an attack on concealment: "You Shall not Give any Counsel or Administer any Herb Medicine or Potion or any other thing to any Woman being with Child whereby She Should Destroy or Miscarry of that she goeth withall before her time. . . . You shall not Conceal the Birth of any Bastard Child. . . ."[14] Pennsylvania statutes enacted in 1718 included penalties for concealment and for advising pregnant women to kill children immediately after delivery.[15]

The second stage of concealment laws came in the early nineteenth century as newly formed legislatures noted the problem. Kentucky in 1801 adopted much of the Virginia law, including the distinction between free and slave women practicing concealment, but adopted a more workable sentence of two to seven years imprisonment.[16] The Georgia legislature in 1816 established a maximum penalty for concealment of one year, but pointedly noted that the woman could also be charged with murder, and then added a section designed to protect the defendant:

The constrained presumption, arising from the concealment of the death of any child, that the child whose death is concealed was therefore murdered by the mother, shall not be sufficient or conclusive evidence to convict the person indicted, of the murder of her child, unless probable proof be given, that the child was born alive, nor unless the circumstances attending it shall be such as shall satisfy the minds of the jury, that the mother did wilfully, and maliciously, destroy and take away the life of such child.[17]

The Michigan legislature passed a similar law but allowed those found guilty of concealment to be fined rather than imprisoned. As the frontier moved west, so did anti-concealment laws, and penalties continued to vary, with attempts to make them severe enough to scare

---

[13]Laws 1792, p. 244; quoted in Eugene Quay, "Justifiable Abortion—Medical and Legal Foundations," *Georgetown Law Review*, Vol. 49 (1960-1961), "Appendix," p. 495.

[14]*Minutes of the Common Council of New York City*, Vol. 3, p. 122.

[15]*The Statutes at Large of Pennsylvania*, Vol. 3 (1712-1724), p. 202.

[16]*Kentucky Acts*, chapter 67, section 2, p. 117.

[17]*Georgia Penal Code*, section 24 (1817).

potential killers, but not so onerous as to make juries unwilling to convict on what was generally circumstantial evidence.

Third stage laws, emerging amidst the growth of prostitution in the 1830s, mandated penalties of six to twelve months or a fine in Wisconsin in 1839, up to seven years in Missouri in 1835 and 1855, up to one year in Nevada's territorial prison in 1861, and up to one year in Wyoming territory in 1869.[18] In all these jurisdictions anti-concealment laws, as would anti-abortion laws soon after, represented a search for a sustainable penalty for actions hard to prove beyond the shadow of a doubt.[19] The trial record of such laws also varied, with convictions generally hard to gain. Overall, the concealment laws represented a run-through of the problem of anti-abortion laws. Statutes — along with enforcement, punishment, and social support for those laws — varied from state to state.[20]

Nineteenth-century legislators were forced to come to grips with abortion as the infant-killing method of choice gradually changed from infanticide (often with concealment) to abortion.[21] The first state legislative response pinpointing abortion came in 1821, when the General Assembly of Connecticut passed a "crimes and punishments" law that included a section without precedent in the United States:

> Every person who shall, wilfully and maliciously, administer to, or cause to be administered to, or taken by, any person or persons, any deadly poison, or other noxious and destructive substance, with an intention him, her, or them, thereby to murder, or thereby to cause or procure the miscarriage of any woman, then being quick with child, and shall be thereof duly convicted, shall suffer imprisonment, in Newgate prison, during his natural life, or for such other term as the court having cognizance of the offence shall determine.[22]

James Mohr has argued that the Connecticut legislators were following the example of Great Britain's Parliament, which in 1803 had

---

[18]Quay, "Justifiable Abortion," pp. 490, 493, 519, 520.

[19]Michigan Code, Section 9, 1815, and Laws, Section 8, 1820; quoted in Quay, "Justifiable Abortion," pp. 482-483.

[20]Eight colonies or states enacted laws to punish concealment before they adopted abortion statutes; eleven states enacted concealment and abortion statutes at the same time.

[21]See also anti-concealment laws of Louisiana (1817), Illinois (1827), New York (1845), and Pennsylvania (1860).

[22]*Public Statute Laws of the State of Connecticut*, 1821 (Hartford, 1821), pp. 152-153.

adopted strong anti-abortion legislation known as Lord Ellenborough's Act, after the English chief justice who was influential in its passage.[23] Since the Connecticut statute, unlike the English law, referred only to abortion after quickening, only to abortion by the use of poisons, and only to the person who administered the abortifacient – rather than the abortifacient user also – Mohr concluded that "America's first anti-abortion law, ironically enough, does not appear to have been greatly opposed to abortion itself." Mohr even wrote that "in a sense, Connecticut's early laws might be viewed as pro-abortion laws rather than anti-abortion laws."[24]

Mohr, however, apparently missed a crucial contributing cause of the Connecticut law, one that hit much closer to home for the state legislators than anything a parliament three thousand miles away had done eighteen years before. The Connecticut legislature acted in May 1821; just seven months earlier a Connecticut minister was sent to prison for causing an abortion through "the use of pernicious drugs."[25] The Rogers case was widely publicized; for example, the Norwich (Connecticut) *Courier* reported that Rogers

> stood charged with a high crime and misdemeanor; 'a deed of nameless note.' The charges ranged between the extremes of seduction and child-murder; and poisons and violence, were shown to be in use to conceal his crime, and shelter from disgrace, the object of his cruelty. It is said, the county never witnessed a trial in which so much baseness and cold calculating depravity of heart were disclosed, and where so black a deed was attempted to be smothered by the Culprit by so much subornation and falsehood. He was convicted. Sentence – Imprisonment two years.[26]

There is no record of legislators' familiarity with Lord Ellenborough, but the Ammi Rogers case shook the foundations of the Episcopal Church in Connecticut and made its way into gossip and discussion throughout the state.

An old town history of Griswold, Connecticut, records some of the background:

---

[23]James Mohr, *Abortion in America* (New York: Oxford University Press, 1978), p. 23.
[24]*Ibid.*, p. 25.
[25]Ammi Rogers, *Memoirs* (Schenectady, NY: G. Richie, 1826), p. 118.
[26]*Norwich Courier*, October 11, 1820, p. 3.

In 1813 one Ammi Rogers learned, polished and eloquent, sanctimo-
nious and representing himself to be a priest of the Protestant
Episcopalian Church, appeared. . . . He began to preach. Crowds
flocked to hear him. Many of the leading men of the community
became his ardent supporters.[27]

Rogers, born in 1770, was graduated from Yale College in 1786 and
received ordination as a priest in New York in 1794. Soon he moved back
to Connecticut, built up several small churches, and involved himself in
theological controversies with the Episcopal bishop of Connecticut. But
trouble soon came, as the town history of Griswold reports: "ugly
rumors concerning Rogers' character here at home became current . . .
in 1818 he was arraigned here before the court charged with seduction
and procuring an abortion, tried, found guilty and served his sentence
in a state prison. And the church which he had founded became scattered
and ceased to exist."[28]

It is hard at this time to sort through all the conflicting evidence in
Rogers' case. The town history concluded that "after a century of gathering and sifting evidence, those best qualified to judge confirmed the
verdict rendered at his first trial. . . ."[29] Rogers, however, always insisted
that he was the victim of a frame-up developed by his theological opponents. He wrote in his memoirs, which went through many editions, that
three of his enemies had convinced Asenath C. Smith, a young woman
who apparently miscarried in 1817, to charge Rogers with impregnating
her and giving her an abortifacient: "The whole story was contrived,
planned and laid out."[30] Rogers, from his many years of ministry, had
both supporters and opponents, but the issues that were debated concerning this case came down to three: Was Asenath Smith actually pregnant, did an abortifacient cause the miscarriage if one actually occurred,
and what kind of punishment was appropriate if the crime indeed had
been committed?

The legislation that was passed a few months after this sensational
trial dealt with all three of these debated points. Rogers contended that
his punishment was unfair because Asenath Smith merely had a

---

[27]Daniel L. Phillips, *Griswold: A History* (New Haven, CT: Tuttle, Morehouse and Taylor,
1929), p. 115.
[28]*Ibid.*, p. 116.
[29]*Ibid.*
[30]Rogers, *Memoirs*, p. 91.

"supposed child." The legislature, evidently taking that objection into account, crafted a law that stipulated punishment only when a woman was "quick with child" and therefore unmistakably pregnant.[31] Rogers made much of Downing's acknowledgement that the abortion, if there was one, might "have been produced by sickness, infirmity, or accident in the mother."[32] The Connecticut legislation dealt with the difficulty of proving actual effect by stipulating the guilt of anyone who administered an abortifacient "with an intention . . . to cause or procure the miscarriage." (Proving "intent" was not easy, but it was much easier than proving in that era the cause of death of an unborn child.)

Finally, Rogers was glad when the judge in his case ordered that his sentence of two years be served in Norwich jail rather than the much feared Newgate prison; when the place of imprisonment was announced, the prosecuting attorney even said to the judge, "I suppose you mean Newgate," but the judge was "merciful," in Rogers' words, and said, "No, I mean Norwich."[33] Some Connecticut legislators apparently thought that two years in a local jail was insufficient punishment, and the Connecticut statute noted that a person convicted of causing abortion "shall suffer imprisonment in Newgate prison during his natural life or for such other term" as the court would determine.

Significantly, Rogers was convicted under the common law that Mohr and his colleagues have argued was easy on abortion. Furthermore, no one during the trial attached importance to the question of whether the unborn child was "quick" or not. Dr. Eleazer B. Downing testified that he had delivered the corpse of a four-month-old unborn child of Asenath Smith, but no one questioned him or anyone else as to whether the child, which could have just reached the quickening transition, had moved in a way that the mother or anyone else might have felt. And yet, that quickening distinction would be written into the legislation of Connecticut and some other states because – in the absence of pregnancy and blood tests – fetal movement was the only legally established indicator of unborn life.

The Rogers case pushed Connecticut legislators to act. Other isolated abortion cases were popping up elsewhere, but the impulse of short-sessioned early nineteenth-century legislatures was to pass laws only when necessary, and generally only after near unanimity was achieved.

---

[31] *Ibid.*, p. 88; *Public Statute Laws of the State of Connecticut, loc. cit.*
[32] Rogers, *Memoirs*, p. 120.
[33] *Ibid.*, p. 149.

Since abortion was not perceived as a significant problem until the mid-century, and even then was somewhat removed from the mainstream, some states were able to avoid abortion legislation for a few years.[34] In addition, if it were known that large numbers of likely abortion victims were what today would be called "hard cases," since they were conceived by disease-ridden prostitutes, fervor to go against legislative minimalism also would be lessened.

What forced reluctant legislative hands in some states was the opening in the 1830s of the "penny press" era that introduced mass newspapers to the United States — how could a containment policy be continued when mass media daily undermined it? The ads were not overt; an indication of abortion's unacceptability throughout the entire nineteenth century is that even when pre-quickening abortion was not explicitly barred, ads did not use the word "abortion." A New York *Sun* ad in 1839 came closest to mentioning the word, but merely spoke of pills "so strong that they should not be taken during pregnancy," because they would "produce a******n."[35] Ads never made the now-familiar distinctions among abortions at different gestational ages; copywriters were generally circumspect. In New York, Dr. Bell promised to cure "irregularity of females."[36] Dr. Ward treated suppression, irregularity and female obstructions.[37] Dr. Vandenburgh contended that his "Female Regeneracy Pills" were "an effectual remedy for suppression, irregularity, and all cases where nature has stopped from any cause whatsoever."[38] Madame Vincent offered her own pills, and ads for "Portuguese Female Pills" and "FRENCH LUNAR PILLS" appeared in 1841.[39] The

---

[34]Hiram Root summarized well the libertarian philosophy that some held: "human laws shall only sanction, and sustain, and encourage, and protect the freshest spontaneity. . . . Every couple should be the sovereign of their own choice and household. . . . Exactly after the fashion of trying to put on infant clothes to a full-grown man, is our way of taking old laws and customs for our guidance . . . . they are not fitted for us. Young America cannot wear them. He likes clothes adapted to his form, suited to his convenience, fashioned for the age in which he lives, and which will leave him free to act, to develop, to expand, to increase, to progress. He does not want to be cramped up by old forms, hemmed in by old usages, restrained by old notions, and he will not be. If there is any thing in the laws of his country not suited to his wants, he will have it abolished, and will institute and develop new and better things. Hurrah! for Young America!" In *Lover's Marriage Lighthouse* (New York: Root, 1859), pp. 8, 359.

[35]New York *Sun*, March 27, 1839, p. 1. For other abortion ads see Marvin Olasky, *The Press and Abortion* (Hillsdale, NJ: Lawrence Erlbaum, 1988).

[36]New York *Herald,* January 6, 1841, p. 4.

[37]New York *Herald,* February 25, 1841.

[38]New York *Sun,* September 14, 1840, p. 4.

[39]New York *Sun,* September 14, 1840, p. 4; January 24, 1840, p. 4.

latter were called "lunar pills on account of their efficacy in producing the monthly turns of females. . . . The effects are truly astonishing. They are never attended with any distressing operation, are always certain, and therefore pregnant women should not take them."[40] Mrs. Mott, Mrs. Bird, Madame Costello, and many others jumped into the market.[41] With all this activity it was clear that the wall of containment built by family, church, and other non-governmental pressure, or by legislation such as the concealment statutes tailored to particular groups, was showing cracks.

The problems inherent in any new general laws were legion, however. The key problem was proof. Just as Virginia legislators in 1713 concluded that it was unfair to hold Jane Ham guilty of concealment unless proven guilty, so abortionists at first had to be given the benefit of the doubt and considered innocent unless the state proved three things: an actual pregnancy, a live unborn child at the time of the abortion, and the death of that child caused by the abortion Two centuries ago it was virtually impossible, even among those who acknowledged the full humanity of the unborn child, to follow that three-step legal process all the way to a *murder* conviction. The pregnancy itself could not be proven until quickening, and the continued life of the child at the time of abortion could only be vouched for by the mother or others who had placed their hands on her body. Autopsies are critical in homicide cases: the coroner must note the position of the bullet wound and cite it causally if the jury is to find guilt. A murder trial without a corpse is hard to win. But abortion cases (when the mother survived) almost never had a corpse or an autopsy, and rarely witnesses. Almost all abortion evidence was secondhand and (when dying declarations were used) a kind of hearsay.

Legislators had to face another troublesome question: How could use of abortifacients be banned when those products were used for other practices considered beneficial? It was believed early in the nineteenth century that unmarried women whose menstrual flow had stopped but whose virginity was still (according to public knowledge) intact were the victims of "suppression" in the uterus rather than suppression of moral-

---

[40]New York *Herald*, August 21, 1841, p. 4, etc.
[41]New York *Herald*, February 25, 1841, p. 4; March 6, 1840, p. 4; December 15, 1840, p. 4; New York *Sun*, March 16, 1840, p. 4. Similar New York advertising continued throughout the 1850s and 1860s. The New York *Tribune*, under the headline "MOST IMPORTANT to the LADIES," advertised "Dr. Geissner's celebrated MENSTRUAL PILLS," which "reach the various irregularities and suppressions of nature. . . . They act like a charm . . . in numerous instances producing regularity of nature after all hope had been abandoned."

ity or honesty. The problem for legislators (and historians) is that at some point there was a connotative transition. Perhaps Madame Restell, New York's leading abortionist from the 1830s through the 1870s, was the innovator who gave women the opportunity to pretend that abortion was actually something else. Her ads mentioned a removal of "female blockages" and "a cure for stoppage of the menses." (Those expressions were accurate in one sense, since pregnancy *is* the leading cause of menstrual stoppage among women of child-bearing age.) She called her abortifacients "female monthly regulating pills," with the pretense that the only goal was regulation of the monthly cycle. There is no doubt about what she meant by that language, since her practice became exceptionally well-known.[42] But what about reputable doctors who spoke of "suppression," "irregularity," or "stoppage of the menses," and provided help in "obdurate," "obstinate," or "persistent" cases? They probably were abortionists, yet was it right to arrest them on the basis of ads, or because they prescribed what had been considered medically valid only a few years before?

The back-and-forth behavior of the New York legislature over the decades indicates the problems. The New York legislature enacted, amended, and reenacted laws concerning abortion ten times from 1828 through 1881, often in regard to current events.[43] A comparison of events and legislation reinforces confidence in the adage concerning the making of sausage and legislation: Don't look too closely. Legislators, like sausage-makers, tended to use whatever ingredients were available. New York's 1846 legislation provides one example. Previous law prescribed use of abortifacients, but surgical abortion was so rare that it had not been explicitly opposed. Sensational press accounts, plus an anti-Restell demonstration on February 23, 1846, led to the new law (passed on March 4, nine days after the demonstration) that forbade not only administration or procurement of abortifacients but also "use or employ[ment of] any instrument of other means, with intent thereby to destroy such child. . . ."[44] In Chapter Seven we will look further at press conduct and consequences, but here it's important to note that there was no happy ending over the short term — Madame Restell's business boomed during the 1850s and 1860s.

New York's 1869 law, like Connecticut's in 1821 and many others,

---

[42]See Chapter One of Olasky, *The Press and Abortion*.
[43]The dates: 1828, 1830, 1845, 1846, 1868, 1869, 1872, 1875, 1880, and 1881.
[44]Law of March 4, 1846, chapter 22, section one (1846), Laws of New York.

followed sensational press accounts, such as those reporting the Philippi/Wolff abortion and homicide case. Magdalena Philippi died in New York City on March 16, 1869, after Dr. Gabriel Wolff aborted her four- to five-month-old child. There was no way of proving the child to have been quick, so Dr. Wolff could not be prosecuted. The bill that became the Act of 1869 was introduced in Albany the very next day. As the grand jury in the Court of General Sessions, during its March 1869 term, was finding insufficient evidence to warrant an indictment of Dr. Wolff, the bill, which eliminated the quickening distinction and thus simplified the prosecutor's problems of evidence, was making its way through the legislature.[45]

The problem with such quick fixes, however, was always sustainability. Following press coverage of a "trunk murder" abortion case in 1871, there was widespread discussion about how severely abortionists should be penalized. Judge Gunning Bedford's charge to the grand jury included a suggestion that the legislature increase the penalty for abortion from second degree manslaughter to "murder in the first degree, and punishable as such with death. . . ."[46] The immediate reaction to Bedford's suggestion was positive; the *Times* reported "Loud applause in court."[47] But members of the Medico-Legal Society of New York argued that a death penalty for abortion "would probably result in lessening the chances for a conviction in any case."[48] The committee expressed no leniency concerning abortion. Its members reported that Bedford's view of abortion as a "capital felony" was "intrinsically just." But committee members were concerned about attitudes revealed during one abortion trial, "when two jurors united in a recommendation to mercy, thus showing a disinclination to convict even on a felony. . . ."[49]

The Medico-Legal Society's Committee on Criminal Abortion proposed, *contra* Bedford, that abortion "should be simply a felony without any specific denomination, and its penalty should be imprisonment for not less than four years. This would give the Judge the power in aggravated cases . . . to sentence the criminals to imprison-

[45]Law of May 6, 1869, chapter 631 (1868), New York Laws; Means, "The Law of New York Concerning Abortion and the State of the Foetus, 1664-1968: A Case of Cessation of Constitutionality," *New York Law Forum*, Fall 1968, p. 646.
[46]New York *Times*, September 7, 1871, p. 8.
[47]*Ibid.*
[48]Cyril C. Means, Jr., "The Law of New York Concerning Abortion and the State of the Foetus, 1664-1968: A Case of Cessation of Constitutionality," p. 475.
[49]*Ibid.*

ment for life."[50] Again, the refusal to make abortion a capital crime did not mean that the committee was viewing the unborn child as less than human life; the committee explicitly stated that the being in question was "alive from conception and all intentional killing of it is murder."[51] The question was one of how best to put abortionists out of business, and the *Times* applauded the Medico-Legal Society's bill as introduced on January 9, 1872, by Assemblyman George H. Mackey, a lawyer who while serving on a coroner's staff had investigated at least one abortion case. The *Times* praised the bill as one "far-reaching enough to catch hold of all who assist, directly or indirectly in the destruction of infant life; it constitutes the crime of felony, and it imposes an imprisonment of not less than four years on . . . the rogues male and female who carry on their hideous trade."[52]

There was still a bit of sausage-making left to go. The legislature added a few words here and there, the most critical of which amounted to a limitation on the maximum penalty for abortion: instead of life imprisonment, no one was to be imprisoned for "more than twenty years."[53] Judges would not have the option of imposing a life sentence, but there is no indication that the legislature, as Means suggested, was equating "one foetal life with one half of an adult life."[54] Instead, the change seemed to be just one more chapter in the search for maximum convictability.[55] The important task, in New York and other states, was to establish the principle that the killing of an unborn child at any period of gestation deserved punishment, regardless of the evidentiary problems involved in pre-quickening abortions.[56] This sometimes meant a lower range of punishment (in Pennsylvania up to three years) for pre-quickening abortions; those cases did not provide the certainty of pregnancy that made a jury

---

[50]New York *Times*, December 15, 1871, p. 1.

[51]Means, "The Law of New York Concerning Abortion and the State of the Foetus, 1664-1968: A Case of Cessation of Constitutionality," p. 476.

[52]New York *Times*, January 12, 1872, p. 4.

[53]Law of April 6, 1872, chapter 181 (1872), New York Laws.

[54]Means, "The Law of New York Concerning Abortion and the State of the Foetus, 1664-1968: A Case of Cessation of Constitutionality," p. 483.

[55]J. C. Stone, "Report on the Subject of Criminal Abortion," *Transactions of the Iowa State Medical Society*, Vol. 1 (1874), p. 31.

[56]Among the states before the Civil War that specified the illegality of abortion at all stages of pregnancy were: Alabama (1840-41), California (1849-50), Louisiana (1858), Maine (1840), Massachusetts (1845), New Jersey (1849), Oregon (1853-54), Pennsylvania (1860), Wisconsin (1858), Texas (1859), Vermont (1846), Virginia (1848).

ready to put away an abortionist for a long period of time. (In Pennsylvania, abortion of a quickened child could bring seven years.)[57] The willingness of jurors to convict, given evidentiary problems, always had to be considered.

Given the difficulties of legislation in this area, we can play off Tolstoy's opening to *Anna Karenina*: The sagas of happily uncomplicated legislation are the same; but every hard-to-draft law has its own story. Some states gave immunity to women from all criminal liability, partly because women pregnant after seduction were considered desperate victims rather than perpetrators, and partly because of the search for any kind of edge in prosecution. New Jersey, New York, and other states gave women immunity from prosecution in exchange for testimony.[58] Wisconsin was among the states that applied a relatively light penalty for abortion of a non-quickened child – three months to one year – and then provided the woman who had an abortion with a one- to six-month sentence and/or a fine.[59] By providing either no or low penalties, so that a woman *would* testify that she had been pregnant, prosecutors had a chance to leap the evidentiary hurdles of convincing a jury an abortion actually had occurred.[60]

Historians who oversimplify this complicated search for penalties sustainable by juries and evidentiary requirements fair to defendants misread provisions such as those which emphasized "intent." Indiana in 1835, for example, added a law stating that

[E]very person who shall willfully administer to any pregnant woman, any medicine, drug, substance or thing whatever, or shall use or employ any instrument or other means whatever with intent thereby to procure the miscarriage of any such woman, unless the same shall have been necessary to preserve the life of such woman, shall upon conviction, be punished by imprisonment in the county jail any term of time not exceeding twelve months, and be fined any sum not exceeding five hundred dollars.[61]

---

[57]Pennsylvania Laws, No. 374, sections 87 and 88 (1860).

[58]See James S. Witherspoon, "Reexamining *Roe*: Nineteenth Century Abortion Statutes and the Fourteenth Amendment," *St. Mary's Law Journal*, Vol. 17 (1985), pp. 58-60, for a useful discussion of incrimination of the woman.

[59]Wisconsin Rev. Statutes, chapter 169, sections 58 and 59 (1858).

[60]Michael Grossberg, *Governing the Hearth: Law and the Family in Nineteenth-Century America* (Chapel Hill: U. of North Carolina Press, 1965), p. 125.

[61]Law approved February 7, 1835, in *Indiana Revised Statutes*, (1838), p. 224.

Mohr contended that such statutes gave abortionists and abortifacient peddlers a victory by allowing them "to plead naivete" when arrested, but such provisions were necessary protection for doctors dealing with those few but real cases of genuine suppression. The law in Indiana and other states was an offspring of medical knowledge in 1835, and *not* an apologia for abortion.[62] Furthermore such a law was a large advance for anti-abortion forces that would no longer have to prove that the operation or potion actually had killed the child: whether or not the attempt was successful, the *intent* could put him out of business. "Intent" clauses were particularly useful since they did not require prosecutors to prove ill will. For example, if a spiritist performed an abortion for reasons that were benign within his own belief system, Wyoming territorial law still held him guilty.[63]

Some states combined "intent" clauses with a two-level penalty: one penalty if intent was shown but there was no proof that the unborn child had actually died as a result of the abortion, and a stiffer penalty if the jury was so angry that it would accept the prosecutor's contention in that regard, even if fetal death by abortion could not be proved beyond the shadow of a doubt. Sections 13 and 14 of the Maine bi-level law of 1840 demand careful reading – I have italicized the subtle clauses – because they provide a good example of the genus:

Section 13: "Every person, who shall administer to any woman *pregnant with child, whether such child be quick or not,* any medicine, drug or substance whatever, or shall use or employ any instrument or other means whatever, *with intent* to destroy such child, *and shall thereby destroy such child before its birth,* unless the same shall have been done as necessary to preserve the life of the mother, shall be punished by imprisonment in the state prison, not more than five years, or by fine, not exceeding one thousand dollars, and imprisonment in the county jail, not more than one year."

Section 14: "Every person who shall administer to any woman, *pregnant with child, whether such child be quick or not,* any medicine, drug or substance whatever . . . *with intent* thereby to procure the miscarriage of such woman, unless the same shall have been done, as necessary to preserve her life, shall be punished by imprisonment in the county jail, not more than one year, or by fine, not exceeding one thousand dollars."[64]

---

[62]See Mohr, *Abortion in America,* p. 142.
[63]See Wyoming laws, first session, 1869, section 25, p. 104.
[64]Maine Revised Statutes, chapter 160, sections 11, 12, 13, 14 (1840).

Juries were given the opportunity to choose.

The evidence of court cases late in the nineteenth century suggests that "intent" clauses sometimes worked well and belies Mohr's notion that they were legislative cop-outs.[65] For example, Texas abortionist Cave advised a young woman, Livie Brown, to take several abortifacients that did not work – her child was born – and further upset his patient by offering her money for sex. She had him arrested. Cave tried to escape an abortion punishment by saying that the potions he recommended did not work, but the Texas Court of Appeals ruled that if "the means shall fail to produce abortion, the offender is nevertheless guilty of an attempt to produce abortion, provided it be shown that such means were calculated to produce that result."[66] Other state courts further strengthened the usefulness of intent provisions by ruling that the drugs recommended by an abortionist did not even have to have proven effectiveness, as long as he believed they would do the job.[67]

We could go on with further examinations of intriguing nuances, but one inference is overwhelming: legislators in state after state were searching for the best sustainable (by judge and jury) ways to put abortionists out of business.[68] When some state supreme court judges made life difficult for pro-life legislators, response was quick. After the Iowa supreme court in 1856 held (perhaps because of a legislative oversight in 1851) that abortion before quickening was not a crime, the next legislature restored the statutory crime by a vote of 27-0 in the Senate and 53-1 in the House.[69] The new statute made abortion of "any pregnant woman" explicitly illegal, with punishment of up to a year in prison, but added the condition that "intent thereby to procure a miscarriage of any such woman" had to be proven.[70] As noted earlier, proving intent to abort before quickening, and in the absence

---

[65]In one Maine case, however, an abortionist did get off; see *Smith v. State*, 33 Maine 48 (1851).

[66]*State v. Cave*, 33 *Texas Criminal Reports* 335 (1894).

[67]See *Commonwealth v. Morrison*, 16 Gray 224 (Mass. 1860); *State v. Van Houten*, 37 Mo. 357 (1866); *Bassett v. State*, 41 Ia. 303 (1872); *State v. Owens*, 22 Minn. 238 (1875); *State v. Fitzgerald*, 49 Ia. 260, 261 (1878). Cited in Grossberg, *Governing the Hearth: Law and the Family in Nineteenth-Century America*, p. 363.

[68]For other statutes with interesting language, see Quay, "Justifiable Abortion," pp. 451 (California), 481 (Mass.), 505 (Oregon), 514 (Texas), 515 (Vermont), 517 (Virginia).

[69]See *Abrams v. Foshee*, 3 Iowa 274; *Journal of the House of Representatives of the Seventh General Assembly of the State of Iowa* (Des Moines: J. Teesdale, 1858), pp. 284, 388, 418, 425, 464, 480, 484, 504, 612-613, 644.

[70]*Journal of the Senate of the 7th General Assembly of the State of Iowa, 1858* (Des Moines: State

of pregnancy tests, was like proving "actual malice" today in a libel case involving public officials or public figures and was very hard to pull off. But if legislation was seen as education, the initiative was successful.[71] Similarly, when citizens in Wisconsin wondered whether an abortion to save the life of the mother was illegal, the legislature made sure its statute covered all unborn children but allowed a life-of-the-mother exception.

> Every person who shall administer to any woman pregnant with a child, any medicine, drug, or substance whatever, or shall use or employ any instrument or other means, with intent thereby to destroy such child, unless the same shall have been necessary for such purpose, shall, in case the death of such child or of such mother be thereby produced, be deemed guilty of manslaughter in the second degree.[72]

The evidence is overwhelming: Despite the legislative minimalist tendencies in pre-Civil-War America, despite all the obstacles inherent in the drafting of effective legislation on such a sensitive subject, when needs became urgent, legislatures wanted to respond, and they did, but with inevitably varying experience.

Let's summarize the overall record. During the 1840s and 1850s alone, at least thirteen states passed laws forbidding abortion at any stage of pregnancy. Three others passed laws making abortion illegal only after quickening. By the end of 1868 thirty states had overcome all the legislative and cultural obstacles to passing an anti-abortion law, and twenty-seven of them punished attempts to induce abortion before quickening. Twenty of the states had bitten the bullet and were punishing abortion at all stages equally, regardless of the added evidence given by quickening; others had an increased range of punishment.[73] Many states provided for increased punishment when a jury could be convinced that the abortion had unmistakably caused the death of the unborn child.[74] Some states, to expedite successful prosecution, dropped

---

of Iowa, 1858), p. 284; *Journal of the House of Representatives of the 7th General Assembly of the State of Iowa, 1858* (Des Moines: State of Iowa, 1858), pp. 612-613.

[71]See *Hatfield v. Grano* 15 Iowa 177 (1863). The plot thickened further in Iowa in 1863 when the court struck back, and after the war as legislators responded.

[72]Wisconsin Revised Statutes, chapter 164, section 11 (1858). See Quay, "Justifiable Abortion," pp. 502, 517, and 520 for other life-of-the-mother exceptions.

[73]See James S. Witherspoon, "Reexamining *Roe*: Nineteenth Century Abortion Statutes and the Fourteenth Amendment," *St. Mary's Law Journal*, Vol. 17 (1985), p. 34.

[74]For a list of the states see *ibid.*, pp. 37-38.

the requirement that the pregnancy of a mother involved in abortion had to be proved.[75] To show the enormity of abortion, some states provided the same penalty for the death of the mother during an abortion operation and the death of the unborn child.[76] To show that the unborn child was considered to be human life, some states defined abortion as "manslaughter."[77]

Again, these laws were not as effective as some of their champions hoped. Shortly after the Civil War, Dr. John Trader of Missouri could still describe a "disgusting" but familiar scene: a man "sneaks into our office and requests us to produce an abortion" on a woman he had seduced, in order to avoid having "his errant duplicity exposed."[78] Physician – and later congressman – J. C. Stone could still note that "The seductionist (for it is reduced to a trade), troubled by the foreshadowing of the fruits of his illicit commerce, has but to apply to the professional abortionist, who is his friend, and he will extinguish the vital spark with less feeling and hesitation than one would have in pulling down a cobweb or plucking a flower."[79] New York journalist James McCabe could still comment on the "class of men and women who make a living by practicing abortion upon women who have been betrayed. . . ."[80] But the goal was to contain abortion, to signal that abortion was out-of-bounds – and signal the legislatures did, by overwhelming votes.[81]

The antebellum legislative record is impressive, for a period largely characterized by legislative minimalism. After the Civil War, when the Reconstructionist impulse was to use the power of the state, passage of abortion legislation is less surprising, but its acceptability throughout the reunited states is impressive. Some southern statute books had treated

---

[75] *Ibid.,* p. 56 has a list.

[76] There were nine by 1868: Florida, Michigan, Minnesota, Missouri, New York, Ohio, Oregon, Pennsylvania, Wisconsin.

[77] The eight by 1868 were: Arkansas, Florida, Michigan, Minnesota, Missouri, New York, Oregon, Wisconsin.

[78] John W. Trader, "Criminal Abortion," paper read before the Central Missouri Medical Association, Sedalia, MO, October 6, 1874, in the Toner Collection, Library of Congress, pp. 588-589.

[79] J. C. Stone, "Report on the Subject of Criminal Abortion," *Transactions of the Iowa State Medical Society,* Vol. 1 (1874), p. 30.

[80] James McCabe, *New York by Sunlight and by Gaslight* (Philadelphia: Douglas Brothers, 1882), p. 493.

[81] Witherspoon, "Reexamining *Roe*: Nineteenth Century Abortion Statutes and the Fourteenth Amendment," p. 69, lists the votes.

abortion with embarrassed silence, but from 1866 to 1870 Alabama leg-islators increased abortion penalties, Florida treated the subject for the first time by making abortion at any stage of gestation punishable by one to seven years in prison, and Louisiana legislators extended to surgical abortion the previous ban on use of abortifacients.[82] Other legislation of that era was repealed or abandoned once northern troops went home, but the abortion statutes remained.

Pro-abortion historians who try to ignore this consistent record end up making statements that the evidence renders ludicrous. James Mohr, for example, contends (with Orwellian "war is peace" flavor) that legis-latures stipulating the illegality of abortion of "any pregnant woman" were actually saying that the law only referred to women with a "quick" child.[83] State legislatures that took the time to pass new legislation expanding protection from unborn "quick" children to any "unborn child" or to "any woman pregnant with a child" of any gestational age must have seen that there was some difference, or else they would have spent a chunk of their brief legislative sessions on meaningless activity.[84] Some states later in the century made their concern for all unborn chil-dren particularly explicit. North Carolina noted its statute's relevance "to any woman either pregnant or quick with child," and Tennessee penal-ized abortionists who went to work on "any woman pregnant with child, whether such child be quick or not."[85]

Mohr overlooked some vital evidence and attempted to explain away clear evidence in other spots. We have seen the misunderstanding of the first explicit anti-abortion law (Connecticut, 1821) that comes from overlooking the Rogers case; that is a miss that can happen to any his-torian, but Mohr's handling of the second and third anti-abortion laws passed in 1825 and 1827 was more curious. He acknowledged that "both the Missouri law and the Illinois law followed Connecticut's 1821 statute closely," but with a major difference – they did not "make any explicit reference to the quickening doctrine; they appeared to make the admin-istration of poisonous substances with the intent to induce abortion ille-gal at any stage of gestation."[86] Mohr contended that "the omission of

---

[82]Quay, "Justifiable Abortion," pp. 447, 457-458, 476.
[83]Mohr, *Abortion in America*, p. 144.
[84]Compare Wisconsin Revised Statutes of 1849, chapter 133, sections 10 and 11, and Wisconsin Revised Statutes of 1858, chapter 169, section 58.
[85]N. C. Session Laws, chapter 351, section 1 (1881), and Tennessee Acts, chapter 140, section 1, pp. 188-189 (1883).
[86]Mohr, *Abortion in America*, p. 26.

explicit reference to quickening in these two early laws probably reflected the fact that the quickening distinction was taken completely for granted rather than any effort to eliminate it."[87] Thus, for Mohr those states that proscribed abortion after quickening supposedly were saying that abortion before quickening was acceptable, but states that banned abortion at all times also were saying it was acceptable before quickening.

Mohr's line of thought in 1978 anticipated the deconstructionist trends of the 1980s. But the overwhelming evidence is that when early nineteenth-century legislators slowly constructed anti-abortion bills, they were *not* leaping through the looking glass and writing words without reference to understood meaning. For the legislators, "with child" (the Illinois usage) or "pregnant" (Missouri usage) meant pregnant, not four and a half months pregnant. If pregnancy could not be proved until that point, then some culprits might get away, but the law would still state that abortion at all times was unacceptable. Legislation, Americans of that period clearly understood, was education.

---

[87] *Ibid.*

PART TWO

Abortion Restrained

5

The Doctors' Campaign
in Context

This book stands in opposition to the oversimplified history that both sides in the abortion wars often prefer. That oversimplification is nowhere more evident than in myths concerning the role of the American Medical Association that have been a staple of speeches and Supreme Court briefs. James Mohr and his followers have viewed the American Medical Association – in the mid-nineteenth century the trade group of one faction of American medicine – as a "politically conscious organization" with the clout to override democratic values in a push for "more comprehensive and forceful anti-abortion laws throughout the United States."[1] That is reading the current lobbying power of the AMA into the past, as we will see.

The story begins in the 1840s and 1850s as married adherents to new doctrines approached their doctors with stunning requests. Middle-class physicians had not had to bother with the problems of prostitutes, but in 1842 Philadelphia physician Charles D. Meigs muttered about "persons so ignorant of their own moral duties, or so uninstructed as to the character and duties of medical men, as to come to them with a bold-

---

[1] James Mohr, *Abortion in America* (New York: Oxford University Press, 1978), p. 146.

faced proposition to procure an abortion. . . ."[2] Meigs offered "the best answer to all such requests: that by the common law such an act is felony, and by the law of God murder."

Not all physicians gave such clear-cut refusals, however. Some popular medical writers, who were themselves influenced by the new theologies of mid-century, took a "pro-choice" position. Dr. W. C. Lispenard wrote in 1854 that abortion "is exclusively the affair of the mother. She alone has a right to decide whether she will continue the being of the child she began. Moral, social, religious obligations should control her, but she alone has the supreme right to decide. We may not approve of the decision; we may look with horror upon the act – but God alone has the power to judge."[3]

Others required medical or psychological reasons for abortion, but were liberal in their definition of need. Dr. Ferdinand Rattenmann, after writing about the "doubtful life of the embryo" and the "mere possible life of the child," saw little problem with induced abortion whenever problems in delivery were possible.[4] Dr. James Soule argued that no woman could be happy when she has "one child crying, 'Ma, ma, I want this, and I want that;' and another at the same time, crying, 'Ma, ma,' and she obliged to carry the third in her arms. . . ."[5]

Doctors who wished to perform abortions had many ways to do so, despite the legal bans. Although increased gynecological knowledge and the advertising acumen of abortionists such as Madame Restell led doctors to suspect patients' claims of "suppression," the verdict still was not clear-cut. "Physicians are frequently applied to by the unfortunate or guilty for relief from 'obstructions,'" Meigs wrote, but he advised doctors to snort at such claims: "Her design is merely to purchase some powerful deobstruent or emmenagogue, which may serve to procure an abortion." Meigs proposed that physicians "compare the complaints of amenorrhoea with the appearance of the patient, and if some evident

[2]Charles D. Meigs, *The Philadelphia Practice of Midwifery* (Philadelphia: James Kay, 1842), p. 134.

[3]Dr. W. C. Lispenard, *Private Medical Guide* (Rochester, NY: J. W. Brown, 1854), p. 194.

[4]Dr. Ferdinand Rattenmann, *Induced Abortion* . . . (Philadelphia: Rudolph Stein, 1858), p. 10.

[5]J. Soule, *Science of Reproduction and Reproductive Control* (Cincinnati: Soule, 1856), pp. 4, 13. Soule did not directly advocate abortion. He argued that contraceptive use "would almost entirely abolish infanticide, and the producing of abortion would scarcely be known of except in history." But he noted that contraceptive devices often failed and appeared ready to use a back-up method. Pp. 14, 60.

malady does not accompany the supposed suppression, to withhold all medical aid."[6] Others were not so firm, and not until after the Civil War were "suppression" excuses no longer tolerated.[7]

One of the masters of abortion apologia was a doctor by his own definition only, but to patients and to the readers of his book he was as much a medic as the next quack. "Dr. A. M. Mauriceau" was remarkable for his brazenness, his long marriage to Madame Restell, and his thirty-year use of an alias (he was actually ex-printer Charles Lohman). Without any formal medical training, Mauriceau claimed he had extensive medical education and had conducted many famous operations which the *Bulletin of the Academy of Medicine* supposedly had reported.[8] Mauriceau traded on his false pedigree as he attempted to describe situations "where it is deemed indispensable to effect a miscarriage, either because of the existence of a deformed pelvis, diseased uterus, or other causes."[9] Many women had small pelvises, Mauriceau reported, and in such common situations the choice was "Caesarian section or miscarriage," with the former almost always fatal to the mother under existing practice.[10] He thus was in the position of advocating abortion to save the life of the mother: "it would seem more humane to sacrifice, before the period of viability, an embryo whose existence is so uncertain."[11] Was abortion dangerous for mother as well as child? Mauriceau said no: "if skillfully effected, it is attended with no danger, especially in the earlier stages of pregnancy."[12]

Mauriceau was a brazen Barnum with an audacious sales technique. First, he provided in his book an unlikely cure for "suppression of menses": seven and a half ounces of prickly ash bark and other sub-

---

[6]Meigs, *The Philadelphia Practice of Midwifery*, p. 133.

[7]J. C. Gleason, "A Medico-legal Case," *Transactions of the Massachusetts Medico-Legal Society*, Vol. 1 (1879), pp. 79-86. *Transactions* reported that in 1879 an abortionist who killed both mother and child while performing an abortion was sentenced to six years in prison despite his plea that he merely was attempting to remove blockages.

[8]A. M. Mauriceau (alias of Charles Lohman), *The Married Woman's Private Medical Companion* (New York: Mauriceau, 1847), p. 281.

[9]*Ibid.*, p. 168.

[10]*Ibid.*, p. 181.

[11]*Ibid.*, p. 281: "I must confess that, if such an alternative were presented to me . . . I should not hesitate to propose these means. The abuse and criminal extension of such a resource is reprehensible, but not its proper and authorized employment."

[12]*Ibid.*, p. 169. Lohman attached a footnote to that comment which stipulated that the "miscarriages" he effected were "perfectly safe, recovery following in about three days." He added, "in no case, if properly effected, with ordinary care on the part of the patient, is it attended with any danger. A skilful and practiced obstetrician will impart no pain."

stances and four and a quarter quarts of Holland gin – slightly more than that spoonful of sugar to make the medicine go down.[13] Since "Mauriceau" did include an ounce of tansy, the potion possibly could "work," but it probably would not, and the patient wishing to abort would move on to the next step:

> The most successful specific, and one almost invariably certain in removing a stoppage . . . is a compound invented by M.M. Desomeaux of Lisbon, Portugal, called the Portuguese Female Pills. . . . It would appear that they are infallible, and would, undoubtedly, even produce miscarriage, if exhibited during pregnancy. . . . A remarkable case is related by Dr. A.M. Mauriceau, during his residence in Paris.[14]

Mauriceau quoted himself describing a difficult case of blockage, noting,

> I must confess, I thought her case desperate, and had but little hope that Desomeaux's celebrated Portuguese Pills, which I determined to put to the test, would here avail [but] the patient entirely recovered, and became possessed of sound health. . . . These proofs of their wonderful powers have induced Dr. Mauriceau, since his return from France, to take the sole agency for the United States. They are to be obtained of him only. . . . For whole boxes the price is five dollars; half-boxes, three dollars. Address to 'Box 1224, New York City.'

Lohman, in short, was (1) inventing a character, "Dr. Mauriceau," and giving him an impressive resumé; (2) introducing another character, "M. M. Desomeaux," and having "Mauriceau" guide the reader to him and his pills; (3), selling the pills for $5, which was then the cost of renting a New York city apartment for one month.[15]

As long as abortionists like Mauriceau were in the public eye and

---

[13] *Ibid.*, p. 15.

[14] *Ibid.*, pp. 15-16.

[15] Lohman further injured the reputation of early birth control by pushing hard for its use: When a prominent abortionist argued that "every reflecting being should hesitate whether it were not better to prevent pregnancy than to thrust human beings into the world [of] disease and wretchedness," the abortion-contraception link seemed tighter. Mauriceau plagiarized from an early birth control proponent, Robert Dale Owen, and used Owen's story of the Kentucky woman who had three children in four years. "Mauriceau" used standard utopian arguments: use of contraception would "banish poverty, vice and profligacy, by enabling the poor to improve their pecuniary condition," with a resultant increase in "rational, reflecting, thinking beings. . . ." But he also came through with, as always, his sales motive, and for that purpose offered "thanks

associated with medical practice, physicians generally were likely to be the Rodney Dangerfields of the era, getting no respect. In addition, some other popular medical writers up to the time of the Civil War, such as Dr. B. L. Hill, still disseminated foggy notions of conception. Hill wrote:

> There are various views as to the cause from which the future being emanates. Some contend that it is produced and originates entirely from the male; others, that it come from the union of a substance in both the male and female; others, that it originated entirely from the female.[16]

Hill himself favored the "egg doctrine," whereby ova were "the real germs of the future being – unconnected entirely from any substance transferred from the male." He suggested that "the male semen serves but to stimulate the germ and cause it to grow," and in that way he made it likely that some abortion-pushing men would feel even less compunction about forcing the death of a being to whom they were barely related.[17]

Many more substantial doctors and medical writers, of course, took strong anti-abortion stands. Dr. Hugh Hodge, brother of the famous Presbyterian theologian Charles Hodge, told his medical school students at the University of Pennsylvania from the 1830s on that the unborn child was not a part of the mother's body, but "an independent being" with its "own independent powers."[18] Similarly, Dr. Stephen Tracy wrote in 1853:

> If examined three to four weeks from the commencement of pregnancy, the embryo will be found to have about the size of a grain of wheat. . . . It is a Human Being. It is one of the human family as really and truly as if it had lived six months or six years; consequently, its life should be as carefully and tenderly cherished.[19]

Tracy agreed with Lispenard's rhetorical statement that God has the power to judge – but Tracy left no ambiguity as to what he believed God's judgment to be. Scientists had proven that life begins "at the

---

to the indefatigable researches of the learned and humane M.M. Desomeaux for his great discovery by which pregnancy can be prevented." Pp. 104, 108, 118-119, 146.
[16]Dr. B. L. Hill, *Midwifery Illustrated* (Cincinnati: J. W. Sewell, 1860), p. 44.
[17]*Ibid.*
[18]Hugh Hodge, *Foeticide, or Criminal Abortion* (Philadelphia: University of Pennsylvania, 1869), pp. 9-10.
[19]Dr. Stephen Tracy, *The Mother and Her Offspring* (New York: Harper & Brothers, 1853), p. 108.

moment of conception; and no person has any right to destroy it by any means whatever." Tracy concluded that

> whoever for the sake of gain, or for any other possible reason, designedly destroys it, excepting in cases (which seldom occur) where it is certainly and indispensably necessary, in order to save the life of the mother, commits a most awful crime, and will be called to give an account therefore at the judgement of the Great Day.

Tracy went on to oppose abortion "even in those lamentable and distressing cases where conception has taken place unlawfully," for

> the life of this new human being is sacred, and no one but God himself either has, or can have, the least shadow of a right or liberty to take it away. To destroy its life, for the sake of saving one's self from exposure and mortification, is but to add a greater to lesser crime.[20]

Tracy recognized that he was now declaring as universally binding what some had shrugged off before as a religious belief, but he did not shrink from the challenge. "Well-informed medical men," he wrote, knew that

> At forty-five days, the form of the child is very distinct, and it is not termed a fetus. The head is very large; the eyes, mouth, and nose are to be distinguished; the hands and arms are in the middle of its length – fingers distinct . . . at two months, all the parts of the child are present . . . the fingers and toes are distinct. At three months, the heart pulsates strongly, and the principal vessels carry red blood.[21]

Tracy thus saw no conflict between his religious beliefs and that which was scientifically established: "The investigation of physiologists have established them as incontrovertible TRUTHS which should be known and felt, and regarded by every human being."[22]

Into this debate between pro-life doctors and those who were publicly pro-choice – few were explicitly pro-abortion – strode Dr. Horatio Storer, a political organizer and joiner. Born in 1830 in Boston, Storer graduated from the Harvard University Medical School in 1853 and began build-

---

[20] *Ibid.*, p. 109.
[21] *Ibid.*
[22] *Ibid.*, pp. 110-111.

ing an enormous list of medical affiliations. He joined not only the American Medical Association and several Massachusetts societies, but was a member of the Obstetrical Societies of Berlin and London, the Medico-Chirurgical and Obstetrical Societies of Edinburgh, the Rocky Mountain Medical Association, the Canadian Medical Association, the Province of New Brunswick Medical Society, the State Medical Society of California, the Louisville Obstetrical Society, and the Medical Society of Sorrento, Italy. Storer clearly was suited by medical training and glad-handing temperament to the anti-abortion tasks of the late 1850s.[23]

Storer's understanding of the abortion problem was circumscribed by his lack of experience with abandoned women and aborting prostitutes. Storer, based on his own experience with fifteen "married and respectable women" who came to him seeking abortion, concentrated on abortion among the married.[24] He evidently did not realize that like attracted like and that the women who came to a middle-class physician such as himself were not representative of abortion-seekers generally.[25] He saw married spiritists, but missed women who could not afford regular medical help or who took advantage of brothel abortion services.[26] To understand abortion's past we need to study more than the limited practice of the most literate doctors.[27]

Another limitation in Storer's analysis was his sense that women generally lacked intelligence and stability. He argued that "their sex lies at the foundation, physiologically and pathologically, of much of the mental derangement that occurs in women."[28] Yes, Storer acknowledged, men also acted erratically at times, but

> allowing every latitude to the influence of the sexual system in the male,
> it must be allowed that in him the genital apparatus is merely subsidiary,

---

[23]R. French Stone, *Biographies of Eminent American Physicians and Surgeons* (Indianapolis: Carlon & Hollenbeck, 1894), p. 495.

[24]Horatio Robinson Storer and Franklin Fiske Heard, *Criminal Abortion: Its Nature, Its Evidence, and Its Law* (Boston: Little, Brown, and Co., 1868), p. 56.

[25]Boston had many proponents of spiritism and free love. It is likely that many of Storer's abortion-seekers were devotees of these doctrines.

[26]See Paul Starr, *The Social Transformation of American Medicine* (New York: Basic, 1982) and *Brought to Bed*, p. 71 for more discussion of doctors' clienteles.

[27]The problem for historians of abortion is heightened by Storer's paradigm-creating ability. Once he opined that abortion was particularly rampant among married women, other physicians tended to emphasize that segment of the population.

[28]Horatio Storer, *Causation, Course, and Treatment of Reflex Insanity in Women* (Boston: Lee and Shepard, 1871), p. 150.

[but] in woman, the case is very different . . . woman is what she is, in health, in character, in her charms, alike of body, mind, and soul, because of her womb alone.[29]

Storer and the coauthor of one of his books, Franklin Heard, also argued that women should not be doctors – even though "women in exceptional cases may have all the courage, tact, ability, pecuniary means, education, and patience necessary . . ." – because the menstrual periods of even these exceptional women, even if "unattended by physical suffering, unfits them for any responsible effort of mind."[30] Overall, it seemed to Storer that women might be unfit for serious thought at many different times: "Woman's mind is prone to depression, and, indeed to temporary actual derangement, under the stimulus of uterine excitation," he wrote, "and this alike at the time of puberty and the final cessation of the menses, at the monthly period and at conception, during pregnancy, at labor and during lactation."[31]

When Storer received some criticism for those views enunciated in 1866, he backed off slightly but argued again, five years later, that women suffered from "transient insanity" at the commencement of each pregnancy and that pregnant women at all times were "subject to grave mental and physical derangement."[32]

Storer also had a nativist outlook that some of his colleagues shared. In discussing the coming settlement of the states west of Missouri and east of California, Storer typically asked, "Shall they be filled with our children or by those of aliens? This is the question that our own women must answer; upon their loins depends the future destiny of the nation."[33] At times he gained support by Catholic-bashing and at other times by promising more than he could deliver. But in a weak organization like the early AMA, his organizing ability paid off, at least on paper, and his youthful energy and dedication helped to unify the small anti-abortion medical cadre, first in Massachusetts and then across the nation.

Storer's first victory came in the form of an anti-abortion resolution passed by the Suffolk County (Boston) Medical Society. He did not even

---

[29]*Ibid.*
[30]Storer and Heard, *Criminal Abortion: Its Nature, Its Evidence, and Its Law*, p. 101.
[31]Horatio Robinson Storer, *Why Not? A Book for Every Woman* (Boston: Lee and Shepard, 1866), pp. 74-75.
[32]Horatio Storer, *Causation, Course, and Treatment of Reflex Insanity in Women*, pp. 133, 148.
[33]Quoted in Carol Smith-Rosenberg, *Disorderly Conduct: Visions of Gender in Victorian America* (New York: Knopf, 1985), p. 238.

have great support among his own Boston physicians, let alone the AMA generally. One Boston physician complained that anti-abortion doctors would "fail to convince the public that abortion in the early months is a crime, and a large proportion of the medical profession will tacitly support the popular view of the subject."[34]

Storer's opponents also were concerned that his committee "seems to have thrown out of consideration the life of the mother, making that of the unborn child appear of far more consequence, even should the mother have a dozen dependent on her for their daily bread. It cannot be possible that either the profession or the public will be brought to this belief."[35] But few doctors wished to be openly identified with spiritists and free-lovers, or with the lowly abortionists themselves, and the published criticism of Storer's push was anonymous.

Storer's next goal was to get others to believe that, despite all the frustrations of legal action during the first three-fifths of the century, laws would be effective. Even the members of an AMA anti-abortion committee he was putting together were not optimistic. When committee member William H. Brisbane of Wisconsin told Storer in 1857 of his "intention to get a law passed by our legislature to meet the case, much too common, of administering drugs and injections either to prevent conception or destroy the embryo," Brisbane added, "it is not probable that any law could be enforced in such cases. . . ."[36] Brisbane, however, had a crucial insight: "the fact of the existence of a law making it criminal would probably have a moral influence to prevent it to some extent." Other doctors also agreed to talk to their legislators.

Storer's major victory came in 1859 when the American Medical Association committee he chaired attacked "the heinous guilt of criminal abortion," recognized the culpability of doctors who were "careless of foetal life," and noted the "grave defects of our laws."[37] The Committee was specific in its recommendation that the AMA declare abortion to be not a misdemeanor but "murderous destruction." The resolution offered by Storer's committee for passage by the full AMA, however, referred to "unwarrantable destruction of human life" rather than

---

[34] *Boston Medical and Surgical Journal*, Vol. 56 (May 28, 1857), p. 346.
[35] *Ibid.*
[36] Quoted in Mohr, *Abortion in America*, p. 140.
[37] *Report on Criminal Abortion*, submitted by American Medical Association Committee on Criminal Abortion at the Twelfth Annual Meeting in Louisville, Kentucky, May 1859; *Transactions of the AMA*, 1859.

"murderous destruction" and merely asked that state legislatures "revise" laws concerning abortions and take other action "as they in their wisdom may deem necessary."[38] Against such vanilla resolutions little objection was likely to be registered, and none was. But their passage did not mean that the AMA, let alone doctors generally, was firmly committed to tough anti-abortion laws.

Storer, as noted, was something of a finagler. His public-relations ability and connections paid off in 1864 when he won a AMA prize competition for an essay on abortion. The awards committee, established on Storer's suggestion, was chaired by his father, D. H. Storer.[39] Storer's own work had little demonstrable effect in a nation focused on fraternal war. Storer's high-powered committee of eight, however, included Dr. Hugh Hodge; southern medical leaders such as Lopez of Alabama and Baron of South Carolina; Dr. Thomas W. Blatchford of New York, who had publicized Madame Restell's activities back in 1845; Dr. Charles Pope of Missouri, a former AMA president who cynically but accurately observed that Missouri's supposedly anti-abortion law was worded in a way that acted as a "screen" for doctors "in the disreputable practice"; and Dr. Alexander Semmes – cousin of a sailor who would soon become the Confederacy's greatest naval hero. All of these doctors had a moral influence, as individuals, in their own communities and states – and all knew if abortion was not stopped it would become, in Semmes' prescient words, "a characteristic feature in American 'civilization.'"[40]

It's interesting and edifying to follow the lives of these individuals. Storer, in his early thirties, stayed out of the war, but Semmes, a physician with Charity Hospital in New Orleans until the war broke out, became brigade surgeon in Stonewall Jackson's corps of the Army of Northern Virginia.[41] He amputated frequently and resumed his position at Charity Hospital after the war, but had no peace back at the hospital, perhaps because his wife had sickened during the closing months of the war and died. Semmes eventually entered the Catholic priesthood and moved to a Catholic college as president and lecturer in literature and history. His anti-abortion beliefs, made firmer in tragedy,

---

[38] *Ibid.*

[39] See Horatio Storer, *Why Not?*

[40] Stone, *Biographies of Eminent American Physicians and Surgeons* and Mohr, *Abortion in America*, pp. 151-155.

[41] Dumas Malone, ed., *Dictionary of American Biography* (New York: Scribner's, 1935), p. 578.

influenced many. Charles Pope also became a professor and taught anatomy and physiology at St. Louis University. He tried to develop among his students a pro-life understanding. As one biographical note explained, "He had a gift of rapid, clear and concise delivery as a lecturer and left a deep impression on the minds of the students of the Mississippi Valley."[42]

Although the effect of massive death on army doctors is hard to quantify — intuitively, it seems as if piles of corpses could have a brutalizing effect on some and a deepening of the tragic sensibility in others — it is moving to read doctors' diaries in the Library of Congress' manuscript division and to see how some physicians were awakened by apparently unnecessary suffering. In 1862 Joshua Taylor Bradford, a doctor from Connecticut assigned to the north's Army of the Ohio, visited several military hospitals and described in his diary the shock he felt at "hundreds, nay thousands in their noisome bunks — some dead, some dying, and many tossing amid fevered limb and delirious foreboding. *There* is a sermon preached to the understanding, more potent than words."[43] Bradford joined anti-abortion activities in Connecticut after the war, as did Maine's Dr. Oren Horr, who in 1864 did what many white physicians would not do: he became assistant surgeon to the 114th (colored) Regiment, U.S. Army.[44]

Samuel Henry Eells, surgeon with the 12th Michigan volunteers, wrote home soon after Shiloh about an experience he said he would never forget:

> The wounded came in pretty fast and soon filled up the hospital and then they were laid down on the ground outside . . . new bullets began to come unpleasantly near and thick. One passed through the tent and within three inches of my head as I was dressing a wounded man, smashing a bottle of Ammonia liniment that stood on a box beside me and sending the fluid right into my face and eyes. . . . I was too busy [to be frightened], and if I had been ever so much scared I don't think I

---

[42]Howard Kelly and Walter Burrage, *American Medical Biographies* (Baltimore: Norman, Remington, 1920).

[43]Diary, March 6, 1862, Library of Congress manuscript division. Following the battle of Shiloh, Bradford was so busy cutting that his notations were minimal. On April 8 he wrote, "Monday was a terrible one. I was in many places where the balls flew thick." On April 12 he added, "Had numerous operations of all sorts."

[44]William B. Atkinson, *Physicians and Surgeons of the United States* (Philadelphia: Charles Robson, 1878), p. 112.

could have run off and left our wounded crying for help. It was a piti-ful sight I can tell you. I hope never to see the like again.[45]

Following the war Eells joined a campaign that produced a new Michigan anti-abortion law in 1869. Eells also took part in other educa-tional efforts under the leadership of Homer Hitchcock, a volunteer sur-geon with the Army of the Potomac, who became president of the Michigan Medical Society in 1871 and the State Board of Health from 1873 to 1877, and backed some hard-hitting anti-abortion prose.[46]

Some doctors contrasted the horrors of war with a prenatal pastoral. Dr. Addison Niles of Quincy, Illinois, wrote,

> The creator has provided the foetus with a house in which to live, with a temperature suited to its wants, with expanding walls to accommo-date its increasing development, and a fountain from which to imbibe his nourishment. Its morals are inoffensive, and no malice is in its heart.[47]

Niles noted that, "A bad man may take the life of an enemy who has done him an injury, but he probably would not murder one who had given him no offense. . . ."[48] Other northern doctors, such as Dr. P. S. Haskell of Maine, compared abortion to slavery, and said both were sins that could bring "the penalty which a Just God, the avenger of the blood of innocents, will mete out to us." Haskell added, "Whether we be innocent or guilty, we shall all suffer, as a people, as a profession and as individuals, just as we all have suffered and are now suffering for the curse of American slavery. . . ."[49] Haskell also expressed admiration for women who carried their children to term rather than aborting them:

---

[45]Letter from Pittsburgh Landing, dated April 13th, 1862, manuscript division, Library of Congress.

[46]Newspaper clippings in Toner manuscript collection, Library of Congress. The *American Lancet* applauded Hitchcock's work and called him an "eloquent advocate of justice."

[47]Addison Niles, "Criminal Abortion," *Transactions of the Annual Meeting of the Ill. Med. Soc.*, 1871, pp. 96-101.

[48]*Ibid.*, p. 97. Niles said of one abortionist, "Who can deny that the blood of the slaughtered innocents cries to God from the ground?" Concerning Niles (1812-1875), the Chicago *Medical Examiner* noted, "To his patients, and especially to those of the poorer class, among whom he had many, he was ever kind and tender." An obituary in Toner's file has Niles "admired by his enemies, loved by his patients, especially the poor."

[49]*Ibid.*, p. 471.

"No public act in the life of woman, however great or good it may be, can any more surely claim our respect and sympathy than this act of patient self-denial which it is the privilege of every family physician so often to witness."[50]

The Civil War, in short, may have led some doctors to think more about issues of life and death, grace and punishment. Dr. Morse Stewart of Michigan called abortion "a deed of darkness. The universal law of the demoralizing effect of all willful violations of the judgement of conscience, in depraving, and, by continued practice, besotting the moral sense, finds no exception here."[51] Stewart noted that "Destruction of the child is not the only result" and wondered about the effect of abortion on those left alive.[52] Dr. James Whitmer of Illinois wrote of a steady path from conception through birth and thereafter: the doctor "sees in the germ the probable embryo, in the embryo the rudimentary foetus, and in that, the seven months viable child and the prospective living, moving, breathing man or woman, as the case may be."[53] He also wondered how a willingness to take innocent life at one time would affect its protection at others.

Dr. O. C. Turner of Massachusetts complained that "Things are not called by their right names . . . how can we expect to recognize as murder that which is simply 'getting rid' of something, or being 'helped' out of trouble?"[54] Turner attacked the definition of "life" that those in favor of abortion were using: "There is no life in the fetus until respiration is established after birth." Turner wrote that if life does not begin until "the child is entirely separated from the mother," then there was a problem of definition when "the child respires and the cord pulsates before it is tied." He went through a logical process, with the goal of establishing a scientific (as well as a theological) pro-life position:

> Surely the child is alive then. It cannot be the mere act of tying the cord that produced life. Then when did life begin? With respiration? That is

---

[50]P. S. Haskell, "Criminal Abortion," *Maine Medical Association Proceedings*, Vol. 4 (1873), pp. 465-473.

[51]Morse Stewart, paper read before the Wayne County Medical Society, published in the *Detroit Review of Medicine and Pharmacy*, Vol. 2 (1867), pp. 1-11.

[52]*Ibid.*, p. 4.

[53]James S. Whitmer, paper read before the Woodford County Medical Society, 1873, published in the *Chicago Medical Journal*, Vol. 31 (1874), p. 392.

[54]O. C. Turner, "Criminal Abortion," *Boston Medical and Surgical Journal*, Vol. 5 (April 21, 1870), pp. 299-300.

only one added function. There was circulation previously, and the power of nervous action and motion. Why is not a fetus alive when it is diving and plunging in its mother's womb? Simply because its lungs are not inflated? Out on such nonsense! One might as well say that a child born blind was not alive because it did not use its eyes. It is on the record, I believe that children have been born by the Caesarean section, after the death of the mother. If there was no vitality in the fetus previous to respiration, then why was it not dead, like the mother? There can be no doubt of it, there was vitality or life. Then if we acknowledge that the fetus had life, how can we say at what period of gestation that life commences? The period of quickening varies, and I do not see why a fetus is not quite as much alive just before it moves as just after. . . .[55]

Turner concluded, "I stand firm in the opinion that there is life in the minutest ovum, and the burden of proof rests with the one who denies it."[56]

We could go on with many such individual statements, lectures, papers, reports, declarations, and so on — but the point is that they *were* individuals. Their anti-abortion message was as potent as the prestige and reputation of the doctors who gave it. Philadelphia's Andrew Nebinger, for example, wrote a precise study of his city's abortion practice and its evil. Unlike Storer, he knew about the wide use of abortion by prostitutes but added, "The commission of this crime is not confined to the harlot." He vowed a continued attack on "an evil of such gigantic proportions as criminal abortion. . . ."[57] But Nebinger was most effective in his anti-abortion teaching because he was loved, "particularly in the lower [poorer] section of the city, where he gave advice, medicine and pecuniary assistance to those who stood in need. It is said that during his long professional life he never asked or accepted a fee from a poor orphan or widow."[58] Nebinger's colleagues recorded that "For more than forty years no man has been more favorably or more widely known in the southern section of the city than Dr. Nebinger. . . . He was a most kindly and considerate friend to the sick poor. . . . He was no respecter of persons, but followed the teachings of the Divine Master, 'In so much

---

[55]*Ibid.*, p. 299.
[56]*Ibid.*
[57]Andrew Nebinger, *Criminal Abortion: Its Extent and Prevention* (Philadelphia: Collins, 1870), p. 31.
[58]Toner Collection, Library of Congress manuscript division.

as ye have done it unto one of the least of these, ye have done it unto me.'" Nebinger's anti-abortion proclamations were heard.

Yes, various state and local medical societies offered resolutions, but these societies were not like the mighty AMA of recent years. Overall, the state of medicine was as Dr. Henry Gibbons, president of the California Medical Society, described it in his address to the Society in 1858:

> We are a heterogeneous mass – an army of incompatibles. No country in the world is supplied with physicians so diverse in character. We have all the peculiarities of all the schools in the world. The physicians of California know less of each other than the physicians of any other land; and they care less for each other. There is no fraternity. Every man is for himself, and thinks the best way to raise himself is by treading down others. All through the country, in every town and village, there can be but one doctor in the same field. We live in continual war with each other – an internecine war, murderous and suicidal.[59]

Gibbons had a Mark Twain style that is worth quoting as we try to savor the flavor of mid-nineteenth-century medicine:

> Surgeons are worse in these respects than physicians proper. Young surgeons are especially quarrelsome; as they grow older they grow wider, unless they were fools from birth. Eclat attaches to operative surgery, and popular applause is more readily obtained by the knife than in the practice of medicine. Operations are talked of by everybody, while treatment without operations is not appreciated by the vulgar. A single bold and successful operation may establish the reputation of a surgeon and make his fortune. He who saves a doubtful limb does well; but he who chops it off dexterously in two minutes and forty seconds, gains imperishable fame. The wooden leg is a walking advertisement.[60]

Physicians had so little honor in their communities that their chief concern often seemed to be getting payment, not influencing policy. As Gibbons put it,

---

[59]Henry Gibbons, *California Medical Society Transactions*, Vol. 3 (Sacramento: James Anthony, 1858), p. 23.
[60]*Ibid.*, p. 24.

We have just four classes of patients to deal with – the first have money without honor; the second, honor without money; the third, neither money nor honor; the fourth, both money and honor. At present it is only in the fortuitous conjunction last named that we have any chance of getting paid. The lawyer demands his fee in advance and gets it. But then his services are more highly prized than ours. He has to do with property, while our concern is only life. And everybody knows that in California the latter is of little moment in comparison with the former.[61]

Medical journals and popular magazines throughout the nineteenth century either bemoaned or applauded the low esteem doctors had *as an organized body.*

The ability of the regular doctors, known as "allopaths," to influence legislators also was limited by the opposition of a variety of alternative medical movements. Hydropaths, botanical physicians, homeopaths, and others criticized the allopaths for drugging and bleeding patients. Another limitation on the political strength of Storer and his allies was the low status of obstetrics and gynecology generally. Even though the University of Pennsylvania established the first medical school chair of midwifery in 1810, the university's guidelines read, "it shall not be necessary in order to obtain the degree of Doctor of Medicine that the student shall attend the professor of midwifery."[62] At the midpoint of the nineteenth century many physicians and women still were questioning the propriety of male physicians conducting vaginal examinations. Allopaths in New Hampshire showed the limited clout of a typical AMA state affiliate at mid-century when they were unable to stop incorporation of the state's Botanic Medical Society, which they considered (for good reason) to be a quack haven; the allopaths lost on a vote of 125 to 107.[63]

Doctors also were in no position to take unpopular stands because they had to remain popular if they were to have any hope of getting paid. They had to take advantage, in Gibbons' words, of a variety of

modes of advertising considered legitimate, if not pushed too far. One uses his horse an advertising medium, and rides into practice. Another offers his services to sundry charitable institution, and has his name pub-

---

[61] *Ibid.*, pp. 28-29.
[62] See *Chapters in American Obstetrics* (Baltimore: Charles C. Thomas, 1933), and Alick W. Bourne, *A Synopsis of Obstetrics and Gynecology* (Baltimore: Williams & Wilkin, 1949).
[63] *Portsmouth Journal*, December 30, 1848, p. 2.

lished accordingly, though his philanthropy may not run out of this particular channel. One has some female friends of extraordinary conversational powers, who talk about him in season and out of season, perhaps much against his will, though motives of delicacy prevent him from rebuking them.[64]

Most doctors yearned for favorable press publicity and tried to stay in agreement with journalists, politicians, and popular opinion generally. Honest and dishonest doctors were united in the hope that "the newspapers will do their filthy work, and give currency to the most mendacious puffs, and the most obscene announcements, column after column, inviting to abortion and to all manner of licentiousness."[65]

Given the heterogeneity, it is not surprising that some doctors supported abortion, if not with their words at least with their instruments, and if not for principle, at least for principal. Dr. Stoddard argued that "blandishments of wealth" led doctors to become abortionists.[66] Dr. George Smith acknowledged that many doctors threatened with loss of business became abortionists, but he recommended that they "take up poverty rather than do abortions."[67] Dr. Mulheron of Detroit saw how self-interested thinking ran over the evidence: "At what period of gestation is the intentional destruction of the foetus criminal? Physiology and morality give but one answer to this question," he argued, but many doctor-abortionists ignored the truth.[68] Dr. Henry Gibbons repeatedly pointed out the economic usefulness of abortion to many regular physicians:

Our profession is not entirely clear of complicity in the crime of feticide. Tempted by thirty pieces of silver . . . individuals may be found in whom

---

[64]Gibbons, *California Medical Society Transactions*, p. 26
[65]*Ibid.*
[66]John P. Stoddard, "Foeticide – Suggestion Toward Its Suppression," *Detroit Review of Medicine and Pharmacy* (November 1875), p. 654.
[67]George Smith, "Foeticide," *Detroit Review of Medicine and Pharmacy*, Vol. 10 (April 1875), p. 211.
[68]J. J. Mulheron, *Peninsular Journal of Medicine*, Vol. 10 (1874), pp. 384-391. Mulheron explained, "the teaching of science and morality agree in pronouncing the destruction of the foetus in the womb of its parent at any period, from the first moment of conception, a crime equal in turpitude to murder, unless there exist justifiable reasons for the destruction. And what are justifiable reasons? There is only one, and that is when the safety of the mother demands it."

the honorable instincts and teachings of the guild are lost in the influence of unprincipled cupidity.[69]

Another doctor noted that "Men who have for years been systematically engaged in this abominable business are recognized in the profession and the community."[70]

Organized physician power may have increased a bit by the 1870s, but its limitations also became apparent during the debate over the legalization of prostitution, which many AMA members favored as a public health measure. In 1867 the New York Board of Health called for legalization with registration of all prostitutes, but the proposal died. Highly regarded Philadelphia surgeon Samuel Gross came out for "licensing" at the 1874 AMA convention.[71] AMA President J. Marion Sims in 1876 made the drive for legalization/regulation a bombastic theme of his presidential address at the doctors' convention; he asked whether "We, the representatives of the medical profession of a great nation, the custodians of the health [can] let the people remain in ignorance?"[72] Sims looked for a repeat of the AMA's anti-abortion success. "We must sound the alarm," he insisted.

Doctors in Washington, Baltimore, Chicago, San Francisco, and Philadelphia followed his lead – but to no avail. Pennsylvania physicians had legislators introduce a bill giving cities the option to legalize and regulate prostitution, but it did not pass. Cincinnati doctors pushed an ordinance to allow inspected brothels, but it also failed. In 1877 the Medical and Chirurgical Faculty of Maryland appointed a committee to lobby the legislature for legalization, and again the doctors' prescription was ignored.[73]

Physician supporters of legalization/regulation had a victory in St. Louis, where prostitution was legalized (with mandatory inspection by Board of Health-appointed physicians) in 1870. However, Clinton Fisk – an abolitionist who became active in the Freedman's Bureau and founded Fisk University – led the fight against legalization, and tens of thousands of residents signed petitions demanding repeal, which came

---

[69]Gibbons, "Observations on Abortion," p. 6.

[70]"Held for Murder," *Western Lancet*, Vol. 7 (May 1878), p. 138.

[71]Samuel Gross, "Syphilis in Its Relation to Natural Health," *Transactions of the American Medical Association*, Vol. 25 (1874), pp. 249-292.

[72]"Address of J. Marian Sims," *Transactions of the AMA*, Vol. 27 (1876), pp. 100-111.

[73]See Neil Shumsky, "Tacit Acceptance," *Journal of Social History*, Vol. 19 (1985/1986), p. 669.

in 1874. Other abolitionists also became anti-prostitution crusaders after the war and were instrumental in defeating legalization/regulation measures in New York in 1876 and Chicago in 1879. William Lloyd Garrison joined the "new abolition" movement, saying it had "the old ring of uncompromising warfare against sin."[74] Garrison said he opposed legalizing prostitution for the same reason that he opposed legalized slavery; he asked, "if one sin can be licensed, why not another?"

The legalization movement apparently failed because it came to be seen as a way for further oppressing the weak rather than liberating them. Aaron Macy Powell – editor of the pre-war *Anti-Slavery Standard* – headed a "social purity" movement that demanded an end to prostitution. Louisa May Alcott, John Greenleaf Whittier, Mrs. Ralph Waldo Emerson, and other ex-abolitionists joined him.[75] The recruitment and transplant of prostitutes, sometimes against their will, became known as "white slavery." Although women from all races were involved, the name became popular because it was seen as parallel to the "black slavery" that the Thirteenth Amendment had ended.

The flavor of continued crusade was evident. The New York Committee for the Abolition of Regulated Vice closed its parlor meetings with the singing of "The Battle Hymn of the Republic." When physicians were on the same side as the opponents of oppression, they could win; such was the situation regarding abortion. When they were seen as compromisers with evil, as in the prostitution battle, they lost. Either way, they were not powerful enough to do much by themselves. The AMA was so weak in and of itself that in 1871 the AMA's Commission on Criminal Abortion expressed jealousy concerning the political clout of Humane Societies:

> We have heard much of late in relation to cruelty to inferior animals, and in many of the States of this Union societies are formed whose sole object is to watch over and to bring to justice those who violate this very humane law. We would ask these *philanthropists*, while engaged in so laudable an undertaking, if it has ever occurred to them that in their midst it is of daily occurrence that men – aye, and women too – are present-

---

[74]David J. Pivar, *Purity Crusade* (Westport, CT: Greenwood, 1973), p. 67.
[75]Some feminists also joined the anti-legalization forces. When Susan B. Anthony attacked legalization/regulation in 1872, Bronson Alcott and other old abolitionist leaders rushed to congratulate her.

ing their poisoned cups and using their stilettoes to spill the blood of human victims, to take the lives of innocent, of unborn infants. . . .[76]

Overall, the post-war years were fertile ground for campaigns that tried to preserve family structure, just as the pre-war years had seen programs for massive social reform. Anti-abortion and anti-prostitution campaigns were liberal causes, carrying forward the solid anti-slavery impulses. Furthermore, anti-abortionists had the advantage of being pro-life in an era which had recently seen such sad and maddening loss of life. Several doctors who understood the political dynamics of the reconstruction era – including Dr. I. H. Bartholomew in Michigan and Dr. Eli Henkle in Maryland – were even able to get themselves elected to the state legislature.

Anti-abortion victories were limited, however, for the laws that were passed contained loopholes big enough for heavily-burdened camels to go through.[77] Even those victories showed how the successes of the anti-slavery and anti-abortion campaigns were parallel. Laws from the 1860s on announced victory, but abortionists and the Ku Klux Klan brought in terror. Discerning doctors still realized that personal involvement and educational efforts, with law as the backdrop, were worth more than words on paper that often were unread.

This was the understanding of Joseph C. Stone, who became a doctor in 1854, fought as a regular officer in the First Iowa Cavalry, reentered medicine, joined state and county medical societies, and was elected to the 45th Congress (1877-79).[78] For Stone, abortion, like slavery, was a "violation of every natural sentiment, and in opposition to the laws of God and man."[79] Stone in 1867 described the abortion record of Massachusetts and New York and then declared, "What is true of Massachusetts and New York is true in a greater or lesser degree of every state, and Iowa fills her quota of crime as surely as she filled the broken ranks of her regiment during the late war."[80]

Stone wrote that the "fertilized human ovum is not like the seed that

---

[76]Report by D. O'Donnell and W. L. Atlee, in *Transactions of the American Medical Association*, Vol. 22 (1871), p. 252.
[77]Mohr's discussion of the Maryland legislation – *Abortion in America*, pp. 211-215 – is good.
[78]Toner collection, Library of Congress, Box 341.
[79]J. C. Stone, "Report on the Subject of Criminal Abortion," *Transactions of the Iowa State Medical Society*, Vol. 1 (1867) (Davenport, IA: Griggs, Watson 1871), p. 27.
[80]*Ibid.*, p. 29.

has been wrapped in some old mummy, and left to await for ages the conditions for its development. Its growth is steady and progressive, physiological and positive."[81] He saw God's sovereignty as a firmer foundation for life than often selfish individual decisions: "but for the providence that blessed them with children in their early married life, many parents would be houseless, homeless, and friendless in their old age."

Stone's suggestion, as he prepared to enter Congress, was to pass good laws when possible, but to stress conversion and education. Legislation, he wrote,

> can do little until this custom is branded as a crime; until the unwarranted discrimination between the murder of a child in one condition of its being, and that in another, is broken down, and a social judgment shall condemn each equally as a violation of human and natural law.[82]

Stone spent only one term in Congress and then returned to Iowa, where he lived for a quarter of a century as a quiet country physician, counseling young women against abortion whenever he could.

In Stone's semi-retirement he could see that after all the activity of the 1860s and 1870s doctors were no more united then they had been at the beginning. Even in 1893 Dr. William H. Parish of Philadelphia noted that "Graduates of the best medical schools have proved false to their noble avocation, and have brought dishonor upon themselves. . . ."[83] Parish recalled that he had turned down one abortion request, only to learn that another regular physician had performed the abortion on grounds of "apprehended insanity."[84] Dr. Edwin Marchel of Alabama also reported with disgust in 1893 that "regular institutes, presided over by men who had received a regular medical education, exist in many of the larger cities of this country, and the work of the criminal abortionist is prosecuted in defiance of law and morals."[85] Marchel argued that the law in Alabama should be tough-

---

[81]*Ibid.*, p. 31.

[82]*Ibid.*, pp. 33-34.

[83]William H. Parish, "Criminal Abortion," *Proceedings of the Philadelphia County Medical Society*, Vol. 14 (1893), p. 153.

[84]*Ibid.*, p. 155. In the discussion that followed Parish's remarks, Dr. Eugene P. Bernardy noted that many people still said, after years of educational effort, "it is only a month old and it certainly is not alive."

[85]Edwin L. Marchel, "The Medico-Legal Aspect of Criminal Abortion in Alabama," *The

ened, but he noted that even under the law citing abortion as a misdemeanor there had been no prosecutions."[86]

In the 1890s, after years of effort, medical societies were still hearing statements about the great difficulty of finding witnesses willing to testify about abortion. "Every person involved in the affair . . . is, for his or her own sake, pledged to secrecy," attorney Robert Taylor pointed out. Even in the relatively small number of cases involving maternal death there was a "practical impossibility of securing convictions."[87] Taylor summarized the problem:

> The explanation of the small number of convictions . . . lies in the secrecy with which this crime in its very nature is committed, and in the fact that such proofs as are attainable rarely do more than cast a strong suspicion of guilt upon the person charged with the offense.[88]

Even dying declarations often were given "little weight" because it was claimed that the dying woman's reason was clouded and her willpower gone, Taylor noted. Witnesses who heard such declarations were said to be emotionally involved.[89]

The inability of statutes and anti-abortion doctors to force out and lock up abortionists meant that other means of containment had to be devised. Work on prevention was crucial. Dr. Parish of Philadelphia probably put it most succinctly: "Those conditions or habits of life which diminish the number of marriages, increase the number of illegitimate pregnancies and the number of criminal abortions."[90] The next chapters of this book examine the initiatives that went beyond anti-abortion statutes to work on habits of life.

Alabama Medical and Surgical Age, Vol. 6 (1893-1894), p. 364. "Drugs such as Savin, ergot, cottonroot, tansy and pennyroyal are made use of. . . . Resort is frequently had to instruments of the crudest nature such as knitting needles, crochet needles, and lead pencils. Several years since, I had a patient inform me that she never expected to have a child so long as she could obtain a lead pencil. . . ."

[86]*Ibid.*, p. 359.

[87]Robert C. Taylor, "Why Do Abortions Go Unpunished?," *American Medico-Surgical Bulletin*, Vol. 9 (1896), p. 453.

[88]*Ibid.*

[89]*Ibid.*, p. 454.

[90]William H. Parish, "Criminal Abortion," *Proceedings of the Philadelphia County Medical Society*, Vol. 14 (1893), p. 160. Chief among the habits was "an underlying immorality, usually on the part of both sexes . . . the only efficient safeguard against" criminal abortion was "preservation of the purity of morals. . . ."

6

A Missed Opportunity

The model of early American generosity toward those in greatest need stressed personal aid in times of disease. Pilgrim leader William Bradford, describing how sickness shrank his small band of settlers following their landing at Plymouth in 1620, commended the "6 or 7 sound persons" who could still move about and

> in ye time of most distress . . . spared no pains night nor day, but with abundance of toyle and hazard of their owne health, fetched them woode, made them fires, drest them meat, made their beads, washed their lothsome cloaths, cloathed and uncloathed them; in a word, did all ye homly & necessarie offices for them.

Bradford wrote that they did "all this willingly and cherfully, without any grudging in ye least, shewing herein true love unto their friends & bretheren."[1]

The early American model stressed hospitality, particularly the opening of homes to those suffering destitution because of disaster. Minutes from the Fairfield, Connecticut, town council meeting of April

---

[1]William Bradford, *Of Plimoth Plantation*, many editions (here, Boston: Wright & Potter, 1898), p. 111.

16, 1673, show that "Seriant Squire and Sam Moorhouse [agreed] to Take care of Roger Knaps family in this time of their great weakness. . . ."[2] Minutes from the Chelmsford, Massachusetts, town meeting in November 1753 show a payment to "Mr. W. Parker for taking one Joanna Cory, a poor child of John Cory, deceased, and to take care of her while [until] 18 years old."[3] But the model also stressed "decent living" on the part of those who were helped. Groups such as the Scots' Charitable Society (organized in 1684) "open[ed] the bowels of our compassion" to widows such as a Mrs. Stewart who had "lost the use of her left arm" and whose husband was "Wash'd Overboard in a Storm."[4] The open hand was not extended to all; the Society ruled that "no prophane or diselut person, or openly scandelous shall have any pairt or portione herein."

Those policies of the seventeenth century – help to the helpless, but a reluctance to help those who had hurt themselves and remained sunk in sin – persisted in the nineteenth. As cities grew, more organization was necessary if those in need through no fault of their own were to be helped. Orphanages were established in New York, Philadelphia, Baltimore, Boston, and other cities. Some groups began providing small monthly allowances to supplement the earnings of widowed mothers who worked for a livelihood. "Widows who have the charge of two, three, four or five children," a Boston association declared, "are unequivocally proper subjects of alms." Female Charitable Societies and Ladies Benevolent Societies, designed initially to aid widows and orphans, started up in New York City and Philadelphia, in smaller northern cities such as Newburyport and Salem, Massachusetts, and then in the South as well. Women in Petersburg, Virginia, petitioned the legislature in 1812 to set up an orphan asylum, for they were "deeply impressed with the forlorn and helpless Situation of poor Orphan female Children . . . and wish to snatch [them] from ignorance and ruin."[5]

We need to keep this history in mind as we look at the response to abortion. "Americans in the early nineteenth century could and did look the other way when they encountered abortion," historian James Mohr

---

[2]Included in Ralph and Muriel Pumphrey, eds., *The Heritage of American Social Work* (New York: Columbia University Press, 1961), p. 22.

[3]Quoted in Eleanor Parkhurst, "Poor Relief in a Massachusetts Village in the Eighteenth Century," *The Social Service Review,* XI (September 1937), p. 452.

[4]Pumphrey, *The Heritage of American Social Work,* p. 29.

[5]Quoted in Suzanne Lebsock, *The Free Women of Petersburg* (New York: Norton, 1984), p. 202.

claimed: "there was considerable compassion for the women involved."[6] But compassion in America never meant looking away. Compassion meant helping people change their lives, not sink deeper into disaster. The real question for urban Americans in the 1830s, as prostitution and abortion became more frequent, was whether the compassion offered to widows and orphans would be extended to women normally considered unworthy of help, and to their children.

The scene of the first attempt to extend compassion was New York, in 1830 a city of promise but with major streets paved with gravel. The municipal idea, seemingly sensible at the time when asphaltum was rare and expensive, was to use larger rocks on the bottom and sand on top. In practice, however, avenues became rutted during the dry season and mud-choked and impassable after heavy rains. A lack of trash collection turned some New York streets into final resting-places for dead cats and broken furniture. Boston overlooked its horse manure and still aspired to be a city on a hill, but strewn garbage made New York a heaven only for porkers. One Manhattan publication, the *Constellation*, mused in 1831 that "A question 'tis, and mooted strong / Between the citizens and swine, / To which the streets do most belong. . . ."[7] Pedestrians watched their steps in order to let sleeping pigs lie.[8] Young women also had to be careful, for the old story of seduction and abandonment followed by abortion or infanticide often was told.

New York City had sections known for brothels, crime, and watchmen who carried clubs but stood on wooden boxes and would not move off them unless desperate citizens offered extra income. The better-off prostitutes wore long dresses with low bodices and flared sleeves. Their hair was piled high, with curls on the side; their faces were powdered and rouged; their bodies smelled of oil of amber. Decked with rings, necklaces, feathers, plumes, combs, and turquoise decorations, they came out in the evening as oil lamps flickered. Other prostitutes remained inside, waiting for strangers on mattresses of straw, cotton, hair, or husks, in rooms sporting rusty tin basins on bare tables. Most were busy through the night, until it was late and the streetlights burned out, making it indeed darkest before the dawn. And most had multiple abortions.

---

[6]Mohr, *Abortion in America* (New York: Oxford University Press, 1978), pp. 17-18.
[7]*The Constellation*, June 4, 1831.
[8]Dogs also roamed at will, and cattle went by under somewhat greater control, but sometimes they got loose; in 1844 a bull gored a man walking down Hester Street on the city's east side.

The central figure in the first American attempt to contain abortion by extending compassion was John McDowall, son of a Canadian preacher, educated at Amherst and Princeton, and a founder of schools in Rhode Island. McDowall, age twenty-nine in 1830, wore a black broadcloth coat and pants supported by suspenders. Young New York gentlemen – "dandies" – carried canes with ivory heads; McDowall did not. Dandies had blue silk umbrellas with white stripes and handles carved in the shape of the heads of various animals; McDowall's umbrella was black. He came to New York to set up Sunday schools in the slums, and he came to wake up the city and himself. As McDowall lingered in bed for a few minutes one Sunday morning, he wrote a complaining note to himself: "Slept late; why did I do it? Why did I not with the morning sun rise . . . ?"[9] The next day he did and soon knew the milkmen from Long Island who came into the city early to sell milk door to door, carrying tin buckets yoked across their shoulders. On October 1, 1830, he was able to record in his diary a significant accomplishment: "Organized the Society for the Moral and Religious Improvement of the Five Points [neighborhood]."[10]

Soon, however, McDowall's diary took on a different tone. On October 5 he wrote of his day's work, "Visited about one hundred families. Saw one house of ill-fame." On October 6 he "visited fourteen families" but was still reflecting on "the harlots! How numerous!" He described on October 16 those "allured by the desire for fine clothing – others by the hopes of wealth, luxury, and ease." By the end of October he was dwelling on a prostitute's spiritual problems: " O woman, woman, think on your ways! . . . Do you mean to brave the terrors of the Almighty? . . . Do you mean to harden your heart, to stop your ears . . . ?"[11]

McDowall also learned more about women who were seduced and abandoned, and he reacted with characteristic fervor: "O, how it moves the heart to look on a young, seduced, broken-hearted female."[12] Visiting a hospital on New Year's Day, 1831, McDowall saw one victim "in deep agitation. She thinks of her guilt, and is troubled."[13] That winter he tried to find shelter in private homes for those who had been seduced and

---

[9]See Phebe McDowall, ed., *Memoir and Select Remains of the Late Rev. John R. McDowall* (New York: Leavitt, Lord, & Co., 1838).
[10]*Ibid.*, p. 101.
[11]*Ibid.*, pp. 101-102, 124-127.
[12]*Ibid.*, p. 144.
[13]*Ibid.*, p. 161.

abandoned: "I found a poor girl 18 years old with a babe in her arms. . . . At her earnest solicitation I aided her . . . a lady with whom the woman's brother once boarded, [took] compassion on her, and received her into her family, for neither father nor brother nor sister would do any thing for her."[14] He was glad that the eighteen-year-old had not had an abortion, unlike many abandoned pregnant women who were "persuading themselves that it is better for their offspring to die thus early than to be born to an inheritance of shame and poverty."

McDowall was well aware that the New York legislature already had passed an anti-abortion law: "Severe legislative enactments exist against those who administer drugs to do this wicked work." He also knew that "the thing is daily done in defiance of penalties" and that advertisements for "'a complete preventive of propagation' are circulated in this city to let persons know how and where the antidote to pregnancy may be had."[15]

For McDowall, the clear answer was compassion, which to him meant both spiritual challenge and the offering of a way out. He quickly learned that the job would be hard. McDowall was shot at verbally and sometimes physically by brothel owners or managers. He was criticized by some female church members who thought that offering "fallen women" second chances might make others see the fall as not so terrible. He was lampooned by men who enjoyed the double standard that allowed them to spend Saturday night on the town and Sunday morning in church. But he kept at it.

McDowall's strategy for fighting the combination was threefold. He proposed both journalistic exposure of brothel-keepers and of men who prided themselves on seduction – a consistent hard line toward the double standard of morality that excused men's conduct – and consistent *compassion* towards the women, in the literal meaning of "suffering with." The last part of his strategy immediately opened him up to gossip. McDowall stressed the need for a large facility at which experienced prostitutes looking for a way out could be housed, but he also suggested that pregnant, recently-seduced unmarried women be placed in private homes. McDowall praised a physician who gave medical care to a woman seduced into a brothel and then "had compassion on her, and took her into his own family, where she resided two months."[16]

---

[14]Remembrance of that winter in *McDowall's Journal*, February 1833, p. 9.
[15]*Ibid.*
[16]*Ibid.*, March 1833, p. 18.

McDowall and his wife – a woman considerably older than himself, the widow of a New Jersey minister – took young prostitutes into their small home at times.[17] There is no indication that McDowall became physically involved with any of the women he rescued, but tongues did wag.

To expose journalistically the conditions of Manhattan morality and to build a large shelter, McDowall needed funds. Having familiarized himself with the city's squalor, he also became a visitor to its solid brick residences, ten yards across and fifteen yards deep, with marble steps and silver-plated doorknobs. Into them McDowall walked to request volunteers and funds for a Magdalen Society that would be devoted to sheltering the seduced and abandoned and exposing seducers and abortionists. It was hard going, and McDowall was often turned down, but he did find one financial angel, Arthur Tappan:

> [I was] going from house to house, reading the scriptures, praying and exhorting all men and women to be reconciled to God . . . the brothel keepers complained . . . the girls themselves began to reflect seriously upon their future prospects. . . . I called on Mr. Arthur Tappan and related these facts to him. He was deeply interested, [and became president of] the New York Magdalen Society.[18]

As a biography of Tappan's relates, the rich merchant "entered into the work with all his heart. . . . Mr. Tappan paid most of the expenses of the Society."[19]

That reliance on Tappan turned out to be a source of great difficulty, however. Born in 1785, by 1830 Tappan had built up one of the nation's largest silk importing businesses.[20] He sold only for cash or quickly redeemed promissory notes and made his profits from low markup and high volume. He had unremitting, torturing headaches. Day after day he sat in the only chair in his cubicle office at the center of his gloomy warehouse store; he found that the lack of another chair speeded the departure of unwelcome visitors. His brother and partner Lewis Tappan wrote a hagiographic biography of Arthur but complained (in his diary)

---

[17]*Memoir*, p. 184.
[18]*McDowall's Journal*, January 1833, p. 2.
[19]Lewis Tappan, *The Life of Arthur Tappan* (New York: Hurd and Houghton, 1870), p. 196.
[20]See Bertram Wyatt-Brown, *Lewis Tappan and the Evangelical War Against Slavery* (Cleveland: Case Western Reserve University, 1969), p. 13.

of the elder's "waspish temper."[21] Tappan spent little on himself or his family – meals of "a few crackers and a cup of cold water" were not unusual – and thus had much to contribute to causes.[22] Those he funded gave him titles. He was president of the American Education Society, life director of the American Seaman's Friends Society, treasurer of the Society for Promoting Common School Education in Greece, trustee of the Mercantile Library Association, and an official of many others.

Tappan became McDowall's "sugar daddy," and the New York Magdalen Society was born in 1831, with the goal of providing shelter and challenge to young women in despair. Tappan became the Society's president and followed avidly the stories McDowall told him of young women like "E.H., an orphan female" who was seduced and became so "suffused with shame [that] she listened to the voice of a procuress and entered a house of ill repute." McDowall met her, told Tappan about her, and gave her a New Testament, noting that it had been "given to me for that purpose by Mr. Arthur Tappan. She often perused it with delight."[23] An ex-prostitute wrote in a letter to McDowall: "When I used to see you, and Mr. Tappan . . . labouring to save us poor creatures, I loved you, for I knew that you loved Jesus, and the souls for which he died."[24]

Tappan also thrilled to the story of a young woman from the country who eloped with a man, slept with him the night before the scheduled wedding, and then – upon the fiancé's receipt of a message supposedly so urgent that there was no time to wait for a clergyman – rushed off with him to New York. "There with redoubled solicitude she renewed her request that he would remove her shame and reproach, by fulfilling his engagement," McDowall later wrote, but the response was maddening: "he put her off, saying, at one time, that they could live together as happily without as with the minister's speaking a few words over them," and also promising to "purchase many fine things for her, if she would be cheerful and contented. . . ."[25]

When the young woman insisted on marriage, he abandoned her, and she resolved to kill herself. She bought a vial of laudanum and almost drank it, but the intervention of a gentleman from her hometown

[21]Lewis Tappan's diary, July 18, 1828, Tappan papers, Library of Congress, manuscript division.

[22]Tappan, *The Life of Arthur Tappan*, p. 45.

[23]*McDowall's Journal*, April 1833, p. 27.

[24]*Ibid.*, October 1833, p. 77.

[25]John McDowall, *Magdalen Facts Number 1* (New York: Magdalen Society, 1832), p. 33.

saved her. The Magdalen Society helped her find shelter with "a genteel family" until she got her bearings back. "She rewarded Mr. Tappan, in giving to him the vial of laudanum, which he kept as a souvenir thereafter."[26]

The result, as Lewis Tappan wrote concerning his brother, was that "Mr. Tappan became deeply interested in Mr. McDowall's labors."[27] Arthur Tappan's support helped McDowall attract backing from others, as Lewis Tappan reports: since "Mr. Tappan was the president . . . [d]onations were made for the support of Mr. McDowall," and "societies were formed in many towns, also in churches, not only in the city of New York, but in other cities and villages."[28] Arthur Tappan had that kind of influence, even among the already committed. One admirer said, "Our great benevolent system owes its expansion and power to his influence. His example inspired the merchants of New York . . . to give hundreds and thousands when before they gave $10 to $15."[29]

Tappan also backed McDowall's plans for journalistic exposure and funded publication of a "First Annual Report" for the Society that would go far beyond the tepid listing of personnel and recital of statistics:

> We have the names, street and number of the houses of ill-fame in this city, notoriously inhabited by abandoned women. . . . Many of these sinks of iniquity are in respectable neighborhoods, disguised under the mask of boarding houses, dressmakers, milliners, stores and shops of various kinds.
>
> Some of them are large and elegant houses, provided with costly furniture, and have brass and silver plates on the doors, on which are engraved the real or fictitious names of the occupants. [Houses have been identified] partly by the girls and women who have been rescued from pollution by the Asylum, and partly by the vigilance of persons male and female employed by the Society.[30]

McDowall's criticism of wealthy philanderers landed him in trouble

---

[26] *Ibid.*, pp. 36, 39.

[27] Tappan, *The Life of Arthur Tappan*, p. 113.

[28] *Ibid.*, pp. 112-113. In Lewis Tappan's words, "The country appeared to be moved. Public meetings were held, lecturing agents were employed, publications were circulated, and the work seemed to advance prosperously. Mr. McDowall was the leading agent, and his labors diffused through the other agencies an enthusiasm seldom evinced."

[29] Wyatt-Brown, *Lewis Tappan and the Evangelical War Against Slavery*, p. 51.

[30] *First Annual Report of the New York Magdalen Society* (New York John T. West, 1831), pp. 8-9.

among some of Arthur Tappan's associates. Some merchants were heavily involved in acts of Biblical compassion, but others prized New York as a city of stores, plays, and brothels. (The Park Theater displayed new gaslights, shops showed goods that came on sailing ships from China and India, and Broadway displayed whores.) Some wives of merchants also opposed McDowall. Dressed in flounces, ruffles, fringes, and lace, with corsets of cloth and whalebone, stockings of silk, shoes of black leather, and large hats with ribbons and flowers, they wanted a firm line of delineation between "polite society" and fallen untouchables. As McDowall wrote:

> We are denounced and condemned as traitors, for . . . visiting lanes, alleys, cellars, garrets, and yards, in New York, to rescue unprotected women from barbarous insult, extreme poverty, starvation, disease, despair, and loathsome death.
>
> We are denounced . . . for sympathizing with her in her sorrows, and laboring to restore her from prison, and the hospital, and the street, and the gutter, and giving to her a clean garment, a mouthful of food, a warm fire, a comfortable bed, a kind mother in her matron, and father in the Society.[31]

McDowall saw sin throughout society, not just in the lives of those designated as "sinners." "The character of a [seduced woman] is as good as the character of a seducer or debauchee," he insisted. He noted that women were blamed for abortion, but it was usually men who "offer[ed] physicians large sums of money" to do the job.[32]

At first the antagonistic comments about McDowall stayed in the parlor, stacked among the knickknacks, bronze busts, vases, cigar stands, alabaster candlesticks, and gift books bound in velvet. Then private irritation went public. City boosters attacked the Magdalen Society "as defaming New York's good name," and public meetings to denounce McDowall were held in Tammany Hall on August 20 and September 9, 1831. "Read this ye base calumniators, and tremble!" was the caption on a handbill announcing the first meeting. A resolution declared the Magdalen report "deserves the reprehension of every honest citizen."[33]

---

[31]McDowall, *Magdalen Facts*, p. 69.

[32]*Ibid.*, p. 36; *McDowall's Journal*, May 1833, p. 36.

[33]Quoted in McDowall, *Magdalen Facts Number 1*, pp. 66, 67. The handbill closed with a stern note concerning McDowall and his associates: "We have been basely calumniated . . . let the curse of Cain be upon their guilty heads – let their names become a by-word

Lewis Tappan reported that "threats of vengeance" dominated the meeting, and one cry went up: "This audacious and libellous man must be put down, and the society that has patronized him must be silenced."[34]

Arthur Tappan worried about the comments of the press and public. "The city press, with few exceptions, commented upon the report with severity," Lewis Tappan wrote. Even worse, several city newspapers denounced Arthur Tappan by name, and some local toughs talked of storming his house.[35] The Tappans and other McDowall allies, the *Episcopal Recorder* noted, "can scarcely go into a hotel, or step for a moment on board a steamboat, without being annoyed by their angry hissing."[36] And, just when the debate might have cooled, McDowall published a new exposé, *Magdalen Facts*, that lambasted church complacency:

> The Church suffers certain persons, unreproved, to teach and to seduce. The Church, as a body, has ceased to teach men that licentiousness is sin. . . . As most ministers carefully omit preaching against it, it is not a matter of surprise that men should plead for the vice as a necessary evil. . . . Are [ministers] not specially charged to lift up their voice as a trumpet to show the people their sins? Are not the lascivious criminals of royal, and of obscure standing too, condemned in the Bible, in plain, bold and decisive terms?[37]

McDowall continued his attacks even though he knew that Arthur Tappan already was feeling uneasy under the pressure of fellow merchants who called him St. Arthur D. Fanaticus.[38]

At this point the problem of relying on a "sugar daddy" became

---

among us – let the finger of scorn be pointed at them wherever they go – let them be proclaimed traitors to their country."

[34]Tappan, *The Life of Arthur Tappan*, p. 113. See also *Journal of Commerce*, August 24, 1831.

[35]*Ibid.*, p. 68, On the other hand, the *Christian Advocate* noted, "It is indeed mortifying to a virtuous mind to be under the necessity of believing that so much licentiousness exists. But must it be concealed for fear of offending the ears of delicacy?. . . [Criminals will triumph if they] succeed in making good men believe that it is an offense against modesty and delicacy to drag the monster to light, and to hold him up to the indignant gaze and just execration of mankind."

[36]McDowall, *Magdalen Facts*, p. 74. The *Recorder* observed that McDowall and his associates "have stirred up (somewhat rudely perhaps) a nest of rattlesnakes and vipers . . . startled by the few rays of light that have been thrown into their hiding place, [they] have lashed themselves into a universal fury. . . ."

[37]*Ibid.*, pp. 26-28.

[38]Wyatt-Brown, *Lewis Tappan and the Evangelical War Against Slavery*, p. 67.

clear. McDowall expressed thanks for the "much money" that Tappan had spent in his support, but he also worried that the Tammany taunts had "dampened the zeal of some of the once-bold champions of the Magdalen cause. . . ."[39] Tappan indeed, according to one biographer, "was taken aback by the volume of criticism and the respectability of some of his opponents."[40] Lewis Tappan gave more detail. His brother, upset by "much unmerited censure"[41] and "apprehensive that reformatory measures had been overdone," withdrew support from McDowall and the Magdalen Society.[42] That withdrawal led to the collapse of the organization, for those who had pledged support because of Tappan's approval or to stay in his good graces also withdrew.[43] McDowall, upset, criticized Tappan publicly and suggested that his cowardice essentially had "turned the females into the street."[44] A stung Tappan responded that McDowall's effort had not failed because of "want of funds" but because his attempt at personal work among the seduced and abandoned "was a waste of moral effort."[45] McDowall, in turn, publicized one minister's comment about those who gave in to sin because of "a profound regard for public favor."[46]

McDowall tried to bounce back by starting in January 1833 a monthly magazine that mapped out the boundaries of the empire of seduction, prostitution, and abortion. He reported that "thousands of children are murdered. Dead infants are frequently found; sometimes in privies, wells, sewers, ponds, docks. . . ."[47] He described "a case of pre-

---

[39] *Magdalen Facts*, p. 80.

[40] Wyatt-Brown, *Lewis Tappan and the Evangelical War Against Slavery*, p. 70.

[41] Tappan, *The Life of Arthur Tappan*, p. 116.

[42] *Ibid.*

[43] As William Goodell recalled in *Memoir and Select Remains of the Late Rev. John R. McDowall* (p. 415), "good men, who, until that time, had given to the enterprise the full share of attention which its importance demands, were induced to withdraw," and from then on McDowall received "little support and assistance. . . ."

[44] *New York Evangelist,* January 26, 1833.

[45] Letter to the *New York Evangelist,* January 26, 1833.

[46] *McDowall's Journal,* July 1834, p. 52. The Minister, A. T. Hopkins of Utica, also spoke of those who opposed Magdalen work "because by its progress their own characters will be exposed, and their guilty pleasures abridged. . . ." Hopkins added, "Let the favorite, but false theory, that his vice is less criminal in man than in woman, be universally discarded."

[47] *Ibid.*, May 1833, p. 36. McDowall also quoted a handbill advertising a medicine by which "the loss of character, ruin and wretchedness may be prevent . . . a complete preventive of propagation." He added, "these cards are handed to gentlemen at dances and theaters . . ." (p. 37).

mature birth, produced, as supposed, by improper means. . . . The mother, a young woman of hitherto unblemished character . . . finally acknowledged, that the physician (a married man) who attended her, was the father of the child."[48]

McDowall's Journal created the sharpest opposition yet. A grand jury called *McDowall's Journal* "a nuisance" that was "degrading to the character of our city," and thus deserved the "interference of the civil authorities."[49] That accusation became the subject of jokes across the country. The *Cincinnati Journal* commented, "Wonderful! New-York can bear three thousand baneful grog-shops, and hundreds of brothels, and gambling halls without number, and all the reality of corruption; but when a person tells the truth with regard to these things, and lifts a note of warning, the 'Grand Jury' – watchful guardians! – are afraid it will demoralize the community!"[50]

McDowall, with the support of six church groups that came to his defense, argued that members of the grand jury and their friends owned brothels, kept mistresses, and wanted to do so without criticism that could drive up rents or drive out customers.[51] He could take pleasure in out-of-town support, such as the *Ohio Observer*'s statement that "never before has there been so general and successful an effort made to ferret out the works of darkness."[52] Within New York City also, there was truth in William Goodell's observation that "no periodical, perhaps, was ever more popular with the plain working class of Christians."[53] Nevertheless, Goodell also noted that it was strongly opposed by "leading and influential" citizens, perhaps because the feature stories he wrote generally told of young women heartlessly trapped by powerful men. In expensive houses, where furniture of walnut and mahogany was set off by cabinets made by Duncan Phyfe, citizens drank Rhenish and Moselle wines, or Madeira and claret, and complained about McDowall's articles. One, entitled "The Reputably-Pious Merchant," told of how a man walking a woman home "in a friendly manner" said he wanted to stop by his store for a moment. "He

---

[48] *Ibid.*, September 1833, p. 65.
[49] *McDowall's Journal*, April 1834, p. 31.
[50] *Ibid.*
[51] *Ibid.* See also *McDowall's Journal*, October 1834, p. 73. (A presbytery includes the elders of Presbyterian churches within a particular geographic area; a group of presbyteries makes up a synod.)
[52] *McDowall's Journal*, April 1834, p. 32.
[53] *Memoir*, p. 417.

requested her just to step in; she did so, and the door was locked. By persuasions and promises and presents, he effected his base designs." Soon the woman was left "shunned and despised; whilst her unprincipled seducer still retains his standing. . . ."[54]

When McDowall was threatened with legal action as a "public nuisance" by those who did not want to see this double standard upset, quarrels also arose over use of the small funds that were available.[55] McDowall lived very simply. A printer who lived with the McDowalls during the fall of 1833 reported crowded quarters and meals of coarse wheat or Indian corn bread, along with wheat mush, molasses, and potatoes.[56] But there were still insufficient resources to keep his journal going. New York newspapers, including the powerful *Courier and Enquirer*, stepped up their lambasting of McDowall, and – after Tappan pulled out – McDowall was without big backers.[57] "The power brought into action against us is immense," McDowall supporter William Brown wrote:

[W]e find arrayed against us the whole corps of unprincipled young men who in a greater or less degree, support the brothels. Secondly, the corps of Newspaper Editors, to a considerable extent. Several of the most influential in this city have openly taken the field against McDowall's Journal, considering it as an unprotected outpost, which it is their policy first to demolish. In aid of these, come a number of country editors.

---

[54] *McDowall's Journal*, April 1834, p. 27.

[55] When criticized, McDowall responded with a harsh answer that turned more wrath toward himself, and Tappan associate John Wheelwright, charging McDowall with "vituperation and slander," joined in the production of a booklet attacking McDowall.

[56] *Memoir and Select Remains of the Late Reverend John R. McDowall, The Martyr of the Seventh Commandment, in the Nineteenth Century* (New York: Leavitt, Lord & Co., 1838), p. 396. Also *Memoir*, p. 212. Occasionally there were apples or applesauce.

[57] *McDowall's Journal*, September 1834, p. 72. A resolution from St. Joseph's Presbytery, Michigan Territory, read: "Resolved, That in order to reform vice of any kind, it is necessary that it should be exposed in all of its enormities to public view. Resolved, that the Rev. J. R. McDowall, of the city of New-York, who is laboring to bring to light the hidden things of darkness, is thus meriting the entire approbation of the Christian community throughout the world. Resolved, that Mr. McDowall's Journal, published in the city of New-York is, in our opinion, an instrument of great good in preventing vice, and in reclaiming the vicious, and ought to be amply sustained and patronized by Christians of all denominations. . . . Resolved, that each member of the Presbytery be an agent to promote the circulation of the Rev. J. R. McDowall's Journal against licentiousness" (May 1834, p. 39). Ministerial meetings in New York, Boston, and Philadelphia, and synod, presbytery, or ministerial association resolutions from as far west as Michigan Territory, came to his defense.

Then, thirdly, importers, publishers, wholesale dealers, and innumerable retailers in city and country, of *obscene books* and *pictures*.[58]

McDowall had to rely on small contributors, and that was not enough.

McDowall's September 1834 issue reported that "The Journal is embarrassed for the want of funds."[59] By the end of 1834 it was time for "The Editor's Farewell Address."[60] The impact of the closing went far beyond New York, because *McDowall's Journal*, as one newspaper noted, was "taken in nearly all the considerable seaports and villages in the country."[61] Reformers in Massachusetts, Vermont, Rhode Island, Ohio, Virginia, South Carolina all wrote that they were watching carefully the events in New York.[62] Newspapers, including the Nashville *Republican*, Rochester *Enquirer*, Baltimore *Working Men's Advocate*, and New Orleans *American*, kept readers posted on the battle of New York. When McDowall's effort sagged, the discouragement was broad.

McDowall, hoping to learn more and revive his supporters, took a speaking tour through upstate New York during the summer of 1835. He also researched the extent of prostitution, seduction, and abortion in towns and hamlets that seemed pastoral by day and made numerous diary entries concerning all that he saw:

July 20th, 1835, Troy: A member of a Christian church [is] criminal in procuring abortions. . . . Truly, the depravity of human nature is complete.[63]

Sept 2nd, Utica: A physician in this region was indicted some years since for procuring an abortion, and escapes punishment merely because the character of a witness was esteemed to be impure. He still lives and practices medicine in this country, though his awful crime is publicly known.

Sept 25th, Rochester: A doctor was indicted for procuring abortions in this city. He boasted of having procured sixty-six in a few months. The trial never came on. It was suppressed, but known to those who managed the public prosecution.

---

[58] *Ibid.*
[59] *Ibid.*, p. 72.
[60] *McDowall's Journal*, December 1834, p. 89.
[61] *Republican Journal*, quoted in *McDowall's Journal*, June 1834, p. 47.
[62] *McDowall's Journal*, May 1834, p. 10; June 1834, pp. 13, 14, 16.
[63] *Memoir*, p. 251.

McDowall returned to New York in time to see the great Merchant Street fire on the evening of December 16, 1835. The temperature was 0 as volunteer fire fighters in red flannel shirts and broad belts, with trumpets attached, raced to the blaze. But what water there was proved to be frozen, and over six hundred buildings burned down. Within a year, astoundingly, the entire realm of destruction was rebuilt, and the city's population was up to two hundred and fifty thousand, a 25 percent increase in five years. McDowall, however, was on a downward path. McDowall's presbytery passed a resolution criticizing his journalistic coverage of prostitution and abortion, which it called "unchristian" for its role in "impeaching and censuring individual conduct and character."[64] The presbytery suspended McDowall from the ministry. The synod, which included the representatives of several presbyteries and acted as an appeals court, backed McDowall, but the infighting weakened the entire movement.[65]

McDowall, hoping to save abandoned women and prove his sincerity, spent most of 1836 furiously pacing from house to brothel in New York and surrounding towns. He ate crusts of bread and walked mile after mile. He became exhausted and finally came down with what his physician called a typhoid-type fever that McDowall's weakened body could not combat. For twelve days a fevered McDowall alternated between visions of depravity and glimpses of glory. Sometimes he screamed about "the filth – the abominations of this city" and exhibited "a shrinking as from something tangible and polluting to the touch."[66] He repeatedly asked his wife to wash him in clean water. But when she asked him, "Are you not afraid to die?" he replied, "Afraid, No. Legions of angels are waiting to conduct me through and Jesus will go with me."[67]

McDowall died on December 13, 1836. His friends memorialized him as a compassionate Calvinist who "poured out the thunders of Sinai, like burning lava, upon guilty head[s]," but showed "the sweet melting of

---

[64]*Memoir*, p. 338. The presbytery was also concerned with the effect of McDowall's coverage on readers, "lest the very efforts to prevent this vice should themselves become the occasions of its spread, by rendering the mind too familiar with indelicate facts and associations."

[65]*Memoir*, pp. 323, 348.

[66]*Memoir*, pp. 360, 365.

[67]Sarah R. Bennett, *Woman's Work among the Lowly* (New York: American Female Guardian Society, 1877), p. 17. "He prayed fervently for his enemies and expressed only sentiments of forgiveness toward them."

mercy" in response to the "tear of contrition."[68] Lewis Tappan, however, commented that "Mr. McDowall was not always so prudent and discreet as he should have been [in discussing] a subject of great delicacy and difficulty. . . ."[69] William Lloyd Garrison, who was also dealing with a subject of great difficulty, commented in a private letter, "J. R. McDowall is dead . . . how he was hated and persecuted! What a weight of glory is his!"[70]

As it turned out, Garrison was a major beneficiary of McDowall's fall from Arthur Tappan's grace. When Tappan gave up on the Magdalen cause in 1832, he switched commitments and began giving Garrison and his newspaper *The Liberator* substantial support.[71] In 1833 Tappan cut his ties with the American Colonization Society and dispatched Garrison to England to gain the support of British anti-slavery leaders for radical abolitionism.[72] Garrison caused a furor with his Constitution-castigating speech at a July 13 mass meeting in London. Arthur Tappan called a New York meeting of abolitionists for October 2, 1833, and promised that Garrison would speak.

The gathering was driven out of its intended meeting-place, but the night was still a milestone, for in another building Tappan and his colleagues formed the New York Anti-Slavery Society. When Garrison at a Philadelphia meeting in December helped to form the American Anti-Slavery Society, he made sure that Arthur Tappan, who was certainly the wealthiest abolitionist, was elected president.[73] At that time Garrison also told Arthur and Lewis Tappan of "the [financial] embarrassments" of *The Liberator* and said that without an influx of cash "the paper must inevitably go down." The Tappans provided funds that, in Garrison's words, "saved the life of *The Liberator*."[74]

---

[68]*Memoir*, p. 369. "With the Bible in his hand, he said to the Magdalens in his family, 'God says thus, and so, and we must do it. Dare you disobey? I dare not.' A pause ensued, when he asked, 'Are you prepared to hear what God says in this holy book?' Then reading, he would apply it, so that each felt herself the one addressed" (*Memoir*, p. 385).

[69]Tappan, *The Life of Arthur Tappan*, p. 114.

[70]Garrison letter to Henry E. Benson, December 17, 1836, Library of Congress, manuscript division.

[71]Tappan had given Garrison $100 in October 1831.

[72]Tappan in 1833 also hired Elizur Wright to come to New York in the Fall as his anti-slavery secretary. In mid-June Tappan wrote William Jay, son of the first Chief Justice, and asked, "Will you give me your opinion as to the expediency of forming an American anti-slavery society? And in doing it now."

[73]Wyatt-Brown, *Lewis Tappan and the Evangelical War Against Slavery*, p. 109.

[74]Garrison letter to Lewis Tappan, February 29, 1836, in the manuscript division of the Library of Congress; see also Garrison letters, Vol. 2, p. 50.

Anti-slavery work did not prove to be an easy go for Tappan. Toward the end of the decade he quarreled and then split with Garrison.[75] Arthur and Lewis Tappan received great personal abuse for their bankrolling of abolitionists who were accused of inciting slave insurrection. Critics of Arthur and Lewis Tappan saw them as "members of the inner circle of merchants and bankers who controlled the financial life of the nation's most flourishing city" and were trying to extend their power.[76] A group of Georgians offered a ten thousand dollar reward to anyone who would kidnap Arthur Tappan and bring him to trial in the South for complicity in murder by aroused slaves; residents of New Orleans raised the bid to twenty thousand dollars.[77] But for better or worse, the priority for many northern reformers became the evil down south rather than the evil in their own backyards. Theodore Weld, for instance, turned down the opportunity to head a post-McDowall society dedicated to exposing the sexual preying of New Yorkers on servant girls and instead wrote a sensational tract attacking the depravity of plantation owners in relation to their female slaves.[78]

For women in trouble in New York, the aborted McDowall campaign was a missed opportunity. Opposition by those who benefited from the double standard, cowardice on the part of some who might otherwise have opposed it, and an unwillingness to extend the boundaries of compassion contributed to the demise of a movement that at one time was on the verge of catching fire. Some of McDowall's work continued through the efforts of the American Female Guardian Society, to which McDowall gave his list of subscribers when he discontinued his *Journal.*[79] With the Magdalen movement scattered and partly discredited, and its leader dead, prostitution and abortion had virtually an open field in New York.[80]

Furthermore, other cities soon became miniature New Yorks. A visitor to the Midwest, J. T. Smith, described in his diary the spread of prostitu-

---

[75]See the useful account in Hugh Davis, *Joshua Leavitt, Evangelical Abolitionist* (Baton Rouge: Louisiana State University Press, 1990), p. 113.

[76]Page Smith, *The Nation Comes of Age* (New York: McGraw-Hill, 1981), p. 606.

[77]*Ibid.*, pp. 607-608 argues that "the major effect of the abolitionists was to enhance enormously the paranoia of the South. . . ."

[78]Gilbert H. Barnes and Dwight Dumond, eds., *Weld-Grimke Letters*, Vol. 1 (New York: Da Capo, 1970), p. 130.

[79]Bennett, *Women's Work Among the Lowly*, p. 17.

[80]See *McDowall's Journal*, April 1834 (extra edition), p 7., and his discussion as to how, if the *Journal* went under, "the devotees of impure lust would keep a year of Jubilee on the occasion."

tion and complained that "physically, morally and intellectually Detroit is the meanest and the vilest spot upon creation's surface."[81] Galena, Illinois, became known for its mining of lead and for its prostitutes, while Natchez (Under-the-Hill) was a center of Mississippi River trade and prostitution. In many cities, McDowall-like attempts were made; in city after city they encountered strong opposition, and the train of prostitution and abortion rolled on. Great opportunities were missed, and good citizens often felt themselves called to deal with the great problems hundreds of miles away rather than the equally severe ones close to home.

George Templeton Strong in 1851 noted that "Philanthropists [were] scolding" about distant causes but ignoring personal compassion. "To have helped one dirty vagabond child out" was worth more than a multitude of lectures, he suggested.[82] Strong commented in 1857 on a sermon by a minister who provoked laughter by saying he seldom visited brothels:

One would think the haunts of fallen women, friendless, desperate . . . are exactly the place for a clergyman to work. But I suppose . . . a thousand conventionalities and respectabilities always keep the door closed tight.

Strong concluded,

Now and then as one walks Broadway at night, the gaslight shines on faces so pretty, innocent and suggestive of everything antipodal to profligacy and impurity, that one is shocked at our indifference and inertness in regard to this calamity and scourge, and feels as if the whole city should go into mourning over it were there but one woman so fallen.[83]

---

[81]J. T. Smith, *Journal in America, 1837-1838* (Metuchen, NJ: C. F. Heartman, 1925), p. 37.

[82]George Templeton Strong, *Diary of George Templeton Strong: The Turbulent 50s*, Allan Nevins and Milton Thomas, eds. (New York: Macmillan, 1952), July 7, 1851.

[83]*Ibid.*, January 11, 1857.

7

Waves of Vigilance

Just as McDowall's concept of compassion toward prostitutes was slow to gain acceptance, so his vision of exposing abortion practice took time to catch on. The only newspaper that regularly attacked abortion during the 1840s was the *National Police Gazette*, the most sensational journal of the era.[1] The *Gazette* typically filled three of its eight pages with ads for patent medicines and the usual run of goods and services, but none for abortion, which editor George Wilkes strongly opposed in editorials. Wilkes proclaimed in 1846 that his newspaper would expose abortionists, although other newspapers would not,

> because we believe that full expositions of the infamous practices of abortionists will tend to present these human fiends in a true light before the eyes of those who may become their dupes. We shall follow up this business until New York is rid of those child destroyers.[2]

---

[1]The *Gazette* began publishing on September 13, 1845, with the stated goal of exposing criminals and vice. It was scorned by "respectable" citizens and feared by both crime lords and police who did not like criticism of corruption. In 1850 a criminal-led mob assaulted the *Gazette* plant; six people died, and the plant was demolished. The newspaper resumed publication shortly thereafter.

[2]*National Police Gazette*, February 14, 1846, p. 205.

The *Gazette* proposed tough action, including police establishment of "a night-and-day watch at the doors of the slaughterhouses of the murderous abortionists of this city . . . miserable and deluded females would never incur the risks of discovery."[3]

The *Gazette* particularly concentrated on exposing the abortion practice of Madame Restell, wife of medical guide writer Charles Lohman, aka Dr. Mauriceau (as discussed in Chapter Five). The *Gazette* called Madame Restell "a monster who speculates with human life with as much cruelness as if she were engaged in a game of chance."[4] One patient, evidently an ex-prostitute, was quoted as saying that "Madame Restell, on previous occasions, had caused her to miscarry five times."[5] The patient also described one Restell abortion in which the aborted baby "kicked several times after it was put into the bowl."[6] The *Gazette* noted angrily that Restell's "advertisements are to be seen in our daily papers. . . . She tells publicly what she can do; and without the slightest scruple, urges all to call on her who might be anxious to avoid having children."[7]

Officials did not respond, and the *Gazette* (on Valentine's Day, 1846) began a campaign directed at New York's richest abortionist: "Restell still roams at large through the influence of ill-gotten wealth and will probably still continue until public indignation drives her and her associates from our midst."[8] *Gazette* editors predicted that a "day of vengeance" would arrive for Restell and other "fiends who have made a business of professional murder and who have reaped the bloody harvest in quenching the immortal spark in thousands of the unborn."[9] As other newspapers were silent, the *Gazette* hit hard: "We are not now demanding justice upon the perpetrater of a single crime, but upon one who might be drowned in the blood of her victims, did each but yield a drop, whose epitaph should be a curse, and whose tomb a pyramid of skulls."[10] The *Gazette* asked that laws on the books be enforced: "We call again for action from the authorities in relation to this woman. She has been for

---

[3] *Ibid.*
[4] *Ibid.*, November 15, 1845, p. 100.
[5] *Ibid.*
[6] *Ibid.*
[7] *Ibid.*
[8] *Ibid.*, February 14, 1846, p. 205.
[9] *Ibid.*, February 21, 1846, p. 218.
[10] *Ibid.*

nearly ten years involved in law, and her money has saved her, as yet, from the direct penalty of a single dereliction."[11]

Authorities, unpressured by any newspaper besides the *Gazette*, did not act. Frustrated, some anti-abortionists took to the streets. At noon on February 23, 1846, a crowd began to gather in front of Restell's house. By 12:30 a crowd estimated by different observers at three hundred to a thousand was faced by forty to fifty policemen who had stationed themselves on her doorstep. The crowd for hours gave anti-Restell cries of "Where's the thousand children murdered in this house?" and "Hanging is too good for the monster." Restell was described as a "wholesale female strangler," and governmental authorities were attacked for not shutting down her business.[12] The New York state legislature quickly passed a law stiffening penalties for abortion, as described in Chapter Four.

The *Gazette* immediately began a strong campaign for enforcement, complaining that police were engaged in "neglect of duty before the face of Heaven" and emphasizing once again that abortion is "murder . . . strangling the unborn."[13] Police finally acted and found a woman willing to testify against Madame Restell. At the trial in 1847, Maria Bodine testified that she had been attracted to Madame Restell's house and operated on by Madame Restell without anesthesia: "She hurt me so that I halloed out and gripped hold of her hand; she told me to have patience, and I would call her 'mother' for it."[14]

Madame Restell was found guilty and given a one-year term on Blackwell's Island in the East River. For a while it seemed as if community pressure had won out over advertising clout. According to later journalistic accounts, however, political connections apparently preserved Restell from any great misery. She was allowed to put aside the lumpy prison mattress and bring in her own fancy new featherbed instead; she also brought into the "prison suite" her own easy chairs, rockers, and carpeting. Visiting hours were altered so that her husband was able to visit at will and "remain alone with her as long as suited his or her pleasure," according to Warden Jacob Acker.[15] By the time Madame Restell

---

[11]*Ibid.*
[12]New York *Herald*, February 24, 1846, p. 1; New York *Tribune*, February 24, 1846, p. 2; New York *Morning News*, February 24, 1846, p. 1.
[13]*National Police Gazette*, April 25, 1846, p. 284.
[14]*Ibid.*, February 14, 1846, p. 205.
[15]New York *Tribune*, April 2, 1878, p. 1.

emerged from such a penalty the excitement had died down, and not much had changed.

The *National Police Gazette* continued its hard-hitting editorials during the 1850s and 1860s. In one, "Our People's Shame," the *Gazette* complained that availability and publicizing of "the deadly drug and the ever alert abortionists" were convincing some women to go against the "maternal instinct."[16] The *Gazette* termed abortion "the monster, wide-spread vice of the day . . . outraging the laws of man, debasing the minds and shattering the bodies of our women."[17] The *Gazette*, however, had more readership than prestige. The *Gazette's* exposure of abortionists provided harassment but not much more, as long as those with greater respectability were on the sidelines. For example, the New York *Times* during the 1860s ran at least sixteen small stories about ten abortion incidents, but *Times* coverage was occasional and unfocused.[18]

During this period, however, some popular books took on abortion. In 1862 James C. Jackson's *The Sexual Organism, and Its Healthful Management* stated that abortion was "among the greatest of crimes."[19] In 1867 Edwin M. Hale's *The Great Crime of the Nineteenth Century* argued that abortion was both "A CRIME AGAINST PHYSIOLOGY," one that stopped "the normal course of the functions of physical life," and "A CRIME AGAINST MORALITY" that should be called by no other name than "murder."[20] S. Y. Richard's *The Science of the Sexes* in 1870, and George H. Napheys' *The Physical Life of Women* – which sold one hundred and fifty thousand copies during the three years after its publication in 1870 – also attacked abortion.[21]

New York newspaper coverage began to change in 1870 as new *Times*

---

[16]*National Police Gazette*, September 28, 1867, p. 2

[17]*Ibid.*

[18]New York *Times*, January 12, 1863, p. 5; January 21, 1863, p. 3; September 28, 1865, p. 5; September 29, 1865, p. 8; May 5, 1867, p. 6; May 28, 1867, p. 5; August 25, 1867, p. 8; August 26, 1867, p. 8; November 24, 1867, p. 5; August 29, 1868, p. 8; August 30, 1868, p. 8; September 4, 1868, p. 2; September 9, 1868, p. 2; March 19, 1869, p. 8; March 24, 1869, p. 11; March 25, 1869, p. 2. See *Times*, July 1, 1867, p. 1; July 3, 1868, p. 7; January 2, 1869, p. 7; etc.

[19]James C. Jackson, *The Sexual Organism, and Its Healthful Management* (New York: Arno Press, 1984; original publication in 1862), pp. 261-263.

[20]See Edwin M. Hale, *The Great Crime of the Nineteenth Century* (Chicago: C. S. Halsey, 1867).

[21]See George H. Napheys, *The Physical Life of Women* (Philadelphia: J. F. Fergus, 1873), and S. Y. Richard, *The Science of the Sexes* (Cincinnati: I. P. Spinning, 1870).

editor Louis Jennings, a conservative Christian, began an anti-abortion crusade with a Biblically referenced editorial entitled "The Least of These Little Ones." He complained that the "perpetration of infant murder . . . is rank and smells to heaven. Why is there no hint of its punishment? Are the Police under the delusion that they are appointed merely for the purpose of dealing with open and public offenses?"[22] Jennings saw the need for public outrage, not just a tightening of laws that would go unenforced. The *Times* gave ample coverage to two more abortion cases early in 1871 but complained about "the extreme rarity of trials for abortion in this City – an offense which is known to be very common."[23] Abortionists, the *Times* reported, "have openly carried on their infamous practice in this City to a frightful extent, and have laughed at the defeat of respectable citizens who have vainly attempted to prosecute them."[24]

Editorials of that sort did not make abortion a much-discussed subject, however. To arouse the public, editor Jennings realized that he needed human interest stories with specific detail that could be acquired only through unconventional reporting. In July 1871 Jennings assigned one of his theological compatriots on the *Times*, reporter Augustus St. Clair, to go undercover in order to gather information for an exposé.[25] For several weeks St. Clair and "a lady friend" visited the most-advertised abortionists in New York, posing as a couple in need of professional services. The result was a hard-hitting, three-column article, "The Evil of the Age," which showed how "thousands of human beings" are "murdered before they have seen the light of this world. . . ."[26]

St. Clair's specific detail skillfully contrasted powerlessness and power. First he described the back of one abortionist's office: "Human flesh, supposed to have been the remains of infants, was found in barrels of lime and acids, undergoing decomposition." He described the affluence of an abortionist couple, Dr. and Madame H. D. Grindle: "The parlors are spacious, and contain all the decorations, upholstery, cabinetware, piano, book case, &c., that is found in a respectable home." He quoted Madame Grindle: "Why, my dear friend, you have no idea of the class

---

[22]New York *Times*, November 3, 1870, p. 4.
[23]*Ibid.*, January 27, 1871, p. 3.
[24]*Ibid.*
[25]George Grant discovered that St. Clair had a Christian Reformed Church background.
[26]New York *Times*, August 23, 1871, p. 6.

of people that come to us. We have had Senators, Congressman and all sorts of politicians, bring some of the first women in the land here."[27] St. Clair named abortionists' names: Mauriceau and Restell, Dr. Ascher, Dr. Selden, Dr. Franklin, Madame Van Buskirk, Madame Maxwell, Madame Worcester. He emphasized the constant cover-up, since "All the parties interested have the strongest motives to unite in hushing the scandal." He ended with a call for change: "The facts herein set forth are but a fraction of a greater mass that cannot be published with propriety. Certainly enough is here given to arouse the general public sentiment to the necessity of taking some decided and effectual action."[28]

St. Clair's article put abortion on the public's agenda, but that by itself was not enough to produce action. Newspaper crusaders know that once the basic facts are laid out and readers are becoming aware of a problem, a specific incident is still needed to galvanize the public. Tragically for a young woman, providentially for the *Times'* anti-abortion effort, the ideal story of horror arrived within the week. St. Clair published his exposé on August 23; on August 27 a *Times* headline at the top of page 1 read, "A TERRIBLE MYSTERY."[29] The general facts of the story were miserable enough. The nude body of a young woman was found inside a trunk in a railway station baggage room. The autopsy showed that her death had been caused by an abortion. But the *Times* provided evocative specific detail:

> This woman, full five feet in height, had been crammed into a trunk two feet six inches long. . . . Seen even in this position and rigid in death, the young girl, for she could not have been more than eighteen, had a face of singular loveliness. But her chief beauty was her great profusion of golden hair, that hung in heavy folds over her shoulders, partly shrouding the face. . . . There was no mark of violence upon the body, although there was some discoloration and decomposition about the pelvic region. It was apparent that here was a new victim of man's lust, and the life-destroying arts of those abortionists, whose practices have lately been exposed in the TIMES.[30]

---

[27] *Ibid.*
[28] *Ibid.* St. Clair also gave figures on the economics of abortion, noting that a Dr. Evans spent $1,000 per week on advertising, received a hundred letters per day requesting services, and had amassed a fortune of one hundred thousand dollars, thus making him the equivalent of a multimillionaire.
[29] *Ibid.*, August 27, 1871, p. 1.
[30] *Ibid.*

The exciting "trunk murder" detective story received full play in the *Times* during the next several days as police tried to identify the perpetrator. A boy who had helped carry the trunk into the station tried to find a man and a mysterious lady who had delivered the trunk. Readers daily absorbed the strategy of the detective in charge, Inspector Walling, who "issued orders which practically put every policeman in the force upon the case." The *Times* also noted that this particular tragedy was not an isolated incident. In a lead column every day on its back page (which functioned at that time as a second front page), the *Times* kept reminding readers that this particular incident showed what went on "in one of the many abortion dens that disgrace New York, and which the TIMES has just exposed as 'The Evil of the Age.'"[31]

On August 29 Inspector Walling arrested a Dr. Rosenzweig, aka Ascher, whose advertisement had been quoted in St. Clair's August 23 story: "Ladies in trouble guaranteed immediate relief, sure and safe; no fees required until perfectly satisfied. . . ."[32] The following day a *Times* editorial, "Advertising Facilities for Murder," quoted that article and noted, "What a ghastly commentary upon such an announcement is the fate of the golden-haired unfortunate who lies, [now] a mass of putrefaction, in the Morgue?" The editorial attacked "the lying notices of men and women whose profession, if it means anything at all, means murder made easy" and asked whether "the lives of babes are of less account than a few ounces of precious metal, or a roll of greenbacks?"[33] The *Times* demanded action: "It is high time that public opinion should be fairly roused. The law must take hold of the abortionists, as it very easily can, and public opinion must set its seal of emphatic condemnation upon every agency which aids and abets the shameful trade."[34]

The back page of that August 30 issue included four columns devoted to a superbly written follow-up by St. Clair and accompanying stories. "A Terrible Story from Our Reporter's Note-Book" revealed how St. Clair, in his undercover research for the exposé, had visited several weeks ago the accused Rosenzweig's Fifth Avenue clinic. Continuing his pattern of showing the affluence of the abortionists, St. Clair described

---

[31] *Ibid.*, August 28, 1871, p. 8; August 29, p. 8; August 30, p. 8.
[32] *Ibid.*, August 29, 1871, p. 8.
[33] *Ibid.*, August 30, 1871, p. 4.
[34] *Ibid.*

the "fine tapestry carpet . . . elegant mahogany desk . . . piano" and so on.[35] St. Clair also inserted a new detail:

> As we entered the room a young girl emerged therefrom. She seemed to be about twenty years of age, a little more than five feet in height, of slender build, having blue eyes, and a clear, alabaster complexion. Long blonde curls, tinted with gold, drooped upon her shoulders, and her face wore an expression of embarrassment at the presence of strangers. She retreated to the end of the hall, and stood there for a moment, and then went to another part of the house. In a few moments the Doctor made his appearance.[36]

St. Clair then described his discussions with Rosenzweig, including the doctor's demand for two hundred dollars and his explanation of what would happen to the aborted infant: "I will take care of the *result*. A newspaper bundle, a basket, a pail, a resort to the sewer, or the river at night. . . ."[37] On his way out, St. Clair glimpsed once again the beautiful young woman, and in his conclusion to his article he drove the point home: "She was standing on the stairs, and *it was the same face I saw afterward at the Morgue. I positively identify the features of the dead woman as those of the blond beauty before described.*"[38]

With one of its own reporters giving a firsthand account, the *Times* sometimes seemed to be convicting Rosenzweig in the press, but it did refrain from editorials demanding punishment for a specific individual still presumed innocent until proven guilty. Still, as more details were discovered, the story more and more resembled the classic pattern of seduction. The young lady was identified as Alice Mowlsby, a poor orphan who lived with her aunt in Paterson, New Jersey. Her seducer was identified as Walter Conklin, son of a mill-owner.[39] The *Times* kept at it, reporting on September 6 "ANOTHER ABORTION MURDER" of "a beautiful girl twenty-two years of age."[40] On September 8 the *Times* gave

---

[35] *Ibid.*, p. 8.

[36] *Ibid.*

[37] *Ibid.* When St. Clair asked more questions, Rosenzweig became suspicious and began to shout, "I'll kill you . . . you spy, you devil, you villain." According to St. Clair's account Rosenzweig's hand then "moved to his breast pocket," and St. Clair had to draw a revolver to make good his escape.

[38] *Ibid.*

[39] *Ibid.*, September 2, 1871, p. 8. As facts of the case continued to be revealed, Conklin admitted responsibility for arranging the abortion and committed suicide.

[40] *Ibid.*, September 6, 1871, p. 8.

prominent play to a judge's discussion before a grand jury of the importance of exposing abortionists: "Let the warning word this day go forth,
and may it be scattered broad-cast throughout the land . . . until these
professional abortionists, these traffickers in human life, shall be exter-
minated."[41]

Rosenzweig's trial, which began in a crowded courtroom on October
26, 1871, received wide coverage. As the *Times* noted, "Notwithstanding
the period which has elapsed since the perpetration of the terrible
tragedy, public attention has never been diverted from this extraordinary
case."[42] On October 29, Rosenzweig was found guilty of causing death
through medical malpractice and was sentenced to seven years imprisonment. The judge told him that he was getting off easy, for "You sent
two human beings to their last account, deliberately, willfully, murder-
ously."[43] The judge said he would join with others in recommending to
the legislature harsher penalties.

The *Times* kept up the crusade. Early in December it reported that
one medical board reported stiffer penalties for abortion and also noted
that "The Press and the Judiciary were thanked for their determined
opposition to this crime."[44] One week later the *Times* gave front-page coverage to another medical group's statement that "the fetus is alive from
conception, and all intentional killing of it is murder."[45] That committee
wanted judges to be given discretion to assign sentences of life imprisonment in abortion cases. It also suggested that passage of new legislation would be possible because New York was "grievously shocked . . .
by the terrible deeds of certain abortionists lately exposed."[46]

The campaign of exposure had an effect because other newspapers,
including Horace Greeley's New York *Tribune*, followed the lead of the
Times. One *Tribune* column (entitled "THE ROOT OF THE EVIL," in
obvious homage to the *Times*' "EVIL OF THE AGE" theme of abortion
as a big money-maker), attacked "an infamous but unfortunately common crime — so common that it affords a lucrative support to a regular
guild of professional murderers, so safe that its perpetrators advertise
their calling in the newspapers, and parade their spoils on the fashion-

---

[41] *Ibid.*, September 8, 1871, p. 8.
[42] *Ibid.*, October 26, 1871, p. 2. The *Times* had been instrumental in focusing that public
attention, of course.
[43] *Ibid.*, October 30, 1871, p. 1.
[44] *Ibid.*, December 8, 1871, p. 2.
[45] *Ibid.*, December 15, 1871, p. 1.
[46] *Ibid.*

able avenues."[47] Popular pamphleteers also followed suit. St. Clair wrote an account, *The Great Trunk Mystery*, that was published in the style of dime novels with a drawing of Alice Mowlsby on the cover and a centerfold of her body (discretely portrayed) stuck in the trunk.[48] A similar pamphlet, *The Trunk Tragedy*, had a cover drawing of Rosenzweig in jail and suggested that the purpose of Alice's death was "to awake the public to the enormity of a great crime that existed to an extent not ever imagined by most people."[49] A third pamphlet from the period used the Rosenzweig furor as an opportunity to go after Madame Restell. *Restell's Secret Life* began, "I have see the wicked flourish like a green bay tree, but the retribution comes at last and crushes them."[50]

The *Times* continued the campaign during the rest of 1871 and into 1872, noting that "The time is opportune to strike quickly, and to strike home."[51] The *Times* emphasized that the fight against abortion was a fight against money and power: "Great mansions on grand avenues are occupied by disgusting 'practitioners' who continue to escape prosecution."[52] It recommended passage of a bill "far-reaching enough to catch hold of all who assist, directly or indirectly, in the destruction of infant life" and backed its recommendation not by emphasizing medical authority but by attaching one additional populist thrust: "The people demand it."[53] With the *Times* and other newspapers pushing, the New York legislature of 1872 passed anti-abortion laws featuring easier rules of evidence and a maximum penalty of twenty years imprisonment.[54]

A few leading abortionists, such as Madame Restell, seemed immune to troubles even when two journalistic "guide books" to New York City portrayed her vividly. Ferdinand Longchamp wrote of how "That Thug of society [Madame Restell] holds in her hands the honor of hundreds of families and it would be dangerous to arouse her resentment."[55] He described a party in Madame Restell's house during which a woman was singing. Her husband stormed in and said, "You are

---

[47]New York *Tribune*, August 30, 1871, p. 4.

[48]Augustus St. Clair, *The Great Trunk Mystery* (Philadelphia: Barclay, 1871).

[49]*The Trunk Tragedy* (Philadelphia: C. W. Alexander, 1871), p. 56.

[50]*Restell's Secret Life*, an undated pamphlet published in Philadelphia, p. 3, in the Rare Books Collection of the Library of Congress.

[51]*Ibid.*, January 12, 1872, p. 4.

[52]*Ibid.*

[53]*Ibid.*

[54]Chapter 181 (1872), New York Laws.

[55]*Ibid.*

certainly much indebted to Madam Killer, but I wonder how you can sing in a house that brought to an untimely death an innocent babe!"[56] James McCabe wrote of Madame Restell as a blackmailer:

> It may be one or ten years after her services were rendered, but at what she considers the proper time she renews her acquaintance with them. She will startle them with a call, or a note regarding the events that they would gladly forget and soliciting a loan for a short time. The appeal is generally made to the man, and is sustained by such strong proofs that he dares not not comply to the demand.

The payer knew that Madame Restell would "never return his money, but he is forced to send whatever sums she pleases."[57]

In 1872 those sums helped to furnish a lavish mansion at Fifth Avenue and 52nd Street.

> On the first floor are the grand hall of tessellated marble, lined with mirrors; the three immense dining-rooms, furnished in bronze and gold, with yellow satin hangings, and enormous French mirror in mosaic gilding at every panel . . . more parlors and reception-rooms; butler's pantry, lined with solid silver services; dining room with all imported furniture. Other parlors on the floor above; a guest-chamber in blue brocade satin, with gold- and ebony-bedstead elegantly covered . . . [many bedrooms and lounges]. . . . Fourth floor — servants' rooms in mahogany and Brussels carpet, and circular picture gallery; the fifth floor contains a magnificent billiards room, dancing-hall, with pictures, piano, etc. . . . The whole house is filled with statuettes, paintings, rare bronzes, ornamental and valuable clocks, candelabra, silver globes and articles of many origins and rare worth.[58]

Madame Restell, once an impoverished printer's wife, traveled the avenues during the 1860s behind a patch of matched grays and a driver with plum-colored facing on his coat lapels. According to one writer, she also carried a small muff of mink in which she hid her hands, much like

---

[56]Ferdinand Longchamp, *Asmodeus in New York* (New York: Longchamp & Company, 1868), p. 19.
[57]Edward Martin [James McCabe], *The Secrets of the Great City* (Philadelphia: Jones, Brothers and Company, 1868), p. 430.
[58]*Ibid.*

the ones "famous pianists or violinists used to protect their hands from harm."[59]

Madame Restell, hoping to avoid earthly retribution, was discreet in her abortion activities from 1871 on. In 1878, however, at age sixty-five but hardly in retirement, the *Times* was able to report in a front-page headline, "MME RESTELL ARRESTED" for "selling drugs and articles to procure abortion."[60] (The purchaser was Anthony Comstock, in disguise; more about his activities in the next chapter.) The *Times* noted that "The residence of Mme Restell is one of the best known in New York. . . . Her wealth is entirely the proceeds of her criminal profession. Her patrons are said to belong to the wealthiest families."[61] This time, though, Madame Restell's patrons were not able to protect her from arrest under very hostile circumstances, or from reporters who followed every detail of her arraignment and trial.

Some of the developments were low comedy. Madame Restell could not immediately raise bail from her own funds, since her investments in bonds and real estate were not liquid. Bondsmen, though, said they would put up sufficient funds only if the judge would order reporters not to print the bondsmen's names in the newspaper. The judge refused, and the bondsmen refused. Madame Restell's lawyer turned to one bondsman and asked him to help out, saying, "Will you not allow a Christian feeling to govern you?"[62] But there was nothing Christian about Madame Restell, the *Times* suggested, as it quoted the bondsman refusing not from opposition to abortion but from dislike of publicity: "I've got a wife and a family of girls, and I'll be hanged if I'm agoing [sic] to have my name in the papers as a bondsman for an abortionist."[63] The threat of press exposure made abortion supporters afraid.

Madame Restell eventually left jail while awaiting trial, but she could not leave behind newspaper attacks. She had lived by the press and was now dying by it. She asked her lawyers if there was some way to suppress the newspapers but was told that nothing could be done, for the press was "without standards." One of Madame Restell's colleagues complained angrily, "Money! We've plenty of that. But what good is it with

---

[59]Alan Keller, *Scandalous Lady* (New York: Atheneum, 1981), p. 6.
[60]New York *Times*, February 12, 1878, p. 8.
[61]*Ibid.*, February 14, p. 8.
[62]*Ibid.*
[63]*Ibid.*

the newspapers against us?"[64] Madame Restell's lawyer asked both judge and editor to have mercy on his client, a "poor old woman," but he was laughed at.

Madame Restell could not seem to understand the causes of the judgment she was facing. "I have never injured anybody," she complained: "Why should they bring this trouble upon me?"[65] Madame Restell at age sixty-five became an avid newspaper reader, but she found no peace. The New York *Times* described how she was "driven to desperation at last by the public opinion she had so long defied."[66] At night she paced her mansion halls like a latter-day Lady Macbeth, looking at her hands and bemoaning her situation. Finally, the night before her trial was scheduled to begin, Madame Restell was discovered in her bathtub by a maid, with her throat cut from ear to ear, an apparent suicide. The *Times* announced this denouement at the top of page 1: "END OF A CRIMINAL LIFE. MME RESTELL COMMITS SUICIDE."[67]

Exposure produced results, as many abortionists were driven into disgrace or despair during the 1870s. This concerted journalistic effort had limitations: "the momentary excitement occasionally roused by the discovery of a criminal of this sort . . . cannot be considered as any proof of an earnest determination on the part of the American people to punish the guilty and protect the weak in all that concerns this dreadful evil."[68] Too often the more visible abortionists, such as Madame Restell, received all the attention. Often the trio of reasons behind the demand for abortion – love of a man outside of marriage, love of money, love of a bizarre theology – went unchallenged. In some communities there was even what anti-abortion feminist Elizabeth Evans decried as the easy attack on "some unlikely quack who has been seized upon as a scapegoat for his more prosperous brethren in wickedness."[69] Nevertheless, each exposure of an abortionist made his "brethren" more cautious.

Another limitation on the power of press exposure was the unwillingness at pulpits to back up the journalistic labors. Some Catholic bishops in New York, Boston, and Baltimore denounced abortion, and the pro-life leadership included Presbyterians such as Rev. Robert Beer of

---

[64]*Ibid.*
[65]*Ibid.*
[66]*Ibid.*
[67]*Ibid.*, April 2, 1978, p. 1.
[68]Elizabeth Evans, *The Abuse of Maternity* (Philadelphia: Lippincott, 1875), p. 50.
[69]*Ibid.*

Northern Indiana; Episcopalians such as Arthur Cleveland Coxe, bishop of western New York; Methodists such as Reverend Dr. Hatfield of Cincinnati's St. Paul's Methodist Church; and Congregationalist ministers such as Rev. W. B. Clarke of Litchfield, Connecticut, John Todd of Pittsfield, Massachusetts, and E. Frank Howe of Indiana.[70] Anti-abortion doctors, however, frequently criticized the performance of many church leaders. The church, Dr. Addison Niles of Illinois complained, did not initiate disciplinary action against abortionists.[71] Niles recorded several cases of clerical cover-up and complained about "a lack of proper religious teaching duly enforced. . . . The clergy should speak out from the pulpit, [and] discipline of the Church should be brought into action. . . ."[72]

The church writings and resolutions that emerged often were powerful, particularly when they played off the Civil War experience. A Congregational church conference in 1868 declared that because of abortion

> full one third of the natural population of our land, falls by the hand of violence; that in no one year of the late war have so many lost life in camp or battle, as have failed of life by reason of this horrid home crime. We shudder to view the horrors of intemperance, of slavery, and of war; but those who best know the facts and bearing of this crime, declare it to be a greater evil, more demoralizing and destructive, than either intemperance, slavery, or war itself.[73]

Minister and best-selling author John Todd told a reporter that "We have rid ourselves of the blight of Negro slavery, affirming that no man may be considered less than any other man. Now let us apply that holy reason to the present scandal."[74]

Some anti-abortion sermons – particularly a "Sermon on Ante-Natal Infanticide" delivered by Indiana minister E. Frank Howe – received wide reprinting.[75] Howe spoke of the "destruction of unborn

---

[70]Martin John Spalding, archbishop of Baltimore, spoke out against abortion and also showed concern for born life by establishing the St. Vincent de Paul Society and, in Baltimore, the House of the Good Shepherd.

[71]Addison Niles, "Criminal Abortion," *Transactions of the 21st Anniversary Meeting of the Illinois State Medical Society* (Chicago, 1872), pp. 98-99.

[72]*Ibid.*, p. 101.

[73]*Christian Mirror*, August 4, 1868. Cited in George Grant, *Third Time Around* (Brentwood, TN: Wolgemuth & Hyatt, 1991), p. 99.

[74]*Christian Monitor*, July 18, 1868.

[75]E. Frank Howe, *Sermon on Ante-Natal Infanticide* (Terre Haute, IN: Allen & Andrews,

children" and acknowledged that "no demonstration of the criminality of this thing will deter some of those who practice it from a continuance of the practice." He argued, however, that many women and men "have fallen into the practice thoughtlessly," particularly since news media were not communicating the truth about abortion.[76] Howe said he would try to get out the message as best he could. "In the ears of the thoughtless I would sound the cry of MURDER! so clearly that henceforth they cannot fail to think."[77] Among the Episcopalians, Bishop Arthur Coxe, in a pastoral letter of January 30, 1869, stressed "the blood-guiltiness of ante-natal infanticide" and cited press accounts to show that "the world itself has begun to be horrified by the practical results of the sacrifices to Molech which defile our land."[78] Coxe told his flock "that they who do such things cannot inherit eternal life. If there be a special damnation for those who shed 'innocent blood,' that must be the portion of those who have no mercy upon their own flesh."[79]

Only one denomination, however, expressly condemned abortion. The General Assembly of the Presbyterian Church in the United States of America resolved, "This assembly regards the destruction by parents of their own offspring before birth with abhorrence, as a crime against God and against nature. . . ."[80] Those guilty of abortion were excommunicating themselves: "except they repent, they cannot inherit eternal life." Abortion had to be fought head-on, the General Assembly argued: "The whole power of the ministry and Church of Jesus Christ should be put forth in maintenance of the truth." Strong preaching was essential.

1869). Howe, in Terre Haute, Indiana, began his sermon with an interesting discussion of why he was speaking on abortion: "It is with extreme reluctance that I touch the subject, not simply because of its delicate nature, but because I cannot doubt that an evil so wide-spread has invaded my own church and congregation." He explained that "to talk of sins lying at the doors of those addressed, when these are friends loved and trusted, this is not so easy or pleasant a task." Howe predicted that "some will be disgusted at the introduction of so delicate a subject into the pulpit," while "the guilty, if such there be, may be angry." He also knew that "those who ever cry 'Peace, peace,' will doubtfully shake their heads." Yet, Howe said he would speak and persevere (p. 1).
[76]*Ibid.*, p. 2.
[77]*Ibid.*
[78]In this way press and pulpit could support each other.
[79]Quoted in Andrew Nebinger, *Criminal Abortion: Its Extent and Prevention* (Philadelphia: Collins, 1870), p. 25.
[80]Minutes of the General Assembly of the Presbyterian Church in the USA (Northern), Vol. 18 (Philadelphia: Presbyterian Publications Committee, 1869), p. 937.

We also exhort those who have been called to preach the gospel, and all who love purity and truth, and who would avert the just judgement of almighty God from the nation, that they be no longer silent or tolerant of these things, but that they endeavor by all proper means to stay the flood of impurity and cruelty.[81]

That call largely went unanswered, and in 1893 Dr. J. H. Kellogg was still castigating ministers for their silence. "Every pulpit in the land ought to send out in stirring and unmistakable tones, warning against the gross immorality of this practice, drawing vivid pictures of its cruelty and unnaturalness, and pronouncing anathemas upon its perpetrators."[82] Kellogg demanded: "The crime should be considered a just cause for church action to disfellowship. . . ."[83]

The *National Police Gazette* also criticized most ministers for remaining silent: "Would that we might hear some strident tones from the pulpits upon this phase of the evil."[84] When a Mrs. Moorhouse of Brooklyn died during an abortion operation, the *Gazette* lambasted those who had not warned her of "the dangers, physical and moral, inseparable from abortion."[85] Instead of hearing abortion denounced "in words of withering scorn and fiery indignation," the *Gazette* continued, Mrs. Moorhouse had "no doubt heard rose water balderdash" and "cream-cheese platitudes" from those who, on abortion, remained silent lest the namby-pamby sensibilities of fashionable "fops" should be hurt.[86] That perhaps was the best explanation. Dr. Winslow Ayer complained in 1880, "Does the reader ask why we so seldom hear pulpit discourses upon this theme? Has he ever considered that a plain sermon upon it from the sacred desk would strike directly at many professed christian members, and give such mortal offence that the offender would preach to slim audiences ever after, if at all?"[87]

---

[81]*Ibid.*

[82]J. H. Kellogg, *Ladies' Guide in Health and Disease* (Battle Creek, MI: Modern Medicine Publishing Co., 1893), p. 365.

[83]*Ibid.*

[84]*National Police Gazette*, September 28, 1867, p. 2.

[85]*Ibid.*

[86]*Ibid.*

[87]Dr. Winslow Ayer, *The Great Crime of the Nineteenth Century and Perils of Child Life* (Grand Rapids, MI: The Central Publishing Company, 1880), p. 5. However, church magazines and journals also ignored abortion. One researcher, Carol Brooks, found that religious journals such as *Catholic World*, *Baptist Quarterly Review*, and *American Presbyterian Review* did not run articles on abortion during the period she examined, 1870-1885. (See Carol Flora

Author Marion Harland in 1883 offered a similar explanation and quoted a clergyman's wife who upbraided her doctor for refusing to abort her unborn child: "And you, who call yourself a humane man, sworn to do your utmost to alleviate the miseries of the human race, condemn me to months of suffering, to the perils of accouchement and subsequent loss of valuable time rather than crush a contemptible *animalcule*?"[88] She quoted another as ready to murder "her unseen, but *living* child" to promote her career.[89] Harland concluded that "Sharp and severe measures are imperatively indicated for consciences thus diseased and twisted."[90]

But laxity in Protestant churches especially was growing in the late nineteenth century. Many who had embraced spiritist doctrine had rejoined theoretically orthodox churches but had not left all of the doctrines behind. Some ministers had also become more accepting of sin in the name of what soon would be called compassion, as Chapter Eleven will discuss. Some were willing when it came to abortion to live and let die. There was little appetite for exposing wrongdoing when many members and some ministers wanted their own wrongdoing to be let alone. In 1891 Brevard Sinclair could note accurately that, regarding abortion, Americans witnessed "the Church asleep."[91]

With ministers hesitant to criticize, journalists took the lead. The Springfield *Republican*, in an editorial entitled "Child Murder in Massachusetts," attacked "child-murdering" by "respectable physicians."[92] The *Republican*, which had dropped its abortion ads, saw a continuity in life from conception through birth and beyond and criticized "the disposal made of infant life, both before and after birth."[93] It even noted that "the prevention of birth (we refer to the destruction of incipient human life by any of the various means of abortion, medical or surgical) has extended widely among married people." A *Republican* editorial ended with a call for "other newspapers and especially the

Brooks, "The Early History of the Anti-contraceptive laws in Massachusetts and Connecticut," *American Quarterly*, Vol. 18 [Spring 1966], p. 20.)
[88]Marion Harland, *Eve's Daughters* (New York: John R. Anderson & Henry S. Allen, 1883), p. 433.
[89]*Ibid.*, p. 434.
[90]*Ibid.*
[91]Brevard Sinclair, *The Crowning Sin of the Age* (Boston: H. L. Hastings, 1891), p. 16.
[92]Springfield *Republican*, August 21, 1880, p. 4.
[93]*Ibid.*

medical journals [to] bear an honest testimony in the matter, – without fear, favor, malice, or hope of reward."[94]

Other New England newspapers covering abortion incidents included the Boston *Journal*, the Manchester (N.H.) *Union*, and the Boston *Globe*.[95] Elsewhere in the country, the Washington *Post* ran a small story headlined "Funeral of the Murdered Girl," noting that Henrietta Carl was "murdered by abortionist Earll" – but there was no follow-up.[96]

Journalism's contribution to the containment of abortion worked when there was consistent and vivid coverage of abortion, with those involved in the practice publicly named. The New York *Times* manned the barricades in the 1880s, giving front-page coverage to the arrests of Dr. M. E. Smith, Dr. Edward Pynchon, Dr. George Kellogg, and Dr. C. H. Orton.[97] The list continued, physician after physician, in 1880 and 1881: Dr. John Buchanan, Dr. George L. Brook, Dr. Vincent Haight, Dr. William Fayen, Dr. Willoughby, and others.[98] As the titles indicate, most of the abortionists who came under police investigation and press attack were doctors.

The *Times* noted more doctor arrests later in the decade. A story in 1884, "Two Physicians in Trouble," noted that two of the "best known physicians in Providence, R.I." were on trial "for alleged illegal practice."[99] A typical story in 1886, "DOCTOR INDICTED," detailed abortion charges against a well-known New Haven physician, Dr. Gallagher, who had operated on a woman known for "wide acquaintance with the bloods of the town and the Yale students."[100] The *Times* emphasized Gallagher's prominent status and noted that lawyers were surprised to

---

[94]*Ibid.*
[95]See Marvin Olasky, *The Press and Abortion, 1838-1988* (Hillsdale, NJ: Lawrence Erlbaum, 1988) for additional material on coverage.
[96]Washington *Post*, August 28, 1880, p. 1.
[97]*Ibid.*, May 19, 1880, p. 1; July 12, p. 1; December 29, 1882, p. 1; February 22, 1883, p. 1.
[98]*Ibid.*, March 14, 1880, p. 12; January 7, p. 2; May 19, p. 1; January 10, p. 3; August 2, p. 1; March 25, 1881, p. 1; April 6, p. 1; April 30, p. 8.
[99]*Ibid.*, January 5, 1884, p. 2. The complainant was Annie Riley, a single "beautiful blonde," seventeen years of age, who said one of the doctors had "betrayed her" (impregnated her in his medical office) and then sent her to a colleague for an abortion. The reporter wrote that "Miss Riley told her story in court with modesty and an air of truthfulness that carried weight with it." With policemen concealed in a room, she had confronted the two doctors; they had offered her a bribe for silence.
[100]*Ibid.*

see him in court.[101] A similar story about a well-connected doctor noted the abortion arrest of Philadelphia physician David Otway.[102]

The *Times* also seized opportunities to play up human interest stories involving abortion. For example, it reported discovery of the corpse of a five-month-old, recently-killed unborn child floating in a cigar box in the water. Inside the cigar box, alongside the body, were a soap dish and a match box. The body, crushed out of shape, was wrapped in a piece of paper. Detectives, drying the paper and finding a hotel inscription on it, learned that a woman in one of the rooms was very ill. It turned out that the father of the dead child, George Davidson, was a wealthy man married to the daughter of a former New Jersey supreme court judge; he had thought to avoid exposure by paying his family doctor two thousand dollars to perform the abortion. The doctor was summoned to the hotel and arrested. The *Times*, willing to confront wealth and power, gave full coverage to the incident.[103]

The *National Police Gazette* showed anti-abortion commitment matching the *Times*. In 1880, for example, it published an indictment that jumped off the page in headline letters half an inch high: "HORROR! The Astounding Revelations Made by a Denver, Colorado, Physician. THE CURSE OF AMERICAN SOCIETY. The Terrible Sins Which Vanity and Fashion Led Their Devotees to Commit." The *Gazette* attacked those who "kill their offspring secretly without the slightest compunction."[104] An interview of one physician ended with a question, "What is the best means of preventing this great crime?" The doctor was quoted as saying,

> Publicity. Let the people know what is going on around them. There is no remedy for a great social secret sin like exposure. Drag it out into the lurid light of day. Do not cover it up and hide it beneath an assumed modesty so shallow that every eye can peep through it and see the false morality beneath.[105]

---

[101] *Ibid.*, July 8, 1886, p. 2.

[102] *Ibid.*, January 22, 1887, p. 2.

[103] *Ibid.*, September 7, 1882, p. 5. The doctor, Theodore Kinne, claimed the child was stillborn, and he eventually was acquitted for lack of proof that he had actually killed the child through abortion, although that was the husband's intention. September 8, p. 8; September 9, p. 8; September 10, p. 7.

[104] *National Police Gazette*, October 16, 1880, p. 7.

[105] *Ibid.* The doctor added, "Many of the women who practice this enormous crime of foetal murder, move in the best society; are looked upon as christian women, yet in secret

Gazette stories followed that suggestion and featured alliterative headlines such as "BLOOM'S BRUTALITY," concerning Dr. Harris Bloom,
and "THE ABORTIONIST'S ART," concerning the Greensburg,
Indiana, trial of Dr. C. C. Burns.[106] A Dr. Gaylord was featured in a
Massachusetts abortion story, and an article from Kansas noted the arrest
of a Dr. H. J. Bennett.[107] An Iowa story concerned the arrest of a Dr.
Gottschall, an Ohio story that of Dr. J. W. Wright, and a Chicago story
that of a Dr. Cook.[108] After an abortion in Pennsylvania, police were "looking for a physician in good standing, who is charged with the crime."[109]

Both the *Times* and the *Gazette* saw abortion as an opportunity for the
strong to oppress the weak – particularly unborn children, and women
victimized by employers who doubled as seducers. In January 1884 the
Times told on its front page the tale of a wealthy man who seduced the
daughter of a courthouse janitor and took her to Philadelphia for an
abortion.[110] That same month another story, "A Victim of Malpractice,"
told of a young woman impregnated by her employer's son and forced
into an abortion that became fatal to both mother and child.[111] A later
story, "Fannie Briggs' Death," told how "Fannie Briggs was an attractive
girl of 19 years and had been employed in the dry goods store of George
A. Hettrick." Hettrick impregnated her and demanded that she have an
abortion. She did, and she died.[112]

The *Times* also told of Dr. Herman W. Gedicke, a wealthy Newark
resident and former alderman, who was sentenced to two years in prison
for criminal abortion. Evidence that he had paid two thousand dollars
to bribe the jury also came to light, and the *Times* quoted Judge
McCarter's characterization of the conviction as "a most signal triumph
of the law over power and influence."[113] (The *Times* gave only cursory

---

they perpetrate a heinous sin, forgetting that they are seen by one to whom darkness
and light are the same."
[106]*Ibid.*, June 26, 1880, p. 5; December 6, 1879, p. 7.
[107]*Ibid.*, April 10, 1880, p. 3, and January 24, 1880, p. 11.
[108]*Ibid.*, March 13, 1880, p. 11; October 9, p. 10; November 5, p. 11.
[109]*Ibid.*, February 7, 1880, p. 11.
[110]New York *Times*, January 19, 1884, p. 1, and January 24, p. 1; see also January 18,
p. 3.
[111]*Ibid.*, January 28, 1884, p. 8: "Jacob was very intimate with Margaret, and her ruin
and death were the results of this intimacy." She was an "unfortunate girl."
[112]*Ibid.*, March 5, 1887, p. 3; March 8, p. 2; March 12, p. 2; March 15, p. 2. See also "City
Lights and Shadows," April 4, 1884, p. 2.
[113]New York *Times*, November 13, 1880, p. 2; January 4, 1881, p. 8. See also stories on
November 6, 1880, p. 8; November 7, p. 2; November 12, p. 2; November 14, p. 2.

coverage to Gedicke's release from prison after serving only five months of his term.)[114] The *National Police Gazette* also did its best to drag abortionists into day's lurid light.

The abortionist briefly mentioned in the Washington *Post* became, in the *Gazette*, "HELLISH EARLL. A Monster Whom it Would be an Insult to Humanity to Call a Man. A LONG RECORD OF INFAMY. Living on the Lives of Innocent Babes and Heartless Erring Mothers."[115] The *Gazette* called Dr. Earll a "human hyena [who] lives upon the crushed and mangled bodies of tender, breathless infants" and published a vision of the abortionist's final judgment, "when the spirits of all the women and babies he has wronged will rise up in testimony against him."[116]

The *Gazette's* headline on a story concerning a womanizing Cincinnati hospital superintendent was, "PATIENTS DEBAUCHED by the Superintendent and Then Furnished with Means to Produce Abortions."[117] A *Gazette* story from Columbus, Indiana, "Sensational Seduction Suit," told of how "Malinda J. Arnold, aged twenty-one, a poor friendless girl, whose father is dead, brings the suit against William Springer, a prepossessing young man, son of Edward Springer, one of the wealthiest and most influential citizens of this county." According to Malinda, William promised to marry her, and she "submitted to his desires on divers occasions." When she became pregnant, "he refused to make good his promise of marriage, and he procured an abortion on her."[118] Such stories of betrayal and abortion were a recurring *Gazette* motif.[119]

Two sensational abortion stories that appeared in the New York *Times* during the last two decades of the nineteenth century showed that the *Gazette* influence (a bringing-to-life of what John McDowall had called for) had the potential to catch on. In 1883 the *Times* gave top placement

---

[114]*Ibid.*, April 12, 1881, p. 1.

[115]*Ibid.*, September 11, 1880, p. 10.

[116]*Ibid.* See also "Shocking Revelation of Betrayal, Abortion and Death Which Horrified a Quiet New Hampshire Neighborhood," the *Gazette* (October 25, 1879, p. 11) told of how a doctor was charged with murder after performing an abortion on a young woman, for "the child was alive."

[117]*Ibid.*, January 10, 1880, p. 6.

[118]*Ibid.*, November 29, 1879, p. 11.

[119]*National Police Gazette*, February 28, 1882, p. 13; October 25, 1879, p. 11; November 15, 1879, p. 13; January 17, 1880, p. 10; May 15, p. 10; July 17, p. 11; November 6, p. 7; April 9, 1881, p. 11; May 29, p. 14; October 15, p. 7; December 31, p. 12.

on page 1 to the discovery of "TWENTY-ONE MURDERED BABIES" in Philadelphia. The lead noted that "the bodies of 21 infants who had been killed before birth" were found in a house formerly occupied by a Dr. Isaac Hathaway. Details were excruciating:

> Only a few spades of earth had been thrown up when Detective Wolf's implement struck something that made a grating sound. The spade had crushed through slender, threadlike bones, as thin and bleached as paper. . . . A few inches further down another skull and more tiny ribs and leg bones were found.[120]

Front-page coverage of the trial was vivid. Hathaway, eighty-three, "a shabby-looking old man, stooping and weak, attired in a very dirty shirt, and with hair and voluminous beard dyed in raven black," looked on as the district attorney held a cigar box with the bones of the "21 infants. . . . Whenever the box was moved, they rattled like hard withered leaves. There were many bits of skulls among them, some almost complete."[121] Hathaway's wife acknowledged that he had done four hundred to five hundred abortions, burying some bodies in the basement and burning others in a stove.[122] Hathaway was sentenced to seven years at hard labor, which at his age was akin to the death penalty.

The *Times'* abortion story for 1890 vividly covered the activities of an arrested abortionist, Dr. McGonegal, who "has the appearance of a vulture. . . . His sharp eyes glitter from either side of his beaked nose, and cunning and greed are written all over his face."[123] The *Times* reporter described McGonegal's accomplice, Fannie Shaw, as "wholly repulsive in appearance, vice and disease having made her a disgusting object."[124] The reporter journeyed to McGonegal's neighborhood in Harlem to learn

---

[120]*Ibid.*, June 21, 1883, p. 1.

[121]*Ibid.*, June 24, 1883, p. 1; June 28, p. 1.

[122]The single longest *Gazette* story concerning abortion came after the same horror story covered in the New York *Times*, the mass murders by Dr. Isaac Hathaway of Philadelphia. *Gazette* editors, like their counterparts on the *Times*, had a sensational headline: "THE DEMON DOCTOR. Blood Curdling Discoveries in a Philadelphia Physician's Cellar. The Remains of Twenty-one Murdered Infants Unearthed by the Police, and More Horrors Promised." The story described the findings in the cellar: "The men had hardly dug down six inches when they struck the skull of a babe . . . 23 infant craniums and a lot of thread-like bones were turned up by the spade." Neighbors gossiped that Hathaway had kept two dogs in the basement to feast on the corpses of the unborn children.

[123]New York *Times*, July 23, 1890, p. 8.

[124]*Ibid.*

how he was regarded by the people he said he was trying to help. The reporter concluded, "To the good people of Harlem, and especially to the poorer class, this grizzly old physician had long been an object of intense hatred. They were certain of his unholy practices, although he had escaped conviction, and when he drove through the streets in his old-fashioned, ramshackle gig, they hooted and jeered at him in derision."[125]

There were dangers in such reporting, not only to the individuals who were accused but to public understanding of the practice of abortion. Hathaway and McGonegal coverage calls to mind Elizabeth Evans' commentary about the scapegoat usefulness of the quack. Stories about these isolated abortionists might suggest the problem was quackery, but by 1890, in New York and other cities, abortionists were becoming better organized and forming group practices. Newspapers generally ignored this economic rationalization of the abortion business, but the *Times* reported in 1894 the arrest of five physicians and ten midwives arraigned on charges of illegal practice.[126] As during the 1880s, the *Times* reported the arrests and trials of many doctors. Van Ziles, Lee, Thompson, and Kolb were just a few of the physicians' names in the headlines.[127] Doctors' offices, not back alleys, dominated the business.

Had more newspapers followed the lead of the *Gazette* and the *Times* by exposing abortionists "Willing to Prostitute Talent, Education and an Honorable Profession to Step into Restell's Shoes," press containment of abortion would have been even more effective.[128] Had more ministers agreed publicly with the *Gazette's* depiction of abortion as a "crime that stands pre-eminent in the list of human infamies . . . it is the duty of the police to at once institute stringent measures for their [the abortionists] extermination," laws might have become more effec-

---

[125] *Ibid.*, July 24, 1890, p. 2. Also see July 25, p. 8; July 26, p. 2; July 27, p. 13; July 28, p. 8; July 29, p. 8; July 30, p. 8; July 31, p. 8; September 19, p. 8; September 23, p. 8; September 24, p. 9; September 25, p. 3; September 26, p. 2; September 27, p. 8; October 1, p. 8; October 2, p. 9; October 3, p. 3; October 4, p. 1; October 16, p. 9 (reporting McGonegal's sentencing to fourteen years in prison for first degree manslaughter).
[126] *Ibid.*, March 25, 1894, p. 13
[127] *Ibid.*, October 24, 1894, p. 16; December 5, 1894, p. 16; September 28, 1896, pp. 5, 8; October 9, 1896, p. 2. See also March 7, 1896, p. 15; April 9, p. 2; June 12, p. 1; June 30, p. 6.
[128] *National Police Gazette*, May 21, 1878, p. 14. For other examples of vivid reporting during this period, see *Gazette* stories of April 23, 1881, p. 11; June 11, p. 3; September 3, p. 2; October 15, p. 11; September 23, 1882, p. 2; September 30, p. 13; October 28, p. 10; November 18, p. 6; January 27, 1883, p. 3; September 15, pp. 2, 4.

tive.[129] Even so, the coverage as it was evidently kept some doctors from performing abortions, some men from procuring them, some women from undergoing them, and some unborn children from dying by them.

---

[129] *National Police Gazette,* January 3, 1880, p. 2. The *Gazette* complained that officials tacitly "winked at and allowed this practice" to go on uninterrupted until some hideous revelation of infanticide makes action necessary.

8

Means of Containment

As press, clergy, and doctors debated during the last decades of the nineteenth century, more women were moving into the most abortion-susceptible part of the population. More unmarried young women were moving to cities and living apart from immediate family or relatives, often in boardinghouses. The female labor force outside of home would increase from 2.6 million to 10.8 million during the half century from 1880 to 1930. Young women in a big city were exposed to many new ideas about behavior, as were young men, but expectations were different:

> *There was a man, it is said one time,*
> *Who went astray in his youthful prime.*
> *Can the brain keep cool and the heart keep quiet*
> *When the blood is a river that is running riot?*
> *And boys will be boys, the old folks say,*
> *And a man is the better who has had his day.*
> *The sinner reformed and the preacher told*
> *Of the prodigal son who came back to the fold. . . .*
>
> *There was a maiden who went astray,*
> *In the golden dawn of her life's young day.*

She had more passion and heart than head
And she followed blindly where fond love led.
And love unchecked is a dangerous guide
To wander at will by a young girl's side.
The woman repented and turned from sin
But no door opened to let her in.[1]

Some contemporary observers applauded and others decried this "double standard," but about its existence there was no debate.

Given the leniency with which their conduct tended to be regarded, it is not surprising that some men became seducers, disregarded the law, and pushed for abortion when pregnant complications arose. Nor is it surprising that some women without family support joined "urban subcultures in which women gave men sexual 'favors' in return for limited economic support, or even became full-time prostitutes."[2] Procurers often tried to entice attractive young women with offers of high pay and baubles – and if a young woman's goal was merely to maximize her paycheck over the short run, prostitution made great economic sense. A Cincinnati woman could trade a five dollars per week starting factory wage for twenty-five to thirty dollars per week as a prostitute.[3] In 1891 a Chicago bookkeeper could trade her salary of eight dollars per week for "massage parlor" work that paid ten to twelve dollars per week in 1891, plus another twenty dollars in tips for sexual intercourse. A New York observer described the temptation for low-salaried employees.

[T]hey see their working companions enjoying good clothes, good dinners, good seats at the theatre, and they know how easily these good things of life may be obtained; they know nothing of the horrors of venereal diseases and believe it is easy to avoid pregnancy; and finally, they have no strong religious or moral principles to keep chaste, nor do they fear the loss of social standing in their set. Is it then to be wondered at that the tens of thousands of working-girls who belong to this class allow themselves to be seduced by the "gentlemen friend," the smooth-spoken flattering "cadet," who is a human hyena in the clothing of a "gentleman?"[4]

---

[1]Ella Wheeler Wilcox, *Refuge Journal,* September 1886, p. 1.
[2]Joanne J. Meyerowitz, *Women Adrift: Independent Wage Earners in Chicago 1830-1930* (Chicago: University of Chicago Press, 1988), p. xix.
[3]*Ibid.,* p. 34.
[4]George T. Kneeland, *Commercialized Prostitution in New York City* (New York: The Century Co., 1913), p. 247.

Alongside prostitution came seduction. Real-life stories emerge from the "unmarried mother" records of several Boston charitable societies:

• [case 12] This girl met the alleged father of her child, a young man of 19, at the home of a friend. He became interested in her and frequently asked her to go to the motion pictures with him. As she was unable to receive him in her home, they spent their leisure time in the park. Here she had intercourse with him very often. She declared, however, that she had never been to his room or accepted money from him and that she believed him when he promised to marry her if she became pregnant. Instead of doing this, he deserted her as soon as he learned of her condition. There is every indication that this girl was sincerely attached to the father of her child and that she had never been promiscuous. In spite of the fact that she was fully acquainted with the possible results of the sex act, having been warned against such dangers by her mother, she states that she never worried over the chance of her becoming pregnant until it was too late.[5]

• [case 19] This girl had known the father of her child, a young machinist of 25 . . . and had associated with him for three months before allowing him to be sexually intimate with her, finally acquiescing, according to her own story, only after much pleading on his part. She went to his room at a lodging house on two occasions. She insisted that she was infatuated with this man and felt certain that her attachment for him would have increased had he lived up to his responsibility for the child. He deserted her when he learned of her condition, having previously asked her to solicit men on the street, which she refused to do.[6]

• [case 26] She met the father by chance coming home from school, when she accidentally ran into him. After this she happened to see him occasionally, and their casual meetings finally terminated in an intimacy. She knew the father three years and had relationships with him in the woods for a year and a half before the birth of her chid. This girl said, "When I was 13 there came to me an awful longing for someone to love me and kiss me at night. I thought it was a mother's love I wanted, but when this man talked to me I thought that was what I wanted. I had no wish to do wrong but longed to be loved." For some time this man made love to her and represented himself as her truest friend. He told her that because she was an orphan she needed such a friendship. For many

---

[5]Percy G. Kammerer, *The Unmarried Mother* (Boston: Little, Brown, 1918), pp. 114-115.
[6]*Ibid.*, p. 132.

months there was no sexual intimacy between them. Finally he began to ask her questions concerning her menstrual periods and afterwards generally instructed her in sex matters. Following this conversation she frequently had relationships with him and did not learn that he was married until some months later. She declared that she loved and trusted the father of her child.[7]

• [case 37] This girl said she first began to have intercourse with men at 17. She tells this story: A traveling salesman, canvassing for a directory, came to her home about noontime, and her mother invited him to come to lunch. Later she was with him a few times, and she said, "I fell very easily. I seemed to have a blind affection for him." . . . She met the alleged father three years ago, and two weeks after their first meeting had intercourse with him. He called regularly at her aunt's house on Sunday afternoon. When she had known him five months, he told her that he was married. She stated that she had never received money from him and did not go with any other man during this time. Efforts to locate the alleged father were unsuccessful.[8]

Opponents of abortion, in an attempt to fight the tendencies and temptations that such stories revealed, developed several strong campaigns during the closing decades of the nineteenth century.

First came educational work on the demand side, since reformers understood that little could be done to reduce the supply of distressed women as long as the demands of men remained so strong. "We hear much about fallen women, [but] there are more fallen men than women," one journalist noted.[9] Reformers publicized organizations such as the White Cross Society, which called on young men to protect women from degradation and "treat the law of purity as equally binding on men and women."[10] For several years thousands of men signed pledges promising chastity. One magazine, *The Philanthropist*, devoted issue after issue to articles designed to "affirm the unity of the moral law for both sexes" and to tell all "that the practice of impurity is as reprehensible in men as in women."[11] The Women's Christian Temperance Union, which during the late nineteenth and early twentieth centuries was the largest women's

---

[7] *Ibid.*, p. 149.
[8] *Ibid.*, p. 172.
[9] "Fallen Men," *Refuge Journal*, September 1895, p. 8.
[10] *Ibid.*, December 1886, p. 6.
[11] *The Philanthropist*, January 1886, p. 4.

organization in the United States (its membership reached two hundred and forty-five thousand in 1911), also made education of men a top priority.[12]

Abstinence education for males helped contain abortion, but lust still ruled many hearts. At a Chicago Gynecology Society meeting in 1910, three female doctors – Rachell S. Yarros, Effa V. Davis, and Effie Lobdell – were still telling the same old, sad, and true story: If men did not pressure women into sex and then abandon them, far fewer abortions would result.[13] Women needed to withstand the pressure, and the late Victorians became famous (and scorned by some recent historians) for their emphasis on chastity.

Alongside the formation of pledge societies came the amplification of law, with the goal of at least protecting the young. *The Philanthropist* asked legislators "to provide exemplary penalties for seduction, with or without promise of marriage, and for the defilement of the persons of girls, without or with consent, under the age of at least eighteen years"; twenty-one was preferable but beyond reach.[14] *The Philanthropist* regularly complained that "bills raising the age to eighteen have been introduced in both branches of Congress, but days, weeks and months pass, and no action thereon."[15] The drive to raise the "age of consent" – the age at which a girl was "regarded by the law as competent to consent to her own seduction" – turned into a major campaign, as *The Philanthropist* criticized

> the statute book in its present low estate, with its flagrantly unjust discrimination against unprotected girlhood and womanhood. Law is a great educator for good or evil. The present statutes of New York and most of the states make seduction easy and comparatively safe for men. . . . Thus does the State pander to impurity, and expose to ruin those whom it should shield and protect.[16]

In 1894 in Delaware the age of consent was seven years, in nine other states (mostly southern but also Idaho, Minnesota, Colorado and South Dakota) it was ten, in six states it was twelve, and in three others thirteen. Seventeen states fixed the age of consent at fourteen, two at

---

[12]In the 1890s there were five times as many women in the New York WCTU group as in suffrage organizations.

[13]*Journal of Surgery, Gynecology and Obstetrics*, Vol. 10 (1910), p. 548.

[14]*The Philanthropist*, January 1886, p. 4.

[15]*Ibid.*, May 1886, p. 4.

[16]*Ibid.*, July 1886, p. 4.

fifteen, and six at sixteen. Only Florida (age seventeen), Kansas (eighteen) and Wyoming (eighteen) came close to doing the right thing, according to social reformers.

The Philanthropist provided sensational stories concerning the need for a higher age of consent:

> [T]wo little girls thirteen and fourteen years old were discovered in the sleeping apartments of two of the popular beaux of the town. The father of the children – pastor of one of the Plattsburge churches – employed a legal adviser and the case was brought to trial. The men, one 28, the other 30 years old, pleaded consent, and although it was proven conclusively that the little girls were drugged with wine, on that plea the men escaped punishment.[17]

When families were intact, *The Philanthropist* editorialized, legal protection usually was not so vital: "Young girls shielded by good home environments do not, it may be said, need for themselves added legal protection." Life was different, however, for "the orphaned or worse than orphaned, the homeless, penniless working girls. These in large numbers, are continually made the prey of sensual, unscrupulous men, who, if able to plead 'consent,' even on the part of the child who just passed her tenth birthday, may evade legal punishment and multiply their victims with comparative impunity."[18]

The movement to raise the age of consent was partly successful. By 1900 only two states or territories had consent laws below fourteen, and twelve had raised it to eighteen. By the 1920s almost all states specified an age of consent at sixteen or eighteen years of age; men who had intercourse with a woman under that age could be charged with statutory rape. Nearly all laws had statutes permitting punishment for seduction and abandonment of women of any age; generally a man who "obtained access" to a woman "of chaste character or repute" by promising to marry her, and who then failed to do so, could be imprisoned for one to ten years. Most states provided that if the accused married the woman before judgment was passed, legal action was ended; in some states prosecution was merely suspended by the marriage and could be revived if the husband deserted his wife within a specified time, usually three to five years.[19]

---

[17] *Ibid.*, February 1891, p. 5.
[18] *Ibid.*, December 1886, p. 4.
[19] Robert South Barrett, *The Care of the Unmarried Mother* (Alexandria, VA: Florence Crittenton Mission, 1929), p. 84.

Yet, once again the law contained sin but did not abolish it. The Vice Commission of Chicago proposed enforcement of laws against "enticing an unmarried female of chaste life to enter a house of prostitution," or "allowing an unmarried female under eighteen to live in a house of prostitution," or "enticing any female under eighteen to come into the state for immoral purposes," or "abandonment of wife and children," etc.[20] But even when courts were willing to encourage prosecution, the trial itself could be a torment, as defendants normally challenged the prosecuting woman's chastity. "One of the difficulties of securing convictions under laws for the protection of women is that so many women prefer to suffer rather than brave the notoriety and unpleasant experiences which they must endure in court trials," Vice Commission members noted.[21] The typical experience was that of a witness who recalled, "The men looked at each other and smiled at what I said, that was what made me get nervous and jerk so."[22]

Furthermore, when an abandoned young mother was able to bring a successful suit for child support, amounts obtained were almost always inadequate. In Illinois in 1910, if a judge gave a father of the child "the highest sentence the law of the state imposes" – and that was rare – he paid child support of $100 the first year, $50 for each of the next nine years, and nothing afterwards. Reformer Clifford Roe commented, "What a travesty is our justice, sometimes. . . . That father came and went as so many fathers do. . . . He was free of all care for a paltry five hundred and fifty dollars . . . she the victim of the double standard of morals."[23] Lump sums required in other jurisdictions – when a paternity case was won – only covered about three years and four months of a child's age. In Delaware, a father was required to pay ten dollars for confinement expense, ten dollars to the attending physician and between five and twenty-five dollars to the mother or custodian of the child. Florida set a maximum of fifty dollars per year. Maryland put a maximum monthly payment at fifteen dollars a month. And so on.[24] Unwed mothers no longer had the economic safety net that had been present in colonial times. Many observers suggested raising the amounts and increasing

---

[20]Vice Commission of Chicago, *The Social Evil in Chicago* (Chicago: Vice Commission, 1911), p. 227.
[21]*Ibid.*
[22]*Ibid.*, p. 274.
[23]Clifford Griffith Roe, *The Great War on White Slavery* (Chicago: Roe and Steadwell, 1911), p. 66.
[24]Barrett, *The Care of the Unmarried Mother*, p. 71.

enforcement, but the most imaginative proposal came from Dr. Lucy Waite of the Chicago Medical Society:

> Make parentage constitute a legal marriage contract and one of the principal temptations to commit criminal abortion will be abolished. This will protect the life and future good name of the innocent of the three, the child, and will give to the mother an honored position in society and, incidently, the father, also.[25]

Dr. Waite concluded, "So long as motherhood means disgrace to the young woman, just so long will she take all the risks involved in destroying the life of the foetus, and in spite of the church, the state and the profession, she will always find someone ready to perform the nefarious deed."[26]

When attention turned to reducing the *supply* of seduction victims, reformers tried to provide help at the point of greatest vulnerability: they focused on the arrival of a young woman in a large city and her need at that moment for a friend on whom she might rely. The Chicago YWCA formed a Traveler's Aid Committee and hired matrons to meet women newcomers to Chicago as they arrived at railroad stations; so did groups in other cities. YWCA annual reports stressed the importance of such help by describing the "luring" strategies used by both amateur seducers and professional, brothel-employed procurers.[27] The importance of having volunteers meet steamers and trains also came through in typical stories published by *The Philanthropist* concerning life in New York City:

> The Castle Garden authorities have been searching for Mary McGowan, sixteen years old, an immigrant who arrived on the White Star steamer Celtic on May 12, and who disappeared on the same day. She is described as being pretty and well developed for her age.... It is feared by Superintendent Jackson that the girl had fallen into bad hands.[28]

---

[25] Dr. Lucy Waite, Chicago Medical Society Symposium, November 23, 1904, in *Illinois Medical Journal*, Vol. 7 (1904), p. 43. She added, "It may be objected that this law would put some men in the position of bigamists, but we have a law covering bigamy and I think these cases would be very interesting ones to bring before the State's Attorney."

[26] *Ibid.*

[27] See YWCA of Chicago, 21st Annual Report (1897), p. 36, and 28th Annual Report (1904), p. 25. For a fictional description of problems, see Louisa May Alcott, *Work: A Story of Experience* (Boston: Little, Brown, 1900).

[28] *The Philanthropist*, June 1888, p. 4.

Immigrants' Protective Leagues in many cities grew out of similar concerns. "The great majority of young immigrant women" found in brothels, according to the Chicago Vice Commission, "were ruined because there was not adequate protection given them after they reached the United States."[29]

Chicago volunteers seemed particularly thorough in their recording of dangers. Most newcomers came to Chicago by train, but

> because of her ignorance of English a girl may . . . be left at the wrong station or persuaded by some unscrupulous person to get off and see some town en route. . . . The delivery of immigrant women upon their arrival in Chicago also needs supervision. At present they are turned over to private expressmen and cabmen and as a result because of incorrect addresses and the carelessness or vicious intent of the drivers . . . many girls do not find their relatives and friends in Chicago.[30]

Groups such as the YWCA also expressed concern about women who moved to big cities when their husbands abandoned them or refused to continue support. One woman came to Chicago from Wisconsin with a dollar and a half in her purse when her husband "fell in love" with another woman and kicked her out. Another woman came to Chicago in 1888 after a farmer in a nearby community seduced and impregnated her.[31] The YWCA in 1912 sheltered a young woman who arrived in the city at midnight without hat or coat, seeking protection from the assaults of her stepfather.[32]

Young women were warned to watch out for brothel recruiters who might trick and then trap them. Some twenty-eight Girls' Protective Leagues in New York City enrolled twenty-five hundred members who learned the importance of spurning "improper proposals when applying for positions through newspapers and employment agencies."[33] The Leagues published a "blacklist of dangerous places." The difficult task was to teach those at risk to follow Biblical principles or at least to think of long-term prospects rather than immediate satisfaction. After all, few women remained at low-paying, entry-level jobs for long. Most married

---

[29]Vice Commission, *The Social Evil in Chicago*, p. 227.
[30]*Ibid.*
[31]Meyerowitz, *Women Adrift: Independent Wage Earners in Chicago 1830-1930*, p. 16.
[32]*Ibid.*, p. 29.
[33]Maude E. Miner, *Slavery of Prostitution* (New York: Macmillan, 1916), p. 284. Miner also demanded stronger laws against rape and abduction.

women, and one-fifth of Chicago single women over the age of thirty-five, held professional jobs, particularly in teaching. Some who remained single gained a degree of independence by running rooming houses. For example, one woman, named Cora, worked as a stenographer for seven years and a general office worker for three years, then rented two houses, furnished them, and sublet the bedrooms. Another woman, Sara, was a hairdresser and waitress until she rented and ran a rooming house. A third, Ann, worked in factories and as a chamber maid, then bought a rooming house.[34] Those women who did stay in retail work typically tripled their pay after fifteen years.[35]

Teaching a long-range perspective was essential in fighting abortion. A century ago, those contemplating a quick fix were asked to think about adoption instead and then compare their own months of troubles with the years of good life that their children could have. The emphasis in the late nineteenth century was on the placement of children in private homes rather than institutions for long periods. Well-publicized placements were helpful not only to born children but to the unborn, whose mothers could say "no" to abortion without consigning the survivors to miserable lives. Most large cities in the late nineteenth century had private placement agencies modeled after the New York Children's Aid Society, founded and run for decades by Charles Brace. Brace's belief was that "the child, most of all, needs individual care and sympathy. In an Asylum, he is 'Letter B, of Class 3,' or 'No. 2, of Cell 426.'"[36] Brace worked to get the orphaned and abandoned into families as quickly as possible. "As Christian men, we cannot look upon this great multitude of unhappy, deserted, and degraded boys and girls without feeling our responsibility to God for them," he wrote. "We bear in mind that One died for them, even as for the children of the rich and happy."[37]

By the 1870s the record was clear: the New York Children's Aid Society alone was successfully placing close to four thousand children each year. One boy who was helped described his experience after he was sent to a farm in Indiana, where "care was taken that I should be

---

[34]Meyerowitz, *Women Adrift: Independent Wage Earners in Chicago 1830-1930*, p. 42.
[35]Charles P. Neill, *Wage-earning Women in Stores and Factories*, Volume 5 of the Report on Conditions of Women and Child Wage Earners in the United States (Washington, D.C.: Government Printing Office, 1910), p. 37.
[36]See Charles Loring Brace, *The Dangerous Classes of New York and Twenty Years' Work Among Them* (New York: Wynkoop and Hallenbeck, 1880), p. 236.
[37]"First Circular of the Children's Aid Society," in Edith Abbott, ed., *Some American Pioneers in Social Welfare* (Chicago: University of Chicago Press, 1937), pp. 132-134.

occupied there and not in town. In sickness I was ever cared for by prompt attention. In winter I was sent to the Public School. The family room was a good school to me, for there I found the daily papers and a fair library."[38] Those who investigated adoption practices found that "Wherever we went we found the children sitting at the same table with the families, going to the school with the children, and every way treated as well as any other children. Some whom we had seen once in the most extreme misery, we beheld sitting, clothed and clean."[39]

During the closing decades of the nineteenth century, much remained to be done to facilitate adoption. The legal framework for adoption was not clear in every state, and courts only gradually endorsed the rights of adoptive parents to move a child's residence and act in every other way as parents do.[40] But as long as public interest in adoption was high, barriers could be overcome. Harvey Rice, trustee of a Cleveland industrial school, reported that "so rapid is the transfer of the child to homes that very few remained for a year in the institution."[41] A Chicago study of adoption groups such as the Children's Aid Society and the Foundlings' Home concluded, "the children generally remain at the homes but a few weeks, there being more calls for their care and adoption than the supply can meet."[42]

That vision of happily placed children would be appealing to unmarried mothers who could be brought to think in long-range terms. Opponents of abortion also tried to make women aware of not just the physical but also the psychological effects of abortion on the mother. In an astounding book published in 1875, Elizabeth Evans described the effects of abortions on women who had them years before, during the heady mid-century days of "free love." One woman, she reported, in *The Abuse of Maternity*, "has mourned for many years the sin committed in her youth."[43] Another told Evans that she once had enjoyed "the contemplation and care of infants," but was now "wild with regret at my folly

---

[38]Quoted in Brace, *The Dangerous Classes of New York*, p. 261.

[39]For more details, see Marvin Olasky, *The Tragedy of American Compassion* (Wheaton, IL: Crossway Books, 1992), Chapter Two.

[40]See Michael Grossberg's very useful history, *Governing the Hearth: Law and the Family in Nineteenth-Century America* (Chapel Hill: University of North Carolina Press, 1965), particularly pp. 271-280.

[41]*Ibid.*, p. 279.

[42]John Moses and Joseph Kirkland, *History of Chicago*, Vol. 2 (Chicago: Munsell & Co., 1895), pp. 390-391.

[43]Elizabeth Edson Gibson Evans, *The Abuse of Maternity* (Philadelphia: Lippincott, 1875), p. 31.

in rejecting the (alas! only once-proffered) gift of offspring."[44] A third said, "I recognized my real condition as a criminal, none the less because undetected and unpunished. [The memory] serves as an effectual damper upon whatever degree of pride or satisfaction I might otherwise feel in the more praiseworthy deeds of my career."[45]

For some, the agony did not go away. One sufferer from what is today called "post-abortion syndrome" told Evans, "From the moment when I began to appreciate my irreparable loss, my thoughts were filled with imaginings as to what might have been the worth of that child's individuality; and especially, after sufficient time had elapsed to have brought him to maturity, did I busy myself with picturing the responsible posts he might have filled, the honors he might have won, the joy and comfort he might have brought to his suffering fellow-creatures; nor, during the interval, have I ever read of an accident by land or by water, or of a critical moment in a battle, or of a good cause lost through lack of a brave defender, but my heart has whispered, 'He might have been there to help and save; he might have been able to lead that forlorn hope; his word or his deed might have brought that wise plan to successful issue!'"[46]

Another sufferer recalled, "I was for a long time as near being insane as one can be without really going mad. . . . I had an idea that I had lost, through that unnatural deed, the normal powers and qualities of a human being. I no longer ate and drank with the old hunger and thirst, nor slept the quiet sleep of innocence; I took no heed of the passage of time, and all that I saw and heard seemed to be the occurrences of a dream, as though life was already finished for me." After a time she "recovered sufficient energy to interest myself [in work, but] the strange feeling of having set myself apart from the rest of my sex, through that sin against my motherhood, will probably always remain to increase the bitterness of my childless and lonely condition."[47]

A third sufferer told Evans, "I envy a mother who goes to weep beside her baby's grave; because she knows where it is laid, and remembers how it looked in life, and is not ashamed to say, 'I have lost a child.' And when I hear mothers lamenting over such a loss, I pity them indeed; but I feel like saying to them, 'You think you are deeply afflicted, but your

---

[44] *Ibid.*, p. 38.
[45] *Ibid.*, p. 67.
[46] *Ibid.*, p. 60.
[47] *Ibid.*, p. 70.

trouble is really light, because it is not mingled with remorse, and you are not to blame for the infant's death.' Truly, all sorrow that I have ever known or heard of is not to be compared with my sorrow, and that of others who have sinned in like manner!"[48]

Her interviews led Evans to conclude, "The enormity of the crime of foeticide may be, in some degree, estimated by the excessive remorse which, sooner or later, is sure to follow its perpetration . . . think what must be the anguish of a mother who . . . sees before her eyes the unfinished wreck of a being whom, a few months later, she would have pressed to her bosom with a tenderness which no other object has power to awaken!" Since there is "grief for the loss of an infant at birth," Evans noted, "how much more terrible, then, must be . . . the keen pangs of a speedily-awakened remorse!"[49]

Nineteenth-century post-abortion syndrome was known to physicians who dealt with "chronic female diseases" and saw the result of "intentional abortion and its attendant remorse in causing nervous maladies. . . ."[50] As Evans and others gathered information on the impact of abortion on women, they also learned more about the causes of the abortion increase of the 1850s. Clearly, the popular medical literature had an impact. One woman who aborted later told Evans, "At the time when I fell a victim to the temptation . . . all the newly-married women of the neighborhood were discussing the ideas derived from certain pamphlets of the 'Medical Companion' order, that had recently been circulated in that region. These women were unanimous in desiring to postpone pregnancy; and I have reason to think that several besides myself took measures to stop its progress after it had begun."[51] Still influential, another woman said, was "the opinion prevalent among my sex that the foetus has no life until it has quickened. . . ."[52]

Evans concluded that "reckless quacks make of the United States mail an agent to carry desolation and death into thousands of widely-scattered families through the dissemination of pamphlets bearing alluring titles, such as 'The Private Medical Companion, 'Secret Physiology,' 'Advice to the Married,' etc., —all of them written with outward decency and in apparent good faith, but all really devoted to the vile object of enriching

---

48 *Ibid.*, p. 71.
49 *Ibid.*, pp. 64-65.
50 *Ibid.*, p. 70.
51 *Ibid.*, p. 66.
52 *Ibid.*, p. 58.

their authors or proprietors through the sins and sufferings of their victims."[53] The idea of inherited non-genetic characteristics, popular at the time, also had consequences. Evans listed some common self-justifications for abortion: "The anxieties caused by insufficient means, and by her unwillingness to become a mother, must react unfavorably upon the disposition of the child; very likely it would be an idiot, or hopelessly perverted in temper . . . there is, as yet, no 'life' in the embryo, and so the strictest moralist could not call its intentional destruction murder."[54]

Elizabeth Evans noted that "in all ages, and among all races and classes," abortion was most likely "where an illegitimate birth is in question."[55] For some married women also, however, "the absence of a visible object prevented a full realization of the nature of the wrong. . . ."[56] It was still common to believe that "prior to 'quickening,' the child in the womb has no 'life,' and may be separated from the parent-body like any inconvenient or hurtful excruscence."[57] Deep down, aborting women knew the truth: "The question naturally arises here, Do not women know that they are doing wrong when they intentionally destroy the fruit of the womb? Yes, they know it, [but often] its character is not rightly understood before its committal, while the remorse that follows is proportionately severe and unappeasable."[58]

The charge to knowledgeable doctors was clear: "now, medical authorities everywhere recognize the fact that life belongs to each human germ with the instant of conception, and law everywhere professes to consider abortion as murder; although the general public is still misled, through the promulgation by unprincipled charlatans of false and obsolete theories. . . ."[59] Tendencies toward theological antinomianism also had to be fought. Evans noted that some "Christian" preachers were saying that sin did not really matter, since all were forgiven in Christ. The natural tendency was to twist doctrine in order to baptize sinful desires. Evans wrote, "The apparent insincerity of this argument is removed when one remembers how the real nature of evil is hidden, or rather, transfigured, through the presence of temptation."[60]

---

[53] *Ibid.*, p. 24.
[54] *Ibid.*, p. 55.
[55] *Ibid.*, p. 13.
[56] *Ibid.*, pp. 13-14.
[57] *Ibid.*, pp. 13-14.
[58] *Ibid.*, p. 52.
[59] *Ibid.*, p. 16.
[60] *Ibid.*, p. 54.

Nevertheless, belief in forgiveness, but only following repentant commitment to change, was essential in the relief of post-abortion syndrome. Evans told of one woman who recalled that following an abortion "I was almost insane with unavailing sorrow," until a friendly counselor told her that her change of heart meant the abortion was not "decisive as to its power to blast my future career. This true woman, true wife, true mother, true friend, saved me from myself. . . ."[61]

Another major cause of abortion was pressure from men who wished to evade their responsibilities. Evans saw "few instances of women committing foeticide where the men most concerned are not at least consenting unto the premature death."[62] She reported "repulsive accounts of husbands or lovers urging, and even commanding, their partners to commit the deed."[63] By the end of the century this intense, short-term pressure was appearing more and more often. The Boston charitable groups recorded some of the results:

• [Case 31] For the last five years she had been intimate with the proprietor of the hotel where she worked. . . . This woman maintained that the alleged father had never paid her money, but had given her expensive presents. When she found that she was pregnant, he gave her money to come to the city for an abortion. She was persistent in her idea to have an abortion, and very reluctantly gave her consent and made plans for her confinement. She admitted that it would be very difficult to break off her intimacy with the father. When interviewed at this hotel, he was very nervous and resented the fact that she had told her story to any one. He was an American man of about 40 and had formerly been a sea captain. He was well known and respected in the community and conducted a prosperous hotel. He was very much afraid that his wife would learn of the affair, and maintained that she and the woman in question were good friends. He said that she did not suspect the relationship, because they had been very careful and had met at another hotel in the city. . . . He admitted intercourse with this woman over a long period of time, but indicated that he had never spent the entire night with her. He called her a promiscuous woman and said that he knew that at one time she had been sexually intimate with three men. He was willing, however, to pay her expenses but would assume no responsibility for the child and urged an abortion. . . . This history was unexpectedly brought to a close when

---

[61] *Ibid.*, p. 52.
[62] *Ibid.*, p. 61.
[63] *Ibid.*

she wrote to the society, stating that she had succeeded in having an abortion performed in her own city.[64]

• [case 34] This girl met the father of her child some three years before its birth, and says that she would have married him had he asked her to. He showed her some attention, taking her to the movies, but she did not become intimate with him until a year before the birth of her child, at which time she began to have sexual relations with him. She claims that he forced her the first time, and had persuaded her on three other occasions to go with him to a hotel, as a result of which she became pregnant. When she told him of her condition . . . he gave her some medicine to produce a miscarriage. This proving unsuccessful, she sought to have an abortion performed by a physician. . . .[65]

Not all unmarried women needed the pull of a seducer to lead them into potential pregnancy and abortion. In 1899 a fifteen-year-old said she left her home in Savannah, Illinois, because "a girl who used to live there . . . induced her to come back with her to Chicago and 'live off the men.'"[66] One eighteen-year-old came to Chicago from Michigan "because she could not have the clothes that she wanted." Another said she wanted more money for clothes than "my mother would give me," and because "When I wanted to be out later they wouldn't stand for that so I left home." Often such individuals ended up complaining about what men did to them:

Teresa Joahn came to Chicago about three months ago to work as a nurse on the North side. On July 1, she meet H.H. at Wilson Avenue beach. He got her to leave that night at 10 p.m. and took her to the Pierce hotel where they took a room as man and wife. He stayed with her that night and part of Sunday. During the next four days he called to see her several times and said he had a lot of business outside. . . . Saturday night he paid the hotel bill and they both left. He took her to the boat landing at the foot of Clarke Street and told her they would take the night boat to Michigan. He left in a few minutes to go and see his doctor and never came back. She thinks that he is a traveling man, but doesn't know his business or the company he works for.[67]

---

[64]Kammerer, *The Unmarried Mother*, pp. 161-162.
[65]*Ibid.*, pp. 166-167.
[66]Meyerowitz, *Women Adrift: Independent Wage Earners in Chicago 1830-1930*, p. 18.
[67]Walter C. Reckless, *Vice in Chicago* (Chicago: University of Chicago Press, 1933), p. 51.

Teresa Joahn properly blamed H.H., but she also needed to look at her own conduct. She had to learn to think of the long run and not only immediate gratification.

The short term reigned supreme, particularly in the thinking of many who became prostitutes. As journalist W. T. Stead wrote, some women with "youth, health and good looks" went to Carrie Watson, a leading Chicago madam,

> as men go to the gambling hall. . . . The misfortune of it is, that women can almost always secure their stakes at first whereas the gambler often as not is deterred by an initial failure. Few people realize that a young and pretty woman can make more money for a short time by what may be called a discriminate sale of her person than the ablest women in America can make at the same age in any profession.[68]

One generally reliable observer estimated that there were forty thousand prostitutes in New York in 1893, ten to twenty thousand in Chicago and Philadelphia, and so on. Prostitutes only survived in the trade for four years on the average, as disease, beatings, alcoholism, drugs, and abortion took their toll.[69]

Reformers often saw abortion advertising as an incitement to the quick fix, and one of their means of containing abortion was a crackdown on advertising. They felt that if abortions were not so easily and immediately attainable, second thoughts would emerge. As early as 1845 opponents of abortion expressed anger that abortion ads "without the slightest scruple" were calling for the "prodigal destruction of

---

A later report read, "Teresa Joahn is now working in a ice cream parlor on South Halsted Street, and she complains October 9, 1912 that the cook, put his hand on her breast, and said she was stuffed with newspapers and he would have five boys meet her tonight."

[68] William T. Stead, *If Christ Came to Chicago* (Chicago: Saird and Lee, 1894), p. 250. "The relations between the spoiling houses and the police on their beats is intimate, not to say friendly," Stead wrote. "The houses are at the absolute mercy of the officer, who can ruin their business by simply keeping it under constant observation. . . . The Keeper of the house, if she is to live and thrive, must make friends with the policemen, and there is usually not the least difficulty in doing so. Tariffs vary in Fourth Avenue as in Washington, but one Madam had succeeded in securing virtual protection on a blackmail scale of $2.50 per officer per week with free drinks, and occasional meals . . . 'police protection' cost the house $15.00 a week or $750.00 a year." Steed also reported "further fees levied by superior officers, fines, money paid to bailsmen, and other incidental expenses . . ."(p. 43).

[69] C. E. Rogers, *Secret Sins of Society* (Minneapolis: Union Publishing Co., 1881), p. 76.

human life."[70] Members of the Massachusetts House of Representatives saw advertising as crucial to the apparent increase in abortion, and in 1847 passed a bill prohibiting advertisements for "any place, house, shop or office where any poison, drug, mixture, preparation, medicine or noxious thing, or any instrument or means whatever" was used "for the purpose of causing or procuring the miscarriage of a woman pregnant with child."[71] The Massachusetts Senate balked at censorship of newspapers and added such large loopholes that a printing press could pass through them without difficulty.[72] Other states followed with generally ineffective bans.

In 1868 the New York Legislature tried to work on the demand side by passing an act that included a provision curtailing the spread of information concerning "where, how, or of whom, or by what means" abortifacients might be obtained.[73] Attacks on "advertising murder" increasingly hit home. By 1873 the idea of stopping abortion by restricting its sales pitches had crossed to the Pacific, as the California legislature passed a law stating that "Every person who willfully writes, composes or publishes any notice or advertisement of any medicine or means for producing or facilitating a miscarriage or abortion . . . is guilty of a felony."[74]

Those anti-advertising efforts had political success, but abortionists who used minimally veiled language could evade penalty as long as doctors, editors, or local governmental authorities did not pin them down by answering the ads, requesting abortions, and then prosecuting. However, during the 1870s one man, Anthony Comstock, became famous for his successful investigations. Comstock, born in 1844, worked as a salesman in New York following the Civil War. But when a friend went from pornography to prostitution and became diseased, Comstock successfully worked to have the pornography-seller arrested. For a time Comstock battled against pornography as an amateur, but he gained attention after he brought along on an investigating trip a New York *Tribune* reporter.

In 1872 wealthy banker Morris K. Jessup gave Comstock the fund-

---

[70]*National Police Gazette*, November 15, 1845, p. 100.
[71]James Mohr, *Abortion in America* (New York: Oxford University Press, 1978), p. 130.
[72]*Ibid.*, p. 132.
[73]Law of April 28, 1868, chapter 430, [1868], New York Laws.
[74]"Advertising to Produce Miscarriage," *The Penal Code of the State of California* (San Francisco: Bancroft-Whitney Co, 1915), section 317. See judicial narrowing of statute in *People v. McKean*, 243 Pac. R 898.

ing to develop an organized campaign, and Comstock headed to Washington in 1873, at a time when bills to expand federal power were receiving ready passage. On March 3, 1873, the 42nd Congress in one of its last spasms passed an act that banned use of the nation's mails to circulate obscene materials.[75] Comstock was appointed Special Agent of the Post Office Department to enforce that law, which became controversial because it unwisely included contraceptive information and devices on its forbidden list. As John Noonan wrote, "In penalizing the possession of contraceptives, Congress went further than any Pope or Canonist."[76]

Comstock followed up that victory with the establishment, in May 1873, of the New York Society for the Suppression of Vice, and in June with passage of a New York state law which defined abortifacients as immoral and indecent and prohibited their sale. Comstock then took direct action, often going undercover into abortion businesses and trapping abortionists at the point of sale. His report of activities for 1873 emphasized the theme of ill-gotten gains and huge profits. One arrested abortionist had a fortune of four hundred thousand dollars, a second registered a twenty-five thousand dollar profit annually, and a third wore a dress valued at over one thousand dollars to her arraignment.[77]

Comstock and his supporters succeeded in sending abortionists into hiding, for a while. One report in 1876 examined

> that class of men who advertise themselves as doctors to treat female diseases. . . . They are usually, if not always, abortionists, and ply their trade with reckless disregard of human life. Forty-nine professional abortionists have been arrested by this society, of whom thirty-nine have been convicted and sentenced, but this is not a tithe of those practicing intentional infanticide.[78]

---

[75]For many years after that law's enactment there was dispute about how it came to be passed, but few disputed its enormous breadth and depth. The greased legislative history of the Comstock Act, as it came to be called, is astounding; for interesting reading see the *Congressional Globe*, 42nd. Cong., 3rd. Sess., II (Washington, 1873), pp. 1240, 1307, 1436-37, 1525-26, 1571, and 2004-05.

[76]John T. Noonan, Jr., *Contraception* (Cambridge, MA: Harvard University Press, 1986 edition), p. 412.

[77]See New York Society for the Suppression of Vice, *Annual Report for 1873*, and Anthony Comstock, *Frauds Exposed* (New York: J. Howard Brown, 1880).

[78]Second Annual Report of the New York Society for the Suppression of Vice, New York, January 27, 1876, p. 8.

Three years later the New York Society rejoiced that "Among notable cases disposed of the past year is that of the closing effectually of the gilded hall of death on Fifth Avenue, kept by Ann Lohman, better known as Madame Restell." Concerning her suicide the society noted, "It is a cause for profound thanksgiving that this city is rid of the disgrace of this woman and her murderous business. . . ."[79]

After Madame Restell's death, however, Comstock did not persevere in the abortion battle. A book he published and amply publicized in 1883, *Traps for the Young*, emphasized pornography and mentioned abortion only in passing, following a discussion of masturbation. "Along this same line come the ante-natal murderers," Comstock wrote. "More than sixty of these wretches have been arrested and imprisoned or fined, through the efforts of the New York Society for the Suppression of Vice. The business now is carried on secretly."[80] But as Comstock's attention turned to other areas, abortionist advertising appeared once more. Organizations similar to Comstock's were organized in other parts of the country, but they also spent their time fighting contraception and gambling. Meanwhile, in the New Orleans *Picayune*, abortionist Dr. E. Berjot and many others like him regularly offered "rooms for confinement and operation; strictly confidential."[81] Ads for abortifacients such as French tansy wafers appeared across the country.[82]

The San Francisco *Examiner* during the 1880s and 1890s, despite California law, ran an average of nine abortion ads daily, with about eight lines per ad. In 1889 Mrs. Dr. Strassmen was writing that "All Female Monthly Irregularities are restored, from whatever cause, by my genuine remedies; real process, without medicine, never fails to regulate in one

---

[79]Fifth Annual Report, New York, 1879, p. 13.

[80]Anthony Comstock, *Traps for the Young* (New York: Funk & Wagnalls, 1883), p. 154.

[81]New Orleans *Picayune*, September 30, 1887, p. 5. See also ads from Bille, Perez, etc., July 10, 1888, p. 3; July 13, 1890, p. 5; September 4, 1891, p. 6, etc. New Orleans towards the close of the nineteenth century became the abortion depot of the South. With railroad competition increasing the number of trains and routes while decreasing ticket prices, it was not hard for a woman to go to a place where she was not known. Newspaper ads frequently proclaimed the willingness of abortionists to treat out-of-town patients and even provide lodging for them if requested. One New Orleans abortionist, Dr. Mason, even advertised in the Houston *Post* (December 7, 1891, p. 6).

[82]*Ibid.*, August 16, 1897, p. 5; August 17, 1897, p. 3. For additional detail, see Marvin Olasky, *The Press and Abortion* (Hillsdale, NJ: Lawrence Erlbaum, 1988), Chapters Four and Five.

day."[83] In 1890 Dr. E. Vice advertised a "process" by which "monthly periods [are] restored in one or two days without medicine."[84] Others offered an "INFALLIBLE REMEDY FOR IRREGULARITY" or the "only safe and sure cure for all female troubles."[85] Mrs. Dr. Gwyer in 1893 advertised "A sure, safe and speedy cure for all monthly irregularities (from whatever cause)." She promised "consultation free and confidential" and suggested a willingness to do what some other physicians (probably male) might refuse to do: "All ladies that are in trouble, sick and discouraged should call on the Doctor and state their case. They will find her to be a true friend to her sex."[86] Other ads also appealed to "All ladies wanting instant relief for monthly irregularities, from whatever cause," and some directly proposed what today is called a first trimester abortion: "ARE YOU WORRIED AND NERVOUS? Are you troubled because your periods are irregular? If you have not neglected attending to them over three months you can speedily be relieved without the least danger or inconvenience . . . Dr. J. V. La MOTTE."[87]

Amidst the abortion ads, small ones of a different character could be found: "Women who have fallen and wish to reform can find a Christian home and friends by addressing Rev. J. W. Ellsworth, 1014 Washington street."[88] But abortion advertisers promised their own brand of compassion: "We will see you through your business, no matter what the cause; no bad after effect."[89] Fast service was available from an abortionist who "Restores monthly periods from any cause in one day."[90] Egalitarian service was available: "ALL LADIES SHOULD CONSULT MRS. DR. LA PHAME: relief at once to those who are in trouble; have arranged my home to suit rich and poor; business strictly confidential."[91] Service in the middle of the night was available from "DR. ANTHAN, THE RELIABLE PHYSICIAN! All ladies assured quick relief of suppression any time or cause."[92] Newspapers in Chicago, St. Louis, and so on ran similar ads.[93]

---

[83]San Francisco *Examiner,* January 13, 1889, p. 7.
[84]*Ibid.,* January 1, 1890, p. 8.
[85]*Ibid.*
[86]*Ibid.,* March 24, 1893, p. 10.
[87]*Ibid.*
[88]*Ibid.,* January 1, 1890, p. 10.
[89]*Ibid.,* July 29, 1898, p. 8.
[90]*Ibid.,* November 1, 1894, p. 10.
[91]*Ibid.*
[92]*Ibid.,* November 1, 1894, p. 10.
[93]J. H. Kellogg, *Ladies' Guide in Health and Disease* (Battle Creek, MI: Modern Medicine Publishing Co., 1893), p. 345 summarized the situation well:

Clearly, the 1890s was a period of containment, not abolition – and even containment depended on sporadic drives to investigate and harass abortionists. In 1904 the Philadelphia County Medical Society commissioned an investigation of abortion ads in newspapers that led to a stoppage of advertising and the jailing of at least a dozen abortionists.[94] Philadelphia physicians worked on both the supply and demand sides by preparing tighter supervision of both physicians and midwives (with removal of licenses from abortionists) as well as elimination of newspaper advertising by abortionists. The St. Louis Medical Society hired an attorney to prosecute advertisers and brought a successful case against one Dr. Nathaniel King. The *Journal of the American Medical Association* reported that "the space usually devoted to these advertisements in the public press has been gradually reduced until now it is 50 per cent less in amount than was formerly the case."[95]

One of the most thorough campaigns was spearheaded by Dr. Rudolph Holmes, a Chicago physician who decided shortly after the turn of the century that books and articles by individual doctors were no longer enough and that resolutions by medical societies were too easy to ignore. With Holmes' urging, the Chicago Medical Society established on November 23, 1904 a Committee on Criminal Abortion.[96] Holmes, who became chairman of the committee, pushed the committee to agree that the best approach lay in "influencing the daily press to discontinue criminal advertisements or inducing them to edit the most flagrant violators."[97]

The newspapers still contain numerous advertisements which the initiated well understand. For almost any sum from $500 down to the paltry sum of $10 these fiends in human shape, the thugs of civilized lands, are ready at any time to undertake the destruction of a human being without the slightest compunction of conscience and with little danger of detection, so imperfect are the laws relating to the crime and so difficult the task of obtaining evidence sufficient to convict the criminal. The fact that jurymen as well as judges and attorneys are not infrequently indebted to the criminal for similar services, also has an important bearing on the results of the case in numerous instances. The impossibility of obtaining a conviction for the crime of abortion, no matter what may be the character of the evidence, is so notorious that persons who are well known as professional abortionists are allowed to ply their horrible trade year after year without being molested.

94Cattell, p. 339.
95*Journal of the American Medical Association*, Vol. 46 (April 28, 1906), p. 1309.
96Minutes of the Chicago Medical Society, Vol. 16, 1903-1904. The committee was established at a special "Symposium on Criminal Abortion" at which several doctors, including Rudolph W. Holmes, read papers about abortion; Holmes' was entitled "A Brief Consideration of Criminal Abortion in Its Relation to Newspaper Advertising."
97*Ibid.* A copy of the minutes is kept at the Chicago Historical Society.

Holmes and his committee members visited James Keely, managing editor of the *Tribune*. They did not ask Keely merely to remove abortion ads from his newspaper; they knew that thinly veiled ads would soon reemerge. Instead, they demanded that Keely accept no medical ads, and Keely agreed. As Holmes reported the victory, Keely "ordered that no more medical advertisements should be accepted by his paper after July 1, 1905, whose purpose was to attract women exclusively or which had the expressed purpose of treating female irregularities or female ailments."[98]

The next step, according to Holmes, was "to influence other papers to follow the lead of the *Tribune*." The committee "visited all the daily papers of Chicago" and told editors they had to give up abortion advertising in any form or face public attack and eventual prosecution by the Medical Society. "Four other papers joined us by agreeing to refuse all advertisements of a criminal nature," Holmes reported, even though "one of the papers lost $50,000 a year by so doing." But four other editors held out: "Two papers announced they always had carefully supervised their advertising columns and for years had accepted no such notices as we described; when we sent them clippings from their papers no comment was forthcoming on their part. The representatives of the two remaining papers heaped upon us the most vituperative insults."[99]

To rope in the recalcitrants, the medical society hired a detective agency. The detectives were to gain proof that the advertisers under question did perform abortions, so that public pressure and sections of legislation could be brought to bear. According to Holmes, "a detective appealed to each advertiser for the purpose of having an abortion produced on herself or on a friend. With two exceptions, all the parties visited either agreed to perform the necessary operation, or to sell a medicine which would correct the female irregularity." The Medical Society confronted the newspapers with that evidence and also informed postal authorities, who issued a "stop order" against mail delivery of the publications that contained abortion ads.[100]

A check of the Chicago press showed that Holmes' strategy worked. For example, a typical issue of the Chicago *Tribune* in March 1905 contained seventeen abortion ads promising to take care of "all difficult female complaints" or "all diseases and complications peculiar to

---

98 *Ibid.*
99 *Ibid.*
100 *Ibid.*

women."[101] By the end of the year, however, there were no noticeable ads for abortionists in the Chicago *Tribune*, and most other newspapers also had emptied their columns of such "medical help."

Similar pressure was applied in other cities, with generally similar results. But Holmes was experienced enough to know that nothing was "permanent" in the abortion wars. He told the Chicago Medical Society, "Now that the advertisements are removed the work of the Committee in the future will be to see that they are kept out; in the course of time they undoubtedly will reappear in a new guise. . . ."[102] For Holmes, the price of freedom from abortion was eternal vigilance.

---

[101]Chicago *Tribune*, March 1, 1905, p. 13.
[102]Minutes of the Chicago Medical Society, Vol. 17, October, 1905 – June 1907.

9

Compassion Coming of Age

Soon after the Civil War's end, one journalist wrote of the charge of the abortion brigade: "Restellism to the right of us — Restellism to the left of us — Restellism in front of us— everywhere meet us. . . . Restellism has become the great crime of our day."[1] One speaker at an American Association of Spiritualists convention presented the accusation, "Murder, red-handed murder, is so popular in Chicago to-day that you cannot go on the principal streets without seeing the signs hanging out by the dozen of scoundrels in the shape of men who stand ready to commit the murder of an unborn innocent for $5 and upward."[2] In the 1870s feminist Elizabeth Evans reported that

> there is scarcely a city or large town throughout the length and breadth of the land but has its druggists' recommendations of Female Pills [designed] to carry desolation and death into thousands of widely-scattered families. . . .[3]

Given abortion's growth during the second third of the nineteenth

---

[1]"Restellism the Crime of This Age," *The Revolution*, Vol. 18 (May 1868), p. 279.
[2]*Proceedings of the Tenth Annual Convention of the American Association of Spiritualists* (1873), p. 71, in Houdini Collection, Rare Book Room, Library of Congress.
[3]Elizabeth Evans, *The Abuse of Maternity* (Philadelphia: Lippincott, 1875), p. 23.

century, users of crystal balls could well predict boom times for the abortion trade during the last third. By 1900, however, Restell was long gone, and Restellism, while still strong, was no longer right, left, and everywhere – it had been at least partially contained. Physicians such as James Scott noted the general view that, regarding abortion, "these times are not so impure" as the previous era had been.[4] Even James Mohr has acknowledged that "Between 1880 and 1900 the practice apparently declined in proportion to the total population from what it had been between 1840 and 1880. . . ."[5]

Containment of abortion was aided by technological change. The vulcanization of rubber at mid-century led to development of mass-produced contraceptives that gave prostitutes an edge in their attempts to avoid conception. While the new rubber pessaries were far from pregnancy-proof, when used effectively they could keep out stray semen as the sponge-on-a-string could not. Theological changes also helped, as spiritism faded. Exposure of abortionists and the grab-bag of containment measures discussed in the last chapter also played a part. Nevertheless, the number of women at risk remained high, and had there not been a growth of compassion toward those seduced and prostituted, it seems likely that abortion incidence would have increased.

The extension of compassion may have begun with the Civil War. Not only did bloodshed have the impact on male doctors that we have discussed, but it also affected women who had volunteered as nurses. In 1867, when minister and popular author John Todd argued in *Woman's Rights* that women belonged almost exclusively in the home, he was answered emphatically by Mary Abigail Dodge's *Woman's Wrongs*.[6] She asked, "Were the thousands upon thousands of women who worked in the ranks of this great army of healers exceptions?"[7] The war experience, she wrote, taught that for "the ideal woman . . . all the children of want, – bodily, mental, moral want, the infant of days or the man bowed with age, – all are children whom the Lord has given her. . . ."[8] Those children of want included illegitimate children and their disgraced mothers, as

---

[4]James Scott, "Criminal Abortion," *American Journal of Obstetrics and Diseases of Women and Children,* Vol. 33 (1896), p. 72.
[5]James Mohr, *Abortion in America* (New York: Oxford University Press, 1978), p. 240.
[6]Rev. John Todd, *Woman's Rights* (Boston: Lee and Shepard, 1867); Mary Abigail Dodge, *Woman's Wrongs* (Boston: Ticknor and Fields, 1868).
[7]Dodge, *Woman's Wrongs*, p. 197.
[8]*Ibid.*, p. 210.

compassion – personal care and challenge, not just the offering of money – began to be extended in the manner McDowall had desired.

That extension becomes apparent if we examine the range of urban charitable activities at the end of the century. By 1895 Chicago had a dozen shelters for the pregnant and unmarried, including the Erring Woman's Refuge, the Florence Crittenton Anchorage Mission, the Life and Hope Mission, the Salvation Army Rescue Home No. 568, the Rescue Mission, Beulah House, the Jewish Home for Girls, and the Boynton Refuge Home.[9] The Home for the Friendless alone cared for 1,291 adults and 1,361 children in 1893, including 1,741 Protestants, 811 Catholics, and 97 Jews. Other cities showed a similar pattern. In Minneapolis, Bethany Home, the Florence Crittenton Home, and the Norwegian Home of Shelter were active; city investigators reported that "[i]n each institution the girls are placed under wholesome moral influences and given practical and industrial training. In each the religious motive is emphasized . . . but in each, girls of all faiths and none are received without discrimination."[10] In Philadelphia, officials applauded the "numerous agencies throughout the city whose object is the rescue and reformation of fallen women. . . ."[11] In San Francisco, Donaldina Cameron's Presbyterian Mission Home became a beacon.

The greatest center of trouble and help, as could be expected, was New York City. Some agencies worked toward prevention of unmarried pregnancy by providing group lodging and affiliation for young women who would otherwise be alone and vulnerable. Among these were the National League on Urban Conditions Among Negroes, the Association for Befriending Children and Young Girls, the Free Home for Young Girls, the New Shelter for Young Women, and so forth. Unmarried pregnant women were offered lodging, help, and training by at least twenty groups, including the Magdalene Benevolence Society, the House of Mercy, the Salvation Army, the Florence Crittenton Mission, and the Heartsease Work for Friendless Women. The Home for Fallen and Friendless Girls admitted 195 young women, and its Annex, designed

---

[9]*Refuge Journal,* December 1895, p. 2, and John Moses and Joseph Kirkland, *History of Chicago,* Vol. 2 (Chicago: Munsell & Co., 1895), pp. 276, 390-394.

[10]Vice Commission of Minneapolis, *Report to His Honor, James C. Haynes, Mayor* (1911), p. 117.

[11]Vice Commission of Philadelphia, *A Report on Existing Conditions* (1913), p. 35. The Commission bemoaned "the moral and physical degradation resulting from the misuse of opium and cocaine. . . . [T]hese drugs are a frequent source of corruption of young girls, and even children become addicted to their use" (p. 34).

"to shelter destitute young mothers with their infants . . . and to keep and train them until able to support themselves," housed seventy.[12] The House of Mercy housed 154 "destitute and fallen women," and the largest refuge, the House of the Good Shepherd, had room for 1,042 women "who wish to reform their lives by deserting the haunts of vice [or] may be in danger of falling."[13]

A host of small shelters such as Waverly House, Lakeview Home, and St. Faith's Home also provided help. Lakeview Home, operated by an association of Jewish women, provided industrial training and personal counseling and cared for twenty-five women and girls and twenty-five infants at the time. St. Faith's Home, established by Episcopalians, sheltered ex-prostitutes and during that time tried to reverse the downward spiral of their lives prior to entry.[14] The Home of the Good Samaritan found jobs for fifty-four women who were "either living in sin and desirous of leaving their old life" or were in danger of "falling into sinful ways."[15]

National organizations also were emerging at the turn of the century. The Salvation Army had thirty-four homes for unmarried mothers, the WCTU's Department of Rescue Work had at least five, and the Protestant Episcopal Church had twelve "Homes of Mercy."[16] The "Door of Hope" group had forty homes "for fallen girls [built] in hopes of not simply sheltering and furnishing them with employment, but through love and sympathy to lead them to a Christian life. None desirous of reforming are refused admission day or night."[17] Crittenton homes – the number grew to sixty-five by 1927 – helped five hundred thousand unmarried girls/women during the five decades from 1883 to 1933.

The crucial understanding underlying many of these activities was simple yet profound: It was fine to contribute money to charities, but the

---

[12]*New York Charities Directory* (New York: Charity Organization Society, 1899), pp. 229-230.

[13]*Ibid.*, p. 231.

[14]See George T. Kneeland, *Commercialized Prostitution in New York City* (New York: The Century Company, 1913).

[15]*Ibid.*, p. 230.

[16]Walter Barrett, *The Care of the Unmarried Mother* (Alexandria, VA: Crittenton, 1929), p. 50. In 1892, with a donation from Charles Crittenton, the WCTU opened Florence Crittenton homes in Denver, Portland, Chicago, Fargo, and Norfolk.

[17]*New York Charities Directory*, p. 229.

larger and more difficult demand was for personal commitment and perseverance. As one minister argued,

> To cast a contribution into the box brought to the hand, or to attend committees and anniversaries, are very trifling exercises of Christian self-denial and devotion, compared with what is demanded in the weary perambulations through the street, the contact with filth, and often with rude and repulsive people, the facing of disease, and distress, and all manner of heart-rending and heart-frightening scenes, and all the trials of faith, patience, and hope, which are incident to the duty we urge.[18]

John McDowall failed in the 1830s, but in the second half of the century many organizations fulfilled McDowall's hopes by persevering in faith and patience; let's begin with a closer look at one.

THE ERRING WOMAN'S REFUGE

On February 13, 1863 seven women from Chicago churches met to discuss the need for a home to which women seeking to leave prostitution (and avoid abortion) could come. The seven set up an "Erring Woman's Refuge" board of managers made up entirely of women and a board of trustees, for fund-raising purposes, comprised entirely of men. According to one manager, men were to raise the money since they were in large part responsible for the problem.[19]

During the next seventeen years over one thousand women came to the Erring Woman's Refuge. At first, most were escapees from brothels, but soon extramarital sexual amateurs and recent victims of seduction, often pregnant, came also. They were treated with firm kindness:

> Proper subjects for this institution are those women of this class who desire to change a dishonorable to an honorable manner of life, who are animated by a wish to reform, and who need friends to help them through the struggle. . . . A woman who is admitted, anticipating the confinement, is required to pledge herself to remain one year in the institution after the birth of the babe. . . .[20]

For the program to work, volunteers who could befriend and chal-

---

[18]William Ruffner, *Charity and the Clergy* (Philadelphia: Lippincott, 1853), p. 141.
[19]Erring Woman's Refuge, *Third Annual Report* (1866), p. 28.
[20]*Ibid.*, pp. 8-9.

lenge the struggling young women were needed, as was a matron/superintendent who could live at the home and lead the way. That last job was exceptionally difficult, and short-term matrons came and went. In 1881, however, a copy of the Refuge's annual report at the Library of Congress shows Miss M. E. Fisher crossed out and the name "Mrs. Woods" written in. A new era for the erring was beginning.

Helen Mercy Woods came from Syracuse, where throughout the 1870s she was in charge of the Onondaga County Orphan Asylum. It is not clear why she came to Chicago, since Helen Woods did not write about herself and was not "important" enough for anyone else to profile.[21] But month after month in her Superintendent's Reports – available at the Chicago Historical Society – she wrote about those she served:

• During the past month five girls have been admitted and two children born. . . . J. B. was brought by her father to remain a limited time; is a very pretty, bright girl, 17 years of age, has been more sinned against than sinning. . . . J. H., very pretty and intelligent girl, hopes the ladies will permit her to remain until after her confinement and then go her way. . . . As the time for spring repairs and cleaning draws near, I would respectfully ask if you have bedding, carpets, chairs, to give away, they would be most acceptable to us.[22]

• March 8th Katie H., brought by her mother, a young, pretty girl, out to service and betrayed.[23]

• During this month ten girls have been admitted. E. L. is nineteen years of age – has a mother living – it is the old, old story, she is anxiously looking each day for the young man who has promised to come and marry her. . . . R. S. came from the west side, she is eighteen, a pretty,

---

[21]The names of some philanthropists of the 1880-1920 era come trippingly to our tongues. We know how John D. Rockefeller, Andrew Carnegie, and others accumulated great fortunes and began to give them away. We know about their good works because they received "the gratitude of society" and because biographers flocked to record such grand benevolence. It seems that no one, however, has written about Helen Mercy Woods; her name is missing from late nineteenth-century Chicago directories of "important" community leaders and from *Bio-Base*, an index to five hundred biographical dictionaries.

[22]*Refuge Journal*, April 1886, p. 1. The *Journal* (actually a newsletter) began in 1886 and was four to eight pages long. It was a monthly through 1891 and a quarterly for the rest of the century.

[23]*Ibid.*, May 1886, p. 1.

quiet girl; she has parents living but does not want to return to them at the present.[24]

• S. B. is a young girl, sixteen years old. She has been betrayed. . . .[25]

• E. A. was brought by her mother, was 'betrayed by promise of marriage,' the old story, nonetheless sad though too frequent. Like most of this class she is amiable, easily influenced and not at all depraved. She is sixteen years old.[26]

By the mid-1880s Mrs. Woods was in charge of over one hundred young women and their babies. She supervised a daily routine, beginning with singing, Bible reading, and prayer followed by breakfast. All residents sewed during the day and had from two to four hours of schooling, along with training in dressmaking, cooking, nursing, and other skills.[27] Helen Woods continued to record the comings and goings:

• Three girls have been admitted. M. H. comes from a neighboring city expecting to become a mother . . . six girls have left . . . we have good tidings from them. One child was adopted. Little Earl has found a home with a kind-hearted and lonely woman.[28]

• E. W. is an orphan and not a very bright girl, 15 years old; she expects soon to become a mother. M. W. is twenty years of age; her parents live in Germany, and she has been in this country only long enough to learn that friendless girls are the prey of the designing men and women who are watching for them. . . . M. L. came because she is friendless and alone. She expects to become a mother.[29]

• M. O. is seventeen. She was brought by her brother. Her mother had been dead five years. She expects to become a mother. . . . L. E. came a

---

[24]*Ibid.*, July 1886, p. 2.
[25]*Ibid.*, August 1886, p. 2.
[26]*Ibid.*, September 1886, p. 2.
[27]*Refuge Journal*, May 1886, p. 3; March 1886, p. 2; June 1886, p. 1. The Chicago *Tribune* quoted Helen Woods on the importance of job skills: "Not long ago a girl came to us from a western town. She was heartlessly betrayed, and if she had not found shelter under our roof she probably would have sunk into a vicious life of helplessness . . . but she stayed with us several months, learned the dressmaking trade, and has now gone back home and is practicing it there." Reprinted in *Refuge Journal*, October 1887, p. 6.
[28]*Ibid.*, May 1887, p. 2.
[29]*Ibid.*, June 1887, p. 2.

long distance from her home to find refuge and to hide her shame from her friends. Are the men never punished, who bring all this sorrow and disgrace on these young, trusting girls?[30]

• We have had calls from a number of our former inmates. L. G. with her little child, now a fine handsome boy in his third year, and the mother looks so respectable and is so full of gratitude to the Home for befriending her when she was homeless and friendless. H. D. . . . insisted on leaving with her so-called friends. She was a sly girl and her influence harmful over younger girls.[31]

• L. D. expects confinement. She is a quiet, not overly bright girl who sincerely mourns over the disgrace she has brought herself and her family. M. L., evidently an assumed name, tells such conflicting stories that only the fact she is here and expects to be a mother can be given. N. A. is a married woman. Love of whiskey has been her ruin – is to remain one year. . . .[32]

• B. T. and child, three weeks old, were admitted. . . . E. B. is a betrayed girl. Parents dead. Says she has no friends. Industrious. . . .[33]

Mrs. Woods was most sympathetic to "young girls who have been betrayed by promise of marriage and have fled from home to avoid exposure and disgrace."[34] She understood the problems of those who had "lost their mother when very young, been allowed to have their own way, or lacked discipline. . . ."[35] She reserved her wrath for the "artful and unscrupulous men" who posed as "patrons and benefactors" and then demanded sexual repayment "for favors bestowed in securing positions or furnishing employment."[36] One of her goals was to fight

---

[30] *Ibid.*, July 1887, p. 2.

[31] *Ibid.*, August 1887, p. 2.

[32] *Ibid.*, November 1887, p. 2.

[33] *Ibid.*, December 1887, p. 2.

[34] *Ibid.*, September 1886, p. 3, from her report to the Thirteenth National Conference of Charities and Corrections, St. Paul, Minnesota.

[35] *Ibid.*

[36] *Ibid.*, April 1887, p. 5. Mrs. Woods then described the situation of many young women drawn to urban areas without family protectors: "Thrown upon the world and compelled in many cases to seek at the hands of men some employment to support themselves, and having that most dangerous endowment of nature –personal beauty – they soon find that they are valued more for their attraction than for their services, and become a victim of man's cruel lust."

abortion, a continuing problem: "[F]requently unmarried mothers are destroying themselves and destroying born or unborn babes."[37] But this, for Helen Woods, was a subset of the need to give careful, personal attention to every newcomer: "Each one has a sad history to relate. How to comfort, how to instill courage and patience. . . . God helping us, we will do our best!"[38]

Month after month, in crowded conditions throughout the 1880s, Helen Woods prayed for God's grace and then did her best. Materially, the Refuge became better off in the 1890s as it moved into a new building that featured Roman red brick, stone trimmings, octagonal rotunda lined with mahogany paneling, a slate roof, and wings radiating in the shape of a Maltese cross. The building, at 5024 Indiana Avenue, was situated diagonally to the street, making it possible for every room on the four floors to have sunshine. But the stories in Helen Woods' monthly reports from 1890 on seemed to become even more somber. By the end of the decade she was writing about one of her residents, "a young girl – a child –who will not be twelve until December first and is nearly four months pregnant. Another girl of sixteen had been married, has a child and deserted her husband."[39] Even the joyful events often were immediately followed by sadness: "F.K. was married to the man who would have been the father of her child had it lived. It was stillborn the day after the marriage."[40]

Mrs. Woods did gain satisfaction, however, when adoptive homes were found for children born at the Refuge. "Two infants were adopted last month, good homes being provided for them. . . . A good home is provided for C.S.'s child, Jane. . . ."[41] Meanwhile, pregnant young women kept coming:

F. C. is an adopted daughter – taken from the Home for the Friendless – is seventeen and pregnant. B.R. is twenty years of age, expects to be a mother. P. H. is fifteen and pregnant four months, brought by her sister. . . . J. T. is sixteen; sent from an Indiana school; is pregnant. H.P. is eighteen years, from the same school and for the same reason. L.M. is a colored girl brought by her mother. She is sixteen years old and

---

[37] *Ibid.*, June 1887, p. 5.
[38] *Ibid.*, February 1888, p. 2.
[39] *Ibid.*, January 1899, p. 6.
[40] *Ibid.*
[41] *Ibid.*, November 1899, p. 6.

pregnant. . . . R. D. was brought by Mrs. Amigh from the German Home. She is pregnant.[42]

At the turn of the century Helen Woods was still at her post, after twenty years, still writing about her "family" of over one hundred women and babies and a half-dozen assistants.[43] Why? What kept her going all those years? Although she never wrote about herself, she and other Refuge leaders often noted the principles that underlaid their perseverance.

First came a classic understanding of the nature of compassion.[44] The *Journal* observed that

> A fallen woman, to be saved, must come in contact not with a system or rule, but with another woman. Not only Christlike charity must go out to meet her, but careful, shrewd sagacity and knowledge of human nature. And underneath all must be faith, downright and absolute, now, as in the days of the first Magdalene, in a power above earthly effort.[45]

Compassion began with realism: "This home of ours has been to many of those whose steps have begun to slide like a ledge of rock midway in the slope of a precipice."[46] Mrs. Woods and her colleagues did not disguise the fact that residents were still on a precipice. Compassion became concrete when it was based on a willingness to suffer *with* those being helped: "the seeking shepherd shares largely in the lot of the lost sheep; if its fleece is torn, so are his garments; if . . . it has strayed away into dank and deadly places, he must breathe the fatal air."[47] Only when personal concern was present was personal challenge likely to be taken to heart. A young woman named Mabel, for example, was cared for by Mrs. Woods and later wrote that the Refuge was "the first place I ever lived that any person cared enough about the salvation of my soul to make it a matter of interest to me. . . ."[48]

Making such concerns a priority was central to the Refuge's task of "changing utterly the physical, mental and moral status of the women." Helen Woods saw work as essential and upheld the Refuge principle:

---

[42] *Ibid.*, September 1899, p. 7; November 1899, p. 6; April 1902, p. 6.
[43] *Ibid.*, April 1902, p. 6.
[44] See Marvin Olasky, "Reclaiming Compassion," *Heritage Lecture* 228, December 1989.
[45] *Refuge Journal*, March 1886, p. 4.
[46] Erring Woman's Refuge, *Eighteenth Annual Report* (1881), p. 6.
[47] Erring Woman's Refuge, *25th Annual Report* (1888), p. 6.
[48] *Refuge Journal*, April 1886, p. 2.

"That nobody shall be idle is an inflexible rule."[49] She saw training as vital for the long run: "As all who the institution shelters are dependent on their own exertions for a livelihood, the need for a thorough industrial training for practical success is evident."[50] But she knew that industrial habits alone did not secure reform.[51] The need for spiritual healing was emphasized through testimonies printed in the *Journal*: "Ah the beauty and joy of living with Christ and of being pure and true to yourself and others. . . . Jesus can and does save even me."[52]

HELEN WOODS' CONTEMPORARIES

Helen Woods disappeared from the historical record following her retirement from the Refuge in 1903, but each shelter that succeeded usually did so because someone like Helen Woods felt called to devote years or decades to the effort. New York City's Heartsease Home, like many others, began with the evangelical impulses of a few women resolving to help their unmarried "sisters." It stayed alive through the dedication of founder Annie Richardson Kennedy, whose goal was "to first bring the girls in touch with their Saviour, then upbuild character."[53] Mrs. Kennedy's letters focused on crises and opportunities:

• A young American girl, 17 years old, who because of her trouble has been abandoned by her mother. [She has] nowhere to go – no home – no work. She remains in the home and is now being trained for a good position. Her life has been changed in every respect.[54]

• A French girl all her life [had] lived in a small village in France, the lady of the village employing her as ladies' maid for the last five years. A young son of the family . . . realizing a child was to be born to them . . . sent her here. . . . [She] has bravely taken up her burden and gone to

---

[49]Erring Woman's Refuge, *Fifteenth Annual Report* (1878), pp. 10-11.
[50]*Refuge Journal*, May 1886, p. 3.
[51]The Refuge's *Fifteenth Annual Report*, pp. 10-11, summarized three vital changes: "Morbid tendencies must give way to wholesome ones, mental activity take the place of inert lethargy in the mind, religious sentiments give rise to good thoughts and insights as to duty. . . ."
[52]*Refuge Journal*, September 1887, p. 3.
[53]Annie Richardson Kennedy, *The Heartsease Miracle* (New York: Heartsease Publishing Company, 1920), p. 35.
[54]Letter to Heartsease Home supporters, September 1910; published in *ibid.*, p. 62.

work with her child and [for] a lady who speaks French and has deep sympathy for the girl.[55]

• A young English girl, age 17, ruined by a widower – this girl remained in the home about one year, during which time her mother died. Now she is in a good position, giving satisfaction and has connected herself with the church and in every way is proving herself true.[56]

• She loved a young man and he ruined her and left her. Inside of six weeks she had lived in an illicit way with three other men. . . . She came to our home through a member of church; she did not know what it meant to be 'born again.' She knows now. The girl was to become a mother. This was what she wrote home to an old heartbroken aunt and uncle whom she had lived with since a baby: 'I am glad this trouble has come upon me, it has saved me from worse things. God has led me here where I have been taught the way of life, and I know now that my Savior forgives and saves.'[57]

For Annie Kennedy, as for Helen Woods, the goal with each young woman was to "work from the inside out."[58] Heartsease's work was "founded on the Lord Jesus Christ and his finished work for humanity. Our first work, therefore, is to bring our girls into contact with our Savior who alone can relieve them of their burden of sin."[59] Mrs. Kennedy and others who worked with women facing crisis pregnancies encountered difficult challenges. The Heartsease Home developed procedures similar to those of the Erring Woman's Refuge but with an even greater emphasis on voluntarism and family relations.

Encouraging voluntarism was essential because Heartsease was staffed almost entirely by contributors of time. Calls for more help went out constantly: "We still need other helpers. Girls need taking to the hospital; positions must be secured; every home for a baby investigated thoroughly. . . . Our boarding-out homes for babies require constant attention."[60] Volunteers did emerge: "Many babies are adopted. We have a long list of prospective foster parents waiting . . . to give a child a

---

[55]*Ibid.*, p. 40.
[56]*Ibid.*
[57]Letter, September 1912, *ibid.*, p. 51.
[58]Letter, September 1905, *ibid.*, p. 65.
[59]*Ibid.*
[60]Letter, September 1913, *ibid.*, p. 59.

chance."[61] So did support from journalists. Jacob Riis wrote of the Home, "No work that I ever came across seems to go nearer the heart of things than that of these devoted women. Heartsease deserves the enthusiastic support of all our people. . . ."[62]

Financially, Heartsease relied on contributors of goods as well as money: "one of our good friends sent us vegetables during last summer in such a quantity that we were able to can enough for our winter supply. . . . We were in need of kitchen utensils – a friend sent in a box of odds and ends. . . ."[63] Another time, when cribs were needed, a wealthy woman whose daughter recently had died told Mrs. Kennedy, "Today is Betty's birthday"; the woman then offered "for your babies" the money she would have spent on Betty over the next year.[64] On a third occasion, "We needed an extra dining room table. After a week of prayer, a friend came in and said, 'My father says that if I don't get rid of the large dining room table he'll chop it up for wood.'"[65] Repeatedly Heartsease returned from the brink of financial disaster – and those whose gifts came out of their homes or out of their own life's crises seemed more tightly tied to the Home's future than those who merely wrote out a check.

The emphasis on "family" also came through in several ways. First, Annie Kennedy wanted young women to recognize their dependence and not assert a false independence. She wrote of a young southern girl who joined a touring vaudeville act, slept around, and became pregnant:

> When her employer discovered her condition, she was practically abandoned in New York and was sent to us from a hospital. When she came to the door she was literally without funds, clothing and alone. We have since written her mother and she will care for the girl and her baby. They are very poor but respectable people. The girl has been led to see the folly of her way.[66]

Second, the Heartsease policy was that every child, whenever possible, should grow up in a home with both a father and a mother: "It has

---

[61]*Ibid.*
[62]Letter, June 18, 1913, *ibid.*, p. 58.
[63]Letter, September 1915, *ibid.*, p. 81.
[64]Letter, December 1910, *ibid.*, p. 42.
[65]Letter, September 1912, *ibid.*, p. 50.
[66]*Ibid.*, p. 82.

been found best that some of these children are adopted into families where they will have the love and care for which they are entitled."[67]

Third, when the mother decided to keep the baby, Heartsease emphasized reconciliation between the mother and *her* mother. When Annie Kennedy was asked in 1912 about a pregnant fifteen-year-old helped seven years before, she recalled that "Mayb and the boy stayed with us nearly 6 months. . . . We also taught her stenography. Her whole life and nature changed, due to her fellowship with her Lord and Master." Annie Kennedy then described a recent visit with Mayb, Mayb's mother, and Mayb's child, now seven: "the boy came in from school while I sat there. First thing he did was to get a book and sit down and read. . . . His school card bears the highest mark. The old mother said to me over and over with tears running down her cheeks, 'Mayb is my good girl, my good girl.'"[68]

By September 1920, even though Annie Kennedy was not any closer to "solving" the problem of seduction, abandonment, and extramarital pregnancy, she was able to rest with the understanding that some sorrows could be surmounted:

> I will give you a few cases. No. 2681, student-teacher, engaged, betrayed. Her beautiful child was adopted. . . . No. 2748, young American girl 19 years, seduced under promise of marriage, well-educated and well-behaved girl, was cast out, but through prayer she went home with her baby. She is doing nicely; she writes that God is leading and that she has his peace.[69]

At this point the Heartsease Home also disappeared into the fog of history.[70]

Similar refuges flowered for a time in every large northern city, and many in the South as well. One southerner, Lem Abbott Odom, began work with pregnancy rescue homes and shelters in 1888 and spent the next fifty years in Montgomery, Alabama; Jacksonville, Florida; and

---

[67]Letter, December 1910, *ibid.*, p. 42.
[68]Letter, December 1912. Kennedy sadly added, "We have been unable to do anything with the father of the child. He has gone selfishly on his way. Although he has known from time to time of Mayb's burden and the growth of his child, there can not have been any growth in his life, only a hardening process. He is greatly to be pitied."
[69]*Ibid.*, p. 61.
[70]Early in 1991 I visited its site – 413 East 51st St. – and found the building there occupied by the consulate of Yemen.

Shreveport, Louisiana. He expressed sympathy for "thousands of girls, who are lured from a life of virtue by those whom they trusted, and have in some unguarded hour yielded to temptation."[71] But Odom also insisted that those lives were not ruined. He recommended that unmarried mothers place their children for adoption and noted that about 85 percent of the girls and women he helped were able to marry or to be restored to "homes, gainful occupations, and positions of trust. . . ."[72]

Odom told many stories of how unmarried, pregnant girls and women fell into and fought their way through trouble:

• In Montgomery, Ida's father died when she was a small girl; Ida, sixteen, "capitulated to the blandishments of a young man," and became pregnant. Odom sent her to a Christian home in St. Louis, where the baby was born and adopted, and Ida then returned to school.[73]

• In a small town Addis, age twelve, was impregnated by her stepfather. Odom had him arrested for rape and had Addis taken into a home where she gave birth to a son who was adopted.

• In southern Arkansas, eighteen-year-old Eudora, daughter of a widow, became pregnant. Her mother sent her to Odom's Montgomery rescue home, where she gave birth to a boy who was adopted by a farmer. Later Eudora married a railroad engineer and had other children.[74]

• Delenia, daughter of a minister, came to Montgomery five months pregnant, after being seduced and abandoned. She gave birth there, and her parents were able to move to a new church at which they could receive her and their grandchild. Odom visited the family ten years later and found them all well; Delenia had become a nurse.

• Josephine, eight months pregnant and sick with malaria and a venereal disease, gave birth to a healthy boy who was adopted and became the chief engineer of a steamship company and the father of five

---

[71]Lem Abbott Odom, *Fifty Years in Rescue Work* (Cincinnati: Revivalist Press, 1938), p. 50. Such language came naturally to Odom, whose father had taught him that "In the Old South, the South of Robert E. Lee, Jefferson Davis, Stonewall Jackson and George Washington, the instinct in every man's and every boy's bosom was to defend the honor of womanhood."

[72]*Ibid.*, p. 72.

[73]*Ibid.*, p. 99.

[74]*Ibid.*, p. 141.

children. Josephine became a nurse and married a minister but eventually died of tuberculosis.[75]

• Myrtle, age eleven, was raised by a grandfather after her mother died and her father ran off. She was impregnated by a local businessman who had a wife and three daughters of his own. Myrtle gave birth to an eight-pound boy who was adopted; Myrtle and the grandfather moved to California.[76]

• Delilah, a sixteen-year-old orphan, eloped with a young man who delayed marrying her when his car supposedly broke down on the way to the county courthouse. While they waited for the car to be repaired, she agreed to "show him" her love. He then abandoned her, and she went to Odom's shelter in Jacksonville where she bore a child who was adopted.[77]

Odom kept going for half a century because he saw himself making an enormous difference in a few lives each year. Odom's stress on adoption also helped. As historian Joan Brumberg noted following her study of a refuge in Elmira, New York:

> Recovery from the multiple crises posed by an unmarried pregnancy was possible so long as the birth remained covert and the baby properly disposed of. A proper disposition meant adoption – either through a private family or through a welfare agency, generally a county orphanage . . . for WCTU women in upstate New York, community aversion to taking on long-term support of illegitimate children worked against retention as did their own ability to make placements in "good Christian homes." In effect, the WCTU appeared to be able to intersect with what may have been a middle-class market for children.[78]

Over two-thirds of the babies born between 1890 and 1907 at the home Brumberg studied were adopted.

Woods, Kennedy, and Odom shared a realistic view of the limits of their work. They did not expect to wipe out seduction and abortion, but

---

[75] *Ibid.*, p. 160.
[76] *Ibid.*, p. 174.
[77] *Ibid.*, pp. 174, 180.
[78] Joan Brumberg, "Ruined Girls . . .," *Journal of Social History*, Vol. 18 (Winter 1984), p. 260.

they were able to see improvements in individual lives similar to those Helen Woods recorded regularly:

> C. S. said her husband had been so kind to her, and was happy and doing her best to make her home cheerful. B. F. brought her marriage certificate to show me she was really married, and said she had a kind husband and good home. . . . M. H., a deaf mute who was here four years ago, brought her little boy of two years and told me of her good husband and nice home.[79]

They also were animated by evangelical beliefs that stressed perseverance even when little earthly reward was evident:

> There is a great deal of good work to be done which demands little sacrifice and yields a sufficient reward in the gratitude of society; but this special work of saving the peculiarly lost has no such reward. The passion for humanity is indulged at the cost of suffering but it is not without . . . the joy of Heaven.[80]

Those same beliefs underlaid the original growth of most of the national organizations designed to help the unmarried and pregnant. The first rescue home of the chain that would become the National Florence Crittenton Mission (NFCM) was founded in 1883 by Charles Crittenton, the "millionaire evangelist." Crittenton had earned his fortune in the pharmaceutical business, but he plunged into despair following the death of his young daughter, Florence. He soon was "born again," however, and felt called to rescue work. Establishing the first home in New York City's red-light district, Crittenton endowed it with the purpose of giving "spiritual redemption to the most despised of all throughout the centuries – the girl on the street." The Crittenton mission was open to any woman "wishing to leave a Crooked Life"; it welcomed prostitutes, "wayward girls," and women suspected of "sexual misconduct," as well as unmarried mothers.[81]

Charles Crittenton, in turn, heavily influenced Kate Waller Barrett, whose life story reflects some typical patterns of the post-Civil War era. Kate Waller was a little girl during the war; when her father became ill

---

[79] *Refuge Journal*, April 1902, p. 6.
[80] Erring Women's Refuge, *25th Annual Report* (1888), p. 6.
[81] Regina G. Kunzel, "The Professionalization of Benevolence," *Journal of Social History*, Vol. 22 (Fall 1988), pp. 21-23.

after Appomatox, it looked as if the family would starve.[82] Help came from an unexpected quarter, however. An officer on Grant's staff, who was orphaned as a boy and cared for by Kate Waller's grandfather, heard of the illness and helped Kate's mother get food and transport.[83] Kate Waller began to forge her own link in a great chain of helping when she married a minister in 1876 and moved with him to a Richmond slum parish. As a pastor's wife she saw all kinds of suffering.

> One night, I shall never forget it, I was sitting in our cozy little parlor, my husband reading aloud to me, and on the sofa lay my sleeping boy, only a few months old. It was just before Christmas and a cold, biting rain was falling. There was a ring at the door, my husband went to answer it, and when he returned he brought with him a young girl who held in her arms a baby. He said, 'Can you not do something for this woman and child? She has no friends and nowhere to go, and she has no money; get some dry clothes for her and the baby.'[84]

That was Kate Barrett's first adult encounter with the helplessness of a mother adrift: "She told me of her ambitions, of her day-dreams of the past. . . ."[85]

Kate Barrett helped other women who came to her. When her husband moved to an Atlanta parish, she entered Women's Medical College of Georgia, received an M.D., and established a small rescue home. Neighbors complained about the home, however, and she backed off. But then she went to hear visiting New Yorker Charles Crittenton speak about how and why he and his "Florence Crittenton Rescue Band," a group of hardy friends, had for two years assembled after midnight and walked through the crime-ridden Bowery talking to anyone who would listen.[86] When she heard him in 1895, her life changed. She wrote, "For the first time in my life I drew a breath of real freedom — freedom from dread of public opinion. . . ." During the remaining three decades of her life, Kate Barrett set up dozens of homes for single mothers in cities

---

[82]Col. Withers Waller was on the staff of Confederate general Fitzhugh Lee; Kate Waller Barrett prized her memories of Robert E. Lee.

[83]Otto Wilson, *Fifty Years' Work with Girls 1883-1933* (Alexandria, VA: National Florence Crittenton Mission, 1933), p. 144.

[84]*Ibid.*, p. 154.

[85]*Ibid.*, p. 166. At that time Kate Barrett was "a nominal Christian" but (she later wrote) had no "definite understanding of what the sacrifice on Calvary meant or the ministrations of the Holy Spirit."

[86]*Ibid.*, p. 120.

around the country and became the head of the Florence Crittenton Association following Charles Crittenton's death in 1909.

The homes under Kate Barrett's influence emphasized personal challenge, training in skills and orderliness, and Bible studies.

> The private, home-like character of the Institution brings the inmates under the personal supervision of the Matrons. Individually they are physically and morally cared for . . . with all those who are not hardened it is a powerful motive to well-doing to know that others are interested in them – that they are not adrift upon the world, with no one to care whether they are saved or wrecked, but that their present and future well-being is a subject of solicitude to many.[87]

Also critical in the success of such homes was an underlying realism concerning possible accomplishments. Volunteers were taught that they could not save the world, but they could help some:

> We cannot purify a whole city – would that we could! But this one thing we do. We try to meet in its early stages, and arrest a sin which contaminates the very heart and life of a community, and, like a terrible disease, if not checked in its progress, destroys body and soul.[88]

Volunteers could see that small changes build up: "Each of these changed lives too, it is to be remembered, is a centre of influence." Ripples went on: "Who can estimate how far and wide may extend the purifying influence of one redeemed life?"[89]

Over this period such homes fought the tendency to turn the unmarried mother into a pariah. Americans, said the president of St. John's College, were to "compassionate, esteem and help the unfortunate victims who keep up the love for their unborn offspring, when by a new crime they might conceal their guilt before the world."[90] Since abortion

---

[87] *Ibid.*, p. 18.

[88] Penitent Female's Refuge, *Annual Report*, 1884, p. 15.

[89] *Ibid.* This small refuge noted, "Although the numbers received here at any one period may seem not very large, the aggregate, when years are taken into account, is by no means small. And when the unquestioned good results are considered – the large proportion of changed lives which results, under the blessing of God, from the influences here exerted – the work must be regarded as anything but small."

[90] Rev. F. Heirmann, S. J., "Ethical and Religious Objections to Criminal Abortion," *Toledo Medical and Surgical Reporter*, Vol. 31 (1905), p. 236; paper read before Academy of Medicine of Toledo and Lucas County, January 27, 1905.

was an illegal but available option, Reverend Peter O'Callaghan argued that "The woman who in conscious knowledge of the obstacles before her, calmly faces the world with her illegitimate child is a heroine, for her path throughout is beset by daily perils and pitfalls that demand all the resourcefulness of her intellect and courage."[91]

Anti-abortion leaders viewed homes to help such women as crucial in their battles. Chicago medical leader Charles Bacon discussed the difficulty of fighting abortion through prosecution of abortionists and concluded, "The only means that we can regard as efficient is the erection of a sufficient number of obstetrical asylums in which the unmarried can be protected . . . and through which the children can be assured a proper existence."[92] *The Illinois Medical Journal* echoed that call: "Let us found and support homes and places for refuge for the woman awaiting confinement. Teach chastity, teach restraint, but above all protect the devoted victim."[93] At a symposium sponsored by the Chicago Medical Society in 1904, Dr. Rosalie M. Ladova called for establishment of more "homes for the care of unfortunate girls and women, so they can be delivered from the physical as well as moral burden. . . ."[94]

Could more homes be established? English journalist William T. Stead visited Chicago and told the story of "Maggie":

> She was 18 full of vigor and gaiety, she was a brunette with long dark hair, a lively disposition, and with all the charming audacity and confidence of inexperience. She fell in love, the man was older than she . . . why could they not anticipate the [marriage] ceremony, did she not trust him? He swore that it was alright, that everybody did it, and they would be so much more to each other. Why repeat the often told story, at first Maggie did not listen to the suggestion, but after time when he pressed her, upbraided her, and declared that she could not love him if she did not trust him, she went the way of many thousands only to wake as they have done with the soft illusion dissipated by the hard reality of motherhood drawing near. . . . Her lover was a married man, and he had skipped the town. . . .[95]

---

[91]Rev. Peter J. O'Callaghan, "The Moral and Religious Objections to Inducing Abortion," *Illinois Medical Journal*, Vol. 7 (1904), pp. 27-28.

[92]*Illinois Medical Journal*, Vol. 7 (1904), p. 24.

[93]*Ibid.*, p. 29.

[94]*Ibid.*, p. 43. Dr. Ladova added, "institutions of this kind would undoubtedly save many a woman from a downward road to a life of shame and child murder."

[95]William T. Stead, *If Christ Came to Chicago* (Chicago: Saird and Lee, 1894), p. 49.

Stead complained that Maggie found a haven only in a brothel; she atypically turned down the offer of an abortion and bore the baby, but he died soon after birth, and Maggie remained a prostitute. As we have seen, Maggie could have gone to the Erring Woman's Refuge and met Hellen Mercy Woods, but she did not — and perhaps she never knew of the alternative. Stead argued that refuges were needed in every neighborhood. After praising the Salvation Army and several other groups, he complained that he did not

> know of any church in Chicago which utilizes the whole of its ecclesiastical plant. . . . Two services a Sunday and possibly a prayer meeting once or twice a week, can hardly be said to be making the best use of an investment in real estate which is estimated to amount to at least to $13 million dollars. All money sunk in church buildings is God's trust money. If it belonged to anyone else and was invested by trustees so as to yield interest only one day out of seven the trustees would be either sent to the penitentiary or the lunatic asylum.

The best use of those real estate investments would be the provision of more havens for more Maggies.

Would more homes be established? Only if the movement for compassion (with its emphasis on not only material help but personal challenge as well) received strong social backing — and only if leaders like Helen Mercy Woods continued to be willing to battle on in a long twilight struggle.

PART THREE

Abortion Breaks Through

10

Weariness Among the Physicians

S ome downward movement in abortion rates from the 1860 high was noted tentatively during the years after the Civil War. In 1875 Dr. John Stoddard wrote of the practice of abortion and noted "some slight check to its boldness, and perhaps to its frequency."[1] By 1893 the trend was clear, and Dr. William Parish could consider a "a half dozen" abortion requests in a year worthy of note; doctors, as James Mohr pointed out, were receiving that many per week at midcentury.[2] In 1896 Dr. James Scott reported the physicians' consensus view concerning the extent of abortion practice: "these times are not so impure [as those of] past generations."[3]

Abortion declined among all three of the major at-risk groups. Contraceptive improvement was probably a leading factor in reducing

---

[1]John Stoddard, "Foeticide– Suggestions Toward Its Suppression," *Detroit Review of Medicine and Pharmacy*, Vol. 10 (November 1875), p. 655.

[2]William H. Parish, "Criminal Abortions," *Medical and Surgical Reporter*, Vol. 68 (April 1893), p. 646; James Mohr, *Abortion in America* (New York: Oxford University Press, 1978), p. 241.

[3]James Scott, "Criminal Abortion," *American Journal of Obstetrics and Diseases of Women and Children*, Vol. 33 (1896), p. 72.

the prostitution-abortion connection, and evangelical efforts also were helpful. Odd circles of married women were less likely to make abortion a rite as spiritism fizzled during the closing decades of the nineteenth century and as a deeper understanding of the consequences of abortion – to unborn human life and to the future peace of mind of aborting women – emerged.[4] By the end of the century, seduced and abandoned young women had a variety of compassionate alternatives to abortion open to them.

And yet, while containment was working, abortion continued, much to the frustration of many physicians. Within state and local medical societies, the crucial turning point on abortion often came not in the 1960s but during the first third of the century, as more doctors told stories like the following three by Robert Ferguson of Charlotte, North Carolina:

• A few years ago there came under my observation a young woman in her first pregnancy and vomiting severely, who had made up her mind that she would not carry the pregnancy to fruition. She was taken to the hospital by her family physician with whom I saw her in consultation. The mother was on hand and took charge of the case. All questions addressed to the patient were answered by the mother . . . this patient had another consultant called in and was curetted immediately.[5]

• The first year I started out to practice, on a Sunday morning, a beautiful young woman wearing many large diamonds appeared at my office and told me her troubles, the same old story, and said she had to have an abortion. I told her that was not my line of work and she would have to look elsewhere. She insisted and said she did not know where to go and if it was the fee that held me back all I would have to do would be to state my price, that she did not care what it cost, she was going to get rid of it. Although I was several thousand dollars in debt for my education I told her that a million dollars would not influence me in the least and that has been my stand ever since I got my diploma. Most doctors are importuned many times each year to produce these abortions of convenience and, inevitably, some succumb.[6]

---

[4]Mohr, *Abortion in America*, pp. 241-243, provides useful evidence concerning the decline of abortion among married women during the late nineteenth century, but he does not note theological connections.

[5]Robert Thrift Ferguson, "Abortion and Abortionist," *Southern Medicine and Surgery*, Vol. 93 (December 1931), p. 889.

[6]*Ibid.*

• About two years ago a lady on whom I had previously operated sent her daughter of 14 years to my office to examine on account of persistent nausea. The girl was three months pregnant and I asked her mother over the telephone to come to my office. She, like all others, wanted to know what she could do to get rid of it — said it just couldn't be permitted to go on. I told her the law and that there was nothing I could do. She said she did not expect that I would do anything for her but thought I might tell her of some doctor who would help her out. I told her I did not know of any such. She remarked that she would go the rounds till she found one. A short time later she visited my office and informed me that she had found a doctor in Charlotte who produced an abortion on her daughter. I asked her the point blank question what he charged and she said he charged $500, and while that was a big fee, she did not mind anything to get her daughter out of trouble.[7]

How long would anti-abortion doctors stick to the task?

Early in the century, although many doctors were performing abortions, the leadership and rhetoric within local medical societies tended to be anti-abortion, and in city after city during the century's first three decades local leaders called meetings to discuss ways to fight abortion.

These meetings developed a typical pattern, beginning with the opening remarks by a theologian who examined religious and ethical issues. In Toledo, for example, doctors in 1905 assembled to hear Reverend F. Heirmann, S. J., criticize an abortionist who had said, "I would as leave kill, if necessary, an unborn child as a rat."[8] Heirmann then posed the question: "Whether abortion is murder or whether the human embryo must be considered a person who has a right to life?"[9] He quoted scientific studies showing the unborn child to be human life from the moment of conception and told the assembled doctors that "the positive law of God" showed them how to react in the face of that knowledge. Heirmann also suggested explicit language: "Instead of resorting to big Latin compounds, foeticide, infanticide, let us use the strong and powerful Anglo-Saxon, child murder, murder of the unborn. . . ."[10]

---

[7]*Ibid.*, p. 892.

[8]Rev. F. Heirmann, "Ethical and Religious Objections to Criminal Abortion," paper read before the Academy of Medicine of Toledo and Lucas County, January 27, 1905; *Toledo Medical and Surgical Reporter*, Vol. 31 (1905), p. 233. Heirmann was president of St. John's College.

[9]*Ibid.*, p. 234.

[10]*Ibid.*, p. 235. Heirmann noted that killing in "just wars" and in self-defense was allowable, as was as capital punishment for crimes committed..

Next on the typical agenda came an estimate of abortion incidence, with commentary by a local medical opponent of abortion. For example, in 1904 Dr. Charles Bacon told the Chicago Medical Society that at least 10 to 13 percent of all pregnancies in Chicago ended in induced abortion.[11] Bacon pleaded with fellow doctors to oppose abortion, since "The right to life is the most fundamental right of an individual."[12] Bacon acknowledged that some said the unborn child's dependence on a mother reduced its rights, but he suggested that such thinking would lead to infanticide, since a baby "needs the breast and the care of the mother for a long period. . . . This human being is just as much an independent being at the beginning of its intrauterine life as after it has reached a condition of extrauterine viability."[13]

Tunes of "Onward, medical soldiers" spluttered to a halt, however, when local district attorneys or lawyers were called upon. For example, W. S. Carroll, an assistant district attorney for Erie County, told the Erie Country Medical Society in 1908 that "under common law abortion was homicide or manslaughter . . . but the modern law does not look upon the offense in such an atrocious light."[14] Anti-abortion laws were virtually "a dead letter," Carroll reported, with no recent cases of offending physicians or midwives being jailed or even having their licenses revoked. Evidentiary hurdles, he observed, were significant. A doctor, called to attempt to repair part of the damage caused by abortion, could not testify about anything the woman told him unless she explicitly answered a series of questions acknowledging her words to be a dying statement. Dying declarations *were* admissible in criminal (although not in civil) cases, but a doctor who attained such information while treating a patient was not allowed to communicate anything that "shall tend to blacken the character of the patient without her consent."[15]

Local officials told doctors that if an anti-abortion case was not devel-

---

[11]C. S. Bacon, "The Duty of the Medical Profession in Criminal Abortion," symposium before the Chicago Medical Society, November 23, 1904; *Illinois Medical Journal*, Vol. 7 (1904), p. 18.

[12]*Ibid.*

[13]*Ibid.*, p. 19. Bacon also opposed euthanasia: a person should not be deprived of life, Bacon said, even if "he be diseased, unconscious, or worthless for any reason whatever unless the State represented by its judicial officers decides that he has forfeited his life by his crimes and rendered its extinction necessary for the welfare of the state."

[14]W. S. Carroll, "The Rights of the Unborn Child," *The Pennsylvania Medical Journal*, Vol.13 (1909-1910), p. 936. Carroll stated that the woman who had an abortion done upon her was not guilty under the statute particularly related to abortion.

[15]*Ibid.*, p. 941.

oped precisely, evidence would not hold up in court. At one medical convention, St. Louis attorney Earnest Oakley reminded doctors that statements by a dying woman to a doctor were not admissible in court unless
she said the required words: "I am going to die. . . . I have abandoned
all hope of recovery."[16] Oakley told doctors they must prompt such statements by asking women hard questions or else give up all hope of convicting an abortionist.

Other officials also strove to lower expectations. M. O. Heckard,
Registrar of Vital Statistics in the Chicago Department of Health, spoke
of "a girl from one of our best families who has made a mistake."[17]
Heckard asked whether he should "report this matter to the proper
inquisitorial officers, and have the distress of the relatives advertised,
who are already bowed down with grief and shame." He said he would
"if there were any possibility of bringing the criminal to justice" but
argued that this would not happen:

> The evidence is destroyed. If the physician does his duty to the law, makes
> this report directly to the Coroner, can he expect another call from that fam-
> ily or their immediate friends? And it is not every physician in the city who
> can afford to sacrifice a family under such circumstances. What can he do?[18]

Frustration showed in the words of attorneys such as prosecutor
Fletcher Dobyns:

> There are approximately from six thousand to ten thousand abortions
> produced in this city each year; there are something like two hundred
> deaths from that evil each year. We can count on the fingers of one hand
> the convictions for criminal abortion that have been secured during the
> last half dozen years. . . . In one case, the physician who took the stand
> for the defense said it would be impossible for a doctor, even after curet-
> ting the parts, as he said he did, to say whether it was fetal tissue. . . .
> Another physician took the stand and showed how the same condition
> could have existed from something else, and that death could have
> resulted from other cause or causes.[19]

---

[16]Earnest F. Oakley, Jr., "Legal Aspects of Abortion," *American Journal of Obstetrics and
Gynecology*, Vol. 3 (1922), pp. 37-41.
[17]Dr. M. O. Heckard, symposium remarks in the *Illinois Medical Journal*, Vol. 7 (1904), p.
42.
[18]*Ibid.*
[19]*Ibid.*, pp. 40-41.

J. M. Sheean, attorney for the Medico-Legal Committee of the Chicago Medical Society. similarly said, "The decisions and enactments on our statute books are but reflections of the public conscience. . . . The law as it stands is further advanced than apparently the public demand for its enforcement would require. . . ."[20] An article in the *Providence Medical Journal* in 1903 reported the "First conviction for Abortion in the State of Rhode Island," but in doing so showed "the difficulties encountered in the effort to convict for criminal abortion in Rhode Island."[21] The convicted offender was a long-time abortionist with a record of previous cases dismissed, and in this case a strong ante-mortem statement and ample evidence of abortion as cause of death made conviction possible. Even so, the sentence of the abortionist was only two years.

After hearing from law officials at local and national meetings, doctors repeatedly bemoaned the difficulty of enforcement. Dr. Henry D. Holton of Vermont told the American Academy of Medicine, "I have seen a good deal of trouble in securing conviction and have experienced it in trying to convict men whom I know, and everybody had a sort of common knowledge, were guilty, but to get the legal evidence was practically impossible."[22] Dr. Edward T. Abrams of Dollar Bay, Michigan, told fellow AMA members in 1908, "For the past two years I have been a member of the Michigan legislature and also chairman of the committee on public health of that body." During that time, he said, he had been unable to find a way to make abortionists' arrest and conviction more likely. In response to one law-tightening proposition, Abrams reported, "I was assured by the best authority in our state that there would be no more powerful inducement for the concealment of abortion than to make a woman a party to the criminality of the act, because it will destroy absolutely the method of getting evidence."[23]

Doctors such as Charles Bacon of Chicago argued that prosecutors could be successful if more physicians cared deeply enough about abortion to take abortionists to court and not let them off the hook. Bacon complained that few doctors put up with

the many disagreeable annoyances attendant upon fighting abortion: the loss of time resulting from attendance at the Coroner's and the Grand

---

20 *Ibid.*, p. 37.
21 *Providence Medical Journal*, Vol. 4 (1903), pp. 57-59.
22 Discussion at 1907 meeting of the Academy, *Bulletin*, Vol. 8 (1907), p. 347.
23 *Journal of the American Medical Association*, Vol. 2 (1908), p. 960.

Jury and finally at the trial . . . attacks to be expected from the defendant's attorney . . . the enmity of the friends of the accused midwife or physician is a factor that will cause many to hesitate to do anything that promises no return except loss of time and money, and worry and annoyance.[24]

Bacon cajoled his fellow doctors to try harder, but he acknowledged,

Ordinarily it is very difficult to get satisfactory evidence against a professional abortionist. The relatives or others interested in the case are generally very anxious to prevent any publicity for obvious reasons, and even in case of the death of the mother it is frequently impossible to get any member of the family to take action in the matter.[25]

Dr. W. H. Wathen of Louisville suggested that doctors "ostracize any man who will produce a criminal abortion," but such unity seemed unlikely.[26]

Even Dr. Rudolph Holmes, who had led Chicago's successful campaign against abortion advertising in newspapers, fell victim to the spiritual depression that seemed to creep over anti-abortion physicians. He had told the Chicago Medical Society that it must maintain vigilance, for the ads "undoubtedly will reappear in a new guise. . . ."[27] And yet, when that event happened in 1910 exactly as Holmes had predicted, he seemed close to despair. Holmes noted that abortionists, denied newspaper advertising space, were printing more business cards and distributing them through brothels and rooming-house landlords. He reported that Chicago abortionists had their own legal department, with witnesses on tap and ready to swear that "the young woman had an operation elsewhere and the doctor was merely performing a life-saving operation."[28] Holmes described the working methods of an abortionist who managed to stay out of jail year after year:

The cardinal principle of their actions is never to perform an operation with a witness present; her companion is rarely if ever allowed in the

---

[24]Bacon, "The Duty of the Medical Profession in Criminal Abortion," p. 21.
[25]*Ibid.*, p. 21.
[26]*Journal of the American Medical Association*, Vol. 3 (1908), p. 957.
[27]Minutes of the Chicago Medical Society, Vol. 17, October 1905 – June 1907.
[28]Dr. Rudolph Holmes, "The Methods of the Professional Abortionist," *Journal of Surgery, Gynecology and Obstetrics*, Vol. 10 (1910), p. 542.

room. If discovery is made it is her word against his; if she dies he stands alone. A very popular way is for two or more operators to work in harmony; one will make all the arrangements for the procedure, and then when all is ready another will slip in to do the work.[29]

Holmes also complained that regular doctors were performing or commissioning abortions. He spoke of three kinds of abortionists: the young doctor "inveigled into committing his first offenses in his pressing need for money"; the established physician "who largely is engaged in ethical practice but who systematically relieves his patients in order that he may hold his families"; and the full-time abortionist, often recruited by established doctors to handle their "dirty work."[30] Holmes noted that doctors in good standing in their local and national societies performed abortions and that their colleagues knew of the practice but were "too weak-kneed to take aggressive action for their expulsion." He also saw governmental complicity and asked, "What can you expect when a member of our legislature is backing financially and politically one of the most notorious abortion hospitals in Chicago?"[31]

What apparently pushed Holmes into despair was the sense that he was virtually all alone. He wrote,

I have come to the conclusion that the public does not want, the profession does not want, the women in particular do not want, any aggressive campaign against the crime of abortion. I have secured evidence. I have asked different physicians, who either had direct knowledge of crime against the prisoner before the bar or who could testify as to general reputation, to come and testify. They promised to come, but when the time for trial is at hand no one appears. On the other hand, so-called reputable members of our Chicago Medical Society regularly appear in court to support the testimony of some notorious abortionist.

Holmes complained that "it is not possible to get twelve men together without at least one of them being personally responsible for the downfall of a girl, or at least interested in getting her out of her difficulty." His conclusion was that "legislation is not needed, at least, in Illinois. We

---

[29]*Ibid.*, p. 543. Holmes added, "In Boston, a coterie of some four or five abortionists adopted this method – the operator would enter the room masked. One of these men confided in a lawyer that he and his associates were doing like 800 to 1,000 a year."
[30]*Ibid.*, p. 542.
[31]*Journal of the American Medical Association*, Vol. 2 (1908), p. 960.

have as good a law as perhaps can be made. It is the enforcement of law that is needed."[32]

Other doctors were angered by silence among societal leaders from other spheres. Walter Dorsett in 1908 told the AMA's Section on Obstetrics and Gynecology that "the clergy do not seem to be at all concerned. Few sermons are preached from the pulpit for fear of shocking the delicate feelings of a fashionably dressed congregation. . . ."[33] He complained that medical students were not being told about the enormity of the crime, and that many "yield[ed] to the temptation."[34] Women contemplating abortion, according to Dr. Edward A. Weiss, then saw "the apathy toward induced abortion on the part of their neighbors, physicians, and the world at large. . . ."[35] Everyone thought "lightly of the offence" and knew that the law was seldom enforced.

Dr. M. S. Iseman in 1912 presented one of the earliest twentieth-century pictures of hopelessness concerning abortion. In New York City, he wrote, "embryonic humanity has no more sanctity nor protection than the rats which infest its docks."[36] Regular M.D.s were the leading practitioners: "So general is the demand and so common the practice, that in the competition for the traffic the ordinary criminal operator has been practically driven out of the business by the highly skilled and respectable members of the medical profession." Well-connected women could gain permission for "therapeutic abortions" from those brilliant specialists of the art, the gynecologists, "whose philanthropic and unfailing tomahawks are whetted for every embryo daring to stray within the confines of a woman's clinic."[37]

Iseman described progressive-era New York as a mecca for abortion. "While the local traffic is as much as the thousand or more abortion specialists can attend to," he wrote, "the outside contingent is simply

---

[32]Holmes also placed hopes on education: young people "will know facts and will live accordingly. Many now make themselves believe that there is no life until the movements are felt. When the false teaching in this respect is put aside good will be accomplished." Holton similarly concluded, "I believe it is a matter of education to a great extent."

[33]Walter B. Dorsett, "Criminal Abortion in Its Broadest Sense," *Journal of the American Medical Association*, Vol. 2 (1908), p. 957.

[34]*Ibid.*

[35]Dr. E. A. Weiss, "Some Moral and Ethical Aspects of Foeticide," a paper read at the Annual Meeting of the American Association of Obstetricians and Gynecologists, Toledo, September 17-19, 1912; *American Journal of Obstetrics*, Vol. 67 (1913), p. 78.

[36]M. S. Iseman, M.D., *Race Suicide* (New York: The Cosmopolitan Press, 1912), p. 140.

[37]*Ibid.*

enormous, and during the season it is difficult to say which is the stronger attraction for the lady visitors to the metropolis – the horse-show, the opera, or the gynecologist."[38] He reported that "The laws against the crime of abortion are no more enforced in the great state of New York than the Revised Statutes of the United States are enforced in China. Out of the scores of thousands committed every year, in some years not a single indictment follows. According to the report of the Secretary of State on the statistics of crime for the ten-year period 1895-1904, there were only nine convictions in the entire State, of which two were in New York City."[39]

Iseman then took his readers on a city-by city tour of abortion law non-enforcement. In the District of Columbia, during the five-year period from 1905 to 1909, thousands of abortions resulted in only nine indictments for abortion and three convictions – not enough to do more than to slow down slightly the traffic to abort.[40] In the District, Iseman wrote, abortion referrals were made even in the "booths of the hairdressing parlors, the sanctums of the dressmaker, and the boudoir of the milliner, and what information cannot be obtained in these directories can be readily learned from the chambermaid or 'wash-lady.'"[41]

Other large cities were no better, Iseman reported. Enforcement was rare. For example, in Atlanta in 1911, "after years of suspended animation, the police made a solitary arrest for the crime of abortion . . ." That was not enough to deter abortionists who hired agents to distribute advertising cards in hotels.[42] Iseman concluded that "except in the formal letter of the statute books, the sanctity which nearly twenty centuries of Christianity has conferred upon the unborn human being is repudiated."[43]

The repudiation of that sanctity also made it easier to broaden indications for therapeutic abortion. "It seems that the wisdom of this can be scarcely questioned," Dr. Frank Higgins argued as early as 1904, because even though some doctors might "perform abortion in many unnecessary cases, it is believed that this will not be true to any large

---

[38]*Ibid.*, p. 141.
[39]*Ibid.*, p. 143.
[40]*Ibid.*, p. 158.
[41]*Ibid.*, pp. 153-154.
[42]*Ibid.*, p. 199.
[43]*Ibid.*, p. 155.

extent. . . ."[44] In the past, Higgins continued, doctors would induce abortion "only when the patient [was] suffering from such grave disease that her life is in eminent peril," but now many believed that the "termination of pregnancy is entirely justified to prevent the advance of what might later prove to be a fatal disease."[45]

Other doctors also discussed therapeutic abortion. Charles Jewett in 1908 wrote that induced abortion was commonly accepted when it could "interrupt morbid processes that threaten to cripple permanently important mental and physical functions." He reported the contention that "melancholia may be taken as a indication for abortion if the woman's condition is manifestly growing worse."[46] Charles Bacon noted in 1910 that Illinois law allowed therapeutic abortion only to save the life of the mother, but "As a matter of fact almost all therapeutic abortions are done to save the health of the mother."[47]

Edward A. Weiss, a Pittsburgh obstetrician, was a persistent critic of lenient standards for therapeutic abortion. He contended in 1913 that "life of the mother" exceptions in state laws were "so flexible that frequently the slightest indisposition of the mother is used as pretext and the life of the fetus is terminated with the conscience-satisfying excuse that it was necessary to preserve the life of the mother."[48] Weiss went on to argue that abortion was too common because students were taught to think of it as a first resort:

It is the exceptional teacher and writer on obstetrics and diseases in women that properly instructs his students on this important subject; more often the contrary is true and his lectures abound with reference and explicit directions as to when and how pregnancy should be terminated.

Weiss, contending that many unborn children were dying unnecessarily, hit hard at the standard teaching: "Is it any wonder then that the student

---

[44]Dr. Frank A. Higgins, "The Proper Indications and Methods for the Termination of Pregnancy," paper read at American Medical Association's 1904 Meeting, Section on Obstetrics and Diseases of Women, in the *Journal of the American Medical Association*, Vol. 43 (1904), p. 1531.

[45]*Ibid.*

[46]Charles Jewett, "Indication for Artificial Abortion in the First Three Months of Pregnancy," *New York State Journal of Medicine*, Vol. 8 (1908), p. 113.

[47]*Journal of Surgery, Gynecology and Obstetrics*, Vol. 10 (1910), p. 548.

[48]*American Journal of Obstetrics*, Vol. 67 (1913), p. 79.

who graduates from the classroom with little or no moral instruction goes forth to follow in the steps of Herod in the slaughter of the innocent?"[49] He argued, "If the unborn child had attorney to represent it at the courts of justice there would be a higher regard for its life. . . ."[50]

A decade later, at a meeting of obstetricians and gynecologists, Weiss still was insisting that "therapeutic abortions" were too common. He asked, "Is it any wonder that so many abortions are being performed by the laymen and the quack, when we, as a profession, give them so much leeway and encouragement?"[51]

Physicians' estimates of the efficiency of law went along with their sense of how much law could accomplish. In 1917 Dr. G. D. Royston questioned fifty-one women who admitted eighty-two illegal abortions (thirty self-induced, twenty done by physicians, twenty by midwives, twelve by drugs) and concluded that nothing would "deter a woman once determined to interrupt her pregnancy."[52] That same year Dr. John Murphy of New York complained that abortionists often dispatched patients to city hospitals confident that the patients would not be pressed to reveal the source of their affliction: "City hospitals are unwitting abettors of the abortionist . . . safe havens for what I might term criminally sick women."[53] Murphy wrote of how he had recently asked one patient if a doctor had "sent her to the hospital, and she answered, 'No one, I always come here after my abortions. . . . And I've told a number of my friends about it.'" Murphy concluded that the hospital "now seems to be a branch of the devil's workshop."[54]

The coming of the "Great War" raised questions about what Americans were fighting for. Dr. Robert McNair wrote in 1918 of "a strong indication of the standing of the criminal abortionist in modern society today, when it is considered how quietly and gracefully his practice is ignored."[55] McNair told of how one abortionist was "cornered, literally red handed" and arrested, but was soon free and "allowed to roam

---

[49] *Ibid.*

[50] *Ibid.*, pp. 74-75.

[51] *American Journal of Obstetrics and Gynecology*, Vol. 3 (1922), p. 46.

[52] G. D. Royston, "A Statistical Study of the Causes of Abortion," *American Journal of Obstetrics and Diseases of Women and Children*, Vol. 76 (1917), p. 582.

[53] John C. Murphy, "Are Municipal Hospitals Unwitting Aids to Abortionists?," *The Medical Times*, Vol. 45 (April 1917), p. 103.

[54] *Ibid.*

[55] Robert McNair, "Status of the Abortionist in the Modern Social Order," *New York Medical Journal*, Vol. 107 (March 16, 1918), p. 503.

at large in accordance with his own sweet will. The reason, it would seem, is quite simple, expressed in two words – public sentiment." The United States in the world war was fighting for a "world wide democracy," McNair commented, "but until we look more carefully to correcting the principles that must serve as the foundation to this great social order of progressive democracy, etc., there is serious danger of history repeating itself in the social conditions of ancient Rome. . . ." McNair concluded that "Huns and the Vandals came from without to pillage and destroy; in reality and it was afterward found out, that the Huns and the Vandals were within the walls of the eternal city."[56]

Complaints continued in the 1920s as Dr. Palmer Findlay of Omaha wrote of how hard it was "to convince the lay public that life begins at the moment of impregnation. . . ."[57] Findlay wrote that "Not one in a thousand [abortionists] is ever held accountable for the crime he commits," due to difficulties of evidence and reluctance to file complaints. Dr. N. W. Moore similarly noted, "notwithstanding our most drastic laws, the criminal is rarely convicted. If a guilty physician is placed on trial there is very often some sympathetic doctor-friend in his community ready to throw a mantle of charity around him."[58]

When the Obstetrics Society of Philadelphia in 1923 discussed ways to limit abortion, no new answers were forthcoming. Dr. Edward Schumann called abortion "an evil which has existed through all time and will continue to exist," with the only hope of limitation "more drastic laws" and "moral training of young people."[59] In the discussion that followed, Dr. John McGlinn said, "We should not ask the Legislature for more laws: we have more laws than we need at the present time and will only have another that will not be enforced because you cannot make people good by legislation."[60]

Doctors who forgot that legislation is education and stated the question that way – can *laws* make people good? – sometimes gave up when

---

[56]*Ibid.*

[57]Palmer Findlay, "The Slaughter of the Innocents," *American Journal of Obstetrics and Gynecology*, Vol. 3 (1922), p. 35.

[58]N. W. Moore, "Abortion, Criminal and Inevitable," paper read before the Kentucky State Medical Association, October 1922, *Kentucky Medical Journal*, Vol. 21 (1923), p. 332. Moore added, "Many places offer help, and when an unmarried woman becomes pregnant and consults me as to how to dispose of her case, I refer her to one of these institutions."

[59]Dr. Edward A. Schumann, "The Economic Aspects," *The American Journal of Obstetrics and Gynecology* (1924), p. 485.

[60]*Ibid.*, p. 486.

they saw that laws could not. At a symposium in 1908, Dr. Rachell S. Yarros of Chicago insisted, "You can not enforce laws . . . with which the public has little sympathy. Even if we could enforce anti-abortion laws the problems would not be solved."[61] At that symposium Dr. J. H. Carstens of Detroit held out little hope for the power of law as long as individuals thought "there is nothing earnest in this world. That it is just made for them and for their pleasure, and everything that interferes with that pleasure they object to and try to do away with . . . we shall never accomplish much by law."[62]

And yet, some doctors understood that the law did deter some abortions and save some unborn lives and that prosecution of a few abortionists sent many more running for cover, at least temporarily. In 1927, for example, Dr. E. A. Ficklen of New Orleans argued that hopes for "total abolition of the practice" would not be met, for in twenty-five states, over a ten-year period, only forty-four abortionists were convicted.[63] Ficklen explained why so few convictions were obtained under a Louisiana law that had been tightened in 1919: "In many instances there was a moral certainty of the guilt of the accused, but . . . drastic changes in criminal law with the requirements for evidence very much reduced would be necessary before we could expect more convictions."[64] Ficklen concluded that those changes would not be forthcoming, since the community was divided on abortion. And yet he did not conclude that current laws, although porous, were worthless. Laws that could not put abortionists in jail could at least restrict their practice.[65]

As early as 1906 some medical leaders who saw partial success as failure spoke of abandoning anti-abortion laws. Those who were pro-abortion then began to take advantage of such weariness. Dr. Henry Marcy argued in the *Journal of the American Medical Association* that "the

---

[61] *Journal of the American Medical Association*, Vol. 52 (1908), p. 548. She added, "Many women say that if they had a little support from the man, they would not think of having an abortion performed."

[62] *Ibid.*

[63] E. A. Ficklen, "Some Phases of Criminal Abortion," paper given before the Orleans Parish Medical Society, March 28, 1927; in *New Orleans Medical and Surgical Journal*, Vol. 79 (1926-1927), pp. 884-893.

[64] *Ibid.*, p. 886.

[65] Other means of restriction also could be useful. Dr. Edwin B. Harvey of Boston, for example, argued for containment by stripping known abortionists of their medical licenses. "The whole business of medical practise is curative, treating diseased persons for the purpose of mitigation of cure," Harvey noted. "What disease is the abortionist trying to alleviate or cure?"

product of early impregnation is of so little importance that abortion will not be seriously established as a criminal offense."[66] Maximillian Herzog closed one meeting of the Chicago Gynecological Society by opposing the idea of treating abortion at all stages as murder: "To look on an embryo four weeks old as a human being seems to be an exaggerated view."[67] Furthermore, Herzog saw doctors as god-like and argued that even dying declarations should not be allowed in court, since the physician's authority should outweigh a judge's: "whatever is confided to a physician is not to be divulged in court under any circumstances. The relations of physician and patient ought to be those of absolute confidence."[68]

Dr. William Robinson, who became a leading spokesman for abortion, told the Eastern Medical Society in 1911 that some unmarried women were right to abort their children, and wrote in 1915 that "The evil of abortion is one of the most terrible evils in our society," but only because of its danger to women.[69] Once he saw the problem as one of avoiding unnecessary risk at the hands of a quack, Robinson was able to conclude that "Under our present social and economical conditions the professional abortionist, much we may despise and condemn him, has more than once proved a real benefactor, in preserving the sanity, the health and the life of a frantic young woman and frantic family."[70]

By the early 1930s there was more such talk, and three different positions on abortion had emerged among physicians. On the left Robinson had become openly pro-abortion; he argued that infanticide (under the guise of accidental suffocation or drowning, medical overdose, exposure to cold, or simple abandonment) still was frequent and that "the legalizing of abortion" would solve the problem.[71] Robinson stated that it was "better to permit the removal of a few inanimate cells" than to have an "unwanted" child born. On the other end of the spectrum from Robinson was Dr. Matthew Liotta, who insisted "on the rights of the

---

[66]Henry Marcy, "Education as a Factor in the Prevention of Criminal Abortion and Illegitimacy," *Journal of the American Medical Association*, Vol. 47 (1906), p. 1889.

[67]*Journal of Surgery, Gynecology and Obstetrics*, Vol. 10 (1910), p. 550.

[68]*Ibid.*

[69]Dr. William Robinson, *Fewer and Better Babies, or the Limitation of Offspring* (New York: Critic and Guide, 1915), p. 121.

[70]*Ibid.*, p. 133. Robinson also cited (pp. 224-225) the European pro-abortion literature that was springing up.

[71]William J. Robinson, "Abortion and Infanticide," *American Medicine*, Vol. 39 (1933), p. 70. He expanded on these ideas in his book, *The Law Against Abortion* (New York: Eugenics Publishing Co., 1933).

unborn child as a human being from the moment of its conception. . . ."[72]
Liotta based his condemnation of abortion squarely on Biblical grounds:
"The commandment, 'Thou shalt not kill,' binds all men."[73] He saw his
fellow physicians as accomplices:

> . . . Never before in all past ages has there been such merciless killing of
> innocent, helpless and unborn human beings as is going on at the pres-
> ent time.

Atheistic "knowledge" and technical skill were fighting Biblical morality,
Liotta argued: "It is all very well to know science. What is most needed
is the art or skill which enables one to apply the principles of science in
a manner pleasing to God."[74]

Many physicians, however, seemed to be in the middle. Robert
Ferguson of Charlotte, for example, saw abortion as killing but wanted
to be "compassionate." The changed understanding of compassion was
evident when Ferguson told of a fourteen-year-old pregnant girl and
asked, "Should not we as organized bodies of medical men apply to the
Legislatures of the various States for relief for these unfortunate young
girls?" After all, Ferguson argued, "Conceptions of right and wrong
change from time to time, and theology, jurisprudence and medicine present radical differences on various points in different countries."[75] He
proposed that "The medical profession should work to the end that certain changes might be made in our National and State laws that would
permit the prevention of the attaching to our girls of 14 years of age and
under the stigma of having borne an illegitimate child."[76] By 1930 the
inevitability of induced abortion was assumed, and articles in medical
journals debated the effectiveness of conservative or radical post-abortion treatments of women without suggesting ways to avoid that choice
in the first place.[77]

At least in hindsight, a reading of hundreds of abortion-related arti-

---

[72]Matthew A. Liotta, *The Unborn Child* (New York: Liotta, 1931), Preface.
[73]*Ibid.*, pp. 9, 12-13. Liotta wrote, "God's punishments are meted out to everyone who
recommends or makes use of any method that will cause an abortion."
[74]*Ibid.*, pp. 11-12.
[75]Robert Thrift Ferguson, "Abortion and Abortionist," *Southern Medicine and Surgery*, Vol.
93 (December 1931), p. 889.
[76]*Ibid.*, p. 892.
[77]H. C. Hesseltine, "Indications for Treatment in Abortions," *Journal of the Iowa State
Medical Society*, Vol. 20 (1930), p. 406.

cles in medical journals from the first third of the century shows that when anti-abortion doctors tried to come up with effective "rationalistic" appeals, they sometimes emphasized arguments that had immediate usefulness but would, as it turned out, backfire later on. Rudolph Holmes, for example, proposed that "Arguments concerning the danger of having the operation done are to my mind more effective than too strong presentation of the moral aspect. . . ."[78] However, as abortion became physically safer for the mother, the downplaying of morality began to hurt.

So did the tendency of some to decree that religious concerns should play no part in the abortion debate. Although a Cleveland doctor, Rolande E. Skeel, complained after one discussion of "a very unfortunate thing indeed that a theological viewpoint has been allowed to enter that which should be a calm scientific consideration of a medical viewpoint," calm examinations apart from Biblical presuppositions tended to lead to more abortions.[79] This was particularly true as – in the words of Dr. J. D. Roberts – "parents of illegitimate children, prompted by the anxiety of the situation with disgrace and ostracism before them," pleaded with doctors to find them "any path out of the difficulty, regardless of law and morals."[80]

Sigmund Zeisler of the Chicago Gynecological Society proposed another method of approach that would haunt the anti-abortion movement. Zeisler wrote, "Whenever a moral question comes up for consideration, I always like to fall back on the old Kantian categorical imperative which is about as follows, 'Always act thus, that the motive underlying your actions may furnish the principle for a general law.'"[81] The categorical imperative for an abortionist, Zeisler wrote, meant

that everybody should commit abortion and that every pregnant woman should allow or consent to an abortion. What then would

---

[78]Rudolph Wieser Holmes, M.D., "Criminal Abortions; A Brief Consideration of Its Relation to Newspaper Advertising – A Report of a Medico-Legal Case," *Illinois Medical Journal*, Vol. 7 (1905), p. 30.

[79]*American Journal of Obstetrics*, Vol. 67 (1913), p. 81.

[80]J. D. Roberts, "Criminal Abortion," *Carolina Medical Journal*, Vol. 46 (1900), p. 135. Roberts asked that educational efforts by doctors continue, but that the vice be condemned from the pulpit; he had heard that done only once, "tho' more murders are annually committed in this way than all others combined."

[81]Sigmund Zeisler, "The Legal and Moral Aspects of Abortion," remarks at the 1910 meeting of the Chicago Gynecological Society, printed in the *Journal of Surgery, Gynecology and Obstetrics*, Vol. 10 (1910), p. 539.

become of this world? . . . That anything should ever become a general practice which would result in the total annihilation of the human race cannot be contemplated with degree of ease of mind. Hence it is self-evident that abortion is wrong, that it really needs no discussion from the moral point of view.[82]

Such an argument would not be compelling in later years when ideas of "overpopulation" became popular.

Some arguments did not take so long to turn around. Dr. Wilbur Krusen, in an echo of spiritist thinking, argued that it "is the right of every child to be well-born," yet "many an embryo is launched even upon an ante-natal career with a justifiable grievance."[83] Five years later Dr. James P. Warrbasse was arguing that the

child should not force itself upon parents that do not want it. It is so apt to find its self in an uncongenial atmosphere that three are caused to suffer where two were happy before. . . . Were the unconceived child to speak it might say, 'Let me be created in love and born only as a gift to parents whose hands are held out with loving welcome to receive me. Spare me from the hostile frown of my creators.' A babe is so important a thing that it is only deserving of loving parents. . . .

From there it was only one small step to aborting the "thing" to save it.[84]

Other attempts to make anti-abortion arguments without regard to theology also have a modern pro-abortion ring. Dr. Allen Gilbert wrote in *Pediatrics* that "Individual self-consciousness does not occur until the 2nd or 3rd year of life. Only then can the child say, 'I am.' Until then the child has the 'possibility of personality.'"[85] Gilbert stated that the possibility occurs with conception, so abortion should not be allowed: "a life *in utero* is sacred in that it represents the possibility of self-consciousness. . . ."[86] But others would take that statement of "possibility" as an opportunity to treat the unborn child as subhuman.

What many of these arguments had in common was their pragmatism.

---

82 *Ibid.*, p. 540.
83 *Therapeutic Gazette*, Vol. 34 (1910), p. 162.
84 James Warrbasse, "Let Me Be Created in Love," quoted in Robinson, "Abortion and Infanticide," pp. 244-245.
85 Dr. J. Allen Gilbert, "The Advent of Self-Consciousness and Its Relation to the Crime of Abortion," *Pediatrics*, Vol. 13 (1902), p. 296.
86 *Ibid.*, p. 298.

Dr. J. D. Roberts of North Carolina complained that the abortion-prone were not listening to doctors:

> Speak with as much authority as we may, urge as we have done for ages past as a profession, frown upon the practice, condemn it as iniquitous, censure the perpetrators as criminals, murderers, remonstrate with them with all our force, still . . . the God-given edict from Sinai's Mount 'Thou shalt not kill' is disregarded [by] the people of a corrupt and profligate time.[87]

Roberts noted that many doctors, either out of frustration or their own religious beliefs, were moving away from moral appeals and speaking against abortion on utilitarian grounds. Increasingly, the anti-abortion house appeared to be built on sand. The utilitarianism was reflected in early twentieth-century popular medical encyclopedias; unlike their late nineteenth-century predecessors, those that contained anti-abortion warnings generally stood only on utilitarian ground. For example, *The Household Physician: A Twentieth Century Medic* warned that "various womb complaints are the usual accompaniments" of abortion and capable of "ruining the future life or usefulness of the woman."[88] The *Century Book of Health* "warn[ed] women of the folly and danger" of abortion and contended that "death frequently results from the employment of such means as are necessary to produce abortion."[89] But with the maternal death rate in abortion about 2 percent, desperate women outside of marriage could take the chance.

Utilitarianism was so dominant that some medical books even had titles such as *The Human Machine: Its Care and Repair*.[90] Other popular books had only brief mentions of abortion. Edgar Maryott's *The New Medical World* simply noted that "Miscarriages criminally procured are to be deprecated, and any man or woman carrying on such unrighteous business should be dealt with as a base criminal."[91] A monstrously long book such as *Health Knowledge* (1,525 pages) discussed suppression of menses and – in the style of an earlier century – recommended use of cotton root, aloes, and other medication.[92] In all of those 1,525 pages just

---

[87] J. D. Roberts, p. 131. Roberts noted that Christian teachings were being overlooked as pagan ideas came back into vogue.

[88] *The Household Physician; A Twentieth Century Medic* (Boston: Woodruff, 1909).

[89] *Century Book of Health* (Springfield, MA: King-Richardson, 1912), pp. 486-487.

[90] *The Human Machine: Its Care and Repair* (Topeka: Herbert S. Reed, 1905).

[91] *The New Medical World* (Springfield, MA: Hampden Publishing, 1906), p. 531.

[92] J. L. Corish, *Health Knowledge* (New York: Domestic Health Society, 1919), p. 69.

nineteen words specifically commented on abortion: "Criminal abortion means that the womb was emptied intentionally. This is caused by taking drugs, or opening the womb."[93] Emphases on illegality and danger to the woman proved to be weak later in the century; once utilitarian thinking became supreme, the battle, in the long run, was lost.

"We are apt to grow sluggish, we are apt to go a little with the tide," Dr. George Phillips had warned in 1896.[94] Three decades later Dr. W. C. Bowers observed that "pressure is brought to bear on every physician from the day he opens his office till the end of his life, to have him commit abortion." Bowers said, "If he loses sight of the criminality of the affair, and the moral responsibility he takes, he is sometimes inclined to aid people who seem in very distressing circumstances, but if he ever does he has started down the hill."[95]

---

[93] *Ibid.*
[94] George A. Phillips, "Criminal Abortion: Its Frequency, Prognosis, and Treatment," *Maine Medical Association Medical Transactions*, Vol. 12 (1895-1897), p. 308.
[95] Fernald, p. 64.

11

The New Compassion

Nineteenth-century doctors such as O. C. Turner did not see abortion as a compassionate solution for a woman who had become pregnant through extramarital sexual relations. "By helping women out of such difficulties," Turner wrote, "the physician invites and encourages them to continue in their sins."[1] At the end of the century, Dr. George Phillips noted that "a produced abortion, if done with care and with antiseptic precautions . . . is free from much danger to maternal life," but that confidence did not lead him either to do abortions or to refer women to abortionists. "It is so easy to send them somewhere else and attend them afterward," Phillips wrote, "to at least grow indifferent in a toil that has no thanks, no money, the toil of teaching those who will not listen." However, Phillips then argued that "there is no other right way, and the responsibility presses more heavily when we remember that almost alone we stand against the wholesale slaughter of infant life."[2]

The new century began with the same understanding. In 1901 Dr.

---

[1]O. C. Turner, "Criminal Abortion," *Boston Medical and Surgical Journal*, Vol. 5 (1870), pp. 299-300.

[2]George A. Phillips, "Criminal Abortion: Its Frequency, Prognosis, and Treatment," *Maine Medical Association Medical Transactions*, Vol. 12 (1895-1897), pp. 306-307, 308.

Jennie Oreman, in *The Woman's Medical Journal*, similarly described her experience and belief:

> Women, ignorant of the right way of living, resort to different means of procuring criminal abortion, in order to escape the responsibilities and duties of maternity. For some reason or other they seek the woman physician and beseech her to rid them of their burden. They attempt to play upon her sympathy as a woman. . . .[3]

Dr. Oreman wrote that her response to such requests was to maintain "the physician's firm determination not to tolerate abortion." By challenging patients rather than adopting a false kindness, Dr. Oreman wrote, "we may control a part of the evil, though not by any means banish it."[4] She concluded, "Our duty as physicians is to be strong and firm in our 'no.' Practical moral sympathy is what the world needs, and not a flimsy sensual sympathy which is not altruism. . . ."[5]

What Jennie Oreman and many other physicians meant by "practical moral sympathy" was a referral not for an abortion but to an anti-abortion refuge. Studies obtainable from Massachusetts charities prior to 1920 show that such compassion often worked. For example, "case 28" in the files examined by researcher Percy Kammerer told of a young woman

> brought up in a home of dissipation and drunkenness. She was allowed by her mother to have intercourse with the landlord and with one of her boarders for financial gain, which reverted to the mother. This girl became pregnant when she was 20. Her father had always been a hard drinker and died of tuberculosis. The mother was alcoholic and immoral.[6]

The young woman had grown up in misery:

> Since her earliest recollection, she could remember only the most deplorable home conditions, which included much sickness and death besides poverty and drunkenness. He mother was drunk six days out

---

[3] Jennie Oreman, "The Medical Woman's Temptation and How to Meet It," *The Woman's Medical Journal*, Vol. 3 (March 1901), p. 87.
[4] *Ibid.*, p. 88.
[5] *Ibid.*
[6] Percy G. Kammerer, *The Unmarried Mother* (Boston: Little, Brown, 1918), p. 153.

of seven and was often insensible for days at a time. . . . Often the children became so frightened with the drinking and carousing that they would stay in the yard all night and once barricaded themselves in the attic to escape abuse.[7]

Nevertheless, all was not lost: "This girl was fond of reading and was familiar with some good books. She lacked self-confidence but had an active mind. . . ."[8] The mother, however, saw profit in renting out her daughter's body, not in developing her mind:

> When this girl was 15, her mother allowed a . . . boarder in their home to have intercourse with her. After this the landlord, who became the father of the child a few years later, frequently reimbursed the mother for her rent because of his sexual intimacy with her daughter.[9]

When pregnancy occurred, the landlord initially "endeavored to blame the paternity of the child on the other man," but he eventually "agreed to pay $5 a week in support of the child."[10] The charity organization that worked with this daughter offered her more than cash and more than mere kindness. It tried to implant a different psychology, so she could view herself not through her mother's depraved eyes: "She showed a keen insight as she reviewed her past experiences and with a good deal of determination resolved to begin a new life. . . ." Once the young woman saw herself as soul and not just body, "she appeared to be willing to win a good reputation at the cost of much patient endeavors."[11]

A change of self-image was also vital to a young woman who never had been taught that some behavior was wrong:

> There was no sort of control exercise during the developmental period; nothing preventing her from sleeping out at any time she so desired and running the streets at will with her immoral friends. . . . She was regularly promiscuous with boys in the parks and doorways before 14. She reports incestuous relations with her father and with her mother's cousin and seems to have been quite accustomed to a life of immoral-

---

[7] *Ibid.*
[8] *Ibid.*, p. 154.
[9] *Ibid.*
[10] *Ibid.*, p. 155. The sum *was* adequate child support prior to the post-World War I inflation.
[11] *Ibid.*, p. 154.

ity. She finds it impossible to remember with how many men she has
had intercourse and from whom she received various amounts. . . .[12]

Immediately before her pregnancy,

> she ran wild around the town with a group of streetwalkers, although
> now and then she would work for a time as a dishwasher or waitress in
> a local hotel. No companionship could have produced worse results;
> when arrested for being a runaway at 14 she was a half-starved, dis-
> eased, and savage prostitute. Under institutional care she showed her-
> self irritable and dishonest. . . . She suffered from spells of depression
> and bursts of temper during which she "smashed things"; her whole atti-
> tude towards life seems summed up in her remark . . . "No one cared
> what I did, why should they begin to now?"[13]

For this young woman pregnancy was the crisis that forced her to make
a choice: death for the unborn child and possibly herself as well, or a
changed life. The Boston charity organization was optimistic:

> The approaching confinement seems to have brought out hidden capac-
> ities in this girl . . . "I will live it down," she says. Her visitor maintains
> that she has never seen a girl feel so remorseful for her actions.[14]

Compassion in her case meant not easy comfort but challenge, with the
goal of producing sorrow for past misdeeds, and resolve to do differently
from that point.

Charitable organizations proceeded on the premise that marriage
was a good way out of unwed pregnancy and that the father of the unintended child should be brought quickly into discussions. One teenaged,
unmarried mother, after growing up in a broken home, sleeping around
from an early age, and using morphine and cocaine, became pregnant
for a second time and showed counselors a "quick temper and vindic-
tive brooding coupled with dishonesty and lying. . . ."[15] They did not
give up on her, however, and paid attention when she said she had slept
only with the father of her unborn child during the past six months and
did not want to lose him. The charity organization tracked down the

---

[12] *Ibid.*, p. 147.
[13] *Ibid.*, pp. 146-147.
[14] *Ibid.*, p. 147.
[15] *Ibid.*, p. 170.

father, "a sailor of about 22, with an unusually frank and generous disposition. He said that he had lived a loose life, never thinking of consequences."[16] The sailor "did not deny intercourse with this girl [but] showed a certain fondness for her and after due deliberation married her." The last report the organization received was that "this man had given up drink and that they had established a happy home life."[17]

Marriage also was the outcome for another young woman who began having intercourse at age eleven and gave birth at age sixteen:

> Her older brother, a drunkard, had relations with her as well as with her mother in her presence for a period of two years. Since the age of 15 she has been promiscuous with more boys, having intercourse at least three times each week.[18]

When a Boston home similar to the Erring Woman's Refuge took in the sixteen-year-old one month before her due date, she "had to be taught how to wash herself and care for her person." Nevertheless, after a year of Bible study, training and housework,

> she showed a marked improvement and a desire to do her duty by the child, so that she received the commendation of all who had to deal with her case. The father of her child settled the suit for $150 soon after the child's birth, and later, after the girl's improvement became evident, he married her.[19]

Such homes (two hundred and twenty-five of them early in the century) made Dr. Jennie Oreman's idea of compassion – "practical moral sympathy" rather than "flimsy sensual sympathy" – a reality each year for about twelve thousand unmarried mothers and their unborn children.[20]

Even as those cases were being recorded, however, other views were developing. The lead article in the first issue of Margaret Sanger's first magazine, *The Woman Rebel*, attacked "all this slushy talk" oppos-

---

[16] *Ibid.*

[17] *Ibid.*, p. 171.

[18] *Ibid.*, pp. 225-226.

[19] *Ibid.*, p. 226.

[20] Walter Barrett, *The Care of the Unmarried Mother* (Alexandria, VA: Crittenton, 1929), p. 6. There was no official figure for illegitimate births in the United States at that time, but one estimate for 1926 proposes approximately thirty-three thousand white births and thirty-six thousand black (about one illegitimate birth for every thirty-two hundred people in the white population and three hundred and twenty-eight in the black).

ing sex outside of marriage.[21] *The Woman Rebel* suggested that, for many unmarried adolescents, sexual intercourse was "an experience which has not 'ruined' them, but rather given them a larger version of life, stronger feelings and a broader understanding of human nature."[22] *The Woman Rebel* attacked institutions such as the Erring Woman's Refuge that turned an abandoned woman into "a traitor to her class and aim[ed] to reform her by means of a scrubbing brush and a club."[23] Every issue presented the credo of a new era: "The Rebel Women claim: The Right to be lazy./ The Right to be an unmarried mother./ The Right to destroy./ The Right to create./ The Right to love./ The Right to live."[24]

Margaret Sanger's publication regularly praised abortion. "The attitude of American law and 'public opinion' on the subject of abortion is about 1,000 years behind even that of Turkey, upon which Christians love to look condescendingly," an article in 1914 declared: "In Turkey abortion is not punished."[25] Author Dorothy Kelly offered her conclusion:

> It is necessary here only to quote the opinion of an expert on the subject, Dr. Klotz-Forest: Legally abortion is a crime. Honestly and scientifically it is not. One can only hope that good sense will triumph in the end, and that abortion, performed by an able practitioner in the best hygienic surroundings, will soon come to be regarded as useful, necessary, and humane, even in a case in which a woman requests it for no other reason than that she does not wish to have a child, that it is not her pleasure to become a mother.[26]

An article by Victor Meric similarly concluded, "If a woman is to free herself effectively, she must make herself absolute mistress of her own body. She must recognize her absolute right . . . to suppress the germ of life."[27]

The Rebel Woman also presented an alternative view of how to find true freedom. Ruth Pickering's poem "The Savior" stated:

---

[21] *The Woman Rebel*, March 1914, Vol. 1, No. 1, p. 1.
[22] *Ibid.*
[23] *Ibid.*, April 1914, p. 11.
[24] *Ibid.*, p. 3.
[25] Dorothy Kelly, "Prevention and the Law," *ibid.*, p. 10.
[26] *Ibid.*
[27] Victor Meric, "The First Right," *ibid.*

O – I am sick of you! . . . / I thought I touched your palm, thought you
were alive . . . /I bathed the ugly paralytic limbs/ Of some one old I cared
no straw about, /And thought you'd put freshness in my heart./ But
today I have broken the image of Christ,/ There is joy in my life, I am
free./ I stand on the threshold, look into the sun/ O, rise yellow butter-
fly/ Out of the road dust/ Up!/ Into blue sky.[28]

In Meric's summary, "Only a ridiculous idea of love and of the act of
reproduction, an idea handed down from the infamous Christian religion, could have led women to forget that she alone has the right to
decide."[29] Those who were truly loving would not have children. George
Lysander warned children yet to emerge,

[Do] not rush into this snare! / You may be born on Fifth Avenue and
be unwelcome./ Or on Canal street, where your brothers fight for food; /
You may grow up to be the prey of greed and lust – / Do you think it is
love who bids you come to us? It is love who bids us, who suffer, bar
the gates against you – / Bar them with tears and hungry longing in our
hearts.[30]

The "hungry longing" covered what might otherwise be construed as a
multitude of sinfulness.

Other ideas about compassion also emerged. By the 1920s many
social workers were describing unmarried pregnancy not as a moral
problem but as an expected activity that demanded "scientific treatment"
rather than "unimaginative and unprogressive" spiritual challenge.[31]
One social worker told Crittenton counselors who advocated marriage,
"You have stood still while the whole procession of social workers have
been marching onward."[32]

Professional social work, in part an outgrowth of the social gospel,
shared that doctrine's tilt toward the political left and its antipathy
toward fundamentalism. Thoroughly modern social workers tried to discourage followers of Helen Mercy Woods, such as the matron of a

---

[28] *The Woman Rebel*, May 1914, p. 45.
[29] Meric, "The First Right," p. 10.
[30] *Birth Control Review*, April 1918, p. 4.
[31] See Regina G. Kunzel, "The Professionalization of Benevolence: Evangelicals and
Social Workers in the Florence Crittenton Homes, 1915-1945," *Journal of Social History*,
Vol. 22 (Fall 1988), p. 21; see also *Florence Crittenton Bulletin*, Vol. 11 (1936), p. 29.
[32] National Florence Crittenton Mission, *Annual Report*, 1931.

Philadelphia Crittenton home who wrote that "my only plan is to remember Jesus and His love. . . ."[33] Secularized professionals saw religious homes as "steeped and saturated in a superheated emotional atmosphere of pseudo-moral indignation."[34]

The battle of worldviews was not fought out explicitly; instead, the philosophical debate was subsumed in an attack on "volunteerism." Social workers complained of an "influx of people, untrained, using our technical terms loosely, taking positions for which they are not fitted, sharing our titles. . . ."[35] For a time old-style compassion held its own, but a crucial blow came in 1929 when Crittenton national headquarters adopted the new thinking and stated that "Volunteer workers seldom have the experience necessary to make adequate investigations or the time to devote to it."[36] Community Chests used a variety of measures to induce their member agencies to "professionalize," and since they controlled the finances of their member agencies, the Chests exerted enormous influence over them. Community Chests encouraged and sometimes forced recipient organizations to drop theological distinctives and yoke themselves to other local agencies.

Some local groups resisted the demands to emphasize material redistribution rather than spiritual challenge. The Chicago Florence Crittenton Anchorage, one of the oldest Crittenton homes, fought off secular social workers, but the Chicago Council of Social Agencies in the late 1930s found the Crittenton Anchorage "deficient in virtually every respect of its program and facility" and refused to refer women to the Anchorage until "problems" were remedied.[37] The Chicago evangelical workers correctly understood the criticism to be, at bottom, a devaluation of the significance of the gospel and their own work, but they were chastised by the chain's national headquarters: "It is regrettable that the home is not used by social workers. It has always been an admitted fact that a good constructive program for the unmarried mother is the greatest need in Chicago."[38]

In Boston, where a similar battle was waged, the general secretary of the Boston home was able to write in 1933 that "In the past century

---

[33]Quoted in Kunzel, "The Professionalization of Benevolence," p. 29.

[34]*Ibid.*, p. 26.

[35]Mary Wheeler, "New Methods of Approach to Volunteers," *Family*, Vol. 2 (1921), p. 142.

[36]*Florence Crittenton Bulletin*, Vol. 4 (January 1929), p. 10.

[37]Quoted in Kunzel, "The Professionalization of Benevolence," p. 27.

[38]*Florence Crittenton Bulletin*, Vol. 16 (January 1941), p. 3.

the work has shifted from the feverishly emotional type of the earlier years to a more careful and thorough study of every phase of the problem of helping girls. The work has become more scientific and practical in its nature."[39] In Denver, Crittenton Home president Mrs. Eugene Revelle happily crooned about "Community Chests and their requirement for efficiency. . . ."[40] In Cleveland, as a study of maternity homes by Marian Morton noted, "Trained professionals took the place of the benevolent ladies who had earlier distributed relief and spiritual salvation."[41] All over, "professional social workers" replaced "evangelically-oriented matrons."[42]

Besides emphasizing secular "professionalism," many of the "progressive" social workers, under the leadership of reformers such as Judge Ben Lindsey of Denver, argued that "progressive compassion" meant accepting without challenge whatever situations arose. Letters to Lindsey (in the Library of Congress manuscript division) provide a fascinating insight into the roaring morality of the 1920s. When a Detroit man wrote to Lindsey asking for advice on the future of a *menage a trois* (husband, male boarder, and pregnant wife, without certainty as to the father of the child, with much jealousy), Lindsey replied that he could not "advise you definitely," for only those "most concerned can settle such a thing."[43] When a Los Angeles man criticized "the complaisant attitude with which thinking people like yourself accept . . . an orgy of licentiousness," Lindsey's wife sent back a letter stating that the judge merely was considering such activities "frankly and candidly" rather than judgmentally.[44]

Underlying the new compassion of Lindsey and many social workers was a new understanding of the nature of man, as popularized by

---

[39] *Ibid.*, p. 26.

[40] *Florence Crittenton Bulletin*, Vol. 13 (August 1938), p. 27.

[41] Marian J. Morton, "Seduced and Abandoned in an American City," *Journal of Urban History*, Vol. 11 (August 1985), pp. 464-465.

[42] Regina Kunzel ("The Professionalization of Benevolence," p. 22) has summarized the war as "a protracted struggle between evangelicals and social workers. This transfer of power did not take place quickly, easily, or without resistance; these styles of reform coexisted, if uneasily, for at least several decades. Evangelical women and social workers perceived each other as antagonists, and the Crittenton homes were one of the battle grounds. . . ."

[43] Letter to Lindsey, October 9, 1926; reply, November 1, 1926, in Library of Congress manuscript division, Lindsey box 355.

[44] Letter to Lindsey from Cyrus Eshelman, Ludington, Michigan, November 18, 1926, and Mrs. Lindsey's response (December 12, 1926, in box 355).

Lindsey both in articles and in books such as *The Companionate Marriage.*[45] Lindsey attacked Christian "teaching about original sin and the fall of man" and demanded of a minister, "why don't you drop all that and commit yourself to the thesis that human beings are only too glad to be good if they can see their way to being so . . . ?"[46] When the minister responded that Lindsey was preaching "paganism," Lindsey responded,

> what I say to these young people is this: you are free agents. . . . The judge that must judge you is your own heart and conscience. . . . Nobody can stop you, and I for one, wouldn't stop you even if I could.

Anti-abortion laws, however, were frankly anti-choice; they were based on the belief that God, not individuals, did the judging, and that abortion should be stopped whenever possible.

In this way the old compassion (helping a woman to do what was right) and the new (helping her do whatever she believed was right) came into conflict. Furthermore, the consensus on what was right became shaky as theological leaders lost prominence in American society and medical leaders backed off from a firm stand against abortion. For over a half-century since the American Medical Association's 1859 committee report condemning abortion, doctors had maintained publicly a united front. But during the 1920s, some editorials in the *Journal of the American Medical Association* began to portend a return to the old quickening distinction dropped in 1859. One editorial, for example, noted that "In a strictly scientific and physiologic sense, there is life in an embryo from the time of conception," but then suggested that doctors abide by the looser view that "it should be less of an offense to destroy an embryo in a state in which human life in its common acceptance has not yet begun than to destroy a quick child. . . ."[47] Soviet legalization of abortion received favorable attention not only in journals of the left but even in the sedate *American Journal of Public Health*, which proclaimed that "good specialists" were performing abortions in the Soviet Union and that "Legalized abortion is the only means for women's emancipation. . . ."[48]

---

45 Ben B. Lindsey and Wainwright Evans, *The Companionate Marriage* (New York: Boni and Liveright, 1927).
46 *Ibid.*, p. 338.
47 *Journal of the American Medical Association*, Vol. 82, (1924), p. 1806.
48 "Ten Years of Legalized Abortion in the Soviet Union," *American Journal of Public Health*, September 1931, p. 1043.

In 1914 *The Woman Rebel* had taken the lead in reviving the idea (proposed by Robert Dale Owen and others in the 1820s) that contraception works well as an alternative to abortion: "Abortions, with their horrible consequences, are quite needless and unnecessary when the subject of preventive means shall be open to all to discuss and use."[49] Dr. William Robinson in 1915 argued that "the knowledge of prevention of conception would do away entirely with the evil of abortion or would reduce it at least to a minimum."[50] Moderate writers also began to turn out articles arguing that contraception was the alternative to abortion. *Medical World* in 1918 called for a repeal of birth control bans, while maintaining the position "that abortion should not be performed except, if ever, as a last resort to save the life of the mother. . . ."[51] Popular medical books began to praise contraception as the compassionate alternative to abortion: "Almost every one of these millions of unhappy abortions are absolutely unnecessary . . . they could all be prevented by telling people how to prevent conception," a book that went through forty editions proclaimed.[52]

Debate about the sale of contraceptives (illegal in many states since the 1870s) raged through the 1920s.[53] Had the different sides accepted the compromise proposed by the *Texas State Journal of Medicine* in 1917 – "an act permitting the dissemination of the knowledge among married women" – the contraception debate, which anticipated the abortion debate, would have been changed for the better.[54] Those who saw the Bible as forbidding birth control even within marriage were determined, however, and the debate soon was polarized. Advocates of contraception shrewdly publicized pleas from the married who already had large families and were economically troubled. During the first half of 1918 the *Birth Control Review* printed nineteen letters requesting birth control infor-

---

[49] *The Woman Rebel*, May 1914, p. 24. The article gave a figure of two hundred thousand abortions per year, with at last six thousand maternal deaths.

[50] William Robinson, *Fewer and Better Babies, or the Limitation of Offspring* (New York: Critic and Guide, 1915), p. 122.

[51] *Medical World*, July 1918; reprinted in *Birth Control Review*, October 1918, p. 4.

[52] Nichols and Jefferis, *Safe Counsel*, 40th edition (Nashville: The Southwestern Co., 1934), p. 98. Nichols and Jefferis also asked rhetorically a question that could not be fully answered for several decades: "If the real facts of birth control were common knowledge, how could the professional abortionist's business flourish?" In recent years, of course, contraception and abortion have flourished alongside each other.

[53] The Supreme Court finally closed out the argument with the *Griswold* and *Baer* decisions that cleared the way for *Roe v. Wade*.

[54] *Texas State Journal of Medicine*, September 1917.

mation, and all were from married people.[55] Opponents of contraception were said to lack compassion when they did not distinguish between sexual conduct within and outside of marriage.

While advocates of sexual liberation concentrated public attention on the plight of poor people with large families and on the lobbying power of the Catholic Church, one fact often was overlooked: use of contraceptives did not necessarily lessen the incidence of abortion. By 1938 the female authors of *Facts and Frauds in Women's Hygiene* could note that "a rather high percentage of failures has been reported from the use of condoms, the birth control clinics finding that almost 50 percent of the women relying upon them have become pregnant despite their use."[56] The trade magazine *Manufacturing Chemist* reported in April 1935 that 45 percent of condoms purchased on the open market contained imperfections, and 20 percent of those (9 percent of all condoms) clearly did not contracept.[57] Diaphragms also were not pregnancy-proof, and one veteran obstetrician wrote to Judge Ben Lindsey,

> I am thoroughly in accord with you in your ideas as to birth control [but] you have a very marked confidence in contra-ceptive methods, much more than I have. . . . I am of course familiar with a number of the so-called contra-ceptive methods and devices, but up to the present time I have found none that were constantly dependable, except of course the complete abstinence from all sexual contact.[58]

If the false security of contraception led to a greater frequency of sexual intercourse outside of marriage, the result could be more crisis pregnancies that might end in abortion rather than fewer.[59]

Furthermore, individuals who became used to immediate gratification were unlikely to think of long-term consequences. For that reason, Dr. Edward Schumann told the Obstetrics Society of Philadelphia in 1923 that he was "very skeptical of beneficial results accruing from the propagation of popular knowledge relative to contraceptive measures."[60]

---

[55] *Birth Control Review*, January 1918, p. 13.

[56] Rachel Lynn Palmer and Sarah Greenberg, *Facts and Frauds in Woman's Hygiene* (Garden City, NY: Garden City Publishing Co., 1938), p. 271.

[57] *Ibid.*, p. 271.

[58] Letter from a Kansas City obstetrician, September 18, 1926, Lindsey papers, box 355.

[59] In addition, contraceptive use could lead to a faith in autonomy, and consequent anger when unplanned pregnancies occurred.

[60] Dr. Edward A. Schumann, "The Economic Aspects of Abortion," *The American Journal of Obstetrics and Gynecology*, (1924), p. 485. Eight years later Schumann added a eugenics

By 1931 Dr. A. J. Rongy, a proponent of birth control, was frankly discussing its limitations: "Through many sad and disappointing experiences" he had learned that

> there is no contraceptive now in use which positively safeguards the woman against pregnancy. No mechanical contrivance used by the woman or the man is always safe. No chemical agent is always effectual. That the most ardent birth control teacher must admit. Now, if this be the case, the birth rate will be affected whether a mishap takes place in a hundred or five hundred times of sexual relationship.[61]

Rongy wanted doctors to combat "birth control propaganda" that led people "to believe that contraceptive agents, properly utilized, never fail."[62]

Conservative forces, in short, could have built an alliance with moderates by accepting contraception among the married and showing that distribution of contraceptives to the unmarried resulted in more abortion rather than less. Instead, moderates who wished to use birth control within marriage and saw no Biblical proscription of it found themselves allied with forces of the left that demanded absolute freedom for individuals. Patterns of alliance thus formed would continue through the 1960s and make possible an eventual abortion victory.

Anti-abortion forces hurt themselves in two other ways also. First, racism was present in the shelter movement, as in American society generally. The Salvation Army's thirty-four homes for unmarried mothers did not discriminate on grounds of color, but at other shelters black unmarried mothers and their unborn children were not welcome.[63]

---

twist: "Among the more intelligent classes of people, where it is so essential that children should be born, there is apparently sufficient contraceptive knowledge to limit the birth rate."

[61] A. J. Rongy, M.D., "Abortion and Birth Control: A Critical Study," *American Medicine*, Vol. 37 (1931), p. 404. Rongy noted that "Statistics gathered in birth control clinics on the effectiveness of contraceptive agents are not always correct, and very often do not furnish a true index for the conclusions arrived at. There are innumerable patients attending these clinics who become pregnant. These women seldom return to the clinic until the pregnancy is gotten rid of. When these women come back to the clinic they seldom tell what has transpired for fear that further treatment will be refused them."

[62] *Ibid.*. p. 405. Rongy hoped that birth control technology would improve and argued that "Birth control education is preparing the soil for a proper reception by the body politic of positive contraceptive agents, which sooner or later will be discovered in some medical research laboratory."

[63] The Crittenton chain had a few homes for "colored girls."

Second, anti-abortion forces sometimes fell into anti-adoption sentiment. Brace's nineteenth-century adoption movement had discouraged abortion by showing that good homes were available for children from the slums. Dr. W. J. Fernald of Illinois argued in 1903, however, that a woman who placed for adoption "the sign of her shame . . . has crucified the tenderest instinct of her womanhood and is unspeakably base."[64] By the 1920s Crittenton policy was, "Motherhood is often the means of regeneration; hence the mother must be kept with the child for the influence it will have upon her."[65]

The influence was not always benign. Sometimes the young mother was able to handle single-parenting, and at other times she and the father of the child would marry following birth, but the emphasis on *always* working to keep the mother and child together became a problem.[66] Adoption continued, of course, with large maternity homes and private arrangements meeting the demand; yet as agencies providing Biblical compassion deemphasized adoption, new problems emerged, for (as Crittenton's Walter Barrett acknowledged), "Commercial agencies [were] not particularly concerned with the moral rehabilitation of the mother. . . ."[67]

If "unwanted children" generally were not to be adopted, and if black mothers and their children were often to receive no help at all, what would happen to them? *Eugenical News*, the popularly written magazine of the American Eugenics Society, attacked in 1917 those who did not "discriminate against the more socially worthless human strains in favor of the more gifted. . . ."[68] *Eugenical News*, however, proposed an alliance of racists: "If the Birth Control League would . . . advocate differential fecundity on the basis of natural worth, it should have the hearty support of true eugenicists."[69] Seven years later, as birth control was catch-

---

[64]*Illinois Medical Journal*, Vol. 5 (1903), pp. 62-63.

[65]Barrett, *The Care of the Unmarried Mother*, p. 49. In 1927, the 44th Annual Crittenton Conference declared that "keeping mother and child together . . . is now approved by the best informed pubic opinion, as shown by audiences of experts in social service."

[66]At the time, given the greater infant mortality in the absence of breast-feeding, it was in the child's interest to be with the mother at first. But after the first year, the child ordinarily would be better off having an adoptive mother and father in a family that desired his presence.

[67]Barrett, *The Care of the Unmarried Mother*, p. 53. Nor, in many cases, was even minimum care taken in placing a child: "All kinds of abuses [became] associated with these [agencies], and adoption often received a bad name."

[68]*Eugenical News*, Vol. 2 (1917), p. 73.

[69]*Ibid*. The American Eugenics Society operated with financing from John D. Rockefeller, Jr., George Eastman, and others.

ing on, *Eugenical News* restated its offer: "We don't want a change of marriage rate, of birth rate, or of death rate per se, but we want selection for quality all the way through . . . if sterilization, if anti-conceptual propaganda will bring about the desired result, they are to be welcomed."[70]

At first there was no alliance, and eugenicists vigorously criticized the contraceptive push:

[T]he more intelligent people learn of the methods of birth control and employ them, whereas the proletariat learns less readily and has stronger procreative instincts. One fears that the end of such a propaganda might be to cut off still more the reproduction of the intellectuals or of the otherwise most successful without diminishing to an important degree the offspring of the less effective, so that our later social state would be worse than the former.[71]

Other American magazines shared such concerns. "Prevention of conception is already an accepted principle among the educated classes of every civilized country," *Critic and Guide* reported, and forecast a "dire" result: the "best elements will gradually be replaced by the worst."[72] On the other side of the Atlantic, eugenics concern also was high. British Socialist Sydney Webb complained that "In Great Britain at this moment, when half, or perhaps two-thirds of all the married people are regulating their families, children are being freely born to the Irish Roman Catholics and the Polish, Russian, and German Jews on the one hand, and the thriftless and irresponsible. . . . This can hardly result in anything but natural deterioration."[73]

Eugenicists seemed particularly concerned about racial issues. "Today it appears an exaggeration to speak of the dying out of the white race," *Eugenical News* argued in 1927. "In two or three decades the problem will have become a vital one, unless a decisive change occurs in the attitude of white people."[74] *Eugenical News* concluded in 1936 that "White America does not realize that the Negro problem is a biological problem, that it is not a problem of environment, but of race . . . the great trouble

---

[70]*Eugenical News*, Vol. 9 (1924), p. 39.

[71]*Eugenical News*, Vol. 10 (1925), p. 132.

[72]Cara G. Stillman, "The Prevention of Conception," *Critic and Guide*, quoted in Robinson, *Fewer and Better Babies, or the Limitation of Offspring*, pp. 187-188.

[73]Sidney Webb, *The Decline of the Birth Rate* (London: The Fabian Society, 1909), pp. 39-40.

[74]*Eugenical News*, Vol. 12 (1927), p. 23.

is that the white man has not thought clearly on the Negro problem."[75]
Clear thinking for *Eugenical News* in the 1930s meant a rash of articles
from Germany. The magazine breathlessly reported the latest Nazi
research:

> Dr. Friedrich Burgdorfer, Chief German Statistician, made some unique
> disclosures which throw light on the dangers to which the white races
> are exposed. . . . If the white nations, from a fear of over-population have
> advocated and practiced birth-control, it does not mean that all races
> have followed their example.

Eugenical News complained that "the colored races do not – so far at
least – practice birth-control. Black, brown, yellow races continue to multiply very considerably."[76]

Eugenical News also praised anti-Semitic programs: "The German
nation has adopted a policy of biological improvement in its racial quality as its major national objective, to which all other objectives are
regarded as subsidiary." According to *Eugenical News*, "farsighted compassion" was present in Hitler's goal of attaining "the increased proportionate reproduction of the more competent eugenic stocks, and the
proportionate decrease of the incompetent and undesirable dysgenic
stocks."[77] In the light of later revelations, the magazine's enthusiasm is
particularly chilling: "These objectives do not stop at perfunctory professions, but the most thorough and complete measures have been
adopted to secure their maximum realization."[78]

When some readers raised questions about Nazi treatment of life and
liberty, *Eugenical News* editorialized that no one need be concerned:

> Special courts have been set up in Germany which carefully weigh the
> racial values pro and con in each case, and in which the legitimate indi-
> vidual interest is fully safeguarded. Every case is considered and decided
> upon its own merits, and there is the further right of appeal. No one who
> knows the strict legality that pervades all German court procedure can
> doubt that these laws will be administered with entire fairness.[79]

---

[75]Earnest S. Cox, "Repatriation of the American Negro," *Eugenical News*, Vol. 21 (1936),
p. 138.
[76]*Eugenical News*, Vol. 20 (1935), p. 12.
[77]Dr. C. G. Campbell, "The German Racial Policy," *ibid.*, Vol. 21 (1936), p. 1.
[78]*Ibid.*
[79]*Ibid.*, p. 27.

As late as 1938 *Eugenical News* was praising Nazi racial policy and its attempt to "decrease and eventually eliminate the poor stock; increase and eventually produce only sound stock."[80] Through such efforts "the morale of the German people has been raised" and a model for the world created: "a nation that is intelligent enough to see that its first necessity is the biological one of improving in its racial quality . . . and to neglect no means of accomplishing, this end."[81]

Furthermore, *Eugenical News* authors from the 1920s through the 1940s did more than complain; they recommended means and methods of reducing the number of "unfit" births." As early as 1923 *Eugenical News* argued that "the high infant mortality rate of [illegitimate] children, which is two or three times the average, is eugenic, in weeding out anti-social strains." *Eugenical News* criticized "proposals to change the laws concerning illegitimacy" that would "sav[e] the lives of these anti-social individuals . . . these changes are nearly all dysgenic."[82] The objective was death of the "unwanted," readers could logically infer. But how could that goal be reached? How could those activities be expanded?

As it turned out, Margaret Sanger had the solution. She was in many ways a Social Darwinist throwback in her criticism of programs (both private and governmental) that provided "medical and nursing facilities to slum mothers."[83] She complained that "The work of the maternity centers in the various American cities . . . is carried on among the poor . . . among mothers least able, through poverty and ignorance to afford the care and attention necessary for successful maternity." She opposed the "dysgenic tendency [of supporting] maternity among the very classes in which the absolute necessity is to discourage it."[84] She argued that "Such philanthropy . . . brings with it, as I think the reader must agree, a dead weight of human waste. Instead of decreasing and aiming to eliminate

---

[80]*Eugenical News*, Vol. 23 (1938), p. 116.
[81]Campbell, "The German Racial Policy," p. 29. Other *Eugenical News* articles praising Nazi innovations included Marie Kopp, "The German Program of Marriage Promotion Through State Loan," *Eugenical News*, Vol. 21 (1936), pp. 121-129. *Eugenical News*, Vol. 21 (1936), p. 58, reported, without criticism, "Nazi recording of racial information and restrictions on marriages between Jews and non-Jews." *Eugenical News* noted criticism of German eugenics but stated, "It is unfortunate that the anti-Nazi propaganda with which all countries have been flooded has gone far to obscure the correct understanding and the great importance of the German racial policy."
[82]*Eugenical News*, Vol. 8 (1923), p. 66.
[83]Margaret Sanger, *The Pivot of Civilization* (New York: Brentano's, 1922), p. 114.
[84]*Ibid.*, p. 116.

the stocks that are most detrimental to the future of the race and the world, it tends to render them to a menacing degree dominant."[85]

Margaret Sanger was explicitly eugenicist in 1925 when she gave the welcoming address to an international eugenics conference. She complained that "the United States shut her gates to foreigners," but "no attempt whatever is made to discourage the rapid multiplication of undesirable aliens — and natives — within our own borders."[86] She suggested that the federal government "expend some of its vast appropriations on a system of bonuses to decrease or to restrict the incessant and uninterrupted advent of the hordes of the unfit . . ."[87] She demanded "a system of bonuses to unfit parents paying them to refrain from further parenthood and continuing to pay them while they controlled their procreative faculties." She said such an approach would "not only be a profitable investment, but the salvation of American civilization."[88]

Had *Time* magazine chosen a "woman of the half-century" in 1950, Margaret Sanger would have been an appropriate honoree. She had contempt for the compassion exemplified in the career of Helen Mercy Woods, and in its place she proposed an alternative. Compassion toward women like herself meant a furthering of their opportunity to be freely autonomous; compassion toward the next generation meant eliminating unwanted children, preferably through contraception, if necessary through abortion; macro-compassion, for the nation and the world, meant a system of keeping the "unfit" (minorities generally included) from becoming parents.

These inclinations did not always fit together, as the history of contraception from the 1920s through the 1950s shows. In the early 1950s *Eugenical News* drew the lessons of the past three decades: "inequality in access to contraceptive information and in skill in applying it is the major factor now operative to produce the well-known tendency of the less favored groups to have more children."[89] The worst period from the eugenicists' perspective was that in which contraception was used by some but not diffused: "Birth control is responsible for an increase in class differentials when it is first introduced, because it tends to be used

---

[85]*Ibid.*
[86]Margaret Sanger, ed., *The Sixth International Neo-Malthusian and Birth Control Conference* (New York: American Birth Control League, 1925), p. 5.
[87]*Ibid.*, p. 6.
[88]*Ibid.*
[89]*Eugenical News*, Vol. 37 (1952), p. 35.

by the upper socio-economical classes before it gets down to general use in the lower."[90] The eugenicist hope was that "present conditions are probably temporary. As birth control gets more firmly established, and the practice of family planning is more widely accepted, class differentials in births diminish."[91] The point to remember was that "not alone the extension of birth control, but more the manner of its extension will determine the future. . . ."[92]

The goal since the 1920s had been the placing of contraceptive offices in low-income areas; *Eugenical News* praised such offices whenever they were "functioning eugenically in so far as they are reaching those in the general population possessed of dull-normal intelligence."[93] Margaret Sanger's "Negro Project" of the 1930s was similarly hailed for its work in spreading contraception among those whom eugenicists most deeply feared. By mid-century, however, believers in the new compassion were contending that not enough was being done. Population increases in the United States and around the world showed that contraception was not saving the world from the suffering to come. When women became pregnant as contraception failed or was not used, they (or their mates/loves/seducers) demanded a way out of immediate distress and charged that anyone who held up a stop sign or even a caution flag lacked compassion.

During the Depression, economic considerations also played a part in public attention to who was having children and under what material circumstances. But so did a new outpouring of anthropological research that attempted to show the universal similarity of human society regardless of worldview. Herbert Aptekar's *Anjea: Infanticide, Abortion and Contraception in Savage Society* was typical of this genre.[94] Aptekar showed that abortion was common in societies around the world:

Certain Eskimo tribes used a thinly carved rib of walrus which is sharpened as a knife on one end, while the opposite end is made dull and rounded. The sharp end is covered with a rolled cover made of walrus skin, which is opened on both ends, and the length of which corresponds to the cutting part of the piece of bone. A long thread made of

---

[90] *Ibid.*, Vol. 38 (1953), p. 83.
[91] *Ibid.*
[92] *Ibid.*
[93] *Eugenical News*, Vol. 13 (1928), p. 95.
[94] Herbert Aptekar, *Anjea: Infanticide, Abortion and Contraception in Savage Society* (New York: William Godwin, 1931).

the sinews of reindeer is fastened to the upper as well as lower end of the cover.

When the probe is being placed in the vagina, the sharp part is covered with the leather covering. After it has been inserted far enough the thread fastened on the lower end of the covering is gently tugged. The sharp end thus being bared, a half turn is given the probe together with a thrust upwards and inwards, which punctures the uterus. Before withdrawing the instrument, the upper thread of the covering is pulled in order to cover the sharp end, thus preventing further injury to the genital organs.[95]

W. E. Masters, a physician who lived among the natives of the Kasai basin in Central Africa tells of a patient: "Several decoctions were prepared from native plants and given to the girl without success, for the girl became pregnant. The natives then administered a black powder which was 'sure to bring the child away prematurely.' The dose was followed by severe vomiting, acute abdominal pain, diarrhoea, and exhaustion for two days. This dose was repeated at intervals of a month and in the sixth month the foetus was expelled."[96]

Aptekar then argued that contraception, despite birth controllers' rhetoric, would not eliminate abortion:

The evolutionary scheme has it that as infanticide diminishes abortion takes its place, and as abortion becomes less rife, contraception takes its place. The truth is, however, that the employment of any one of these practices extensively does not necessarily entail the diminution of the others. Given a strong enough desire to restrict the size of families, both abortion and infanticide, or abortion and contraception might be – and in fact have been – used more extensively than either alone.[97]

Aptekar then summed up:

Contraception and abortion are tools. Like most tools they are laden with potentialities for both destruction and construction. . . . As matters stand now, we have failed utterly to prove that as a people we are intelligent enough to direct these instruments for the welfare of our society. Birth rates in Western Civilization race, unbridled, toward a precipice.

---

[95] *Ibid.*, pp. 142-143.
[96] *Ibid.*, pp. 143-144.
[97] *Ibid.*, pp. 150-151.

Pointing to the United States, Aptekar particularly criticized "antiquated laws [that] impede intelligent efforts to equalize the most uncalled for differences in the birth rates of the laboring and upper classes."[98]

The anthropological acceptance of abortion was part of a larger theological shift, as Harry Elmer Barnes made clear in his foreword to Aptekar's book: "The outstanding revolution in the perspective of man in our time is the development of a truly humanistic outlook upon life and its problems." Previously in Western civilization

> our primary interests have been otherworldly. It was natural and logical that this should be so. What was the longest human life, never far exceeding a century, compared to the limitless expanse of eternity where man lived on forever either in matchless happiness or in the most unspeakable torments? Now that science has at last destroyed any possible basis for the belief in a literal immortality . . . we are free at last to devote our intelligence and energy to the problems of making this life here and now more worthwhile. . . . The first step is to develop a rational and tolerant attitude towards the philosophy and practice of birth control [and] civilized medical ethics in the handling of abortion policy and practice.[99]

During the 1920s and 1930s theological liberals took charge of several mainline American denominations. Although an outright shift in policy regarding abortion took another generation, the practical "pro-choice" application was a natural outgrowth of a liberal faith that opposed God's sovereignty and placed "reason" above revelation.

Economic depression, anthropological teaching, and theological change formed the background for the most influential pro-abortion book of the 1930s, Dr. Frederick Taussig's *Abortion*. Taussig recommended legalized abortion whenever "the mother is physically depleted by childbearing and poverty" or "clearly irresponsible."[100] He argued that the primary concern of doctors should not be the life of the unborn child along with the life of the mother. Instead, Taussig suggested a "freedom from religious bias" that would lead to "consideration for the health of the mother," including mental health, and concern for the welfare of the family as a whole. Socioeconomic and mental health rationales for

---

[98]*Ibid.*, p. 185.
[99]*Ibid.*, pp. v, vii.
[100]Frederick J. Taussig, *Abortion* (St. Louis: C. V. Mosby, 1936), p. 448.

abortion were radical steps that, when taken, could open wide the doors of abortion businesses. Taussig embedded such proposals, however, in a suggestion that the number of abortions, legal or not, would always be high and that the only way to reduce the number of non-doctors performing illegal abortions was to allow more legal ones.

Taussig's nationwide estimates of 681,600 abortions and eight thousand maternal abortion deaths annually received a boost when a full-page review in *Time* magazine pronounced his book "authoritative."[101] *Time*, which was famous for snide attacks on individuals its editors did not like, simply described Taussig as "a handsome man" with a "great" family and an emphasis on "strict and meticulous clinical work."[102] Editors also accepted Taussig's contention that the cause of maternal deaths in abortion was not the general inability of doctors to stop infections at that time, but the "secretiveness growing out of laws which declare abortions criminal unless performed to preserve the health or life of the mother."[103] Furthermore, *Time* relayed Taussig's encouragement of abortions when there were "eugenic reasons," "suicidal tendencies," and "economic reasons in women of high fertility."[104] The change in thinking among some leading doctors was beginning to have broad public repercussions.

By 1942 doctors sympathetic to abortion were able to hold a conference on the practice at the New York Academy of Medicine. There Dr. Sophia Kleegman charged that restrictions on abortion were formulated largely by the "theological dogma" of "one particular church." Other conference speakers argued that when abortion was a possibility for a woman, the only compassionate response was that "the ultimate decision should be hers."[105] As in medical meetings of earlier years, theologians were invited to speak on moral aspects of abortion, but this time the guest speaker was not an evangelical minister or a Catholic priest, but Algernon Black of the Ethical Culture Society. Black opposed the view that "abortion is the destruction of a human being" and contended

---

[101] *Time*, March 16, 1936, p. 52.

[102] *Ibid.*

[103] *Ibid. Time* did use the word "abortion," at a time when other newspapers still referred to "illegal operation."

[104] *Ibid.* A few years later abortion in cases of probable infant deformity, women's mental health, and family poverty would become part of the liberalization package that pro-abortion forces would demand.

[105] *The Abortion Problem: Proceedings of the Conference Held Under the Auspices of the National Committee on Maternal Health, Inc.* (Baltimore: Williams and Wilkins, 1944), pp. 50-52, 104.

that an unborn child "has not the selfhood [sic], the relationships, or the consciousness of human personality – save potentially."[106] Conference speakers overall enumerated themes that received great play over the coming years: anti-abortion laws violated church-state separation, attempted to save that which is not yet human, and did not stop abortion anyway. The underlying argument, however, was that the anti-abortion position lacked compassion for the mother and realism in a world which did not need more poor mouths to feed.

By 1955 the idea of abortion as eugenic compassion had come so far that medical mainstream leaders such as Dr. Theodore Lidz of Yale University were publicly contending

> that abortion is preferable to the birth of a child that might be injurious to the well-being of the mother and perhaps to other children in the family as well as to the specific child to be born, because the mother and the family, for emotional, physical, social, and economic reasons are not in a position to take care of another child.[107]

The emotional reasons alone could lead to abortion for one third to one half of women, Lidz contended:

> At any given moment, about 7 per cent of a population is psychotic and about 30 to 40 per cent is seriously disturbed emotionally. This gives us a basis for estimating the number of mothers who may be unable properly to raise their children.[108]

A Planned Parenthood-sponsored conference at which Lidz spoke agreed that "the mounting approval of psychiatric, humanitarian, and eugenic indications for the legal termination of pregnancy" should lead to new laws.[109] When the conference proceedings emerged in book form, *Time* publicized the work, and Lester David in a popular magazine of the period, *Coronet*, called it "the most comprehensive and authoritative book of information ever compiled on the vital subject of abortion."[110]

---

[106] *Ibid.*, pp. 100-101.
[107] Mary Calderone, ed., *Abortion in the United States* (New York: Hoeber-Harper, 1958), p. 166.
[108] *Ibid.*
[109] *Ibid.*, p. 183. Guttmacher insisted that participants "include humanitarian reasons in our statement." Taylor argued that "to include this indication makes it so completely uncontrollable that such a recommendation is unrealistic" (p. 175). Guttmacher won.
[110] *Time*, June 2, 1958, p. 70; *Coronet*, June 1958, pp. 78-86.

12

The New Portrayals

As the meaning of compassion turned upside down during the first half of the twentieth century, so did the way abortion was portrayed in the press. The change went through several phases: quiescence of the old leaders, divergent coverage among the flagship publications of New York, the triumph of sympathy for abortion, and then a redefinition of press purpose.

The old leaders at exposing abortion, the *National Police Gazette* and the New York *Times*, had grown quiet by the turn of the century. The *Gazette*'s retirement followed its acceptance of abortifacient advertising in the mid-1880s. "LADIES. Tansy Pills are perfectly safe, and never fail; sent sealed, with directions, for 25 cents," the *Gazette* proclaimed.[1] Some ads attempted to package drugs in more palatable ways: "LADIES. If you are in trouble send for the French Medicated Lozenge; acts like a charm; is Sure, Speedy and Safe."[2] Some remnants of anti-abortion coverage remained while those ads proliferated. A

---

[1] *National Police Gazette*, September 19, 1885, p. 15. Variations from other ads: "PILLS OF TANSY are Perfectly Safe and always Effectual," or "LADIES Try the old reliable and you will not regret it. Caton's Tansy Pills are perfectly safe and never fail."
[2] *Ibid.*, March 20, 1886, p. 15.

headline in May 1886 told of "A SAD STORY. The Horrible Secret Revealed by the Death from Malpractice of a Popular Boston Church Singer."[3] But the old coverage seemed out of place amidst columns selling not only abortion but "12 pictures of beautiful women, full view, very spicy. . . . In the Act, all different positions."[4] It would have been philosophically inconsistent and historically unprecedented for the *Gazette* not to transform its news policy when its advertising procedures changed.[5]

After the turn of the century, however, new practitioners of abortion exposure emerged. The New York *Journal,* a newspaper owned by William Randolph Hearst, gained the largest daily circulation in the United States (about eight hundred thousand in 1914) by running sensational stories, including testimony from coroners of deathbed conversations with post-abortion women:

When I arrived at the hospital I saw that the woman was dying. Then word was brought to me by an assistant that he had heard that the doctor who had performed the operation had arrived at the hospital to seek an interview with his patient. I gave orders that under no circumstances should he be allowed to see the woman alone. . . . Then I proceeded to take the woman's ante-mortem statement. She had rallied for the moment and proved to be the bravest woman in the face of death I have seen for a long time.

"Do you believe you are about to die?" I asked. "Yes I know I am going to die very soon," she answered. . . . She told me the doctor had performed three operations upon her. . . . [Then] somebody said, "There's Dr. Stein who is accused of performing this operation." I stepped over to him and said: "Dr. Stein, I want to confront you with your victim." Then I said to the woman, "Turn. Look at this man. Who is he?" "That is Dr. Stein . . . the doctor who attended me."[6]

---

[3]*Ibid.,* May 29, 1886, p. 7.
[4]*Ibid.,* June 18, 1887, p. 14. A section of not-too-subtle come-hither notices such as "Young Lady, 18, will correspond with gentlemen or sell my photograph (not in tights) at 25 cents" also must have brought in tens of thousands of dollars.
[5]Publisher of the *Gazette* during the 1880s was Richard K. Fox, who turned his newspaper from exposure of crime and vice to promotion of burlesque queens. In the 1890s the *Gazette* was not available at reputable newsstands but could be found, printed on pink paper, in barrooms and barber shops throughout the United States. In the twentieth century the *Gazette* fell into declining circulation and eventual bankruptcy.
[6]New York *Journal,* May 10, 1909, p. 5.

The *Journal* reported that the woman died and abortionist Stein was arrested. The undercurrents of the story were typical for the era: a wealthy, established abortionist (not a back-alley amateur) oppressing a victimized woman.

Another Hearst-owned newspaper, the San Francisco *Examiner*, reported a similarly compelling situation the following year. Six of the seven columns on page 1 of the September 24, 1910, San Francisco *Examiner* – and almost all of pages 2, 3, 4 and 5 – were devoted to the story of Eva Swan, a schoolteacher who died after having an abortion and was buried in a doctor's cellar.[7] Details were like those of the New York *Times'* "trunk murder" in 1871: Eva Swan died, and Grant "packed the body of the girl in a trunk."[8] The *Examiner* included details of how Grant and an assistant carried the trunk at night to a house the doctor rented, tore up a section of the wood flooring of the basement, dug a hole, and saturated the earth with nitric acid.

[T]hen they took the body of the girl from the trunk, wrapped it in a blanket and flung it into the hole. They covered it with loose earth and poured in more nitric acid. Then over the grave they had dug they built a cement floor four inches thick.[9]

The crime came to light only when Grant's assistant, with troubled conscience, talked about the incident to another Grant employee, Ben Gordon. Gordon went to the police after he quarrelled with Grant over eighteen dollars Gordon said the doctor owed him. "Crime Hidden For Months Revealed by Boy as Act of Revenge," the headline concerning that aspect of the story proclaimed.[10]

Accompanying the main articles were large pictures of Eva Swan, Dr. Grant, and other principals of the tragedy. *Examiner* stories about the horror covered most of the first four pages of September 25, the first three pages on September 26, and the first three pages along with page 5 on September 27.[11] Throughout that coverage the *Examiner* lambasted Grant, who was said to have "spent money very freely" and "owned a

---

[7]San Francisco *Examiner*, September 24, 1910, p. 1.
[8]*Ibid.*
[9]*Ibid.*
[10]*Ibid.*, p. 2.
[11]After slipping to page 13 on September 28, the story roared back to the first two pages on both September 29 and September 30, before dying down to page 3 on October 1 and page 39 on October 2.

big automobile."[12] The *Examiner* revealed that Grant's real name was Robert Thompson, that he was a graduate of Dartmouth and Baltimore Medical College, and that he appeared heartless; when booked for murder, Thompson "squeezed a puffed cheek with pudgy hand . . . never blinked an eyelid . . . chew[ed] gum as he heard the charge read against him."[13] Thompson's nurse testified that she saw him "saw off the young woman's legs with a common wood saw, and then jam her mutilated and blackened body into the trunk."[14]

Over the next two decades, the New York *Times* covered abortion very sparingly, but Hearst newspapers continued to label abortionists as evil and corrupt.[15] The New York *American*, for example, told readers in 1916 that "Confession Bares Trust of Illegal Physicians / Dr. Andre L. Stapler, Convicted of Manslaughter, Tells of Widespread Malpractice / Gives Names of Twelve Doctors in New York City and Also Man in Office of Coroner."[16] The story noted bribes of two hundred dollars to five thousand dollars and explained that Stapler

> gave the names of twelve physicians who are the principal malpractitioners in New York. . . . He gave in detail the methods which are used by the members of the trust to conceal the true causes of death in cases where illegal operations were performed. He showed how false certifi-

---

[12]*Ibid.*, p. 2.

[13]*Ibid.*, September 27, p. 1. The Eva Swan story was played up outside San Francisco as well. An Associated Press account offered sensational detail, noting that "Gallons of nitric acid had been poured upon the body, which had been crushed into a shallow grave in the basement." The AP also reported the confession by Thompson's nurse that Thompson had "packed the girl's body in a trunk, first cutting off the legs at the ankles."

[14]Some West Coast newspapers also sent their own reporters to cover the criminal investigations. Los Angeles was still a small city in 1910, but a special Los Angeles *Times* reporter was present at the inquest to report that Thompson had "the appearance of a vulture" and sat "practically unmoved" during the hearing, with "his cruel mouth twisted into a cynical smile."

[15]A change in the *Times* coverage took place in the mid-1890s as the *Times* was introducing a slogan that would become famous, "All the News That's Fit to Print." (The *Times*, a morning newspaper, had a second slogan as well: "It Does Not Soil the Breakfast Cloth.") When *Times* editor Elmer Davis wrote the official history of the newspaper in 1921, he explained the sloganeering as an effort to tell the public that the *Times* would be free of "indecency" or "sensationalism," with "contaminating" material left out. During the two decades after 1896 the *Times* apparently defined abortion as something not fit to mention, since it definitely did soil the breakfast cloth. Elmer Davis, *History of the New York Times* (New York: The New York Times Company, 1921), pp. 199-200.

[16]New York *American*, January 14, 1916, p. 11. The *American* was William Randolph Hearst's morning and Sunday newspaper in New York. In 1914 it had the largest Sunday circulation in the United States (about seven hundred and fifty thousand).

cates of death are obtained and the Board of Health is deceived. He referred repeatedly to dealings with certain officials in the Coroner's office, who aided in concealment. He also told of instances in which the police aided in the concealment of deaths from malpractice.[17]

The next day the *American* kept at it with a headline, "Doctor Held; May Exhume Many Bodies / William McCracken, Accused of Criminal Practice, Is Arrested in Eighteenth Street Office / Charge Is First to Follow the Disclosures of Dr. A. L. Stapler, Convicted of Manslaughter."[18]

By 1924 the *Times* was showing sympathy for abortionists as long as they were "respectable." For example, the *Times* portrayed one arrested abortionist, Dr. Hadley Cannon, as a family man collapsing in a police station, to the sorrow of his wife and their two children.[19] The New York *Journal*, however, gave more detail concerning the crime, reported that Cannon had fled his previous home in upstate New York because of a previous malpractice case, and noted that his wife divorced him there and was given custody of their children.[20] A larger difference in coverage emerged in 1925 when the *Times* briefly noted the arrest of Henry L. Mottard, alias Dr. H. L. Green, while the *Journal* played the story at the top of its front page, with pictures and text that emphasized the search of Mottard's farm on Long Island "for surgical instruments and bodies of infants."[21]

The *Journal's* style was reminiscent of nineteenth-century coverage. As Mottard confessed to crimes, reporters expressed horror and amazement: "The blandness with which Mottard uttered his remarkable professions leads the authorities to believe that . . . he has been a veritable Molech in his destruction of infants' lives."[22] The *Journal* also implied

---

[17]*Ibid.*

[18]*Ibid.*, January 15, 1916, p. 9. The story noted that the bodies of at least ten women who may have died following abortions would be exhumed and quoted the city coroner's statement that "there is undoubtedly a very large illegal practice in this city." The *American* noted that "many women who patronized these illegal establishments are said to have been socially prominent" and that deaths had been covered up by falsification of death certificates.

[19]New York *Times*, August 9, 1924, p. 5; August 10, p. 14; August 14, p. 17.

[20]New York *Journal*, August 8, 1924, p. 4; August 10, p. 5.

[21]*Ibid.*, April 10, 1925, p. 1.

[22]*Ibid.*, p. 2. Molech was the Ammonite god mentioned fifteen times in the Old Testament, in passages such as "Do not give any of your children to be sacrificed to Molech" (Leviticus 18:21). The Hebrew prophets vigorously protested such human sacrifice.

that abortion was a pagan ritual when it described Mottard's farm as a "temple . . . where women came in considerable numbers to sacrifice."[23] It emphasized Mottard's wealth by noting that his house was "lavishly furnished and has especially handsome furniture in the music room [and] a fully equipped operating room." But that indication of competence did not save Mottard from depiction as an evil man.[24]

The following year brought another *Journal* front-page story of a body cut into pieces following "an illegal operation."[25] While the New York *Times* briefly covered the death on page 26, the *Journal* graphically described the butchery and noted that the legs of the corpse still had stockings on them.[26] *Journal* and *American* stories continued for the next several days with more sensational detail and identification of the "pretty 18 year old victim of the box tragedy" as Edith Green, whose fiancé confessed that he had taken her "to Doctor Walsh's office for an operation to forestall approaching motherhood."[27]

The coverage difference between mass circulation newspapers such as the *Journal*, the *American*, and the New York *Daily News* on the one hand, and the elite-oriented *Times* on the other, persisted through the 1920s: the former exposed and criticized abortionists, while the *Times* briefly noted the occasional arrests.[28] For example, the *Daily News* went on the attack in 1927 after Robert Thompson, the San Francisco abortionist (aka James Grant) who had buried Eva Swan in 1910, moved to New York, and (using the alias "Robert Malcolm") was charged with attempted abortion and possession of narcotics.[29] The case was dismissed by a local magistrate, with Thompson boasting that "he could beat any police case because he had the pull,"[30] but reporter John O'Donnell of the *Daily News* exposed thirty physicians who were send-

---

[23] *Ibid.*

[24] *Ibid.*

[25] *Ibid.*, July 14, 1926, p. 1.

[26] New York *Times*, July 14, 1926, p. 26; New York *Journal*, July 14, 1926, p. 1.

[27] *Journal*, July 15, 1926, p. 1; *American*, July 16, pp. 1, 5 and July 20, p. 2.

[28] The *Daily News* was a tabloid featuring photographs and short, sometimes hard-hitting articles, many of which featured crime and sex. In 1924 the *Daily News* attained the highest daily circulation in the United States (seven hundred and fifty thousand); circulation grew to 1,320,000 in 1929 and peaked in 1947 at 2,400,000 daily.

[29] Thompson, sentenced to twenty years for the abortion murder of Eva Swan, received parole after nine years and moved to Boston. There he once more opened an abortion business, this time under the alias "Stanton A. Hudson." In August 1922 he was arrested on the charge of procuring an abortion but was discharged.

[30] *Journal of the American Medical Association*, Vol. 92, No. 7 (February 16, 1929), p. 579.

ing patients to Thompson "in return for generous commissions."[31] Police, pushed by public opinion and the board of health, eventually raided Thompson's office, but lack of evidence let Thompson get away with only a one-year prison term for practicing medicine without a license, which he had lost after his California sentencing.[32]

The New York *Times* from 1929 through 1938 continued to downplay abortion rites, burying on inside pages the news placed by the New York *Journal* on page 1.[33] The New York *Daily News* portrayed one doctor's abortion business as one more in a series of scams: "On one occasion he established what he announced would be a model dairy farm near Freeport and purchased a herd of infected cows to supply the milk. Health authorities condemned them."[34] The New York *Journal* scorned the doctor's argument that he performed illegal operations only when "necessary to save his patients."[35] The New York *American* noted that another abortionist also had been arrested for attempted grand larceny and felonious assault on a widow: "Mrs. Laura Baird . . . exhibited a broken nose . . . and contended that Dr. Sturm had tried to keep $25,000 in jewelry, stocks, certified checks and cash that belonged to her."[36]

The implication in the popular press was clear: an abortionist's life was filled with greed, fraudulent behavior, lying, and abuse of women. The New York *Journal* quoted one judge's comments about abortionist Dr. Jacques Alper: "This man's eagerness for money caused him to go

---

[31]New York *Daily News*, September 7, 1928; clipping in *Journal-American* archives, The University of Texas at Austin.

[32]*Ibid.*, September 5, 8, 27, and 28, and October 2, 1928. The raid was botched, probably intentionally, with the *Daily News* charging "that policewomen had been bribed by Thompson to destroy evidence of the clinic's criminal operations and had assisted the quack doctor in spiriting away his semi-conscious women patients." The policewomen actually helped the key witnesses into taxicabs, according to the *Daily News*. At the trial's opening O'Donnell described how Thompson "laughed at the law . . . cursed and swore at newspapermen." O'Donnell noted that Thompson "often boasted he couldn't be prosecuted because 'What I know about the girl friends of some officials will burn them up.'" Thompson believed, apparently justifiably as long as his profile was low, "that his knowledge of prominent politicians' love affairs would prevent legal interference with his so-called death clinic" (*Daily News*, January 12, 1929).

[33]Compare New York *Times*, December 26, 1934, p. 12, and December 27, p. 42, with New York *Journal*, December 26, p. 1.

[34]New York *Daily News*, December 2, 1928.

[35]New York *Journal*, January 24, 1929; New York *American*, January 30, 1929.

[36]New York *Evening World*, March 18, 1930, p. 16; New York *American*, March 27, 1930; see also New York *World*, November 26, 1914.

into this racket. Why he was such a fool, I do not know. Doctors who do such things have no place in the medical profession."[37] Popular newspapers in cities other than New York also covered local abortion activities during the 1930s, without portraying abortion as a compassionate solution to problem pregnancies.[38]

Most newspapers depicted abortion as a device of the powerful. The *Journal-American* played up the arrest of the "socially and politically prominent" Dr. Louis Duke, a former president of the Brooklyn Civic Club, who used "political influence" to build himself a "sumptuous establishment" and perform abortions without great concern in a "richly-furnished Bedford Avenue office."[39] Newspapers suggested that there was nothing inevitable about the spread of abortion, because there were not that many people professionally involved in it. The *Journal-American* reported that:

> For a number of years, a small but influential group of doctors, numbering about 20, controlled the Brooklyn abortion business, earning illicit fees averaging from $100 to $500 an operation. . . . Powerful political connections helped them escape the law when police raided their offices and arrested them. . . . Bank accounts of the abortion group have been examined and it has been discovered that large withdrawals from certain doctors' accounts were made at the time of their arrests. Part of these amounts were paid to officials as bribes.[40]

The press goal was to wipe out that small group and keep the heat on potential successors.

The pressure, however, was not kept up. In part, reporters and readers seemed to become bored. One attorney in 1939 called press attacks on abortionists a "Roman holiday" – and such festivals were often followed by hangovers. As Elizabeth Evans had noted in the 1870s, and

---

[37]New York *Journal*, April 15, 1936.

[38]On the West Coast, for example, the Los Angeles *Times* ran brief articles on abortion arrests and convictions: "Two local physicians . . . have been arrested [and] charged with performing an illegal operation," a typical lead began. Such stories generally emerged when a woman suffering after an abortion operation went to a local hospital, hospital authorities notified the police, and crime beat reporters relayed the story. ("Physicians Accused by Girl Dancer," Los Angeles *Times*, May 1, 1929, p. 8; see also Los Angeles *Times*, May 1, 1931, p. 4.)

[39]New York *Journal*, December 10 and 11, 1938. Dr. Duke regularly set aside 10 per cent of his gross income for payoffs to prosecutors and police and even deducted these essential business expenses from his income tax returns.

[40]*Ibid.*, March 11, 1939, p. 1.

H. L. Mencken four decades later, many newspapers avoided discussion of issues and instead conducted "emotional wars upon errant men: they always revolve around the pursuit of some definite, concrete, fugitive malefactor, or group of malefactors . . . the impulse behind them is always far more orgiastic than reflective."[41] Sometimes, Mencken wrote, the Roman holiday atmosphere led to a reaction, with press and public eventually turning on the reformer, "butchering him to make a new holiday."[42] Although nothing so dramatic as a new butchery resulted this time, more newspapers and magazines toward the end of the 1930s began to report abortion stories neutrally, and sometimes portrayed abortion leaders positively. *Time* praised Dr. Frederick Taussig, as noted in the last chapter, and the New York *Times* merely noted, without a critical word concerning abortion, arrests of Dr. Anthony Renda, Dr. Aloysisus Mulhollard, Dr. Dukoff, Dr. Morris Weiss, the father-and-son physician team of Leslie and Leslie, and Dr. Alice Chairman.[43]

Increasingly, other newspapers also began to present the new perspective proposed by pro-abortion doctors: the problem was not abortion but the "unscrupulous abortionist." The New York *World-Telegram* in 1942 proclaimed that one office where abortions were performed was similar to "a regular hospital."[44] Scathing sarcasm was reserved for reporting of the trial of a non-doctor abortionist, Erminia L. Pugliesi, who weighed 412 pounds and had to come to the courthouse in a specially built car, remodeled to have one large door in place of two.[45] The New York *Daily News*, at the height of its economic success in the late 1940s, ran one long article attacking "practitioners of medicine's black art – disreputable midwives, disgraced nurses and quack doctors" who were employees of "chain-store abortion enterprise."[46] Then, as if in contrast, the *Daily News* ran a long, sympathetic article about "an outstanding physician" who allegedly performed a few abortions on the side.[47] The story suggested that some abortionists were altruistic and ended with the notion of "debating the question: Medals of honor or lamp posts

---

[41]H. L. Mencken, "Newspaper Wars," *Atlantic*, March 1914, p. 292.

[42]*Ibid.*, p. 293.

[43]New York *Times*, April 1, 1943, p. 25; January 27, 1944, p. 21; January 29, 1944, p. 7; January 28, p. 10; February 3, 1944, p. 20; February 4, p. 17; February 20, 1944; February 24, p. 17; March 5, p. 37; June 1, p. 21; July 6, p. 17; July 19, p. 21.

[44]New York *World-Telegram*, March 18, 1942.

[45]New York *Times*, February 16, 1946, p. 15,

[46]New York *Daily News*, September 15, 1946, p. 20.

[47]*Ibid.*

and gallows for abortionists?"[48] The story implied that "good" abortionists should be praised and only unscrupulous ones punished.

Newspapers in many cities began presenting such ideas. The San Francisco *Examiner*, which had played large the abortion case of Robert Thompson in 1910, had a dramatic opportunity to examine abortion issues in 1946 during the San Francisco trial of Dr. Charles B. Caldwell, a well-established physician accused of committing an abortion that led to a maternal death. The evidence seemed ample. Two women testified that he had committed abortions on them; Caldwell's office receptionist testified that she had watched him doing four abortions; the deceased woman said on her deathbed that Caldwell had done the abortion; California prosecutors charged that Caldwell's business "has been almost entirely that of performing illegal operations."[49] The *Examiner*, however, praised Caldwell's competence and merely reported that his former receptionist was allowed "to testify in somewhat lurid detail regarding operations which she claimed to have witnessed in Dr. Caldwell's offices."[50] Increasingly, only abortionists considered unscrupulous received the antagonism once aimed at all abortionists.[51]

Dr. Leopold Brandenburg was portrayed positively following his arrest on abortion charges for the third time in 1947. Brandenburg had gained notoriety two years before for a fingerprint-removing operation on Roscoe (Cocoa) Pitts, an Alcatraz alumnus trying to avoid connection with his past entrepreneurial activities; Brandenburg, after slicing the skin from Pitts' fingers, inserted the raw ends into "pockets" cut into the flesh of Pitts' chest. As the New York *Journal-American* reported, "It took six very uncomfortable weeks for each hand before the flesh of the fingers and chest grew together so that the hand could be cut away."[52] (The story did not have a happy ending, as a few telltale whorls remained; Pitts, arrested in Waco, Texas, on a motor violation, was identified as the person who had dynamited a safe in North Carolina. When

---

[48]*Ibid.*

[49]San Francisco *Examiner*, May 22, 1946, p. 8.

[50]*Ibid.*, May 29, 1946, p. 3. See also May 13, 1946, p. 6; May 14, p. 8; May 15, p. 8; May 16, p. 28; May 17, p. 5; May 18, p. 22; May 20, p. 24; May 21, p. 10; May 23, p. 5; May 24, p. 28; May 25, p. 5; May 27, p. 24; May 28, p. 15; May 30, p. 11; June 4, p. 13; June 5, p. 28; June 6, p. 30; June 7, p. 30; June 10, p. 9; June 11, p. 26; June 13, p. 32; June 18, p. 26; June 19, p. 24; June 21, p. 28; July 2, p. 30; July 4, p. 13; July 10, p. 28; July 11, p. 7; July 13, p. 1; July 14, p. 14.

[51]See, for instance, "Four Seized in Alleged Illegal Operation Raids," Los Angeles *Times*, September 30, 1948, p. 2.

[52]New York *Journal-American*, July 8, 1945.

police asked Pitts for the name of a physician who would operate with such creativity, Pitts was understandably irritated enough at the failure of the operation to recommend Brandenburg.)

Brandenburg also was indicted when ten thousand dollars taken from a U.S. mail truck in North Carolina made it to his bank account, but the doctor went free because there was no evidence that he knew the money had been stolen.[53] Clearly, there was enough here for reporters to attack Brandenburg sharply – but they did not, for he had "better equipment than most hospitals."[54] Newspapers emphasized Brandenburg's "white surgical suit,"[55] and *Time* magazine reported that Brandenburg's patients were getting the same drugs and precautions that they would in a hospital.[56]

Other New York abortion stories of the late 1940s noted the excellent educational backgrounds of some abortionists; one arrested doctor was said to be a medical school graduate of Johns Hopkins and a former physician to Rutgers University.[57] As the number of maternal deaths due to abortion fell by over 90 percent through the use of penicillin (whether the abortions were legal or illegal), the threat of abortion to the lives of mothers did not loom so large, and increasingly the question was whether anyone cared deeply about the unborn children.[58] The Houston *Post* in 1950 reported that a man who had done yard work for one accused abortionist, Mrs. Diane Banti,

> said women would come to the Banti house and after Mrs. Banti took them into the back room he could hear them screaming. Within about 10 or 15 minutes Mrs. Banti would bring a package out to him, he said, and he would bury it. He pointed out the place where the skeleton of a premature baby was found Thursday and said he is pretty sure he buried one of Mrs. Banti's packages there about three months ago.[59]

The *Post* included a photo of some two dozen people standing on the Banti garage. According to the article, "Officers were continually chas-

---

[53] *Ibid.*
[54] New York *Daily News*, March 4, 1945.
[55] *Ibid.*, September 5, 1947.
[56] New York *Journal-American*, September 4, 1947; *Time*, September 15, 1947, pp. 49-50; New York *Times*, September 4, 1947, p. 52; September 5, p. 11; September 6, p. 30.
[57] New York *Tribune*, February 22, 1948.
[58] See Thomas W. Hilgers, "The Medical Hazards of Legally Induced Abortion," in *Abortion and Social Justice* (New York: Sheed & Ward, 1972), pp. 57-88.
[59] *Ibid.*

ing people off the garage in back of the house," but the "curious" kept coming back.[60] If the curious came back to the Houston *Post* the next day they were disappointed, however. There was no follow-up story, nor were there any more stories about other young lives lost.

Similarly, the Los Angeles *Times* in 1952 gave the top left quarter of its second page to a headline, "Wealthy Woman Dies in Mystery," and two accompanying pictures.[61] The lead mystery included not only the finding of her corpse in a downtown alley, but the reason why a woman described by friends as "always in good taste" ended her life with a doubly fatal operation.[62] Los Angeles *Times* readers intrigued by the mystery would be frustrated: there was no follow-up. Other newspapers ran shorter stories and also let them drop.[63]

By the early 1950s, New York newspapers were mentioning only in passing that official city physicians were charged with performing abortions.[64] When a hospital administrator revealed that he was not reporting abortion cases to the Brooklyn district attorney, as he was legally required to do, no one in the press seemed to care.[65] Instead of attacking abortion generally, newspapers continued to distinguish between the activities of "bonafide doctors" and others.[66] For example, Dr. Henry Blank, when rearrested and taken away for two years in Sing Sing, went with the accolade of one newspaper that he was considered "one of the best in the business."[67] Abortionists who had "an elaborate layout of surgical instruments and drugs" generally received positive portrayal.[68]

---

[60]*Ibid.*, p. 2.

[61]Los Angeles *Times*, May 28, 1952, p. 2.

[62]*Ibid.*

[63]See "Illegal Operation Nets M.D. 3 Years," New York *Journal-American*, May 5, 1950; also September 6, 1951; November 21, 1951; March 30, 1952; and July 14, 1952. See also "3 Doctors and 4 Others Plead Guilty of Abortion," New York *Tribune*, February 18, 1952. All articles without page numbers in this chapter were found in the *Journal-American* archives at the University of Texas Austin.

[64]New York *Tribune*, August 23, 1951; New York *World-Telegram-Sun*, August 22, 1951; August 31, 1951. For additional stories of certified doctors performing abortions, see also New York *Daily News*, January 13, 1951; New York *Journal-American*, January 24, 1950; July 2, 1950; September 6, 1951; March 29, 1952; January 1, 1953; New York *Times*, November 22, 1953, p. 35.

[65]"Charges MDs, Hospitals Hush Abortion Cases," New York *Post*, December 10, 1953.

[66]New York *Daily News*, April 4, 1951. See also New York *Times*, April 4, 1951, p. 25; April 5, p. 26; May 11, p. 19; February 16, 1952, p. 8.

[67]New York *Journal-American*, May 2, 1955. Blank, after cooperating with the Amen investigation and receiving a pardon, had returned to the abortion business and enjoyed an estimated annual income of $115,000.

[68]New York *Journal-American*, June 28, 1954.

Depiction of abortionists at mid-century both reflected and encouraged the changing understanding of compassion. Journalists generally ignored deaths of unborn children — weren't those born out of wedlock likely to have miserable lives anyway? — but commented that maternal deaths showed a lack of compassion. Beneath the headline "Life Gamble Lost by Ex-Swim Star," the Los Angeles *Times* told how "A former woman world's champion swimmer gambled her life against the promise of a motion picture career here and lost."[69] The story explained that Virginia Watson had an "illegal operation . . . in order to accept the promise of a minor screen role with actor Johnny Weissmuller"; the story implied that had she won her gamble, all would be well.[70] Compassion meant improving the odds for a desperate woman to have her abortion. In 1954 Max Lerner in the New York *Post* wrote of "between 5,000 and 6,000 deaths a year" — that was an estimate from twenty years before, pre-penicillin — and argued, when one woman died, that "It is you and I who must share the blame for Gertrude Pinsky's death. . . ." Ignoring the pails and jars and shrouds in which the aborted unborn were placed, Lerner turned his wrath on illegal abortion's "cruel cloak of darkness and furtiveness."[71]

By the mid-1950s press accounts regularly distinguished between abortions conducted by regular physicians and those performed by "butcher quacks." The New York *World-Telegram-Sun* publicized abortion-as-compassion in a story beneath the headline, "How Do Doctors Justify Abortions?"[72] Wire service stories told of one physician whose "operating room and procedure were very sterile . . . only one woman in 1,000 might have had any trouble,"[73] and of a second abortionist whose "clinic" had "21 beds and the latest scientific equipment."[74] A few madmen had to be run out of business: Articles in 1956 described the abortionist who killed both mother and child, with the larger corpse "cut into fifty pieces, placed in Christmas wrapping paper and dumped into

---

[69]Los Angeles *Times*, December 1, 1954, p. 2.
[70]*Ibid.* The story made coast to coast headlines, sometimes with errors. The December 1, 1954, New York *Tribune*, under a headline "Death of Movie Aspirant Is Blamed on Abortion," incorrectly identified Virginia Watson as the sister of movie swimming star Esther Williams. See also "Swimming Star Dead: Abortion to Aid Film Career Fatal to Virginia Hopkins," New York *Times*, December 1, 1954, p. 36.
[71]Max Lerner, "Death and Abortion," New York *Post*, April 9, 1954.
[72]New York *World-Telegram-Sun*, July 6, 1957.
[73]New York *Herald Tribune*, June 27, 1954.
[74]New York *News*, March 10, 1956.

various trash cans."[75] But there were also the "good abortionists." The Washington *Post* described one as "a practicing physician since 1924. . . . The county medical examiner said that his examination indicated the operations were performed with high surgical efficiency."[76]

By 1962 the changed depiction was becoming standard. Newspapers across the country reported how a woman who died during an abortion operation was cut up piece by piece, with bones and pieces of flesh stuffed down a sewage line.[77] When the line became clogged the crime was discovered, and newspapers provided gory details as in the past. But this time the problem was said to be not abortion but *illegal* abortion, with the implication that if abortion were legalized such things would not happen. Readers could look up from their newspapers and buy at local bookstores a paperback, *The Abortionist*, which portrayed abortionists as kindly but victimized public servants who risked their freedom for the sake of many.[78] The message of press and paperback was spread to millions more when an episode of the CBS television drama "The Defenders" gave an abortionist a similar halo.

These views accompanied the year's largest abortion story, that of Sherri Finkbine, twenty-nine, the "pretty mother of four healthy children" and the wife of a high school history teacher.[79] As Miss Sherri, she starred in the Phoenix version of "Romper Room," a nationally syndicated program for children. She seemed to have an all-American life. But she had unwittingly taken the drug thalidomide, then surfacing in Europe as the reason why some children were born with phocomelia (flipperlike limbs) or without any limbs at all.[80] Thalidomide had not

---

[75]New York *Tribune*, January 31, 1956.

[76]Washington *Post*, June 28, 1954, p. 7.

[77]The abortionist evaded police but eventually was captured in France and extradited. See "Queen's M.D. Admits Girl's Abortion Death," New York *World-Telegram-Sun*, September 12, 1962, p. 1, and "Runaway M.D. is Indicted in Death of Coed," New York *Journal-American*, September 26, 1962, p. 1.

[78]Dr. X and Lucy Freeman, *The Abortionist* (New York: Grove Press, 1962), p. i. The book suggested widespread hypocrisy in its tales of "the lawyer who brought his wife for an abortion – and two days later his mistress," or the policewoman whose lover, a high police official, offered to let the operation be performed on the steps of police headquarters – with a cordon of police protection.

[79]Washington *Post*, August 3, 1962, p. A-4. For more detail on the Finkbine episode, see Marvin and Susan Olasky, "From Murder to Liberation: The Crucial Crossover in Abortion Coverage, 1962," *Journalism Quarterly*, Spring 1986.

[80]*Newsweek*, August 13, 1962, p. 52. Known in England as "The Sleeping Pill of the Century," thalidomide was used by European mothers beginning in 1958 to relieve the nausea of early pregnancy. It was distributed to children as a pacifier and termed "West

been cleared for use in the United States, but Mrs. Finkbine's husband, while traveling in Europe during 1961, had purchased tranquilizers that contained the substance. One year later, when Sherri Finkbine was in the first trimester of her pregnancy and had trouble sleeping, she found the "Distaval" in a medicine cabinet and took some pills. In the succeeding weeks of her second month of pregnancy she took more.

On July 16, 1962, Sherri Finkbine read a newspaper story about babies born in Europe with serious birth defects after their mothers had taken thalidomide. She called her doctor to ask about her tranquilizers, and the doctor found out she had been taking thalidomide.[81] He suggested abortion, legal at that time in Arizona when the mother's life was in danger. That would ordinarily have been no barrier for Sherri Finkbine, since a committee of three doctors appointed by the Arizona Medical Society regularly stretched the law to give approval for abortion in special situations. In this case a Finkbine abortion was approved by a three-member medical panel on July 23, just three days after Sherri Finkbine first approached her doctor; the grounds were psychological danger to the mother. The abortion was scheduled for July 25 or 26 and apparently would have taken place then had not Finkbine told a Phoenix newspaper about her story, in order to "alert others" to thalidomide dangers.[82]

Once the story hit the press, hospital administrators feared protest and possible legal action and refused to authorize the abortion that doctors already had approved. With Sherri Finkbine cast as the Pauline amidst perils and thalidomide as the train about to run her over, the legal and judicial system became Oil Can Harry. Planned Parenthood's Alan Guttmacher argued that anti-abortion laws "just haven't kept up with the medicine."[83] Abortion was not merely the refuge of the seduced and abandoned or the sellers of body and soul for money; abortion was the goal of "pretty Sherri Finkbine," the perfect suburban housewife and mother, a "deeply tanned brunet [sic] wearing a sleeveless dress of white linen who tapped the toe of an orange spike heeled pump."[84]

Germany's Baby-Sitter." Tragically, doctors soon learned that women who took thalidomide during their second month of pregnancy ran, according to Dr. Frances Kelsey of the Food and Drug Administration, about a 20 percent chance of bearing a deformed child.

[81] *Arizona Republic,* July 23, 1962, p. 1.

[82] *Ibid.,* July 24, 1962, p. 1.

[83] *Ibid.,* August 21, 1962, p. 1.

[84] Los Angeles *Times,* August 4, 1962, p. 1.

During July and August 1962 hundreds of newspaper reporters hung on the Finkbines' words as they first considered Japan and then went through the process of securing visas and making travel arrangements to Sweden.[85] Reporters suggested that those who might criticize the Finkbines' decision lacked compassion. The Atlanta *Constitution* wrote that Sherri Finkbine "had to go to Sweden to find a more civilized attitude toward her plight" and that Americans "ought to have a look at their abortion laws in light of what they did to her."[86] Reporters accepted the Finkbine contention that the "operation" would be performed for the good of the baby.[87] Although many people throughout the United States offered to adopt the child if born, the Finkbines were said to be continuing abortion plans for altruistic reasons. A Washington *Post* reporter told Finkbine of one such offer and noted that she burst into tears, saying, "It doesn't change our minds. It wouldn't be fair to the child."[88] The New York *Times* quoted Finkbine as saying, "I burst into a rage when a San Francisco couple offered to adopt the baby."[89]

As these last quotations show, even Sherri Finkbine referred to the being in her womb as a "child" or "baby." So did most journalists, at first. Headlines used the word "baby" and came up with euphemisms for abortion. The New York *Times* reported, "Couple May Go Abroad for Surgery to Prevent a Malformed Baby," a Los Angeles *Times* headline stated that the Finkbines planned "Baby Surgery," and the New York *Journal-American* described an operation to "lose the baby."[90] Three decades before, the anthropologist Aptekar had proposed changes in vocabulary since "the word abortion used in Western Civilization carries with it the connotations of the word murder. Mention of the word always brings up the feeling-tones connected with a host of other terms designating despicable and dishonorable acts."[91] Since the Finkbines did not seem like murderers, reports disassociated them from abortion, and soon the word "fetus" — which previously had been used only when

---

[85]Chicago *Tribune*, August 4, 1962, p. 5, and August 5, 1962, p. 1.

[86]Atlanta *Constitution*, August 18, 1962, p. 30.

[87]New York *Journal-American*, July 25, 1962, p. 1.

[88]Washington *Post*, July 31, 1962, p. A-3.

[89]New York *Times*, August 5, 1962, p. 64.

[90]New York *Times*, August 1, 1962, p. 19. Los Angeles *Times*, August 1, 1962, p. 1; New York *Journal-American*, August 18, 1962.

[91]Herbert Aptekar, *Anjea: Infanticide, Abortion and Contraception in Savage Society* (New York: William Godwin, 1931), p. 131.

reporters focused on the medical aspects of the situation – began to replace the words "unborn child."[92]

Clearly, the pro-abortion conferences and publications of the 1940s and 1950s were bearing journalistic fruit. Abortion was receiving front-page justification across the country, and restrictions on abortion were portrayed as cruel and unusual punishments. Coverage was always from Sherri Finkbine's perspective. In Sweden, upon receiving the news that her abortion was approved, she is said to have "dropped the telephone receiver and buried her face in her hands weeping. 'I can't tell you how relieved I am. I don't know what I would have done if it had not been granted.'"[93] Earlier she had said what she would have done: "If we should have an abnormal child we would love the child, and give it the best care in the world. . . ."[94] But as the story developed, journalistic identification with Finkbine was so intense that alternatives were ignored.

Overall Sherri Finkbine was the heroine and the legal system was villainous. Reporters ignored or did not stress facts not fitting that story structure. No major newspapers emphasized the fact that only two of seven babies aborted in Sweden for thalidomide were known to be deformed, or the statement of the Food and Drug Administration's Dr. Frances Kelsey that only 20 percent of German thalidomide babies were deformed. Not one of them seriously examined the lives that the 20 percent who were deformed could still expect to have. On August 18 the Finkbines' unborn child died from abortion in Sweden, and coverage dribbled off with some final praise for Sherri Finkbine's assumedly compassionate decision.

In late 1962 a question on abortion was included for the first time in a Gallup Poll. The poll asked whether Sherri Finkbine did right or wrong "in having this abortion operation." Some 52 percent of those responding thought she had "done the right thing," 32 percent felt she had done wrong, and 16 percent had no opinion.[95] Those favoring abortion would have to work hard over the next three decades to widen the circumstances under which a majority of Americans favored abortion. But by the end of 1962, a decade and a month before *Roe v. Wade*, and before

---

[92]See, for example, New York *Times*, August 5, 1962, p. 12 and August 19, p. 12; New York *Journal-American*, August 18.

[93]New York *Journal-American*, August 17, 1962.

[94]Los Angeles *Times*, August 4, 1962, p. 15.

[95]*The Gallup Poll, Public Opinion 1935-1971* (New York: Random House, 1972), p. 1984.

most Americans even realized that a major advance for abortion was occurring, the crucial foothold for abortion was won.[96]

---

[96]For more detail on press coverage of abortion, see Marvin Olasky, *The Press and Abortion 1838-1988* (Hillsdale, NJ: Lawrence Erlbaum Associates, 1988).

13

The Uses of History

The history of abortion is messy. The patterns are complex. Yet, there are answers to questions raised in the Introduction. Essentially, I have found that pro-life forces have been wrong to assume that abortion was rare in the nineteenth century, that tough laws virtually ended the practice, that doctors and ministers led the way, and that the anti-abortion consensus remained philosophically intact until the 1960s. Pro-abortion groups have been wrong, however, in their typical assertion that abortion was widely accepted before this century, that abortion was diffused throughout the population, that abortion became illegal because regular doctors sought to drive out competitors, and that abortion rates generally are unaffected by illegality or the development of alternatives.

This history will be useful, I hope, because both sides in the abortion debate have lived for so long not by banners alone but by myths as well. A pro-life placard that proclaims, "The Natural Choice Is Life" ignores the sad fact that in many cultures, and among many American women seduced (as in the early nineteenth century) by men, money, or radical theology, the natural choice is and has been death. A pro-life activist who believes a change of law will eliminate abortion ignores the late nineteenth-century lesson that law by itself avails little unless programs emphasizing prevention and offering true compassion are in place and effective. A pro-life talk show guest who blames abortion on the sexual revolution of the 1960s and the Supreme Court edicts of the 1970s ignores the trends culminating in 1962 that made legalization likely.

The side favoring a right to abortion has been dominant in academia and in publishing, so its arguments have been presented at greater length. In 1968 Cyril Means, Jr., contended that abortion was not a common law offense and that late nineteenth-century anti-abortion laws were concerned solely with the health of women (rather than the lives of unborn children). His arguments provided a crucial prop for the Supreme Court majority in *Roe v. Wade*.[1] In the late 1970s James Mohr did not hide the fact that the mid-nineteenth-century American Medical Association expressed concern for unborn children, but he explained away such comments by imputing and emphasizing self-seeking motivation on the part of the "regular" physicians who led the anti-abortion drive. Their goal, Mohr wrote, was to drive the competition (including non-AMA doctors and midwives) out of business. "By raising the abortion question and by highlighting the abuses and dangers associated with it, regular physicians could encourage the state to deploy its actions against their competitors," Mohr argued.[2]

Proponents of abortion came up with imaginative interpretations during the 1980s. Carroll Smith-Rosenberg added an explicit class angle to the Mohr thesis:

> The "regulars" claimed one powerful ally – the mercantile elite in the major seaports. . . . During the opening decades of the nineteenth century, these old families began to endow medical schools and hospitals,

---

[1]Cyril C. Means, Jr., "The Law of New York Concerning Abortion and the State of the Foetus, 1664-1968: A Case of Cessation of Constitutionality," *New York Law Forum*, Fall 1968, pp. 455-487.

[2]James Mohr, *Abortion in America* (New York: Oxford University Press, 1978), p. 160. Another reason "why organized regular physicians sustained an anti-abortion crusade involved their desire to recapture what they considered to be their ancient and rightful place among society's policymakers and servants . . . physicians in America had fallen into low repute during the period of democratized and wide-open medicine that characterized the first half of the nineteenth century," and the anti-abortion drive "provided the exhilaration of helping once again to make public policy . . . it was time for the enlightened once again to come forward and guide the benighted public on a key question of social and moral policy. In that way the medical profession might recapture some of the luster of its golden past, when the physician had been a major voice in his society and enjoyed the status of a 'god'" (pp. 163-164).

which their sons would then direct and staff. These older and powerful families thus had a vested interest in maintaining the status and control of the Eastern urban medical establishment.[3]

Smith-Rosenberg also stressed "psychologically primitive male fears of the aborting mother."[4] According to this theory,

> The aborting matron served as the scapegoat for all that was problematic in the new social order. The dependent and domestic True Woman asserted that, despite its emerging problems, the bourgeois order, rooted in women's biology, was natural and God-ordained. . . . If, as Roland Barthes argued, the object of bourgeois myth is to make the bourgeois order seem natural, the AMA had constructed a complex and classic bourgeois myth.
>
> The image of the lethally powerful aborting woman not only bespoke men's professional anxieties; it expressed far more universal and psychological primitive fears and projections. Indeed, the psychosexual is as revealing as the professional. Each constitutes one pole in a complex bipolar symbolic language. Both meanings were deeply appealing. We must decipher both if we are to understand the mass appeal the anti-abortion movement wielded.[5]

The anti-abortion movement was successful, in other words, because the American Medical Association

> created a new Oedipal triangle, linking the male physician with the male fetus against the mother. The mother was potentially lethal and insane; only the male physician could protect the male fetus.

Rosenberg concluded that, "when the physician actually prevented an abortion, it was he, not the mother, who gave the fetus life."[6]

This psychohistory was too farfetched for all but the most avid proponents of abortion. The Mohr analysis, however, has become common coin. In 1989, when Lawrence Tribe was attempting to explain the advent of anti-abortion laws, he wrote that "physicians were eager to halt

---

[3]Carroll Smith-Rosenberg, *Disorderly Conduct: Visions of Gender in Victorian America* (New York: Knopf, 1985), p. 230.
[4]*Ibid.*, p. 226.
[5]*Ibid.*, p. 239.
[6]*Ibid.*, p. 242.

the competition in abortion services from medical irregulars."[7] That year the New York *Times* tried to explain (on the day after the Supreme Court's *Webster* decision) how the debate over abortion began; it proclaimed that in the nineteenth century,

> when efforts arose to make abortions illegal, the discussion turned less on the moral issues that preoccupy the contemporary debate than on questions of health and medical professionalism.[8]

The "medical profession," according to the *Times'* reflection of the Mohr thesis, was "struggling to establish itself as authoritative." In 1990 *Senior Scholastic*, a magazine distributed to high school students, taught a new generation elements of the Means and Mohr views: "abortion was banned because it was dangerous to women . . . and the American family. . . . Historians say that doctors were also concerned about business."[9]

Mohr's analysis by then was also the basis for a brief filed by 281 historians in connection with the *Webster* case. The remarkable document began, "Never before have so many professional historians sought to address the Honorable Court in this way."[10] The brief acknowledged that the knowledge of the 281 signers was "widely diverse" – few had any record of sustained research on abortion history – but that nevertheless all signers were "united in the conviction that *Roe v. Wade* is essential to women's liberty and equality and consistent with the most noble and enduring understanding of our history and traditions."[11]

Later other historians jumped onto the bandwagon, until over four hundred had signed onto the brief's assertions that abortion was broadly accepted throughout most of American history and opposed largely by men concerned with their own status or opposed to women's "labor force participation and independence."[12] Rather than expressing concern over the chilling effect on historical debate that such a juggernaut would have, signer Estelle B. Freedman wrote of her happiness when "as far as

---

[7]Lawrence Tribe, *Abortion: The Clash of Absolutes* (New York: Norton, 1990), p. 30.
[8]New York *Times,* July 4, 1989, p. 1.
[9]*Senior Scholastic*, April 20, 1990, p. 11.
[10]*Brief of 281 American Historians as Amici Curiae Supporting Appellees*, p. 1. This may be because the unwritten historians' code was, "Do not sign your name to an historical account unless you can vouch for its accuracy."
[11]*Ibid.*
[12]*Ibid.*, p. 23.

I could tell, no historians came forth to support Webster or to attack the hundreds of historians who supported this *amicus* brief."[13]

The monolith made it difficult for historians to uphold what Mohr himself saw as their role:

> helping society by reminding us all the time of complexity, paradox, alternative explanations, mixed motives, and inconvenient facts. Ultimately, I suppose I see historians functioning most of the time as society's "trimmers": people who not only suggest new perspectives on subjects germane to the intellectual and social world of the present but also question and correct views that rest upon flimsy evidence and interpretations that have become dysfunctional paradigms.[14]

Mohr himself came under fire for signing and defending a brief that at the least oversimplified his book (which itself, as we have seen, laid out a path straighter than warranted by historical reality).[15]

The debate over the brief is interesting, but the major question for historians is not the brief but the book. Did Mohr, in *Abortion in America*, accurately answer the basic questions: How many women were having abortions? Why were they having abortions? Was the practice of abortion widespread in American society, or was it generally restricted to particular groups? Did opponents of abortion eventually reduce the extent of the practice? If so, how?

Let's recap the historical developments, starting with the Maryland archives that show abortions in 1656 and 1663. Both, significantly, involved maidservants forced to it by their masters. Massachusetts court records show abortions in 1678, 1681, and thereafter; those first two, and almost all the others, involved unmarried women impregnated and

---

[13]Estelle B. Freedman, "Historical Interpretation and Legal Advocacy: Rethinking the *Webster Amicus* Brief," *The Public Historian*, Vol. 12, No. 3 (Summer 1990), p. 27.

[14]James Mohr, "Historically Based Legal Briefs: Observations of a Participant in the *Webster* Process," *The Public Historian*, Vol. 12, No. 3 (Summer 1990), p. 22.

[15]For a critique of the brief and Mohr's role in it, see Gerald V. Bradley, "Academic Integrity Betrayed," *First Things*, September 1990, pp. 10-12. Bradley wrote, "The brief made two central claims: (1) abortion was not illegal at common law, and (2) the moral value attached to the fetus became a central issue in American culture and law only in the late twentieth century. Both claims are false. Key signatories knew, or had ample reason to know, that they were false. Worse, one of the principal signatories, himself a key authority cited in the brief, has in his scholarly work reached and published conclusions that contradict the brief's conclusions. Worst of all, when the contradiction was brought to his attention, this scholar actually *defended* the duplicity as a public service."

abandoned. Given the great physical risks of abortion to the mother at the time, infanticide was more frequent than abortion, but records show both practiced in Connecticut, New York, and points south. The colonists knew that infanticide or abortion was knocking at every unmarried, pregnant woman's door; the goal was to minimize the number of killings by promoting abstinence and, if sexual relations and pregnancy did occur, marriage.

In colony after colony, premarriage social pressures worked to contain abortion. Colonial records indicate that by the 1760s, among the non-slave population, as many as one of every three Americans was conceived out of wedlock, but not more than one out of fifteen was a bastard at birth. Whenever the identity of the father of the unborn child was clear, the father could choose between marriage, disgrace (with forced payment of child support anyway), and flight to another colony under an assumed name; most men chose marriage. For those unborn children at greatest risk, with no paternity established, another form of containment at least prevented dire poverty. An unwed mother could assert that a particular man was the father, and if it was proven that he had slept with her – even if others had also – he had to pay child support through about the first twelve years of life. Statutory proscriptions on the concealment of birth and some local ordinances also made abortion more difficult.

Early in the nineteenth century, the early system of containment began to break down as urbanization, increased mobility, and theological liberalism made it easier in practice and conscience for men to impregnate and run. Prostitution was also on the increase at this time. Journalists and doctors from 1830 through 1860 suggested that prostitutes, devoid of any reliable contraception, became pregnant and had abortions, sometimes several a year, often with drastic physical repercussions for mother as well as child. The average life expectancy for a women in the trade was four years. Reliable estimates from 1860 had sixty thousand prostitutes at work and getting pregnant, so the abortion rate must have been rising. (That was certainly the case in Paris where prostitution was legal and public health researchers could document its connection to abortion.)

The theological tidal wave that rolled over many northern cities during the 1850s certainly led to an abortion increase. Hundreds of books from the pre-Civil War decade describe the channeling of spirits during weekend retreats, seances, and other meetings attended regularly by several million people. Manifestations of "spiritism" accompanied a philosophy that claimed absolute freedom from earthly conventions, such as marriage, for the "truly spiritual" person. When adultery among nineteenth-century New Agers led to unwanted pregnancy, for the first time in American history thousands of married women were having abortions.

These are crucial findings. James Mohr wrote of the "many American women" who sought abortions during the first two-thirds of the nineteenth century and declared that "this practice was neither morally nor legally wrong in the eyes of the vast majority of Americans, provided it was accomplished before quickening."[16] Mohr repeatedly suggested that everyone was doing it: "Abortion entered the mainstream of American life during the middle decades of the nineteenth century. . . ."[17] But that is just not true. Abortion was never part of the American mainstream as Mohr contends. It was a recourse of those adrift on particular sidestreams: victims of seduction, prostitutes, and spiritists.

How many were on those sidestreams? Questions of quantity can be approached in two ways, through statistics or through contemporary narratives that carry authenticity. Scientific statistics, prior to recent decades, simply are not available. Judith Leavitt noted in her useful book *Brought to Bed* that even when we turn to the honorable data of childbirth generally,

> It is only in the twentieth century that the recording of births (live and still) began to be noted reliably by local and state health departments, and even today we cannot calculate precisely the risks women face each time they become pregnant.[18]

Quantitative researchers on both sides of the abortion question, including Christopher Tietze of Planned Parenthood, have acknowledged the difficulty in developing scientifically accurate numbers concerning what for decades was done in secret.[19]

Historians have a partial alternative to statistics, however: descrip-

---

[16]Mohr, "Historically Based Legal Briefs: Observations of a Participant in the *Webster* Process," p. 16. The Supreme Court brief-writers emphasized this theme.
[17]*Ibid.*, p. 102.
[18]Judith Leavitt, *Brought to Bed: Childbearing in America, 1750 to 1950* (New York: Oxford University Press, 1986), p. 24.
[19]Tietze paper in Mary Calderone, ed., *Abortion in the United States* (New York: Hoeber-Harper, 1958), p. 180.

tions of the situation made by reliable contemporary observers. Mohr used a variety of estimates to conclude that up to 17 to 20 percent of pregnancies were ending in induced abortion during the 1850s and 1860s.[20] Since there were about 1.4 million births in 1860 (in a national population of thirty-one million), Mohr's abortion rate translates into approximately two hundred and eighty thousand to four hundred thousand abortions annually (depending in part on whether he factored in Dr. Hugh Hodge's calculation of a 14 percent miscarriage rate).[21] Such a figure is probably too high, since some of the doctors Mohr quoted may have been exaggerating for political effect, and others used the word "abortion" to include what is now called miscarriage. (For example, *The Matron's Manual of Midwifery* in 1848 reported that "when the foetus is prematurely expelled before it can survive, it is called an abortion.")[22]

I am not a fan of numbers – I like them as much as Indiana Jones likes snakes – but in this project I have been confronted by the need to go among them. At first, when asked how many abortions there were at particular points in American history, I would point to the lack of scientific statistics and say, "I don't know." When pushed – "Can't you make an estimate?" – I would say, "I cannot." But, of course, I could. I have now written two books about abortion history and four more books about other aspects of the American past generally and the nineteenth century specifically. After all that research, it was a lie to say that I could make no estimates. When editors and others persisted in their questioning, I finally steeled myself to make them . . . always with the proviso that any number be preceded by "roughly" or some other term to avoid suggesting the arrogance of precision.

With all these caveats, and putting together the evidence I have found, with particular emphasis on the abortion-prostitution connection, I estimate that in 1860 there were roughly one hundred and sixty thousand American abortions, in a non-slave population of twenty-seven million. (There is very little accurate information about what was going on among slaves.) Roughly one hundred thousand of those one hundred and sixty thousand abortions probably were undergone by prostitutes; Chapter Two quotes contemporary testimony and explains the logic of

---

[20]Mohr, p. 50

[21]Hugh Hodge, *The Principles and Practice of Obstetrics* (Philadelphia: Blanchard and Lea, 1864), p. 459.

[22]Frederick Hollick, *The Matron's Manual of Midwifery* (New York: Excelsior, 1848), p. 340.

that figure, given what we know about the extent of prostitution in 1860 and the unavailability of technologically advanced contraception at the time. When pressed on the number of non-prostitute abortions in 1860, I estimate roughly sixty thousand, with most of them occurring among married women involved in theological radicalism of one kind or another, particularly spiritism.

Chapter Three provides the admittedly speculative basis for the numbers concerning spiritists. What about young women who were not disposed to abortion by theology but felt driven to it by an imminent illegitimate birth? Information about nineteenth-century premarital pregnancy is poor, but what there is points to, as historian Daniel Scott Smith reported, "a substantial decline in prenuptial pregnancy in the nineteenth century."[23] One survey, for example, shows 12.6 percent of first-born children during the 1841-1880 period born within nine months of marriage, compared to 33 percent during the 1761-1800 era.[24] And what of the pregnant young women who did not get married? Smith writes of "the distinctive character of the American experience in the nineteenth century" and "the strikingly low illegitimacy ratios" of the era.[25] Probably only one of one hundred children born in 1860 – about fourteen thousand – was illegitimate at birth.[26] Judging by contemporary testimony, it is likely that an equal number of children in the wombs of abandoned women were aborted.[27]

And so we come to an admittedly rough estimate of about one hundred and sixty thousand abortions in the 1860s non-slave population of twenty-seven million. Could there have been one hundred and forty thousand abortions? Yes. Could there have been one hundred and twenty thousand? Possibly. Could there have been fewer than one hundred thousand? That does not seem likely, given the contemporary accounts. Although my overall figure is lower than Mohr's, it is shocking to some pro-life advocates, because – given U.S. population growth – it is virtually the equivalent of our current figure of 1.6 million abortions

---

[23]Daniel Scott Smith, "The Long Cycle in American Illegitimacy and Pre-nuptial Pregnancy," in Peter Laslett *et al.*, eds., *Bastardy and Its Comparative History* (London: Edward Arnold, 1980), p. 370.

[24]*Ibid.*

[25]*Ibid.*, p. 372.

[26]*Ibid.*; see estimates from Massachusetts and Maine.

[27]See discussions of proclivity to abort in documents such as the *First Annual Report of the New York Magdalen Society* (New York: John T. West, 1831), and John H. Warren, Jr., *Thirty Years Battle with Crime* (Poughkeepsie, NY: A. J. White, 1874).

in a population of close to two hundred and sixty million. Of course, a lower percentage of pregnancies ended in abortion then because those in the American mainstream were bearing children frequently.[28] But a similarity of overall abortion/population ratios surprises many pro-lifers, because abortion then was sometimes doubly fatal and because the nineteenth century has been depicted as a time of "no compromise" anti-abortion laws and strong anti-abortion lobbying by the American Medical Society and by church leaders.

To pro-lifers disturbed by the fact that there were many abortions in the mid-nineteenth century, I suggest that a grasp of historical reality, not fable, is the key to building a successful movement. But to abortion proponents who might contend that big numbers prove the acceptability and universalism of the practice, I suggest contemplation of the Civil War. In that most famous mid-century shedding of American blood, over six hundred thousand soldiers died; it clearly would be wrong to pretend that only a few died. It would be equally wrong to contend that the six hundred thousand deaths were spread generally among the population and widely accepted. They were not: some people led lives of enormous hazard, others were far from the front lines, and very few people applauded the killing. So it was with abortion: it was frequent but not common.

It was a rite among certain groups, but it *was* contained in the late nineteenth century.

Mohr's story of how abortion was fought in the late nineteenth century is also wrong. The American Medical Association did not have the power to do what Mohr said it could do. Laws by themselves, while important as educational tools, were not grandly effective. Laws clearly dissuaded some women from having abortions, but Eliza Sowers, Olive Ash, sixteen-year-old Marty Kirkpatrick, and thousands of other abandoned, unmarried women were not dissuaded. Sixty thousand prostitutes were not dissuaded. Abortion was risky for women – perhaps one in twenty died during the process – but an abortionist such as New York's famous Madame Restell was able to build a millionaire's mansion on Fifth Avenue, brick by brick, risk by risk.

Opponents of abortion, of course, did not always agree on strategy.

---

[28]Eleven or 12 percent was the likely percentage then, compared to about 29 percent now. The 1990 U. S. census figure was 249 million, but statisticians suggest that was a significant undercount.

In law, for example, some wanted to make penalties exactly fit principles. The 1871 debate in New York was a classic. When one judge proposed that abortion become a capital crime, he initially received loud applause. Members of the Medico Legal Society of New York, however, argued that a death penalty for abortion, while "intrinsically just," was unsustainable; no jury would convict when such a penalty loomed. The New York legislature eventually approved an abortion sentence of four to twenty years.[29] The attempt to make penalties socially acceptable sometimes meant a lower range of punishment (in Pennsylvania up to three years) for abortion before quickening; those cases did not provide the certainty of pregnancy that made people willing to put away an abortionist for a long period of time. Many states gave immunity to women from all criminal liability,[30] others gave women immunity from prosecution in exchange for testimony, and virtually every state allowed abortion to protect the life of the mother.

Punishments calibrated not to intimidate juries or female victims of abortion had an effect. Although few abortionists were convicted, the threat was always there. As spiritism waned, and as the introduction of diaphragms and rubber condoms reduced pregnancy among prostitutes, it appears that the abortion rate fell during the late nineteenth century and stayed *relatively* low through 1960. Had abortion been as frequent in 1910 as in 1860, there would have been over five hundred thousand abortions in the latter year, but early twentieth-century articles by doctors suggest a rough figure of two hundred thousand to two hundred and fifty thousand.[31]

---

[29]See discussion in Chapter Four.

[30]Partly because women pregnant after seduction were considered desperate victims rather than perpetrators, and partly because of the search for any kind of edge in prosecution.

[31]See Charles Bacon, "The Duty of the Medical Profession in Relation to Criminal Abortion," *Illinois Medical Journal*, Vol. 7 (1905), p. 18; Palmer Findley, "The Slaughter of the Innocents, *American Journal of Obstetrics and Gynecology*, Vol. 3 (1922), pp. 35-37; and J. B. Eskridge "The Management of Abortions," *Journal of the Oklahoma State Medical Association*, Vol. 25 (1932), p. 471. Findley's estimated percentages yield a total of two hundred and fifty thousand abortions in 1922, but my sense is that reputable doctors in this period tended to overestimate slightly; a few journalists, then as in more recent times, overestimated wildly. Also see Taussig, p. 388, and his citation of the study by Macomber, p. 25. In citing estimates from that period, it is vital to take into account that generally included among "abortions" was what we now commonly call "miscarriage." For information about typical percentages of known miscarriages, see books ranging from Hodge, *The Principles and Practice of Obstetrics*, to Gillian Lachelin, *Miscarriage* (New York: Oxford University Press, 1985).

Pro-lifers were not happy with that total, but they knew that abortion could not be abolished, though it could be limited.

And it was limited. Throughout the first six decades of the twentieth century, unmarried young women often placed children for adoption or, during pregnancy, married the father. Contraceptive improvements made a difference in pregnancy among prostitutes, who proved to be technologically adept. Abortion among the married was low, except in neighborhoods like Greenwich Village and, perhaps, among several immigrant populations. Use of birth control by married couples reduced the pressure for abortion in many instances. We have no statistics concerning the incidence of abortion among married women in the 1920s, but one study of the sexual habits of one hundred married men, and an equal number of married women, suggests that the number was not great. Most of these New York City residents were under forty and had "attained a relatively high level of culture. A considerable number of them are persons of outstanding intellectual or artistic achievement."[32] These individuals were willing to answer very detailed questions about their sexual activities in a way that set them apart from most Americans at the time, who were not so "liberated." Ninety-two of the men and ninety-seven of the women used contraceptives; eighty-two of the women had been pregnant a total of two hundred and twenty-eight times, with thirty to thirty-five induced abortions resulting. In other words, of every seven pregnancies in this abortion-likely group, there were about five births, one miscarriage, and one abortion.

The role of advances in medical technology is important to understand. The advent of antiseptic techniques during the late nineteenth century reduced estimates of maternal mortality during abortion from 6 percent (Michigan, 1881) to 1 or 2 percent (numerous studies, 1906-1929).[33] But improved safety for mothers did not lead to a rush to the abortionist, as long as values backed up by law suggested alternatives to abortion. Further reductions in maternal hazard following the introduc-

---

[32]G. V. Hamilton, *A Research in Marriage* (New York: Boni, 1929), pp. 24-43.

[33]See, for example, E. A. Ficklen. "Some Phases of Criminal Abortion," *New Orleans Medical and Surgical Journal*, Vol. 29 (1926-1927), pp. 884, 893, and W. O. Johnson, "Two Years Resume of Abortions," *Louisville Journal of Obstetrics*, Vol. 22 (1931), pp. 778-782. Ficklen argued that he could not hope for "the total abolition of the practice" because financial rewards for abortionists were great and "the present situation is simply an outgrowth of the law of supply and demand." He noted, however, that "the rigorous training given to midwives and physicians have robbed the procedure of many of the dangers from sepsis, which formerly existed" (p. 889).

tion of penicillin in the 1930s also did not lead to any evident abortion increase during the 1940s and 1950s. Technology did not determine action; the abortion surge came in the 1960s with a change in values.

The sexual revolution of the 1960s made extramarital intercourse and its pregnant results a mainstream activity. The employment revolution of the 1970s made the major economic loss that could result from pregnancy a major concern. Many young women became career-oriented, and – among some young couples – worry about one more mouth to feed increased when pregnancy could also mean one less paycheck. A century ago some women saw "their working companions [prostitutes] enjoying good clothes, good dinners, good seats at the theatre, and they know how easily these good things of life may be obtained."[34] Some of those women would also decide to maximize their incomes. Today there is a far better way for women through their own work to enjoy good clothes and dinners, but that may also involve having an abortion in order to avoid severe disruption of the income flow.

Sex education in schools and through the media has virtually eliminated the ignorance of a century ago, a time when some young women knew "nothing of the horrors of venereal diseases."[35] However, many more unmarried young women today "have no strong religious or moral principles to keep chaste, nor do they fear the loss of social standing in their set."[36] In the 1960s the advent of birth control pills contributed to the belief that unwanted pregnancy could be eradicated. Many college students and feminists viewed that technological breakthrough as essential to their liberation. No longer would women have to worry about a double standard that allowed men to be sexually active outside of marriage, while women were either bound to virginity or left at risk of unwanted pregnancy.

The technological change came along just as marriage began to be portrayed as a "trap" for women. Betty Friedan accurately wrote in her early-sixties manifesto *The Feminine Mystique* that "By 1962 the plight of the trapped American housewife had become a national parlour game. Magazine issues, newspaper columns, books learned and frivolous, educational conferences and television programs were devoted to the

---

[34]George T. Kneeland, *Commercialized Prostitution in New York City* (New York: The Century Co., 1913), p. 247.
[35]*Ibid.* Moral ignorance has been on the rise.
[36]*Ibid.*

problem."[37] As opposition to marriage became common among journalists and academics, and as marriage became merely an optional center for sexual activity or childbearing, many journalists accelerated the attack on a "confining" tradition.[38] No-fault divorce laws gained favor in most states because marriage itself was seen as the guilty party. Anti-marriage sentiment and reality began to feed on each other. Educated women who were most influenced by feminist ideology advocated "shacking up" and even avoidance of all entangling alliances, so that women could advance as rapidly in the workplace as men. Children increasingly were viewed as obstacles. Abortion became an integral part of the anti-family ideology because even the most avid birth control advocates realized that some unplanned pregnancies still would occur.[39]

During the 1960s and early 1970s these changes primarily affected persons over eighteen and were particularly evident on college campuses. Not surprisingly, the revolution could not be contained at that level. By 1985, about 40 percent of the unmarried teenagers between ages fifteen and nineteen were sexually active.[40] Expansion of the sexual wars outside the adult battlefield changed the nature of concerns. Feminists had pictured autonomous adults freely choosing sexual relationships and then dealing rationally with the consequences. Women who were poor or uneducated, it was felt, would act "rationally" by using contraceptives or getting abortions. That was not always the case, it turned out. But the trickle-down of sexual revolution and devaluation of marriage ideas to younger and younger teenagers became even more of a problem. Since birth control was not foolproof and was often unused by those educated in technical details but little more, the twin goals of planned childbearing and sexual liberation for all were on a collision course.[41]

As sexual practice changed, theological beliefs that were once on the fringe have also entered the mainstream. Abortion in the nineteenth cen-

---

[37]Betty Friedan, *The Feminine Mystique* (New York: Norton, 1963), p. 21.

[38]See Samuel Blumenfeld, *The Retreat from Motherhood* (New York: Arlington House, 1975).

[39]For additional discussion of these ideological changes, see Susan and Marvin Olasky, *More Than Kindness: A Compassionate Approach to Crisis Childbearing* (Wheaton, IL: Crossway Books, 1990.)

[40]Children's Defense Fund, *An Advocate's Guide to the Numbers* (Washington, D.C.: CDF, 1988), p. 4.

[41]Concern over AIDS during the 1980s increased sales of condoms and may have cut down some extreme promiscuity, but the basic acceptance of sex outside marriage has not changed.

tury was never generally acceptable among the married, but it was linked to religious innovations among some members of the "fashionable and intellectual communities."[42] Nineteenth-century statements that it is "less criminal to kill children before they were born, than to curse them with an unwelcome existence" have a decidedly modern ring.[43] Such ideas are now common in many parts of American society, as is the belief that "the authority of each individual soul is absolute and final in deciding questions as to what is true or false in principle, and right or wrong in practice."[44]

Such a faith in self fed, and feeds, abortion. Nineteenth-century spiritists claimed "a God-given right to rectify any mistakes they may have made, and do so as often as such mistakes occur"; their counterparts claim the same right today. The spiritist code was that "if another can develop in me more love than my husband or wife, in virtue of that very love I am newly married, and the old should be absolved, for we should be true to nature and no law has any right to interfere in my affections."[45] Similar beliefs today lead to the frequent changing of partners, as we demand and receive "the liberty that allows each one alone to judge conscientiously for himself, in regard to matters pertaining to his affectional nature."[46]

In summary, recent decades have produced the mainstreaming of what once was marginal. Premarital intercourse, but with no intent of marriage, is common, and parents who care about their children are told to make sure they are using birth control. Young women are told to keep their eyes on the prize – careers and income maximization – rather than family and children. Students are taught to do whatever they feel is right for themselves, regardless of what Biblical commandments (now seen as suggestions, at most) might demand. The mainstreaming of the marginal, along with legal change, has led to more abortions and has made the task of pro-life forces far more difficult.

And yet, a kiss is still a kiss, and the fundamental things still apply, as time goes by. Analysis of nineteenth-century activity is relevant in three ways to the efforts of abortion opponents today. First, men and

---

[42] *Cincinnati Lancet and Observer*, 1867, p. 139.

[43] Henry C. Wright, *The Unwelcome Child or The Crime of an Undesigned and Undesired Maternity* (Boston: Bela Marsh, 1858), p. 111.

[44] *Proceedings of the Free Convention, Rutland, Vermont, July 25-27, 1858* (Boston: J. B. Yerrinton), p. 9.

[45] *Ibid.*, p. 18.

[46] *Ibid.*, p. 9.

women fighting abortion applauded legislation protecting the unborn, but they did not live by laws alone, nor by the efforts of a few professional lobbyists. Doctors were not powerful enough as a lobbying force to do much, but individuals with demonstrated moral integrity and compassion became the ethical rocks of their communities and were able to cast shame on abortionist colleagues by calling them "educated assassins" and "monsters of iniquity." Some ministers were bold and courageous enough to do the work of "sounding the cry of murder" in the ears of their congregations. Some journalists provided not merely screaming editorials but the specific details needed to show what went on in offices of abortion. Anti-abortion forces began to gain success not because of a conspiracy among physicians or anyone else, but because people from widely diverse backgrounds did what they could in their own spheres of influence.

Second, the anti-abortion forces examined the needs of populations disposed to abortion and found ways to keep some women from falling into the roles, situations, and beliefs that made abortion likely. Young women moving to big cities were met at train stations by matrons who could steer them away from exploiters and toward secure homes and rooming houses. Clubs and other leisure-time activities were provided so that women could, essentially, "just say no" without ending up starved for fun and friends. "Social purity" forces tried to educate and prod men out of double-standard belief and behavior. Urban missionaries went into bars and brothel living rooms, whenever possible, to offer prostitutes a way out, and evangelists such as Dwight Moody spoke directly to those who realized most readily that they were among the lost.[47] Homes such

---

[47]See sermon delivered in a Chicago brothel-area hall by Dwight L. Moody, "Christ and Fallen Women," in Norman Roumane, ed., *Social Abominations* (Harrisburg, PA: Whitman, 1892). Moody spoke of one prostitute who said, "I have fallen from everything pure, and God cannot save me; there is no hope." Moody said that if she repented, God would forgive her. "She said, at last, she could not abandon her course, as no one would give her a home. But that difficulty was got around by my assuring her kind friends would provide for her; and then she yielded, and that same day was given a pleasant place in the home of a Presbyterian minister. But, for forty-eight hours after entering her new home, that poor reclaimed woman cried, day and night . . . when I was last in Philadelphia, she was one of the most esteemed members in that Presbyterian church." Moody told his audience, "And so every one of you can begin anew; and God will help, and man will help you. Oh, turn and do not die. . . . And let me say, right here, if there is any person here who keeps a brothel, if you will allow Christian ladies admittance, they will go gladly and hold meetings. This idea that Christian ladies do not care for your class is false – as false as the blackest lie that ever came out of hell . . . ladies of

as the Erring Woman's Refuge did not try to cover up the past but offered a transition to honorable self-support.

Third, opponents of abortion did not consider their job done when women decided not to abort. They hoped to find stable homes for children, whether through marriage of parents or adoption by others. Probably the most relaxed moment for an experienced refuge manager like Helen Mercy Woods was when she could report that a "child was adopted. Little Earl has found a home. . . ."[48] Those refuges of a century ago have modern counterparts, both large and small. Member homes of the Christian Maternity Home/Single Parent Association (CMHA), most of which are licensed as foster care agencies so they can provide housing for minors, have six to eight women in residence at one time. Each operates as a family, with members responsible for doing chores and taking part in family prayer and discussion. Residents decide to live in these maternity homes for many reasons. Some feel uncomfortable at home or are pushed out by parents angry or embarrassed about a pregnancy. Others seek a supportive environment in which to explore adoption or the friendship of women in similar situations.[49]

Both the past and the future of anti-abortion success can also be seen in the work of small organizations such as the Christian Family Care Agency (CFCA) in Phoenix, Arizona, a licensed foster care and adoption group. The CFCA provides in-depth counseling, shepherd homes for pregnant women, foster care for parenting teens and their children, and support groups for pregnant and parenting teens, as well as for those choosing adoption.[50] CFCA's foster care program for parenting teens allows a young mother and her new baby to live in a group home under the supervision of houseparents. The foster home's goal is *not* to ease the burden of parenting for the teen but to combine a lesson about reality with protection for the child.[51] Crucially, the knowledge comes in the safe environment of a family home, not in the dangerous terrain of a soli-

---

the city have lately been visiting these houses personally, and have been trying to save their erring sisters . . . many houses have been visited. We have a place to shelter you. . . . If you are sincere, there are hundreds and thousands of people in this city whose hearts will go out to you."

[48] *Refuge Journal*, May 1887, p. 2.

[49] All CMHA homes are open to non-Christian women, but the program stresses spiritual as well as material needs.

[50] For more about the CFCA and other current organizations, see Olaskys, *More Than Kindness.*

[51] The roles are important. Housemothers do not assume infant care nor offer to baby-sit; if a teen is desperate, a housemother may take over for a short time, but

tary apartment filled with sounds of a crying child and a tired parent who might respond in anger.

In short, the practice of compassion, a century ago and today, means giving a woman undergoing a crisis pregnancy a physical home and a spiritual rock. It means the adoption of hard-to-place children. It means counseling and standing by desperate women. Particularly in a politics-obsessed age, the one-on-one practice of compassion may be less thrilling and may seem less important than dramatic protests or power politicking, but it is the major way in which lives have been saved. Yes, the slow pace of such efforts means that many lives have been lost also, but opponents of abortion need to realize that all have never been saved, even when law was firmly on the anti-abortion side. Yes, protective laws and enforcement help, but the most effective pro-life efforts have always concentrated on one life at a time.[52]

Whenever a society or a part of it becomes concerned largely with personal peace and affluence, abortion rates rise. The children of unmarried parents are always in greatest danger, and children of minority and poor parents are also easy victims. When the self-gratification emphasizers in northern cities during the mid-nineteenth-century almost moved abortion into the mainstream of American life, Henry Wright concluded, "It is no matter of wonder that abortions are purposely procured; it is to me a matter of wonder that a single child, undesignedly begotten and reluctantly conceived, is ever suffered to mature in the organism of the mother."[53] It is no matter of wonder that in the 1960s and 1970s, as many political leaders emphasized absolute freedom and a Great Society of material prosperity, abortion entered the mainstream.

---

only in exchange for doing laundry for the household or mowing the lawn. "We're trying to avoid those situations where a teen and her baby are indulged by parents or foster parents for three, six, or nine months, until the teen is spoiled, the parents are exhausted, and a break occurs," CFCA director Kay Ekstrom says. "The girls we get here are usually not very open to suggestion until the reality of parenting comes home to them." Houseparents, Kay Ekstrom says, need to have "inner strength and a conviction that the child will be better off in the long run by maintaining a hands-off situation. They have to let the child cry longer than they would let him cry. They have to let his diaper be wetter than they would allow. The teenager has to learn that it is her responsibility – and if she can't handle it, then she can make life different for the baby by placing him with parents who can." (Interview by Susan Olasky.)

[52]Even Kristin Luker, who was not on the pro-life side, observed concerning some of her opponents, "what they all have in common is a tough patience that waits for small improvements . . ." (*Abortion and the Politics of Motherhood*, p. 189).

[53]Wright, *The Unwelcome Child or The Crime of an Undesigned and Undesired Maternity*, p. 35.

The popular acceptance of abortion was a long time coming, as the last section of this book shows. The wave moved through the physicians' ranks and spread via journalistic acceptance into the larger society. As abortion was on the verge of nationwide legalization, the Long Island *Press* presented a typical portrayal of abortion anguish: "'Oh, thank you, thank you,' she told the abortionist. 'Within the next hour she will have some cookies and a soft drink . . . and be on her way back home.'" The Chicago *Sun-Times* reported that "Women who elect abortion show love . . . the current movement is to regard abortion as a positive experience."[54]

By 1971 mainstream publisher Prentice-Hall was presenting author Edgar Chasteen's "moderate" proposals:

> The third plank in a compulsory birth control program is to recognize parenthood as a privilege extended by society rather than a right inherent in the individual.[55]
>
> Once we establish the principle of compulsory birth control the number of children permitted by law can be raised and lowered depending upon social conditions at any given time. Though we set family size at two children now, at some future date it might be necessary to raise or lower permissible family size to accomplish some socially beneficial objective.[56]
>
> If more than two children are born to a woman, we could take those children from the parents and offer them for adoption and/or fine or imprison the parent. Laws presently governing parenthood provide certain punishments for parents deemed by the courts, for reason of abuse, neglect or inability, to be unfit. Such laws could be extended to include overly prolific parenthood as a type of unfitness.[57]

During the 1970s the abortion train was moving so fast, and concerns about "overpopulation" were increasing so sharply, that it was no longer inconceivable for "compulsory birth control" to become an item on the national agenda.

That compulsory birth control and abortion are not on the

---

[54]See Marvin Olasky, *The Press and Abortion* (Hillsdale, NJ: Lawrence Erlbaum, 1988), pp. 103-122.

[55]Edgar R. Chasteen, *The Case for Compulsory Birth Control* (Englewood Cliffs, NJ: Prentice Hall, 1971), pp. 202-203.

[56]*Ibid.*, pp. 205-206.

[57]*Ibid.*, p. 209.

national agenda at present is no small accomplishment of the pro-life movement. During the two decades since the publication of that Prentice-Hall book, fast-food restaurants, high schools with cafeteria-style curricula, and television sets with zappers for quick channel changes have become cultural shrines. Choice, convenience, and comfort form a cultural trinity. Supporters of legal abortion offer women a quick change of channels (without mentioning the ghost that remains), while opponents of abortion offer the need to accept a certain amount of suffering. It is remarkable not that abortion has continued, but that opponents of abortion have pretty much held their own.

Current, generally reliable statistics, combined with historical perspective, throw the containment of aggressive abortion into sharper relief. The national figure of 1.6 million abortions per year has held steady for a decade even as the group of unborn children at greatest risk – those conceived out of wedlock, with no marriage forthcoming – has expanded sharply. The number of illegitimate births increased from six hundred and sixty-six thousand in 1980 to one million in 1990, but the number of abortions to unmarried women stayed steady at 1.3 million, or about 80 percent of the total number of abortions. This means that the chance of making it to birth for unborn babies in that situation increased from 34 percent to 44 percent. That is small consolation for pro-lifers, since 56 percent die (and most of the 44 percent who survive face life without a father and often in impoverished and dangerous circumstances). But it is a sign that the abortion mindset has not taken over totally, as it threatened to do twenty years ago. It is also worth noting that the ratio of abortions to births among married woman is about one to ten: three hundred thousand abortions, three million births.[58]

The pro-life movement, in short, is asking itself at this point a question that leads to self-abuse: why haven't we been able to stop abortion? It is not asking at this point a more helpful question: Why aren't things worse? Might it be that some pro-lifers are doing some things right? What about the volunteers at several thousand crisis pregnancy centers who have opened up their homes, provided material help and spiritual challenge, and done many other things in the face of defamation cam-

---

[58]See two publications from the Department of Commerce, Bureau of the Census: *Historical Statistics of the United States* (1975), pp. 8, 49, and *Statistical Abstract of the United States* (1990), p. 62.

paigns waged against them by the abortion lobby? What about those lawmakers and legal experts who are working in the nineteenth-century tradition to develop sustainable legislation?

All of these "moderate" advocates of life sometimes face attack not only by the abortion lobby but by those pro-lifers who stand with a few short ladders outside a towering inferno and cry, "no exceptions." For example, "adoption, not abortion" is the most potent slogan the pro-life movement has, and groups such as the De Moss Foundation and Michigan Right-to-Life have recently conducted successful television advertising campaigns on that point, but such an approach is insufficiently radical for some. New groups such as the Nurturing Network have shown initiative in targeting specific abortion-prone segments of the population (young professional women desperate to avoid career-sidetracking, for example), but others have been content to repeat an "abortion is murder" mantra.

Some dedicated opponents of abortion continue to waste their energies and stock of potential goodwill in a mad dash that ends first at a brick wall and second, as frustration grows, in either extreme action or a long winter's nap. "Pro-life ultra-ism" is partly the result of theological errors (including a superficial view of evil) and juvenile millennialism (non-negotiable demands, now); but it also emerges from historical ignorance. Some pro-life leaders like to equate their movement with that of the abolitionists, but they choose the wrong heroes. Men such as William Lloyd Garrison and John Brown precipitated a tragic civil war in which six hundred thousand died, but the enslaved objects of their compassion ended up leaving the Scylla of slavery only to fall prey to the Charybdis of sharecropping, lynching, and the Ku Klux Klan.[59]

A better model for the pro-life movement now would be the containment policy that the United States successfully used in regard to the Soviet Union from the late 1940s through 1991. The containment policy, as skillfully enunciated by George Kennan in his famous *Foreign Affairs* article of 1947, stressed that the United States should avoid military adventures but should concentrate on the "long-term, patient but firm and vigilant containment of Russian expansive tendencies."[60] Kennan understood that it was unusual not for dictators to emerge, but for a web of ideology and tyranny to extend so far. He understood that

---

[59]Brown also practiced terrorism, which the pro-life movement opposes.
[60]George Kennan, "The Sources of Soviet Conduct," *Foreign Affairs*, Vol. 25 (July 1947), p. 575.

"Soviet power . . . bears within it the seeds of its own decay, and that the sprouting of these seeds is well advanced."[61]

Proponents of containment did not have it easy. Some Americans criticized the approach because it did not kill Communism immediately. Some demanded military action and argued that it was immoral to leave hundreds of millions of souls in a totalitarian hell while life went on in America. Containment doctrine was embraced by Dwight Eisenhower in the 1950s and maintained by the United States, despite some wavering in the 1970s, for forty years. Now that the West has won, all of us can see how immoral it would have been to resort to war in order to gain a slim chance to achieve ends, at enormous cost, that were attainable with peaceful perseverance.

The pro-life movement today needs Eisenhowers, not John Browns. It needs leaders who understand that in America there has always been some abortion among women seduced by men, money, or the religion of self. That is sad, but the tragedy becomes gargantuan only when those three groups expand to become part of an evil empire and when those on the outskirts of the groups come to consider abortion normal. The pro-life goal should be to help Americans see abortion not as a right but a rite, a non-normative practice engaged in by sidestream groups and not given societal approval. As abortion is contained in that way, the provision of compassionate alternatives will reduce the likelihood of abortion being used as a desperate recourse.

Containment of abortion, in short, requires use of all the legal, educational, and political nineteenth-century pro-life forces. Anti-abortion laws are crucial to containment, not primarily because abortionists would be jailed – the history suggests that few would be – but because making abortion (or most abortions) illegal would make the practice of abortion a costly one for physicians. A cynical or existentialist doctor may well decide to double his income by performing abortions when there is no risk but for some verbal harassment. That same doctor may settle for delivering babies if the killing alternative might result in loss of license. On the demand side, the illegality at least deters many women from rushing into the practice.

A rollback of abortion will be possible if fewer women and girls enter those three population groups that are most at risk for abortion and if those in the groups are offered a compassionate way out of crisis preg-

---

[61]*Ibid.*, p. 580.

nancies. Anti-abortion laws will have limited effectiveness as long as schools, television shows, and other education outlets frequently equate premarital and extramarital intercourse with true romance. Young women embarking on careers will still have abortions if they either turn their work into an idol or see continuation of pregnancy as the road to ruin. Those who take after spiritists of the past and attempt to make themselves divine will not look kindly on a little creature that interferes with them. Containment/rollback requires a continued expansion of those churches and other organizations that espouse uncompromised Biblical doctrine.

Pro-lifers must realize that the killing of some children by secret abortion or brutal infanticide will continue to some extent. Over two centuries ago a colonial news-sheet headline read, "Inhuman Cruelty, or Villainy Detected." The story was of the "cruel and barberous Intended Murder of a Bastard Child belonging to John and Ann Richardson, of Boston, who confined it in a small room, with scarce any victuals, or cloathing to cover it from the cold or rain. . . ." Exposure and punishment of the Richardsons did not stop such "villany," but at least it was accurately named: "Inhuman Cruelty." Some humans always will act cruelly, sometimes through inherent selfishness and sometimes out of desperation, but pro-life priorities for the next several decades should be honest naming, tightening of laws, patient containment, and long-term development of compassionate challenge.

Those pro-lifers who charge machine guns in the belief that their own blood atones for societal sin will find the scenario I have laid out unheroic or depressing. But is the success of Mothers Against Drunk Driving depressing, even though the effort does not stop most of the fifty thousand vehicular homicides that occur annually? Are laws against murder unimportant because they cannot stop thousands of murders? Besides, we have seen with our own eyes in recent years how containment can lead to rollback. Who would have dreamed that the Soviet empire, after decades of constant pressure, would finally fall so fast? But it did, and that is why a doctrine of perseverance is not depressing for those who have a Biblically realistic view of human nature and a trust in God's timing and justice.

The abortion empire can begin to fall only if it faces steady pressure over decades through all the means that worked a century ago and are beginning to work anew: education about abstinence, refuges for the abandoned, provision of adoption and many other services. Pro-lifers even have one big advantage over their predecessors: now, wonderful photographs of unborn children at every state of gestation are available. Whittaker Chambers dated his initial break with Communism to the time his young daughter smeared porridge on her face. Chambers found himself looking at her "intricate, perfect ears." He saw immense design, not a chance coming together of atoms – and "at that moment, the finger of God was first laid upon my forehead." Millions of Americans, at the moment they see an intricately made unborn child sucking his thumb, may hear not a great and powerful wind nor an earthquake but a gentle whisper.

What, then, are the uses of history for the pro-life movement? The adage "those who forget the past are condemned to repeat it" states the problem backwards as far as today's movement is concerned. The goal of today's pro-lifers *should be* to repeat a nineteenth-century past in which abortion was successfully fought by moderate means under conditions that were spiritually far from ideal. Mature opponents of abortion a century ago did not say "all or nothing" and thus save lives. Most did not demand that abortion be legislatively designated as murder, but worked for penalties that were sustainable in public opinion and in the jury box. Most appreciated the educational impact of anti-abortion laws but did not expect much in the way of enforcement, and instead concentrated on ways to provide women with alternatives to abortion. Many had great stamina because they were not laid low by a sense of failure when, despite their efforts, many unborn children died. They rejoiced that, in a fallen world, many were saved. So should their successors.

GENERAL INDEX

This index does not cover the footnotes except for additional material given beyond source information in those notes.

INDEX OF PERSONS